Rentz's
STUDENT AFFAIRS PRACTICE
IN HIGHER EDUCATION

Third Edition

Rentz's
STUDENT AFFAIRS
PRACTICE IN
HIGHER EDUCATION

By

FIONA J. D. MacKINNON & ASSOCIATES

CHARLES C THOMAS • PUBLISHER, LTD.
Springfield • Illinois • U.S.A.

Published and Distributed Throughout the World by

CHARLES C THOMAS • PUBLISHER, LTD.
2600 South first Street
Springfield, Illinois 62704

© 2004 by CHARLES C THOMAS • PUBLISHER, LTD

ISBN 0-398-07468-2 (hard)
ISBN 0-398-07469-0 (paper)

Library of Congress Catalog Card Number: 2003061558

With THOMAS BOOKS *careful attention is given to all details of manufacturing
and design. It is the Publisher's desire to present books that are satisfactory as to their
physical qualities and artistic possibilities and appropriate for their particular use.*
THOMAS BOOKS *will be true to those laws of quality that assure a good name
and good will.*

Printed in the United States of America
JB-R-3

Library of Congress Cataloging-in-Publication Data

Rentz's student affairs practice in higher education / [edited by Fiona J.D.
MacKinnon & associates].—3rd ed.
    p. cm.
    Rev. ed. of: Student affairs practice in higher education, c1996.
    Includes bibliographical references (p.) and index.
    ISBN 0-398-07468-2 (hard) — ISBN 0-398-07469-0 (paper)
    1. Student affairs services—United States. I. Title: Student affairs
practice in higher education. II. Rentz, Audrey L. III. MacKinnon,
Fiona J. D., 1939–

    LB2343.S7936 2004
    378'.194—dc22

                                       2003061558

ABOUT THE EDITOR

FIONA J. D. MACKINNON is Associate Professor of Higher Education and Student Affairs at Bowling Green State University and Interim Associate Dean of the College of Education and Human Development. She received a B.A. in English from Denison University and a Ph.D. in Higher Education and Student Affairs from The Ohio State University. She has served on the editorial board of the *Journal of College Student Development* (ACPA) and the *Career Development Quarterly.* She was the recipient of a Fulbright Senior Scholar Award to Beijing Normal University, People's Republic of China.

ABOUT THE CONTRIBUTORS

IRVIN W. BRANDEL has held the positions of Director, Associate Director, and Training Director of the Counseling Center at the University of Akron. He received an M.S. in College Student Personnel at Michigan State University and a Ph.D. in Counseling from the University of Akron. He has served on the Executive Board of the Association of Counseling Center Training Agencies, the Accreditation Board of the International Association of Counseling Services (IACS), and as a site visitor for the American Psychological Association and IACS.

ELLEN M. BROIDO is Assistant Professor of Higher Education and Student Affairs at Bowling Green State University. She received the B.A. degree from Columbia University, the M.S.Ed. in College Student Personnel from Indiana University, and the D.Ed. in Higher Education and Student Affairs from the Pennsylvania State University. She serves on the editorial board for *The Journal of College Student Development* and is a Directorate Member for the ACPA Commission for Professional Preparation. She received the ACPA Annuit Coeptis award for Emerging Professionals.

D. STANLEY CARPENTER, Professor of Educational Administration and Director of the Center for Leadership in Higher Education at Texas A&M University, holds a B.S. in Mathematics from Tarleton State University, an M.S. in Student Personnel and Guidance from Texas A&M-Commerce, and a Ph.D. in Counseling and Student Personnel Services from the University of Georgia. He has served as the Executive Director of the Association for the Study of Higher Education (ASHE), as Editor/Chair of the ACPA Media Board, and as a member of the NASPA Board of Directors.

MICHAEL D. COOMES is Associate Professor, Chair of the College Student Personnel program, and Interim Director of the School of Leadership and Policy Studies at Bowling Green State University. He is a member of ACPA and coeditor of the Commission XII Graduate Preparation Program Directory. He is a member of ASHE and NASPA. From 1973 to 1981 he served as student financial aid administrator at St. Martin's College (Lacey, Washington) and at Seattle University.

MICHAEL DANNELLS, Professor and Director of the Higher Education Administration Doctoral Program at Bowling Green State University, received the B.S. degree from Bradley University and the Ph.D. in College Student Development from the University of Iowa. He has held the positions of assistant dean of students, director of residence life, director of new student programs, and Chair of the Department of Counseling and Educational Psychology at Kansas State University. He is a member of the editorial board of *The Journal of College Student Development* and a Faculty Fellow in NASPA.

JUDITH J. GOETZ is Senior Associate Director of the Division of Undergraduate Studies at The Pennsylvania State University. She received a B.A. in History from Hamline University, the M.A. in College Student Personnel and M.Ed. in Guidance and Counseling from Bowling Green State University, and a Ph.D. in Higher Education Administration from the University of Toledo. She is active in the National Academic Advising Association (NACADA) serving as a member of the Commissions for Graduate Student Advising and Advising Undecided Students.

KATHRYN S. HOFF is Assistant Professor of Human Resource Development in the College of Technology at Bowling Green State University. where she earned her Ph.D. in Higher Education Administration and M.Ed. in Career and Technology Education. She serves as the Managing Director of the Academy of Human Resource Development (AHRD). She has prior experience as a human resource development practitioner responsible for internships, cooperative education, college relations, recruiting, career development and management for employees, organizational change management, and training and development.

DON HOSSLER is Professor of Educational Leadership and Policy Studies, Associate Vice President for Enrollment Services for the Indiana University System, and Vice Chancellor for Enrollment

Services at Indiana University, Bloomington. He has served as the Executive Associate Dean for the School of Education and Chair of the Department of Educational Leadership and Policy Studies. He earned his baccalaureate, with honors, at California Lutheran University and his Ph.D. in Higher Education from the Claremont Graduate School. He is the editor of *The CASE International Journal of Educational Advancement.*

JOSH KAPLAN is Director of the Student Health Center at Bowling Green State University. A graduate of Princeton University, he received the M.D. from Downstate Medical Center, State University of New York, and is certified by the American Board of Internal Medicine. He has served as president of the Ohio College Health Association (OCHA) and is chair of the clinical medicine section of the American College Health Association (ACHA).

JOANN KROLL is Director of Career Services at Bowling Green State University. She earned the M.Ed. in Higher Education Administration from Kent State University. The National Association of Colleges and Employers (NACE) has twice honored her department with its prestigious Award of Excellence for Educational Programming. She served as a consultant in Russia helping to establish the first Career Services Center and a national network of Career Services professionals.

JOHN WESLEY LOWERY is Assistant Professor of Higher Education and Student Affairs at the University of South Carolina. He earned the B.A. degree in Religious Studies from the University of Virginia, the M.S. in Student Personnel Services from the University of South Carolina, and the Ph.D. in Higher Education Administration from Bowling Green State University (Ohio). He is a recipient of the ACPA Annuit Coeptis Award for Emerging Professionals.

RENA K. MURPHY is Coordinator for Research for University Housing at The University of Michigan. She received a B.S. in Physics from Eastern Kentucky University, an M.A. in College Student Personnel, and a Ph.D. in Higher Education Administration from Bowling Green State University (Ohio). She holds memberships in ACPA and NASPA. Publications and research interests include factors that influence student learning outside the classroom setting.

WANDA I. OVERLAND is the Assistant Vice President for Student Affairs and Dean of Students at Bowling Green State University. Prior to assuming her current position, she worked at North Dakota State University as the Assistant Dean for Student Life and Director of the Memorial Union. She earned her Ph.D. in Higher Education Administration at Bowling Green State University.

CAROLYN L. PALMER is Associate Professor in Higher Education and Student Affairs at Bowling Green State University (Ohio). She received the B.A. from the University of Massachusetts in Human Development, the M.A. from the University of Connecticut in Counseling, and the Ph.D. from the University of Illinois in Quantitative and Evaluative Research Methodologies. She is the recipient of service and research awards from the Association of College and University Housing Officers–International (ACUHO-I). Recent research interests are in the areas of campus violence, hate speech and hate behaviors, and outcomes assessment in student affairs.

AUDREY L. RENTZ is Professor Emeritus of Higher Education and Student Affairs at Bowling Green State University (Ohio). She received the A.B. from the College of Mount St. Vincent (Mathematics), M.S. from The Pennsylvania State University (Counselor Education), and Ph.D. in Counseling, Personnel Services and Educational Psychology from Michigan State University. She has served on the editorial boards of *Initiatives* (NAWE), *The Journal of College Student Development* (ACPA), and *The Journal of Psychological Type* (APT). She was honored by OCPA as the recipient of the Philip A. Tripp Distinguished Service Award.

BETTINA C. SHUFORD is Assistant Vice President for Student Affairs and Director of the Center for Multicultural and Academic Initiatives at Bowling Green State University (Ohio). She earned the B.S. in Psychology from North Carolina Central University, the M.S. in Guidance and Counseling from the University of North Carolina at Greensboro, and the Ph.D. in Higher Education Administration from Bowling Green State University (Ohio). She is the past chair of the NASPA Educational Equity and Ethnic Diversity Knowledge Community.

JOHN H. SCHUH is Professor and Department Chair of Educational Leadership at Iowa State University in Ames, Iowa. He has held administrative and faculty assignments at Wichita State University, Indiana University (Bloomington), and Arizona State University. Currently he is editor-in-chief of the New Directions for Student Services Sourcebook Series and associate editor of *The Journal of College Student Development*. He is the recipient of awards from NASPA and ACPA for contributions to the literature and for service from ACPA and ACUHO-I. He received a Fulbright fellowship to study higher education in Germany in 1994.

EDWARD G. WHIPPLE is Vice President for Student Affairs and adjunct Associate Professor in Higher Education and Student Affairs at Bowling Green State University (Ohio). He received the B.A. from Willamette University (Oregon), the M.A.T. from

Northwestern University, and the Ph.D. from Oregon State University. Previous student affairs administrative positions were held at Montana State University–Billings, the University of Alabama–Tuscaloosa, Texas Tech University, and Iowa State University. He is an active member of NASPA and a consultant for the Northwest Association of Schools and Colleges.

MAUREEN E. WILSON is Assistant Professor of Higher Education and Student Affairs at Bowling Green State University (Ohio). She was awarded the B.S.B.A. degree in Business Administration and Communication Arts from Aquinas College, the M.A. in College and University Administration/Student Affairs Emphasis from Michigan State University, and the Ph.D. in Higher Education and Student Affairs from The Ohio State University. She is the recipient of the Emerging Scholars Award and the Nevitt A. Sanford Research Award from ACPA.

JEANNE M. WRIGHT is Assistant Professor in Health and Human Services at Bowling Green State University (Ohio). She is a Certified Health Education Specialist with the M.Ed. and the Ph.D. in Health Education from the University of Toledo (Ohio). She is the principal investigator for a statewide HIV Prevention Grant evaluating outcome monitoring measures for Health Education/ Risk Reduction programs funded by the Ohio Department of Health and Centers for Disease Control and Prevention. Areas of expertise and publication focus on a variety of college health and wellness topics.

ELIZABETH YARRIS is an Associate Professor, Associate Director, and Psychologist on staff of the Counseling Center at Bowling Green State University (Ohio). She received the B.S. in Psychology, the M.A. in College Student Personnel, and the Ph.D. in Counseling Psychology from the University of Iowa.

PREFACE

It should be possible to help every student to build an "educational package." Rather than saying "Let's admit good students and not get in their way," we should admit our students and then get in their way, in the most constructive sense, to help them make . . . powerful connections. (Richard Light, *Making the Most of College*, 2001).

The landscape of higher education has changed dramatically over the past 15 years. Nationally acclaimed reports have evolved from blue-ribbon panels and have challenged the status quo. As colleges and universities, learned societies, and accreditation bodies have attended to the national agenda with particular initiatives such as assessment and student learning outcomes, student affairs has also responded to the call to action. But our work is not yet complete. What should we be able to do to ensure student success?

Three particularly important paradigm shifts in recent years have realigned the nature of student affairs work: (1) the focus on student learning outcomes, (2) the systems perspective of enrollment management, and (3) the potential and power of technology. Within each functional area the paradigm shifts have reframed the central mission of student affairs work: to think about what it is that students need to know, how we can help them know and understand, and what they should be able to do with that knowledge.

The paradigm shifts provide the emerging vision of the profession in this book. Student learning has been the vital core of student affairs work since the beginning of the field; nonetheless, concentration on services, programs, and functional areas has been easier to define and to orchestrate than the vague notion of supporting students in their quest for higher learning. The current focus on student learning outcomes makes learning the responsibility of all. The enrollment management movement has captured all functional areas and banded them together as interrelated subsystems providing an organizational context for the enhancement of student learning and retention. Understanding the nature of the university as an organization with a critical societal mission, but limited resources, is part and parcel of pragmatic administration. Technology enhances our relationships with students and informs our professionalism. It expands our reach and helps the profession respond to this new generation of students who have grown up with instant messaging, DVDs, MP3s, and multitasking.

I invite all who read this book to pause and consider the assumptions undergirding the profession and higher education. The first two chapters, thoughtfully revised from the previous edition of the book, provide the philosophical and historical tools to clarify assumptions, values, and concerns. The enrollment management chapters on admissions, financial aid, academic advising, and orientation interweave conceptually into one package loosely constructed at one institution and tightly constructed at others. Residence life, orientation, judicial affairs, career services, student activities, financial aid, and multicultural affairs provide an interesting, united focus on learning and living skills. Counseling, career services, and health services help focus on an integrated, wellness orientation to life. The final chapter of the book examines three central issues (social justice, student learning, and professionalism) that typify the current challenges facing our continually evolving profession and higher education.

I am deeply grateful to the authors for their contributions and for their expertise as this project moved forward. It has been a pleasure to work with experts who are consummate professionals and committed to the mission of the field.

I am most indebted to Audrey Rentz, who has been a mentor to me in the very best sense. Her support and guidance throughout my years at Bowling Green State University have been both personally and professionally empowering.

Fiona J.D. MacKinnon
July 2003
Bowling Green, Ohio

CONTENTS

Rentz's
STUDENT AFFAIRS PRACTICE
IN HIGHER EDUCATION

Chapter 1

THE PHILOSOPHICAL HERITAGE
OF STUDENT AFFAIRS

Stan Carpenter

INTRODUCTION

O g and El, our Neanderthal ancestors, had a problem. To be sure, Og and El, and their tribe, had lots of problems, but this was the most vexing yet. Although they did not know it or even understand the problem, they were beginning to think too much about their children, about the tribe, and about life generally. Og and El did not understand that the issue really was that their brains and minds were becoming more complex and more differentiated. Having a good brain was an advantage and was necessary for survival. Og and El were not very big or very fast compared to other animals. They were not particularly strong or keen of sight, smell, or hearing. But they could think and plan and remember. The problem was that this ability to conceptualize caused them to wonder—to need to know, to speculate, and to be unhappy when they did not have answers. Perhaps it was something poignant, like the death of a child, or just the mundane cycle of the seasons that first elicited a search for a larger meaning to life, but whatever it was, the quest could have soon led to depression, insanity, and death for the members of the tribe and therefore the tribe itself.

Thus was philosophy invented, or as some would say *discovered*, in an attempt to supplant powerlessness with knowledge. It did not matter that the knowledge was "incorrect" (in modern terms)—simply that it explained otherwise terrifyingly uncertain and uncontrollable things such as fire and rain, birth and death. It was necessary to have something to believe in and it was important to strive to learn more.

Over time a tribal culture developed, encompassing all the beliefs, knowledge, and skills that made the group unique and contributed to their survival. The culture was instilled in the children by formal and informal means in a process of education not materially different from that of today. As the tribe became a village, then a city, then a sovereign state, philosophical knowledge grew and differentiated. Eventually, it became necessary to attend to the higher learning of some members to prepare them to lead, to teach, and to press the search for new knowledge.

Student affairs professionals are the direct descendants of early educators, and hence heirs to a long tradition of thinking and writing about educational philosophy. The purpose of this chapter is to examine the impact of philosophy generally and several specific philosophical positions that influence higher education and the practice of student affairs work.

WHAT IS PHILOSOPHY?

At first, all learning was philosophical. The word *philosophy* from the Greek philosophia, literally means love of wisdom or learning. Only in the past 200 years has there occurred a separation of natural philosophy (or sciences such as chemistry and physics), mental philosophy (or psychology), and moral philosophy (e.g., political science, economics, and sociology) from the general concept (Brubacher, 1982). For thousands of years, the study of philosophy was the same as advanced learning, a wide-ranging intellectual quest. The explosion of knowledge and specialization have changed that—but philosophy is still a broad and deep field.

Philosophy is a poorly understood concept. People begin sentences with "My philosophy on that is . . ." and proceed to give unsupported opinions, sometimes inconsistent with their behaviors or facts.

Philosophy can be thought of as simply a general approach to the world or it can be a process of disciplined inquiry. Gracia (1992) captured it this way:

Philosophy may be interpreted . . . :

I.   . . . as a set of ideas or beliefs, concerning anything, that an ordinary person may hold.

II.   . . . as a view of the world, or any of its parts, that seeks to be accurate, consistent, and comprehensive.

III. . . . . as a discipline of learning.

    A. Activity whereby a view of the world or any of its parts, that seeks to be accurate, consistent, and comprehensive, is produced.

    B. Formulation, explanation, and justification of rules by which the production of a view of the world, or any of its parts, that seeks to be accurate, consistent, and comprehensive, is produced (philosophical methodology). (p. 56)

This chapter concerns itself primarily with the second interpretation (a view of the world), and with elements of the third (a discipline of learning.) In essence, the reader will apply the information presented (a view of the world), using the proper methods (through the discipline), to modify personal beliefs in such a way that they are accurate, consistent, and comprehensive.

THE THREE GREAT QUESTIONS OF PHILOSOPHY

Originally, philosophy was concerned with virtually all knowledge, but in modern times it has come to consist of three main (very large and important) questions: What is real? How do we know? What is of value?

Ontology

Ontology is concerned with the ultimate question of existence. Some people also call it metaphysics (literally "beyond physics"). Og, El, and their descendants desired to know what was real and what was ephemeral. Is the universe friendly, neutral, or malevolent? Is there order in the universe or only probabilistic chaos? Is physical existence real or is only our intellect, the goings-on in our minds, real? What is life? Is there a God or some other supernatural entity? Is this all there is?

Clearly, such questions are overwhelming and demand a systematic and satisfying answer. Just as clearly, they call for speculation, at least in the early stages of theory building and maybe for a long time after that. Every action taken by an individual, every decision, every thought will be colored by beliefs about the nature of reality.

Ontology can be usefully broken up into other areas of questions: anthropology, cosmology, theology, and teleology (Johnson, Collins, Dupuis, & Johansen, 1969). Anthropology concerns the nature of the human condition. Are people innately good or evil? What is the relationship between the mind and the body? Is there a soul or spirit and does it have precedence over the worldly flesh of the body? Do humans have free will?

Cosmology involves the study of the nature and origins of the universe, including questions about time, space, perceptions, and purpose. Theology considers questions of religion. Is there a God? More than one God? A "good" God or an indifferent one? Is God all-powerful? All-knowing? Some ontological theories depend heavily on theological theories.

Teleology, or the study of purpose in the cosmos, cuts across the other areas mentioned. Is the universe a chance event or is there some larger purpose? Much of what troubled Og and El, and continues to trouble humankind, is the province of ontology. Questions of ontology, while difficult, are at least straightforward. But how can data be gathered to answer them?

Epistemology

Epistemology examines the nature of knowledge itself, sources of knowledge, and the validity of different kinds of knowledge. Generally, knowledge can be gained in the following ways: from sensory perception (empirical knowledge); from revelation (knowledge from a supernatural source or being); from an authority or by tradition; from reason, logic, or intellect; or from intuition (nonsupernatural insight, not resulting from reason). These sources of knowledge are all subject to criticism. What is truth? Is truth subjective or objective, relative or absolute? Is there truth external to human experience? Can finite beings understand infinite truth?

Different philosophies have very different epistemologies. One fundamental issue is whether truth is unchanging—or does it vary with the situation or the individual? Can truth be discovered or constructed? Some philosophers hold that some truths are self-evident and do not need to be proven. These might be called Truths. Others reject this notion out of hand, suggesting that there is no truth except that leading from experience and that context is paramount. Speculations and theories about the origin and nature of reality and the ways that knowledge may be best gathered lead quickly to choices.

Axiology

Axiology, the third great question of philosophy, concerns values. Values necessitate choices—and choices require evaluating options. What is good? What is beautiful? Individuals, communities, countries, and societies may develop value systems based on their philosophies. When value systems conflict, tension develops. The impact of philosophy on personal and professional behavior is most clear in the process of valuing. What someone believes and thinks is likely, although not certainly, a determinant of action.

Axiology is divided into ethics and aesthetics. Ethics is the study of proper behavioral choices. What is moral? Are ethics contextual or absolute? Is there a connection between what is believed to be right and proper action? Is the good of the societal unit superior to the good of the individual? Who has the right to set ethical standards? Are the laws of society subordinate to the laws of a supernatural entity, such as God? What is the proper relationship between teacher and student? These (and many others) are all questions of ethics.

Professions develop more or less enforceable, formal and informal codes of ethics, based on shared philosophies. It is incumbent upon the practitioner (1) to learn to apply these ethics in such a way that students or clients are best served, and (2) to participate in ongoing dialogue to update the ethics of the profession.

Aesthetics involves questions about beauty and art. What is beautiful? Is there some ideal that is impossible to attain? Is beauty affected by individual experience? Are there absolute standards, or should experts be called upon to judge what is excellent and what is not? Who is to choose? The phrase "beauty is in the eye of the beholder" suggests that the finger painting of a four-year-old is beautiful to some, but the world art market suggests otherwise. Aesthetics allows discussion of such choices and values.

EDUCATIONAL PHILOSOPHY

Philosophy as a general discipline is often applied to specialized areas. There exists, for example, lively literature on the philosophy of science, the philosophy of law, and the philosophy of education.

Educators study educational philosophy to undergird their practice. Because of the unique and pervasive place of education in the culture, the distinction between the general and the specific is not easy to determine. Education is the very transmission of the culture and all accumulated knowledge. Through the process of education the student is equipped to continue learning and eventually contribute to the whole. In this sense, education is philosophy in action, a point most clearly made by John Dewey (1916) when he defined philosophy as the general theory of education.

Philosophical positions are central to the practice of education. Two different educators, for example, holding disparate philosophies would be unlikely to agree on any coherent curriculum The educational implications of assuming that humans must somehow overcome their sensory impressions in order to use their intellect or reason to understand reality are far-reaching. An alternate view is that experience is the only worthwhile learning. This is just one example of differing viewpoints taken from epistemology. There are many more epistemological examples available, to say nothing of ontological questions of value. Obviously, everything done in the name of education has a basis in some philosophical notion and/or "teaches" some philosophical tenet to the student.

In a pluralistic society such as the United States, philosophical differences between and among teacher and student, college and teacher, school and parent, college and society at large, and any permutation of these, can and do cause great conflict. This is not necessarily bad, especially at the college or university level, where a certain amount of conflict and challenge of views contributes to learning. Nevertheless, to the extent that education is an intentional activity, educators and institutions should examine and be aware of their philosophical bases. Practices inconsistent with espoused views and beliefs are confusing at best—and may be damaging.

Hence, the study of educational philosophy. Professionals have an obligation to learn and know more than techniques and approaches to problem solving. Only by studying and applying deeply held assumptions and underlying premises can a practitioner of student affairs hope to bring insight to a novel problem, a different student, or a new situation. If a practitioner holds one view and an institution holds another view, conflict is likely; if neither knows what the other believes, then conflict is certain and may not be easily resolved. Student affairs professionals cannot always tell what an institution truly believes, but they can and should always determine their own educational philosophies.

MAJOR PHILOSOPHICAL SCHOOLS

Student affairs and higher education practices are based on a variety of different philosophies. Therefore, it is necessary to acquaint the reader with several influential Western schools of thought that have had the most impact on U.S. education: idealism, realism, neo-Thomism, pragmatism, and existentialism. A treatment of Eastern philosophy and other thinking is beyond the scope of this book.

IDEALISM

Plato offered the basis of idealism, the notion that the "real" world is accessible only through reason, in his writing on the teaching of Socrates and through his own work. The thinking here is that the world as perceived by humans is transient, changeable, always becoming but never quite finished, and hence deceptive. The real world is perfect, not needing and not having physical manifestation. Thus, the idea of a chair is more important, a higher order of reality, than the chair which is seen or sat upon.

Ontologically, reality depends on a superordinate mind that is capable of conceiving reality in its ideal state. Humans possess a spark of this Mind and can communicate with the real world through (and only through) reason and intellect. Material existence (the things of the flesh) inhibits this communication and reason. Things of the flesh are not to be trusted. Truth is unchanging and permanent, infinite and ultimately unknowable. Since humans are finite, they can know about the truth, but can never know all. The ethical goal is to live a moral life by following the will of the mind or of the universe. Some people (such as teachers, priests, and political leaders) are closer to the Ideal than others and they should be heeded. Beauty is defined as an approximation of the Ideal, usually the Divine. Idealism allows, almost requires, a supernatural entity and is therefore very compatible with religion. Later thinkers have worked out idealistic philosophies without the use of a God, but these philosophies are largely unsatisfying.

Educationally, idealism posits that each individual should be helped to actualize the spark of the ideal that is within. However, the test of the actualization is correspondence with the Ideal, much of which has already been discovered over the years. Hence, students are taught using materials that have stood the test of time and societal examination. The Great Books are used and the primacy of the state is emphasized. The assumption is that a consensus ideal is a better approximation than an individual conception. Idealism is one of the cornerstones of a conservative approach to curriculum and education emphasizing essential truths.

REALISM

Aristotle believed that observed reality is the only Reality. He was not satisfied with the Platonic view that sensory data were distorted and not to be trusted. That is, the universe exists without a mind standing behind it and whether humans perceive it or not. Natural laws are permanent and unchanging, and humans can discover them through the use of their minds. If there are things that are not yet understood, then there simply has not been enough research.

Truth, then, is external and independent of knowledge. Epistemologically, realism makes use of inductive logic. The observer gathers particular bits of knowledge and fits them into theories, propositions, and laws according to the rules of science. Truth is completely knowable and may be judged by its correspondence with reality. Values and beauty have to do with conformance with the laws of nature. That is good which allows people to live in accordance with nature, the so-called moral law; and that is beautiful which reflects natural harmony. Human nature is everywhere the same, and a distinction is made between the natural and the accidental. The essential nature of anything does not change, even though some variations may be noted (Brubacher, 1962).

Educationally, realism calls for the student to be acquainted with rational methods of observation and logic. Hence, science and mathematics have a large place in the curriculum. However, the traditional humanities are important as well because there are natural ways for society to function and the student must be made aware of the best thinking to date. Students are not left to learn what they think they want to know, since this would take away time from what they should be learning, what is already known. After all, it is inefficient for students to arrive at their own conclusions about that which is already known, let alone the fact that no one can be expected to contribute to new knowledge without a grounding in research to date. Realism is also, clearly, a foundation for conservative educational thinking, with its reliance on knowledge external to the student.

NEO-THOMISM

St. Thomas Aquinas saw much to like in both Idealism and Realism. On the one hand, Aristotle's ideas were very persuasive, were grounded in common sense, and seemed to reflect human experience. On the other hand, it was necessary to bring into account the known (to Roman Catholics like Aquinas) existence of a supernatural being (God). The solution was to combine the two, retaining the duality between mind and body proposed by Plato, but assigning faith a preeminent role over reason. That is, humans were free to observe the material world in scientific, logical ways with the proviso that when reason contradicted the revealed truth of religion, then reason was simply faulty. Much of realism is inherent in neo-Thomism, so much that some call this philosophy religious realism (Kneller, 1964). The basic notion is that there is no inherent conflict between faith and reason, so long as it is understood that God is perfect and therefore faith is preeminent.

Aquinas lived in the thirteenth century (the philosophy was originally called Thomism), but his ideas have endured so strongly that the Roman Catholic Church acknowledges this philosophy as its official position (Johnson et al., 1969) and it is the basis of much of Catholic education. There are also lay philosophers who subscribe to neo-Thomism, with their axiology being based upon a rationally derived and unchanging moral law that is not supernaturally based.

Education for neo-Thomists consists of teaching the perennial truths derived from faith and reason. Because humans have free will, the student must be taught the discipline of learning and must be encouraged to make good choices. Knowledge and values are permanent and unchanging, and the purpose of learning is to live by rational and moral standards. The student is educated in a moral atmosphere that forms the framework for knowledge. Again, time-honored and established methods and materials form the base of the curriculum.

PRAGMATISM

Pragmatism defines reality as the interaction of humans with nature. Reality is the sum total of human experience, and that is true which is proven useful after a careful investigation and analysis. Pragmatism represents a major break with the other philosophies thus far considered in that it rejects the idea of permanent, unchanging truth. Although it has roots in the empiricist tradition (developed from realism as explicated by Charles Sanders Peirce, John Dewey, and William James), pragmatism suggests that even so-called natural "laws" are not eternal.

Indeed, reality is defined by the interaction of humans with nature. While nature has an objective, albeit changeable, existence, it has no real meaning except as it relates to human experience. Speculation about the infinite or supernatural is idle, by definition, since it cannot be verified by human means. Pragmatic epistemology does not allow humans to simply make up truth; rather, truth is determined using the experimental method. As a problem is confronted, data are gathered, hypotheses are generated, mental testing is conducted, and finally solutions are implemented. The best or most workable solution is the truth—for these circumstances, using these data collection methods. Given that things change, techniques improve, and different approaches give different answers, this truth is temporary and not absolute. For example, based on everything scientifically known, the sun will very likely rise in the morning. But it is possible for conditions to change and, therefore, dawn is never a certainty.

Values are relative and situational, chosen through a logical process. That does not mean that morality changes willy-nilly, but that there are no absolute precepts, always true and never violated. Morals are not handed down from some higher authority, but rather are decided by individuals and groups, by agreement and consensus if possible, in a dynamic process. Pragmatism is thought to require democracy for best use.

Educationally, the student is thought of as an integrated whole, thoroughly involved in his or her own education. Since experience is the only determiner of reality, the student should be allowed to learn whatever is of interest. Abstract concepts are important, but they should be studied later in the education process rather than earlier so that the student develops a lively style of experiencing and then organizes the experiences from the beginning. This project method should allow for the education of the biological, psychological, and social aspects of the student. The teacher or other educator should not be ascendant, but rather facilitative. The curriculum and materials used should be flexible and learner-centered. Readiness and enthusiasm are keys to learning and teaching.

EXISTENTIALISM

Jean Paul Sartre (1947) wrote, "existence precedes essence." This apparently simple phrase is fraught with meaning. The fact of "being" carries with it the awful truth that humans are only and totally what they make of themselves by their own choices. The universe exists and the order that science finds is present, but these facts matter only as backdrop for the confrontation that is inevitable in the life of every person. People find themselves, when they become truly aware of their condition, in an indifferent universe that has no purpose and in which they are doomed to die.

Truth is that which each individual concludes in a passionate encounter with the self and the choices available. There is complete freedom because of the indifference of nature, the absence of rules; there is complete responsibility because no one else chooses, or if they do, the individual chooses his or her response. The human condition causes "angst," searching for meaning in a meaningless world, possessing freedom and aware of finitude or existential dread. Knowledge is gained in an active way involving both thinking and feeling. Existentialism does not allow detached analysis. Information is less important than what the person does with the data. Values are meaningless unless chosen. However, freedom does not imply anarchy: A commitment to freedom for self leads inevitably to a conception of freedom for all. Responsibility for choices that restrict the freedom of others is its own kind of limit. Additionally, true freedom is the freedom to commit to others in an authentic relationship. Still, the fundamental value of existentialism is to be true to oneself.

The existentialist educator walks a tightrope between encouraging freedom and bridling immature choices. Students must be confronted with the reality of the human condition and must take responsibility for their choices. The educator must also interact with the students in an authentic way, modeling mature behavior and attending to his or her own growth. The educator stimulates student involvement with learning on a personal level and commitment to understanding—not to following the crowd or bowing to expert opinion. Every person in every situation is treated with dignity and respect, even if some behaviors are not tolerated.

Humanities, literature, art, and history (Kneller, 1964) are heavily utilized since they reflect the struggles of people to understand their own existence. Students undertake a careful study of traditional knowledge in order to grasp the world in which they live. Students makes the subject matter their own by seeking out interpretations (e.g., in historical accounts) and considering counter conclusions. Education is an active process that never ends.

A BRIEF PHILOSOPHICAL HISTORY OF HIGHER EDUCATION

The history of higher education is, in some sense, a history of thought and therefore a history of philosophy. This section treats philosophical influences on Western higher education from the time of the Greeks through the present.

As ancient Greece was settled and city-states were established, the life of the mind began to take on more importance. The democratic assemblies put a premium on erudition and persuasion. The Sophists, itinerant teachers, were among the first to meet this need. They focused on utilitarian education—they were not concerned about the ends to which logic and rhetorical skills were turned (Domonkos, 1977). This moral relativism caused a countermovement to use the discipline of learning to attain ethical wisdom and absolute truth. Chief among the philosophers engaged in this quest were Socrates and his student Plato. Most importantly, they each established schools for the edification of both teachers and students. To all intents and purposes, these institutions are the precursors of modern colleges and universities.

Plato was an idealist and believed that only the elite, defined as the intellectually able and educated, should be allowed to rule. Not surprisingly, his notion of education was focused on reason and ideas, a striving for knowledge that was absolute and unchanging.

On the contrary, Plato's student, Aristotle, did not distrust sensory data, but rather sought to organize it according to logical and scientific principles. Aristotle did believe that truth is unchanging, as seen in the previous discussion of realism, and he advocated a search for the laws of nature. These ideas, along with other minor philosophical schools, as well as some attention to law and medicine, dominated higher education through the fall of Rome.

During the so-called Dark Ages, higher education was essentially the domain of clerics in the Christian West, but there were thriving academic communities among the Jews, Moslems, and Byzantines. In fact, it is through contact with these other cultures that interest in the ancient Greek philosophies reemerged to challenge the rather sterile, faith-based notions of the church hierarchy. The history of all of the early institutions of higher education in the West is too extensive to go into here.

The best of the early universities was the University of Paris, which housed lively philosophical debate around theology and the conflict between religious idealism and Aristotelian realism. Eventually the university found it necessary to succumb to church doctrine in order to gain papal support in a struggle against the Parisian authorities. But this debate was not confined to Paris and raged on. St. Thomas Aquinas successfully joined realism and religion (see preceding), and his ideas of reason and science as permissible but subservient to faith became the philosophy of the church and more specifically the universities and schools. Consequently, most of the great discoveries of science for hundreds of years took place independently of the universities either in the academies or as a result of private patronage of great thinkers,.

Even the onset of the Reformation, the ecclesiastical revolt against the Roman Catholic Church, did not materially change the philosophy of higher education. Universities were intellectual captives of whoever their sponsors were, whether state governments or state religions, usually both. But the Reformation had allowed the camel's nose under the tent of Catholic theological hegemony. Sect after sect sprang up, eventually leading to the notion that no one group owned the truth. This fertile climate spawned thinkers who came to speculate about the place of the supernatural in their conceptions of the universe and humankind. Writers and philosophers in this Enlightenment, such as Locke and Voltaire, and the people they influenced, notably Benjamin Franklin and Thomas Jefferson, spoke of inalienable rights and contracts between the rulers and the governed. Effectively, they were seeking the natural laws of society, just as scientists were discovering the natural laws of physics, astronomy, chemistry, and biology. Knowledge and education were becoming too important to be dominated by religious authorities. The power of ideas was beginning to manifest itself.

Still, the colleges and universities were reflective of the society, and by and large the society was pietistic. If education was too important to be dictated by the church, it was certainly too important to be left to professors, and so there evolved an uneasy equilibrium between lay control and teacher autonomy. In England, higher education was primarily for the elite, intellectually and/or financially, who were being groomed for ecclesiastical and political leadership. They were provided a classical liberal arts education with little science and much orthodox theology. Their spiritual growth and social progress were monitored as heavily as their intellectual progress. They were taught to strive for the Ideal.

This model of education was lifted whole cloth and set down in the American colonies. All of the original nine colonial colleges were sectarian except the University of Pennsylvania (then the College of Philadelphia) and all followed the British model. Standards for behavior, for learning, and for spiritual development were absolute and individuality was not brooked. But new ideas were brewing. In the later part of the colonial period and much more so in the early federal period of the United States, there was a proliferation of colleges, mostly sectarian, but some state-sponsored. At first, these were much the same as those that had gone before, but market forces, increased specialization of disciplines, and the onrush of scientific discovery began to engender diversity and differentiation (Potts, 1977). To counter this drift toward the secular, and worse, the non-classical, the faculty of Yale published the Yale Report in 1828. This was the first formal statement of the philosophy of higher education in the United States (Brubacher & Rudy, 1976). The Yale Report held that the traditional, classical curriculum was the only way to provide higher learning to students because of its emphasis on (1) mental discipline (based on faculty psychology), and (2) its steadfast refusal to accord status to the transitory, the ephemeral, or the worldly. In other words, economically or scientifically useful knowledge should be learned elsewhere. The Yale Report was influential for decades, but its very publication signaled the beginning of the end for strictly Idealist higher education.

Realism, in the form of science, empiricism, and practicality, was pushing its way into the curriculum. The latter half of the nineteenth century saw the advent of the German model university, the bastion of research and academic freedom to teach and to learn. The Morrill Act of 1862 led to the creation of a distinctly U.S. style institution, the land grant university, with its curious combination mission of research, teaching, and service. As secular and current course content displaced religious and ancient knowledge, pressure to focus on the intellect only increased. The out-of-class habits of students, the extracurricular activities, the sports they engaged in—these were distractions from the "real" business of education. However, the United States was still a moralistic nation and was not about to surrender its young men (and certainly not its young women!) to colleges and universities unconcerned about anything but their minds. Hence, institutions took on obligations that had not existed in other parts of the world, the role of parents without true control, a concern for the out-of-class behavior of students in ways that were unconnected to the curriculum (as opposed to the earlier British model).

TWENTIETH CENTURY PHILOSOPHICAL INFLUENCES ON U. S. HIGHER EDUCATION

As the twentieth century began, the hegemony of realism, embodied as Newtonian science, was cracking, as had idealism before it. To be sure, the receiving of intellectual knowledge was still the primary role of students, but Pragmatism and later Existentialism were making inroads in almost all disciplines and hence were working their way into the thinking of those guiding colleges and universities. Until the early 1960s, the dominant philosophical mode for colleges and universities was still a focus on intellectualism tied to an almost formless attitude of *in loco parentis*.

In many ways, the conflict boiled down to one of epistemology. Is the student to be educated about the truth or does the educated student participate in shaping the truth? Is the content of a liberal education more or less constant or does it change in relation to context?

On the one hand are the essentialists, variously identified as rationalists, rational humanists, neo-humanists, or perennialists, among other labels. These philosophers and educators did not all hold the same beliefs, differing in views about the nature of knowledge, the existence of God, and the importance of reason versus revelation. Nevertheless, they united in their opposition to the corrupting influences of the vocational and the worldly on higher education. Thorstein Veblen's (1918) assertion of the value-free nature of research was one example, but the best-known advocates of this position in the early twentieth century were Robert Maynard Hutchins (1936) and Mortimer Adler (1951). Both men extolled the virtues of intellectual excellence to be gained by the assiduous study of the Great Books, the so-called Western Canon. This kind of study and education were thought to prepare the mind in the best way for any field of endeavor. Indeed, these ideas were timeless and essential. Furthermore, education without moral content was considered useless. Hutchins and Adler were ostensibly secular in their suggestions, but their ideas resonate clearly with the views of the religious perennialists. Truth is something that does not change: It needs to be discovered and once discovered it must be learned by each succeeding generation. Ideas that have stood the test of time are to be returned to again and again. Fundamental to this viewpoint is the conception of the mind as separate from the body—knowledge uncontaminated by experience.

On the other hand were the pragmatic naturalists, the experimentalists, the instrumentalists, the progressivists, and the reconstructionists. Such thinkers as John Dewey (1937), Sidney Hook (1946), and Alfred North Whitehead (1929) thought that the split of intellect from the world of theory from practice was wrong. Liberal education is and should be based in the context of the time and the place, and reason should be informed by passion and emotion. Humans are whole and must be educated as such. Experience and rationality should be used as means rather than ends to help solve the problems of society. Indeed, the reconstructionists dared to dream of Utopian goals and sought to involve education in their plans. Truth, in this conception, is something that works and is meaningful to each individual in different ways.

It is not a long leap from this pragmatic viewpoint to that of existential-ism, postmodernism, critical theory, and constructivism (Lincoln, 1989). If knowledge is not external and unchanging, if it is defined as what is work-able based on experience, and if the society is working toward democracy, then who is to define truth? If one conception of truth is just as good as any other, then truth ceases to be universal and becomes intensely individual. Reality is constructed rather than discovered. Not only are the mind and the body not separated, but also they are one with context. Pluralism, as opposed to assimilation to the dominant culture, is cultivated and acted upon. As should be immediately clear, these ideas have drastic implications for higher education and student affairs.

Considerations of philosophy were largely settled on the side of the prag-matic by the influx of students after World War II. Returning soldiers had little patience for the parental function of colleges—and the nation needed technically trained graduates. The early stirrings of the civil rights move-ment and the unrest of the 1960s refocused the philosophical lens on high-er education. For most schools, the parental role perished in the fiery heat of the social revolution of the 1960s and the aftershocks in the 1970s. Of course, Roman Catholic and many other sectarian institutions continued to adhere to a neo-Thomist view, but in most colleges students experience a mishmash of philosophical influences. Colleges are by turns moralistic in some regulations, scientific in some attitudes and services, existential in their assigning of responsibility for learning, and withal pragmatic. The typ-ical institution harbors individuals in important faculty and administrative positions who exercise great authority and who firmly believe in each of the major philosophies. And the school that acts consistently on only one of the philosophies is rare and probably sectarian.

EDUCATIONAL PHILOSOPHY
AND STUDENT AFFAIRS

For the first 200 years or so, higher education in the United States large-ly followed an idealist model. Education was thought of as mental discipline and things of the flesh were to be conquered so they did not get in the way. Young people (students) especially needed help to control their impulses—all that energy and all those hormones. Faculty psychology dictated and spiritual needs reinforced that students should invest all their resources into training their intellects and moderating their base desires. To this end, edu-cators controlled living and eating arrangements, and arranged curricula in such a way as to leave little free time and less discretionary behavior. Since humans were thought to be flawed and incapable of innate understanding of absolute, eternal truths without restraint and focus on reason, colleges took on a parental role.

The explosion of science and specialization, coupled with a growing democratic mindset and the influx of German ideas of higher education, eroded this position by the latter part of the nineteenth century. In the realist mode, depending as it did on the mind-body split articulated by Descartes and others, things of the flesh did not really matter. Professors and researchers at the new universities were quite simply not interested in anything but knowledge and did not care to participate in students' out-of-class lives. Again, truth was conceived as external to humans, something to be discovered and understood rationally. Human nature was not thought to be inherently negative or positive, simply not relevant to learning and thinking.

Still, higher education as an institution is known for its inertia, and the graduate and research universities required a feeder system of undergraduate colleges. Accordingly, the United States developed a model unique in the world. Excellent universities conducting state-of-the-art research were joined with undergraduate colleges that continued to follow the British model. U.S. society was not prepared to abandon adolescents to their impulses, even if faculty members thought they had better things to do. The necessity of traveling long distances to attend colleges, the relative youth of U.S. students, the essentially Christian character of the nation, and hundreds of years of tradition in higher education contributed to the need to regulate student conduct on campus. Thus, in rough strokes, was born the student affairs worker.

Philosophically, *in loco parentis* provided not only a framework for idealistic rules in order to bring the student into compliance with age-old social mores, but also an outlet for emotional and psychological needs unmet, and properly so, in the classroom. The roots of the services and control models of student affairs, then, are in the essentialist philosophical tradition. Knowledge is something absolute to which students must accommodate. Since students needed help to do this, and since faculty were increasingly unwilling to provide this help, it was necessary to hire a new kind of educator.

By the beginning of the twentieth century, early student affairs workers were filling much of the parental role of the colleges, thereby relieving the faculty of the task. Colleges and universities were growing and becoming more complex organizationally, requiring other administrators and managers, as well. Additionally, psychology was finding its niche as the "science" of human behavior, particularly with the testing movement. The idea was that people were suited to certain careers and that systematic counseling would help with a match. Well into the 1950s, Cowley (1957) held that the field was dominated by three types of student affairs workers—humanitarians, administrators, and counselors, each with a role, but rather uncoordinated.

THE STUDENT PERSONNEL POINT OF VIEW (1937)

Confusions about the field of student affairs and its goals for students are reflected in the first and second statements of the Student Personnel Point of View (SPPV) (American Council on Education, 1994). In the 1937 statement, importance is placed on coordination with the academic enterprise with the goal of ensuring the maximum improvement of the student meeting his or her potential. Emphasis is also placed on scientific research to learn how to best serve institutions and students. In fact, the SPPV would be unremarkable philosophically except for its insistence on the impact of education on the "whole student." While this philosophical statement is grounded in a rational humanist context, overtones of existentialism and pragmatism are clearly present. The student is presumed to have a role in his or her own education—a radical notion at the time.

THE STUDENT PERSONNEL POINT OF VIEW (1949)

The revised SPPV (American Council on Education, 1994) is philosophically much more straightforward in its pragmatic approach. Democracy and social reconstruction are presented as the bases for education. There are nods toward standards of conduct and self-control. The clinical findings of the social sciences are not left out, but problem solving is clearly preferred as a goal. Again, the student is responsible for his or her own education, but enrichment and facilitation are coming to the fore instead of simply services.

STUDENT DEVELOPMENT

The radicalism of the 1960s disturbed the uneasy equilibrium that student affairs had reached with the academic establishment. Obviously, societal standards were in flux and could hardly be transmitted wholesale. Students were demanding an increasing amount of attention—the role of education had to shift. The student affairs response was to counsel a focus on the person rather than on the course content. Colleges were to teach students rather than subject matter. In fact, the argument went, if the focus is really to be on the whole student, then human development principles must be applied across the curriculum and the extracurriculum (Brown, 1972; Miller & Prince, 1976). Furthermore, the student is in control of what is to be learned and what is to be valued. The university was to be construed as a place where learning was facilitated, where the student learned to make choices and understand that every choice has consequences that must be considered and accepted. In *loco parentis*, dead in a legal sense since the 1960s, died in a practical sense in the 1970s despite recent attempts to revive it.

The student development model, with its underpinnings in the self-confrontational struggle of existentialism and the utilitarian foundation of pragmatism, changed student affairs practice completely. The merging of the goals of the academic and the "other" education recognizes that, to the student, college is a seamless web of growth and development. All aspects of education are interdependent—one cannot be accomplished without the others being in place. Focus on the student means that wellness, support for nontraditional students, alcohol awareness, learning assistance, and many other areas are not only just as essential as housing, financial aid, counseling, and student activities, but also crucial if optimum learning is to occur. Student affairs educators stop being purveyors and become facilitators and consultants. Colleges do not pronounce appropriate choices for students, but rather propose them for the students to choose from—and sometimes not even that.

A student development focus does not mean that values are abandoned by institutions or student affairs professionals, but that expectations are clearly stated up-front in such a way that students can make good choices for themselves. Likewise, science is not forsaken; rather, student development theory is based on research into developmental psychology, causing some controversy among practitioners who have to reconcile somewhat lockstep conceptualizations with undeniable student uniqueness. Finally, student development capitalizes on diversity, celebrating and enhancing differences as necessary and educational.

It may seem that existentialism and pragmatism give too much authority to the individual to be used as bases for transmitting a culture. However, pragmatism has a strong emphasis on the social, with an acknowledgment that the individual lives in a group and that growth for all is a goal. Existentialism emphasizes self-confrontation and acceptance of responsibility for choices. This responsibility is understood to include the impact of personal choices on other free beings. Rights for one are rights for all and must be respected.

THE 1987 NATIONAL ASSOCIATION OF STUDENT PERSONNEL ADMINISTRATORS (NASPA) STATEMENT

In 1987, NASPA published "A Perspective on Student Affairs: A Statement Issued on the 50th Anniversary of the Student Personnel Point of View." This paper acknowledged articulately the growing diversity of U.S. higher education and strongly emphasized the place of institutional mission in education. Under the label of shared assumptions, the perspective statement argues for the preeminence of the academic mission for higher education and suggests that student affairs should not compete with, or substitute for, the academic mission. Instead, student affairs enhances and supports the principal goals of colleges and universities. Other parts of the statement go on to reiterate (1) the notion of the whole, unique student; (2) the importance of involvement in learning; (3) the crucial nature of the college environment; and (4) personal factors in education. Philosophically, the perspective statement is a mixed bag, with a seeming nod toward essentialism (the emphasis on cognitive learning), an expression of existentialist tenets (worth and uniqueness of the student), and recognition of pragmatism (importance of involvement, environment, and diversity). This is partially because the statement was not intended to be a philosophical tract, but rather a political statement, and therefore it tried to be all things to all people. Still, to the extent that the statement represented the mainstream of student affairs leadership, there was a clear turn toward institutions and academic content as foci, at the expense of emphasis on students and their choices.

THE "REASONABLE EXPECTATIONS" STATEMENT

A document entitled "Reasonable Expectations: Renewing the Educational Compact Between Institutions and Students" was published by NASPA in 1995 (Kuh, Lyons, Miller, & Trow, 1995). While not strictly philosophical in tone, the statement takes the form of an examination of the pragmatic contract between colleges and universities, and their students. The focus is on mutual respect and high expectations going in both directions, with integrity and communication strongly emphasized. There is an existential recognition of choice and responsibility and a bias toward action and involvement. While the statement is careful to be vague with regard to underlying ontological and epistemological beliefs, presumably so that many and varied institutions are covered, idealist and realist educators would be hard-pressed to follow all the tenets espoused. Similarly, although the statement is aimed at the broader institution, it is clear that professional student affairs workers are best able to provide the interface called for between the college and students.

THE "STUDENT LEARNING IMPERATIVE" (SLI)

The SLI was published by ACPA in 1994, ostensibly as a call to change student affairs practice so that there is more focus on "student learning and personal development" (ACPA, 1994, p. 1). However, the document makes no clear differentiation between student learning, personal development, and student development, at one point calling all three terms "inextricably intertwined and inseparable" (ACPA, p. 1). Philosophically, the statement leans toward the essentialist, with its insistence on "educationally purposeful activities" (ACPA, p. 2). Presumably, some activities are more important for learning than others, and student affairs professionals, along with other institutional agents, know which are which and should guide students accordingly. One way to learn about appropriate activities for students is scientific research. To be sure, process is emphasized, the seamless nature of education as perceived by the student is recognized, and a holistic approach is advocated in the SLI. Withal, however, the tone suggests that student affairs has failed in some way and must get on the academic productivity

bandwagon in order to help institutions and students become more efficient learners. Student affairs is relegated to a "complementary mission"
(ACPA, p. 2), involving more emphasis on learning theory and assessment.
This is an apparent abrogation of existentialism as a fundamental base of
student affairs practice and pulls back from pragmatism, as well.

THE PRINCIPLES OF GOOD PRACTICE

In 1996, the presidents of NASPA and ACPA jointly commissioned a committee, cochaired by Elizabeth Whitt and Greg Blimling, to draft a statement
and inventories to assess good practice, with a report being issued in 1997
(ACPA & NASPA, 1997). Concepts espoused were (1) active learning, (2)
high expectations, (3) collaboration, (4) effective resource use, (5) inquiry-
based practice, and (6) community. Holistic emphasis and diversity were
clear assumptions, and the report breaks no really new ground but serves as
a cogent and coherent restatement of modern student affairs values and
practices. Philosophically, learning and development are conceived to be the
responsibility of the student interacting with a caring and intentional institution in which all parties are working toward a positive learning setting.

POWERFUL PARTNERSHIPS

The American Association for Higher Education (AAHE) combined with
ACPA and NASPA to publish the document entitled "Powerful Partnerships:
A Shared Responsibility for Learning" in 1998 (Joint Task Force on Student
Learning, 1998). The report is a far-reaching prescription for reform of
higher education that envisions the application of learning research and
theory being applied by boundary-spanning academic and student affairs
professionals. This vision is truly powerful, encompassing students, faculty,
student affairs professionals, and other staff in the context of external stakeholders, including parents, boards, and governmental parties, among others. Cutting-edge programs are highlighted, and principles of diversity,
student agency, supportive environments, and intentional development are
implicitly and explicitly emphasized. Students and institutions are considered to be linked in a common enterprise—that of full learning and development. Cognitive learning is not privileged over holistic development;
instead the two are seen as mutually necessary. This statement virtually epit-
omizes the philosophical notions of pragmatism and existentialism, allow-
ing also for a crucial role to be played by the institutional mission.

THE SEARCH FOR A STUDENT AFFAIRS PHILOSOPHY GOES ON

The several statements published in the 1990s are not the only attempts
to codify the philosophical tenets of student affairs. Knock, Rentz, and Penn

(1989) detailed significant influences on student affairs' philosophical heritage, arguing that professional practice had moved past rationalism and neo-humanism into pragmatism and existentialism as the basis of student development. Whitt, Carnaghi, Matkin, Scalese-Love, and Nestor (1990) asserted that emergent paradigm thinking (Lincoln & Guba, 1985) and the complexities of practices and diversity in higher education made a unified philosophy of student affairs impossible to divine—indeed, unwise and inappropriate. Context and cultural considerations should be paramount.

Manning (1994) introduced liberation theology into the mix and in 1996 also debunked the myth that student affairs has no philosophy, asserting that pragmatism and existentialism are inherent in most current thinking and practice. Young examined the values of student affairs several times in work that has clear philosophical underpinnings, most recently in a special issue of the *Journal of College Student Development* on the ethos of scholarship as a guiding model for student affairs practice (Young, 2001). Young's consistent theme is that student affairs core values serve the causes of both individuation and community.

Several articles in the same issue of the *Journal of College Student Development* have philosophical implications. The most relevant is that of Evans with Reason (2001), whose extensive analysis of many of the documents explored previously (and others) concludes with the identification of several underlying themes that suggest that learning, conceived broadly as development, has been the focus of the student affairs field all along. She also highlights appreciation of diversity, holism, and student self-responsibility, as well as accountability. She argues that there is little new under the sun, but it is always useful to restate our core goals. What is new in the Evans analysis is a call for advocacy and activism on campus. She believes that the time has come for student affairs workers to push harder for critical aspects of social justice and other student needs on campus. Evans characterizes this new role as going past Deweyan pragmatism, but it may well be a natural extension of an evolving philosophy of the student affairs field. Clearly, it can be argued that pragmatism and existentialism, taken seriously, imply that student affairs workers should examine campus conditions and work to change those that adversely affect students and/or do not facilitate optimum development and learning for everyone in the community.

A careful reading of all the statements and assertions detailed here (and of others not mentioned) leads to the position that sufficient evidence exists to determine that student choice is a sine qua non for quality in higher education. Students inarguably make choices as individuals. They decide which classes to attend, what to study, and in which activities to become involved. By their choices, students determine the level of benefit that will be derived from college and its attendant milieu. Students decide which choices work for them, which consequences they are willing to undergo. In short, students are in charge of their own lives.

While professional judgment is and should be exercised in matters of curriculum and in student affairs practice, students cannot be coerced to follow such advice. Students create their own meaning based on their own phenomenological world. This philosophical stance is largely existentialist, with a generous helping of pragmatism. But, principally, it revisits the distinction made earlier in this chapter about the nature of truth. It is argued here that truth, as we understand it in student affairs practice, is largely constructed by individuals rather than located outside human experience, waiting to be discovered or divined or revealed. The goal of student affairs practice is to facilitate the process of collecting information, undergoing experiences, and making meaning by students. Along the way, student affairs professionals may advise, suggest, cajole, and counsel, but they may not live, know, or choose for the students. Nor can any institution.

BUILDING A PERSONAL PHILOSOPHY OF STUDENT AFFAIRS

This chapter has focused on the philosophical heritage of student affairs and higher education and the importance of philosophy in the formulation of policy and programming. It has been argued that the philosophical terrain of colleges and universities is hotly contested and uncertain. In such loosely coupled organizations, multiple missions exist, multiple actors behave with varying motivations, and multiple choices must be made. For the professional to navigate successfully in these seas, he or she must have reference points, guiding stars to chart a course. A knowledge of one's personal philosophy helps provide such direction.

In developing or examining a personal and professional philosophy the following questions may be considered:

- What is the place of humans in the universe? Are people here to fulfill God's purpose, at the whim of an uncaring supernatural power, as the result of chance, as the ultimate in existence, or does it even matter why? Are people inherently of value or do they need to earn value? Do behaviors matter more than simple existence? Do humans have free choice or is their behavior predetermined by fate, science, or God?
- Does the universe exist in some objective sense external to the understanding of humans? Is reality for any person only what he or she perceives it to be? Is there some larger purpose to creation that is unknown or unknowable?
- Is truth unchanging and eternal, either in an infinite, supernatural way or in an immutable, scientific way? Are there discoverable laws of nature? Is truth what works or makes sense to individuals or communities or societies? What is the best way to determine truth—the scientific method, experience, reason, or revelation and intuition?

- Are the laws of God more important than the laws of the society or the country? Is the greatest good for the greatest number a measure of behavior or policy? Are individual rights preeminent? Are people free to act in any way that pleases them? Does any person owe any obligation to any other person or state or the world? What is the nature of responsibility?
- Is beauty in the eye of the beholder? Are there objective standards for art or music or love? Do some people know what is best and most beautiful for other people?
- How can cultural standards be best defined? Should children be given instruction on the tried and true best ways to think and live, or should they be given the tools of critical thought and left to create their own worlds? Is it better to educate for mastery or understanding or even something else? Do appropriate educational practices differ depending on the subject matter and the age of the student?

The answers and the search for answers to these and hundreds of similar questions influence actions, thoughts, and behaviors for everyone every day. Philosophers in all fields of endeavor have tried to create consistent, coherent systems to help make large and small decisions, but ultimately the individual must choose and act on the choice. But even the choices that are perceived to be available as options are circumscribed by individual circumstances, education, religion, and custom.

No philosophy or set of beliefs is prescribed here. However, it is strongly urged that every student affairs professional make a continuing and intentional effort to understand his or her own worldview. Expediency and reaction are tempting and too easy. Professionalism demands active thought and thoughtful action. The Three Great Questions of Philosophy

TECHNOLOGY RESOURCES

American College Personnel Association (ACPA). (1994). The student learning imperative: Implications for student affairs. Washington, DC: Author.American College Personnel Association and National Association of Student Personnel Administrators (1997). *Principles of good practice for student affairs* [Online]. Available: http://www.acpa.nche.edu/pgp/principle.htm

American College Personnel Association and National Association of Student Personnel Administrators. (1997). Principles of good practice for student affairs. [Online]. Available: http://www.acpa.nche.edu/pgp/principle.htm

Joint Task Force on Student Learning. (1998). Powerful partnerships: A shared responsibility for learning [Online]. Available: http://www.aahe.org/teaching/tsk_frce.htm

REFERENCES

Adler, M. J. (1951). Labor, leisure, and liberal education. *Journal of General Education, 6,* 175–184.

American College Personnel Association. (1994). T*he student learning imperative: Implications for student affairs.* Washington, DC: Author.

American Council on Education, (1994). The Student Personnel Point of View (1937). In A. L. Rentz (Ed.), *Student affairs: A profession's heritage* (pp. 66–78). Lanham, MD: University of America Press.

American Council on Education (1994). The Student Personnel Point of View (1949). In A.L. Rentz (Ed.), *Student affairs: A profession's heritage* (pp. 108–123). Lanham, MD: University of America Press.

Brown, R. D. (1972). *Student development in tomorrow's higher education—A return to the academy.* Washington, DC: American College Personnel Association.

Brubacher, J. S. (1982). *On the philosophy of higher education.* San Francisco: Jossey-Bass.

Brubacher, J. S., & Rudy, W. (1976). *Higher education in transition.* New York: Harper & Row.

Cowley, W. H. (1957, January). Student personnel services in retrospect and prospect. *School and Society, 85,* 19–22.

Dewey, J. (1916). *Democracy and education.* New York: Macmillan.

Dewey, J. (1937). President Hutchins' proposals to remake higher education. *Social Frontier, 3,* 103–104.

Domonkos, L. S. (1977). History of higher education. *International encyclopedia of higher education* (pp. 2017–2040). San Francisco: Jossey-Bass.

Evans, N. J., with Reason, R. D. (2001). Guiding principles: A review and analysis of student affairs philosophical statements. *Journal of College Student Development. 42(4).* 359–377.

Gracia, J. J. E. (1992). *Philosophy and its history: Issues in philosophical historiography.* Albany, NY: State University of New York Press.

Hook, S. (1946). *Education for modern man.* New York: Dial.

Hutchins, R. M. (1936). *The higher learning in America.* New Haven, CT: Yale University Press.

Johnson, J. A., Collins, H. W., Dupuis, V. L., & Johansen, J. H. (1969). *Introduction to the Foundations of American Education.* Boston: Allyn & Bacon.

Kneller, G. F. (1964). *Introduction to the philosophy of education.* New York: John Wiley.

Knock, G. H., Rentz, A. L., & Penn, J. R. (1989). Our philosophical heritage: Significant influences on professional practice and preparation. *NASPA Journal, 27(2),* 116–122.

Kuh, G., Lyons, J, Miller, T., & Trow, J. A. (1995). *Reasonable expectations: Renewing the educational compact between institutions and students.* Washington, DC: National Association of Student Personnel Administrators.

Lincoln, Y. S., & Guba, E. (1985). *Naturalistic inquiry.* Beverly Hills, CA: Sage.

Lincoln, Y. S. (1989). Trouble in the land: The paradigm revolution in the academic disciplines. *Higher education: Handbook of theory and research, 5,* 57–133. New York: Agathon Press.

Manning, K. (1994). Liberation theology and student affairs. *Journal of College Student Development, 35(2)*, 94–97.

Manning, K. (1996). Contemplating the myths of student affairs. *NASPA Journal, 34(1)*, 36–46.

Miller, T. K., & Prince, J. S. (1976). *The future of student affairs.* San Francisco: Jossey-Bass.

National Association of Student Personnel Administrators. (1987). *A perspective on student affairs.* Washington, DC: Author.

Potts, D. B. (1977). 'College Enthusiasm!' as public response, 1800–1860. *Harvard Educational Review, 47(1)*, 28–42.

Sartre, J. P. (1947). *Existentialism.* New York: Philosophical Library.

Veblen, T. (1918). *The higher learning in America.* New York: D.W. Huebsch.

Whitehead, A. N. (1929). *The aims of education and other essays.* New York: Macmillan.

Whitt, E. J., Carnaghi, J. E., Matkin, J., Scalese-Love, P., & Nestor, D. (1990). Believing is seeing: Alternative perspectives on a statement of professional philosophy for student affairs. *NASPA Journal, 27(3)*, 178–84.

Young, R. B. (2001). A perspective on the values of student affairs and scholarship. *Journal of College Student Development. 42(4)*, 319–337.

Chapter 2

STUDENT AFFAIRS:
AN HISTORICAL PERSPECTIVE

Audrey L. Rentz

The student personnel movement constitutes one of the most important efforts of American educators to treat . . . college and university students as individuals, rather than entries in an impersonal roster. . . . In a real sense this part of modern higher education is an individualized application of the research and clinical findings of modern psychology, sociology, cultural anthropology, and education to the task of aiding students to develop fully in the college environment. (American Council on Education, 1949, p. 110)

INTRODUCTION

Seeds of the student personnel movement lie quite naturally within the American system of higher education and yet are also influenced by the larger society outside the walls of academe. A description of the history of student personnel requires a description of this educational context. Thus, this chapter begins with an overview of American higher education from its early colonial period until the mid-1800s. Events leading up to the early 1900s are generally thought of as catalysts for the development of student personnel work. In broad terms, these catalytic factors are the evolving and changing nature of American society, the expanding pluralism of higher education, and the differing educational philosophies that shaped higher education's mission. Material describing student personnel work is organized according to the widely held perception that student personnel work experienced three major movements or stages as it progressed to its present form of practice known as student affairs. Each movement or period of growth reflects a somewhat different philosophy, mission, and style of interaction or practice with students. Significant statements of principle and practice as well as personalities that helped define and operationalize practice for each movement are identified. These movements are: (1) student personnel work (late 1800s to mid-1960s), (2) student development (mid-1960s to late 1980s), and (3) the contemporary emphasis on student learning. Because of the limited nature of this chapter, the reader is encouraged to consult *Student Affairs: A Profession's Heritage* (1994) for complete statements of principles and values that are only highlighted here.

COLONIAL HIGHER EDUCATION (1636–1780)

Responsibility and concern for the whole student, described by the concept *in loco parentis*, is linked to the earliest colonial college, Harvard. Chartered in 1636 by its Puritan founders, this English-American institutional prototype was created to mirror Emmanuel College, Cambridge University. The goal was to bring about a *translatio studii*, the transference of Old World higher learning to the new colonies (Brubacher & Rudy, 1958). The founders were motivated to build institutions *pro modo Academarium in Anglia*, ("according to the manner of universities in England." Brubacher & Rudy, 1958, p. 3). The English models were "organized residential associations . . ." founded ". . . for the purpose of inculcating specific patterns of religious belief and social conduct" (Pierson, cited in Brubacher & Rudy, 1958). Curriculum, student discipline, degree requirements, and policies reflected those of Emmanuel College. The bachelor of arts was the initial degree with a concentration in ministerial preparation. For Harvard's clerical faculty (dons), the education of the intellect was viewed as secondary in importance to the salvation of an individual soul. These dons, deeply committed to their faith and to their students, labored to achieve Harvard's aim, that "Every one shall consider the mayne End of his [*sic*] life & studyes, to know God & Jesus Christ, which is Eternall life" (Harvard College Records, cited in Brubacher & Rudy, 1958, p. 8). Early entrance requirements reflected a classical concept of a liberal education:

> When any Schollar is able to read Tully or such like classicall Latine Authour ex temporare, and make and speake Latin verse and prose *Suo (ut aiunt) Marte*, and decline perfectly the paradigms of Nounes and verbes in the Greeke toungue, then may hee bee admitted into the Colledge, nor shall any claim admission before such qualification. . . . (Colonial Society of Massachussetts, cited in Brubaker & Rudy, 1958, p. 12)

Once admitted, young (aged 11–15) male students' lives, in and out of the classroom, were rigidly controlled and supervised by paternalistic dons. Daily visits to student rooms, meals taken in common, and strictly supervised chapel services and classes were thought to help guard the young students against temptations of sin. The hope was that these "gentleman/scholars" might learn to serve as examples of Puritan piety and civility. A somewhat sarcastic analysis of these early paternalistic efforts saw them as "a persistent emphasis on extracurricular religion, and also a considerable snooping into the lives of the students" (Cowley, cited in Mueller, 1961, p. 51). And yet, for the early Harvard scholars, the college level–educated man was viewed as a member of the long line of succession from the early prophets and apostles.

In subsequent years, members of other religious sects (e.g., Anglicans, Calvinists, and Dutch Reform) were motivated to establish institutions to promote their set of Christian values and to prepare literate, college-educated clergy. Duplication of the English collection of like colleges became less important as unsolvable factors mitigated against it as a goal. In comparison to England, colonial campuses were separated by rugged terrain and a lack of satisfactory transportation. In addition, both the founders and the local community residents most often lacked adequate financial resources. As a result, subsequent institutions were less similar to their Emmanuel prototype than Harvard and offered degrees somewhat broader in scope. Among these early institutions and their purposes were William and Mary (1693) to prepare piously educated youth and spread Christianity among the Indians; Yale (1701) to prepare youth for employment in the public state and the church; College of Philadelphia (1740), Princeton (1748), Kings College (1754), and College of Rhode Island (Brown) (1764) to provide education of Baptist ministers who previously lacked formal preparation; Dartmouth (1769) and Queens College (1770) to prepare youth in languages, liberal and applied arts, and sciences for ministerial and other civic roles.

While institutional purposes varied, *in loco parentis* was constant. At Yale, for example, 16 required chapel services weekly, 4 voluntary noon prayer sessions, and frequent revival gatherings were meant to help students experience "distinct effusions of the Holy Spirit" (Cowley, cited in Mueller, 1961). During these early formative years, these institutions were private, limited to young male students, residential, and staffed by clerical or lay male faculty and administrators.

A unique hallmark of the colonial system of higher education was the close and personal relationship between its faculty and students. It did not take long for certain campus and societal events to change this orientation. Historians frequently cite the Harvard food riot of 1766, labeled the "butter rebellion" as one such event. Triggered partly by the presence of rancid butter in the warm Spring dining commons and probably more by the repressed volatile behavior of male students, this outburst escalated to such an extent that several deaths were recorded. Subsequently, dons were less willing to continue to worship, eat, and live alongside their youthful students. This personal interest in the whole student and the attitude of *in loco parentis* would not reappear on American campuses for almost another 275 years.

THE PLURALITY OF HIGHER EDUCATION INSTITUTIONS (1780–1865)

AN OVERVIEW

As the number of collegiate institutions increased, the profile of the American system of higher education as male-centered, private, paternalistic, and residential was considered to be permanent. From approximately 1780 to the outbreak of the Civil War in 1862, a number of societal needs emerged that can be linked to major changes in this profile. Several of these major changes are introduced here. Curricular offerings were expanded by the creation of the elective system. Professional education was enhanced with the establishment of graduate institutions using the older Germanic institutions of scientific thought as prototypes. Degree programs increased as different types of institutions were established to offer curricula in response to expanding societal demands for lawyers, accountants, physicians, merchants, scientists, elementary and secondary schoolteachers, engineers, and farmers trained in the application of technology and science.

Numbers of enrolled students grew as women were accepted as students and later served as faculty members. In addition, women were called upon to fulfill local community needs for hundreds of public elementary and high school teachers. Closely allied to the growing number of women in higher education was the development of a number of women's institutions. Previously private male institutions faced new competition from the creation of land grant institutions, women's colleges, state-supported public institutions, traditional denominational or church-related institutions, and coeducational campuses. Cheyney College in 1830 marked the beginning of Black institutions established to provide education for a group of minority people for whom such opportunities had been almost nonexistent. As the profile of higher education changed, leaders of American institutions intensely debated the significance of each new feature while trying both to maintain tradition and to respond to society's changing needs. During this same period, many students reacting to negative campus environments moved off campus. In so doing, they created a somewhat parallel collegiate structure that eventually included student debate clubs, literary societies, housing arrangements, and athletic groups. This resulting structure later became known as the extracurriculum and thrived for many years (Brubacher & Rudy, 1958). These major changes in the profile of American higher education are frequently considered as antecedents of a movement that by the mid-twentieth century had become student personnel work.

CURRICULAR INNOVATIONS

Curricular innovations were viewed as one of two kinds: vertical expansion or lateral expansion. The founding of Johns Hopkins (c. 1876) as the first graduate institution represented what Brubaker and Rudy (1958) referred to as a vertical expansion of the American curriculum. Perhaps a more important development was the lateral expansion of the curriculum, the creation of the elective system, an idea that ignited considerable controversy. Advocated by Thomas Jefferson, this innovation gave rise to an examination of several key questions that would dramatically alter the future profile of higher education. At the center of many debates were such fundamental questions as "Should higher education be 'practical' or 'liberal', a means to an end or an end in itself? Were the 'new' studies (such as science) more important than the 'old' studies (such as the classics)? Should the college be predominantly secular or religious in orientation? Should it aim to be aristocratic, and train the elite, or...seek to attain a democratic all-inclusiveness?" (Brubacher & Rudy, 1958, pp. 96–97). In the middle of what was probably the most significant educational controversy of the nineteenth century, Yale President Jeremiah Day undertook a bold and defining role. On behalf of his faculty, Day published the Yale Report of 1828, providing an authoritative statement about Yale's future. The document, ". . . became a classic statement in defense of the old order" (Rudolph, 1990, p. 130). "The thorough study of the ancient languages was the only proper system for a college" (Brubacher & Rudy, 1958, p. 101). The case to preserve Yale's classical and narrow curriculum "was made with such finality that not until the next generation would another band of reformers assail the old course of study" (Rudolph, 1990, p. 131).

Not all higher education leaders agreed. Their response was the creation of yet another type of higher education institution. They founded independent schools whose purpose was to teach nonclassical subjects. Among such institutions were the United States Military Academy at West Point (1802); Rensselaer Polytechnic Institute, where initially in 1824 teachers were prepared to instruct both "sons and daughters of local farmers and mechanics in the art of applying science to husbandry, manufactures, and domestic economy" (RPI Annual Register as cited in Brubacher & Rudy, 1958); the United States Naval Academy (1845); and later the Massachusetts Institute of Technology in 1865. As a result, the variety and the breadth of academic degree programs available multiplied. The young nation continued to mature and as it did, colleges and universities consistently responded to the constantly changing society outside their walls.

The effects of secularization and industrialization were experienced not only outside the ivy-covered walls of the academy, but also within. Male students attended public colleges and universities whose status was confirmed by the 1819 decision in the Dartmouth College case providing that state legislatures may not exert governance or control over such institutions. Similarly, Thomas Jefferson in 1825 established the University of Virginia as the first state-supported but not state-governed institution. The traditional, somewhat narrow, liberal arts curriculum of the colonial colleges was no longer the only curriculum offered.

Lincoln's endorsement of the Morrill Land Grant Acts of 1862 and 1864 affirmed the importance and the permanence of public higher education. These laws to bring about "the liberal and practical education of the industrial classes in the several pursuits and professions of life" (Solomon, 1985, p. 44) set aside acres of public lands in states on which institutions would be built to provide instruction in agriculture and mechanical arts. The result was the development of a large system of agricultural and mechanical colleges, referred to as "utilitarian institutions" or "aggie schools" (Mueller, 1961, p. 52). Their curricular offerings combined concentrations in liberal arts with practical education. Additionally, these legislative acts required states either to admit Black students to existing colleges or to provide separate but equal educational facilities for them. Thus, two systems of higher education, Historically Black and Predominantly White, separate but equal, existed side by side (Roebuck & Murty, 1993).

As different types of curricular offerings were created, various institutional settings emerged. From 1850 to 1870, several prototypes of higher education institutions emerged: the private women's college, the religiously oriented coeducational college, the private women's coordinate colleges, the secular coeducational institutions (both public and private), and the public single-sex vocational institution (Solomon, 1985).

WOMENS' PARTICIPATION IN HIGHER EDUCATION

Women's education has been a cause of debate for centuries. The advocates of women's education have been few, the enemies many. The arguments against it have included women's immorality, their transcendental virtue, their fragile bodies, and feeble minds. If taught to read, women will give themselves to promiscuity; if they go to college, they will never bear children (*Better Than Rubies*, 1978, jacket cover).

Phyllis Stock reminds us that "women often gain in status and power in society, not with the advent of a new social structure, but with the breakdown of an old one" (Stock, 1978, p. 26). The validity of this observation would be demonstrated repeatedly as American society and its system of higher education evolved. Women were allowed to assume greater and more powerful roles and responsibilities simply because those roles and responsibilities previously assumed by men became unattended. The young nation's needs for teachers at the elementary, secondary, and collegiate levels added considerable weight to the proponents of access for women into higher education.

As early as 1776, the words of Abigail Adams written to her husband, President John Adams, expressed her views concerning the need to educate women. Those words, still quoted by contemporary authors, became a clarion call to all women:

If you complain of neglect of Education in sons, What shall I say with regard to daughters, who every day experience the want of it. With regard to the Education of my own children, I find myself soon out of my depth, and destitute and deficient in every part of Education (as cited in Solomon, 1985, p. 1).

Undergraduate study, formerly considered by many a "forbidden world" to women (Solomon, 1985, p. 1), was now becoming a reality.

Women's colleges shared a common purpose with their female seminary predecessors. They perceived their mission to be to educate women so that female graduates might be better prepared to assume roles within the domestic sphere, as wives and mothers and, only if needed, as schoolteachers (Solomon, 1985). Within several years, granting women access to colleges and universities was viewed as an appropriate and proper way to address societal needs.

With female boarding schools, academies, and seminaries serving as a foundation, women were quickly educated to become teachers and in turn established and taught at colleges for women with a curriculum that varied from high school courses to that equal to neighboring male four-year colleges and universities. Mount Holyoke, established by Mary Lyon in 1836 as a seminary, became one of the earliest women's institutions and served as a model for others in the Midwest, the West, and the South (Solomon, 1985). Other women's institutional pioneers were Emma Willard, founder of Troy Seminary in Troy (New York) in 1821, and Catherine Beecher, who started Hartford Seminary (Connecticut) in 1828 (Rudolph, 1990). The pace quickened and in 1836, Georgia Female College (Wesleyan) offered a curriculum that combined both secondary and collegiate courses. Mary Sharp College (Tennessee) in 1853 went one step beyond the usual course offerings by offering a curriculum that emphasized Latin, Greek, and higher mathematics (Solomon, 1985). In 1837, an alternate form of higher education emerged when in an evangelical community, Oberlin College (Ohio) became the first coeducational undergraduate institution to allow four women to enroll. Ultimately, "coeducation . . . became the dominant mode, as early feminists had hoped, . . . but women's colleges did not perish" (Solomon, 1985, p. 43). The profile of American higher education would from here forward always include women.

Once admitted, women were able to pursue the traditional baccalaureate degree program or receive a diploma following completion of a special Ladies Course (Rudolph, 1990, p. 311). Women's presence brought with it a new concern for those responsible for campuses. Worried about the perceived dangers of having women on Oberlin's predominantly male campus, President Charles Finney said ". . . you will need a wise and pious matron with such lady assistants as to keep up sufficient supervision" (Holmes, cited in Mueller, 1961, p. 53).

Several pioneer public women's colleges were founded in the post–Civil War years by religiously motivated persons: Vassar (New York) in 1865; Wellesley (Massachusetts) and Smith (Massachusetts) in 1875; and Bryn Mawr (Pennsylvania) in 1884, patterned after Johns Hopkins University, was awarding graduate degrees by 1888 (Rudolph, 1990). In addition, the Women's College of Baltimore (Maryland), opened in 1884 and, sponsored by the Methodist Conference, held similarly high standards for academic rigor as its Virginian Presbyterian-sponsored neighbor Randolph-Macon

College for Women (Virginia). The former is today's Goucher College (Solomon, 1985).

By 1882, with coeducation flourishing, the lady matrons and principals had proven that their existence had merit. Citing improved relationships between male and female students, it was observed that "there is comparative freedom from the dangers and conditions ordinarily incident to college life" (Holmes, cited in Mueller, 1961, p. 53). These lady principals, later titled Deans of Women, were given administrative and disciplinary functions when appointed by institutional presidents.

As the nineteenth century ended, yet another aspect of higher education was added. Several Catholic girls' schools moved toward collegiate status. The Academy of the Sacred Heart at Manhattanville (New York) became a college in 1900 and Washington Trinity College was founded in the same year (Rudolph, 1990). The Catholic system of higher education developed single-sex and later parallel coeducational institutions.

THE BEGINNINGS OF BLACK INSTITUTIONS

The profile of American higher education was to be altered yet again. This time the enhancement came with the establishment of Black institutions in the North. Cheyney College opened in 1830, and both Lincoln College and Wilberforce University were established in 1856 by the Methodist Episcopal Church (Hill, 1984; Roebuck & Murty, 1993; Thomas & Hirsch, 1987; Thomas & Hirsch, 1989). Alexander Lucius Twilight was the first recorded Black graduate of Middlebury College in 1823 (Ranbom & Lynch, 1987, Fall 1988, Winter). In the South, Black students were restricted in their pursuit of higher education because collegiate education had previously been "declared" illegal (Fleming, 1984; Hill, 1984; National Advisory Committee on Black Higher Education and Black Colleges and Universities, 1979; Thomas & Hirsch, 1989). In 1860 there were approximately 4 million Black slaves in America, with more than 90 percent living in the South. In each southern state except one, Black slaves and free Blacks were excluded from formal instruction, which helps explain why over 90 percent of the southern Black population was illiterate in 1860. Before the Civil War, the number of Blacks who had received undergraduate degrees from American colleges and universities did not exceed 28 (Roebuck & Murty, 1993). Two perceptions formed the basis of the rationale for not educating Blacks: (1) the intellectual inferiority of Blacks, and (2) once educated, Blacks would "get out of their place" and inevitably become competitors of whites within economic, political, and sexual spheres (Goodenow, 1989, p.152).

In the years after 1865, with the passage of the Thirteenth Amendment abolishing slavery, Virginia Union, Shaw University (1865), and Howard University (1867) marked the beginning of formal Black higher education institutions (Rambon & Lynch, 1987, Fall 1988, Winter). Alcorn College, the recipient of federal land grant funds was the first Black land grant college (Rambon & Lynch, 1987, Fall - 1988, Winter). From 1866 to1890, 16 of the historically Black public colleges in existence today were created. Hampton University, considered one of the most influential institutions in the history of Black education, was established in 1868 in Virginia (Roebuck & Murty, 1993). The decision of the U.S. Supreme Court in *Plessy v. Fergusson* in 1896 made constitutional "separate but equal" schools and Harvard awarded the first honorary degree to a Black, Booker T. Washington (Rambon & Lynch, 1987, Fall 1988, Winter, p. 17). These early historically Black institutions served an important function within the larger system of colleges and universities, and their courageous students made possible prototypes for additional institutions in the years ahead.

ANTECEDENTS OF STUDENT PERSONNEL WORK

Most new educational and societal movements arise as a reaction against a situation or an outcome that becomes perceived as undesirable. Such was the case as a series of issues in American higher education and American society influenced the development of student personnel and supported its transition from an early emphasis on *in loco parentis* to today's focus on student learning. To what set of needs were the early proponents of student personnel work responding? What factors helped to create the positions and roles they assumed as the movement grew on college and university campuses? Who were the early pioneers? And what did they bring to the evolving movement that provided it with stability, strength, and a sense of common mission? An exact date for the beginning of student personnel remains a matter of conjecture among historians. W. H. Cowley reminds us that the practice of (student) personnel enjoyed a long history and was characteristic of much earlier systems of higher education: ". . . what might be called Alma Maternal ministrations to students had characterized the universities of the Middle Ages. . ." (cited in Williamson, 1949, p. 16). Efforts on the part of students to move away from the campus' narrow classical curriculum and the emphasis on piety and discipline led ultimately to the establishment of debate clubs, literary societies and eventually the Greek-letter social fraternity movement.

> In a sense, the literary societies and their libraries, the clubs, journals and organizations which compensated for the neglect of science, English literature, history, music and art in the curriculum—this vast developing extracurriculum was the student response to the classical course of study. It helped to liberate the intellect on the American campus. It was an answer to the Yale Report of 1828, an answer so effective that by the end of the cen-

tury at Yale itself there would be a real concern over which was really more fundamental, more important, the curriculum or the extracurriculum (Rudolph, 1990, p. 144).

Between 1825 and 1840, so popular were student groups that several national Greek-letter social fraternities were created from former debating societies and drinking clubs: Kappa Alpha, Theta Delta Chi, Sigma Phi, Delta Phi, Chi Psi, and Psi Upsilon (Rudolph, 1990). According to Rudolph ". . . Greek-letter fraternities were intended to bring together the most urbane young men on campus into small groups that would fulfill the vacuum left by removal from the family and the home community. . ." (Rudolph, 1990, p. 146). In addition, they "offered an escape from the monotony, dreariness, and unpleasantness of the collegiate regimen . . . and from the dormitory with its lack of privacy" (Rudolph, 1990, pp. 146–147).

A PERIOD OF INTELLECTUALISM (1855–1890)

The profile of higher education would not remain inviolate for long. This time change came in the form of an educational philosophy that espoused a much narrower mission for American higher education. Its existence and influence came about as a result of our society's need for scientific and technical professionals prepared in the hard sciences: mathematics, physics, astronomy, and so forth. As more and more American and European faculty, educated in German universities, joined American college and university faculties, they introduced the educational philosophy known as intellectualism. Generally speaking, this school of thought placed primary emphasis on the training of the intellect; the rational mind was valued above all else. Also associated with this school of thought was the concept of academic freedom represented by two words: *lernfreiheit* and *lehrfreiheit*. The first term implied that students were to be free of administrative control and regulation. They could travel from campus to campus, and could live wherever they chose. The latter term conveyed a faculty member's right to engage freely in research or scientific inquiry and to report research conclusions or findings without fear of reprisals (Rudolph, 1990). With the primary focus on rational development, other aspects of students' social, psychological, physical, and spiritual development were devalued. The years when intellectualism was in favor were later known as the period of Germanic influence, approximately 1855 to 1890. Faculty and student roles were redefined. Increasingly, faculty found it both necessary and desirable to devote considerable time to the pursuit of scientific research in addition to teaching, and had little time or concern for student life outside the classroom.

The previous interest and value associated with the residential aspect of many colleges and universities all but disappeared. Yale was the only campus to maintain its position of endorsing a residential setting. The personal quality of student–faculty interactions that had marked American higher education changed dramatically. Institutional or administrative attitudes toward students shifted as well. Earlier handbooks that contained excessively stern rules of student conduct were replaced by pamphlets that were considerably thinner and set forth more liberal rules. Higher education's previous definition of the student had cast him as an adolescent. This perception changed so that the student came to be viewed more as an adult. Male students were perceived to be capable of solving their own problems, academic, religious and social, as they saw fit. "Overweening paternalism gave way to almost complete indifference" (Cowley, 1937, p. 221). Harvard in 1886 altered its class attendance policies to require only that juniors and seniors pass examinations. Male students left campuses to initiate student-governed off-campus living accommodations and to develop out of class activities. Intercollegiate athletic programs were initiated with a crew race between Harvard and Yale in 1852 and a football game between Princeton and Rutgers in 1869. Later these intercollegiate programs included baseball and track (Brubacher & Rudy, 1976; Rudolph, 1990). By the 1870s, a major element of higher education had taken form, an array of activities referred to as the "era of the extracurriculum"

> In the extracurriculum the college student stated his case for the human mind, the human personality, and the human body, for all aspects of man that the colleges tended to ignore in their single-minded interest in the salvation of souls. In the institutions of the extracurriculum college students everywhere suggested that they preferred the perhaps equally challenging task of saving minds, saving personalities, saving bodies. On the whole the curriculum would still be intact, and compulsory chapel was only beginning to give way. But in the extracurriculum the students erected within the gates a monster. Taming it would now become as necessary a project as the long-delayed reform of the curriculum itself (Rudolph, 1990, p. 155).

THE PIONEER DEANS (1870–1920)

From approximately 1875 to 1930, the undergraduate student body increased nearly 30-fold (Brubacher & Rudy, 1958). Presidents were concerned about their ability to administer an ever-growing institution while also assuming responsibility for student life issues. Presidents increasingly endorsed the need for an administrator to coordinate or supervise students. Others voiced a concern for women students on previously predominantly male campuses, while some spoke out publicly against the previous devaluing of the residential component. In 1889, President Gilman at Johns Hopkins established the first system of faculty advisers by appointing Professor E. H. Griffin as the "chief of the faculty advisers" and announcing that "in every institution there should be one or more persons specifically appointed to be counselors or advisers of students" (Cowley, 1949, p. 20).

Presidents became critical of the prevailing philosophy of intellectualism and its hands-off attitude toward students. Responding to both faculty persuasion and parental pressures, Harvard's President Charles Eliot recommended to his Board of Overseers that this most recent wave of treating students impersonally be challenged. Previous policies governing student attendance should be reinstated. It was a time when university governance became a very complex responsibility. As a consequence of all segments of an institution reporting to the president and the growing size and scope of the extracurriculum, Eliot appointed Professor Ephraim Gurney in 1870 as the first college dean. Although the position was considered academic, Gurney's task, in addition to regular teaching, was to relieve Eliot of the responsibility of student discipline. Later in 1891, when the dean's position was reorganized into two separate offices, LeBaron Russell Briggs, age 35 and already a respected professor of English, assumed those duties related to students considered to be nonacademic: discipline, registration and records, and various other aspects of students' lives outside the classroom (Brown, 1926).

Briggs is generally regarded as the earliest dean of students, and the "official sponsor of undergraduates" (Brown, 1926, p. 95; Brubacher & Rudy, 1958; Mueller, 1961). His appointment was part of Eliot's call for a new system of student discipline, a system that would emphasize self-discipline and a developed sense of self-responsibility (Morison, 1930). Briggs's attitude toward dealing with student discipline was evident in the goals he established for his deanship: "(1) To help the student disciplined, and not merely to humiliate him [sic]; (2) to make it easy for the faculty to do its work; and (3) to develop a sentiment among the students which would render discipline less and less necessary" (Brown, 1926, p. 101). In 1897, he organized a group of 60 upperclassmen to assume responsibility for meeting and assisting entering students, "to stand ready in time of need . . . [as] unpretentious counselor(s)" (Brown, 1926, p. 127). Briggs served in the deanship until his retirement from Harvard in 1925.

"Everywhere two types of deans made their appearance: 'academic deans' of colleges or special faculties . . . and 'dean of students' . . . whose concern was with the extracurricular life of undergraduates (Cowley, 1937, pp. 224–225, cited in Brubacher & Rudy, 1958, p. 322). The University of Chicago's President William Harper was among the first to argue for a resurgence of on-campus living. Greek-letter social group members slowly returned to campuses. Clubs and student organizations flourished and the campus "became an arena in which undergraduates erected monuments not to the soul of man but to man as a social and physical being" (Rudolph, 1990, pp. 136–137). Rudolph's observation reflects the new priority assigned to total human development of students that would help usher in the early stages of student personnel work. Following the years of the Germanic influence, the role of the extracurriculum had come full circle: administrators now valued its existence on their campuses. The effects of this student-established extracurriculum were vast:

The extracurriculum which these young men developed—the agencies of intellect, the deeply embedded social system, the network of organized athletics—would become the repositories of their power. Through the extracurriculum the student arrived at a position of commanding importance in the American college. By opposing the literary societies, journals, and other clubs to the curriculum, by opposing the fraternities to the collegiate way, and by setting up in the athletic hero a more appealing symbol than the pious Christian, the students succeeded, although not really intentionally, in robbing the college professor of a certain element of prestige and of a sizable area of authority (Rudolph, 1990, p. 157).

By 1882, the increasing numbers of matrons, wardens, and lady principals had successfully convinced academic administrators of their value within the collegiate environment. Although male and female students dined together, "relations between them are such that there is comparative freedom from the dangers and conditions ordinarily incident to college life" (Holmes, 1939, p. 9). Historians generally concur that at the University of Chicago in 1892, the hiring of Alice Freeman Palmer, former president of Wellesley, constituted the appointment of the first dean of women. At the same time, Marion Talbot, a friend of Palmer's, was appointed assistant dean and assistant professor of domestic sciences (Solomon, 1985). Talbot later replaced Palmer as the first full-time dean of women. Educated in Latin, Greek, and modern languages abroad, she received her B.A .and M.A. from Boston University, and later a B.S. from the Massachusetts of Technology, majoring in sanitation, the field that later evolved into home economics. Talbot cofounded the American Association of University Women in 1881 and convened female colleagues to help establish the National Association of Deans of Women in 1916 (Fley, 1979). No one could claim that Talbot fit that times' narrow stereotype of a woman dean. From the late 1920s until and early 1930s, she served as acting president of Constantinople Women's College in Turkey (Fley, 1979).

These women deans' responsibilities spanned far beyond the single charge of supervising women's behavior. Their goal was to "champion the intellectual and personal ambitions of young women" (Knock, 1985, p. 31). To achieve this, they recognized that additional educational preparation was needed. Teachers College at Columbia University offered the first M.A. degree program and Diploma of Dean of Women in 1914. An early handbook entitled *The Dean of Women* and written by Dr. Lois Kimball Mathews, Dean of Women at the University of Wisconsin, was published in 1915 and served as an initial text (Lloyd-Jones, 1949). Enrolled women studied

the hygiene of childhood and adolescence, . . . biology as related to education including sex education, . . . educational psychology, . . . history of the family, . . . sociology, educational sociology; philosophy of education, . . . management of the corporate life of the school, . . . problems of administrative work, . . . the psychology of religion, and a practicum. . ." (Lloyd-Jones, 1954, pp. 262–263).

The University of Illinois claims the first recorded appointment of a dean of men when Thomas Arkle Clark accepted the position in 1901. Eight years before he had been appointed dean of undergraduates and assistant to the president. A former student of L. R. Briggs at Harvard, Clark's contributions were primarily in the arena of discipline. By 1919, the number of men who held the position of dean on college and university campuses had grown significantly. In that same year, a group from the Midwest decided to formalize their relationship across institutional lines and established the National Association of Deans of Men (NADM).

These student personnel pioneers, male and female, valued the uniqueness and the individuality of each student. They were committed to the holistic development of students and held an unshakeable belief in each student's potential for growth and learning. These core values would become the foundation of future statements and documents that would define the new field's mission and goals.

As the availability of on-campus living facilities grew, the number of students enrolled in higher education increased dramatically. Administrative staffs increased dramatically. During the early 1900s, college and university campuses were being served by large numbers of student personnel practitioners: deans of men, students, and women; registrars; counselors; vocational guidance counselors; placement counselors; residence hall directors, admissions, food and health service staffs; and coordinators and advisors of student organizations and activities (Rudolph, 1990). All were devoted to providing programs and services required to help students derive the maximum benefit from their undergraduate experience, both in and out of the classroom.

Some historians perceive student personnel as emerging solely as a reaction to the dominant German-based intellectualism and its resulting impersonal attitude toward students. However, other factors can also be viewed as causal. W. H. Cowley (1949) explains his viewpoint regarding the rise of student personnel work:

> The usual explanation . . . is that scientific psychology led to the application of research findings to the problems of military, of industry, and of education. . . . But it struck me that for *student* personnel work at least three other considerations were antecedent to scientific psychological research: first, secularization of education; second, the increase in student populations beginning about 1870; and third, the attacks upon the intellectualistic impersonalism imported by American Ph.D.s trained in Germany (p. 16).

THE EMERGENCE OF STUDENT PERSONNEL AND ITS ASSOCIATIONS (1916–1936)

As early student personnel professionals gathered to talk about their evolving field, discussions inevitably turned to the need for a standard definition, a set of criteria to guide practice, and a statement of values to help clarify the new field's role on campuses. What would later be known as the Student Personnel Point of View, a statement of core values and principles of student personnel work, evolved from such a conference of college personnel officers from Purdue University and Wabash College in 1929, in cooperation with the American Council on Education and the Personnel Research Foundation of New York. During that meeting, J. A. Humphreys (Dean of Personnel Services, Oberlin College) proposed five guiding principles to serve as the foundation of student personnel work:

1. Personnel work is, and should be, first of all an idea rather than a tangible organization. It stands for individualization in college education. Personnel work among college students consists of those activities or procedures which have as their objective assisting the individual student.
2. The logical outcome of this principle is the idea that there should be brought to bear on all student problems, either individual or group situations, the point of view which concerns itself with the individual student. The application of established policies and the forming of new ones ought to be made with reference to individual needs. After all the college exists for the student and not the student for the college. Specific personnel problems arise out of situations, not out of a clear sky.
3. Every member of the faculty, every administrative officer and assistant is a personnel officer in the sense that responsibility for serving the individual student rests upon all those who come in contact with the students.
4. College personnel work is not an activity set off apart from the educative process of the college. True personnel work functions as a part of the educative process. (Humphreys, 1930, pp. 11–12.)

Elements of the preceding can be found in the following definition offered by Clothier two years later, now considered a classic, as he wrote for the Committee on Principles and Functions of the American College Personnel Association:

Personnel work in a college or university is the systematic bringing to bear on the individual student all those influences, of whatever nature, which will stimulate him [*sic*] and assist him [*sic*], through his [*sic*] own efforts, to develop in body, mind and character to the limit of his [*sic*] individual capacity for growth, and helping *sic*] to apply his [*sic*] powers so developed most effectively to the work of the world (Clothier, 1931, p. 10).

Small meetings at neighboring campuses brought student personnel deans together to discuss common issues and concerns. These efforts resulted in the creation of three early student personnel professional associations: as cited previously, (1) the deans of women established the National

Association of Women Deans (NAWD) in 1916, which became the National Association of Women in Education (NAWE); (2) the deans of men convened the National Association of Deans of Men, (NADM) in 1919; and (3) the deans of men in conjunction with the early deans of students created today's National Association of Student Personnel Administrators (NASPA). Members of the National Association of Placement Secretaries, established in 1924, later changed their name in 1931 to the American College Personnel Association (ACPA). In the early 1950s, a conglomerate of professionals within education established the American Personnel and Guidance Association (APGA), which was later renamed the Association for Counseling and Development (Mueller, 1961). For information about professional associations of interest to specific student affairs practitioners, such as orientation, financial aids, student activities, and so on, the reader is advised to consult appropriate chapters within this book.

Not only was the new field not readily understood, but also academic administrators were dubious about its proper place on a campus. Esther Lloyd-Jones suggested the appropriate role and administrative location for the division or the field within institutional governance. She proposed that student personnel be considered a separate but equal partner to the other two main divisions (instructional and operational) of college and university administration (Lloyd-Jones, 1934, p. 22).

Two years later, Cowley in *The Nature of Student Personnel Work* (1936) attempted to bring order to the existing confusion surrounding the amorphous nature of the evolving field by providing a rather detailed discussion of many of the definitions in use. Rejecting several, claiming they were too inclusive, and disregarding others because they were too restrictive, he offered his own definition. At the same time, he sought to differentiate the new field from guidance and personnel work and from the broader concept of education, already an area of some misunderstanding among many practitioners. "Personnel work constitutes all activities undertaken or sponsored by an educational institution, aside from curricular instruction, in which the student's personal development is the primary consideration" (Cowley, 1936, p. 65). He continued,

> The personnel point of view is a philosophy of education which puts emphasis upon the individual student and his [*sic*] all-round development as a person rather than upon his [*sic*] intellectual training alone and which promotes the establishment in educational institutions of curricular programs, methods of instruction, and extra-instructional media to achieve such emphasis (Cowley, 1936, p. 69).

THE STUDENT PERSONNEL POINT OF VIEW (1936)

As noted earlier, numerous definitions and terms were being used interchangeably not only by practitioners, but also by administrators and faculty trying to understand this new movement's purpose. Clearly, an authoritative statement of principles and practice was needed. The Executive Committee of the American Council on Education (ACE) convened a group of professionals in Washington, D.C., in April 1936 to clarify the "so-called personnel work, the intelligent use of available tools, and the development of additional techniques and processes" (American Council on Education, 1937, p. 67). In attendance were F. F. Bradshaw, W. H. Cowley, A. B. Crawford, L. B. Hopkins, E. Lloyd-Jones, D. G. Paterson, C. G. Wrenn, and others, with E. G. Williamson serving as chair. Their deliberations resulted in the document entitled *The Student Personnel Point of View*. This constituted the first statement of philosophy, purpose, and methods of practice that formed the foundation for the field's future growth and put appropriate emphasis on students. (The reader is encouraged to consult *Student Affairs: A Profession's Heritage* [1995] for a complete copy of the 1937 and 1949 documents.) It is significant that in the initial paragraph of the 1937 statement, labeled Philosophy, committee members affirmed the concept of holism as the fundamental assumption that would guide future practice:

> One of the basic purposes of higher education is the preservation, transmission, and enrichment of the important elements of culture—the product of scholarship, research, creative imagination, and human experience. It is the task of colleges and universities so to vitalize this and other educational purposes as to assist the student in developing to the limits of his [*sic*] potentialities and in making his [*sic*] contribution to the betterment of society. This philosophy imposes upon education institutions the obligation to consider the student as a whole—his [*sic*] intellectual capacity and achievement, his [*sic*] emotional make-up, his [*sic*] physical condition, his [*sic*] social relationships, his [*sic*] vocational aptitudes and skills, his [*sic*] moral and religious values, his [*sic*] economic resources, his [*sic*] aesthetic appreciations. It puts emphasis, in brief, upon the development of the student as a person rather than upon his [*sic*] intellectual training alone (American Council on Education, 1937, p. 76).

Twenty-six separate student personnel services were identified, from interpreting institutional objectives and opportunities to prospective students and their parents, to "keeping the student continuously and adequately informed of the educational opportunities and services available to him [*sic*]" (American Council on Education, 1937, pp. 77–79). Coordination was cited as a key concept that the committee believed should be implemented not only within individual institutions, but also between student personnel work and instruction, between student personnel work and business administration, and between higher education and secondary education. The communication of information about students, among all those who worked with them, was viewed as beneficial for students and their development.

Illustrative of the need for student personnel work is the following perception of students held by personnel counselors in a report to their administrative supervisors at a large urban university in 1938:

1. Our students are markedly lacking in social skills, the ability to meet people and to get along with them. They frequently feel ill at ease in a social group and cannot engage in conversation in other than argumentative fashion.
2. Our students are constantly being frustrated by financial difficulties, by their immaturity, by their social awkwardness and by their lack of practical and social experience (Rudolph, 1990, pp. 86–87).

THE STUDENT PERSONNEL POINT OF VIEW (1949)

Both national and individual priorities changed during the years of World War II, 1939 to 1945. America's involvement in this war to end all wars began in 1941 and demanded sacrifices from all segments of society. The value of the individual lessened as the country's spirit of patriotism grew. Economic goals were defined by a war machine or war production mentality. The manufacture of ammunition, equipment, airplanes, uniforms, and health supplies was geared toward the success of the war effort fought on two continents. While thousands of young men were drafted and others enlisted, food and other commodities were rationed at home to ensure that military troops would be fed and well supplied. Americans believed that this war was a struggle to prove the superiority of democracy, and their goal was to liberate those countries and peoples who had been oppressed by ruthless enemies. In 1945, with the defeat of Hitler's European military effort and the explosion of atomic bombs on Nagasaki and Hiroshima, Japan surrendered. America's long war effort came to an end.

In the period following World War II, values and priorities reverted to the previous peacetime attitude. Families, now able to think about today and to plan for tomorrow, worked to provide material goods for their children that a few years ago were scarce or unavailable. Individual needs and comforts were highly valued. The Serviceman's Readjustment Act of 1944 (the GI Bill) provided funds for direct college costs and subsistence that allowed returning veterans to pursue a college education. College and university enrollments swelled. The American undergraduate student body was becoming somewhat less homogeneous. Student services and programs previously planned for large groups of homogeneous students (e.g., freshmen) were in need of revision. In 1949, with higher education booming, the Committee on College Personnel of the American Council on Education released a revision of the 1936 SPPV document. The goals of higher education were expanded and now reflected the interconnectedness of the world at peace. Among the new goals, three are of particular significance:

1. Education for a fuller realization of democracy in every phase of living;
2. Education directly and explicitly for international understanding and cooperation;
3. Education for the application of creative imagination and trained intelligence to the solution of social problems and to the administration of publications (American Council on Education, 1949, p. 108).

Paragraphs that described student needs and services for the first time described higher education's awareness of its new types of students—married, veteran, and international.

From these two seminal documents (1937 and 1949), a set of fundamental assumptions arose that would guide professional practice for years. Many professionals believed these assumptions represented the spirit of student personnel practice. Certainly they reflected post–World War II democratic values. They were

1. Individual differences are anticipated and every student is recognized as unique;
2. Each individual is to be treated as a functioning whole;
3. The individual's current drives, interests, and needs are to be accepted as the most significant factor in developing a personnel program appropriate for any particular campus (Mueller, 1961, p. 56);
4. Teaching, counseling, student activities and other organized educational efforts should start realistically from where the individual student is, not from the point of development at which the institution would like to find the hypothetical student; and
5. The student is thought of as a responsible participant in his [sic] own development and not as a passive recipient of an imprinted economic, political or religious doctrine or vocational skill (American Council on Education, 1949, p. 109).

STUDENT PERSONNEL PRACTICE

Student personnel work continued to flourish during the 1940s and 1950s. Professionals believed they understood the needs of students. They planned and offered services and programs to help students function effectively, not only on the campus but also later in society. Practice was motivated by the spirit of the SPPV, and techniques were grounded in principles from sociology, psychology, philosophy, and anthropology intermingled with educational administration, and guidance. Practitioner roles were varied, including caring parent, adviser, programmer, counselor, and disciplinarian. Students were free to choose to consult or use available student services or to decide to participate in programmatic offerings.

Higher education administrators became aware that several services offered to students were being duplicated, in part because of the dual organizational structure of the two offices of dean of men and dean of women. Standards of practice were not always consistent across these administrative lines, and neither were the educational requirements and backgrounds of those supervising these offices. Nevertheless, practitioners believed that the extracurriculum provided opportunities for students to learn a variety of skills as they moved toward personal and social maturity. The distance between student affairs and the academic side of the campus increased. Programs and services were viewed as extras, extracurricular, and not necessarily linked to the curriculum. Always the aim was to help individual students grow and develop as fully functioning human beings able to survive, thrive, and contribute to society.

With the Russian launch of *Sputnik* in 1957, the United States experienced a new and pressing need for scientifically and technically prepared individuals. The race to demonstrate America's prowess and commitment to space exploration and travel had begun. Increased federal funds were channeled into higher education at an unprecedented rate to ensure the availability of science-oriented programs, students, and teachers. Large numbers of high school students who had demonstrated superior intellectual abilities, were encouraged to pursue degrees in the hard sciences. The National Education Defense Acts provided funding for the professional development of elementary and high school teachers. Undergraduate student enrollments swelled as students flocked to universities to study science and the new computer technology. Other high school graduates, desiring to avoid the military draft linked with the developing Vietnam War, enrolled as well, viewing the college campus as a safe refuge.

STUDENT DEVELOPMENT

In contrast to the prevailing attitudes of tranquility and pride that marked the 1950s, the decade of the 1960s was characterized by turmoil, upheaval, and confrontation. Some years later this period was referred to as the age of student activism, the years of civil disobedience, and the downfall of *in loco parentis*. Many student affairs administrators found themselves in difficult situations. They perceived a conflict among their multiple roles. They desired (1) to be advocates for students, (2) to be sensitive to student needs, (3) to help students learn to navigate bureaucratic organizations and participate in social causes, and (4) to serve as counselors and advisors. At the same time, however, they were being told by their institutional presidents to control student behavior. With exploding student enrollments, large classes, an increased use of graduate teaching assistants, and residential overcrowding, undergraduate students began to react to a deep sense of impersonalism they believed was invading higher education. In addition, the use of new computerized technology to efficiently process class registrations and other institutional procedures seemed to strip them of their personal identities as they became known only by their student identity card and number. Discontent escalated as students viewed undergraduate coursework as irrelevant to the solution of major contemporary societal issues. "Flower power," "take time to smell the roses," "do not fold, staple, or mutilate" and other chants filled the campus air along with shouts of demonstrators protesting the involvement of universities in federally funded research programs to assist military operations. Institutions struggled with federally imposed affirmative action quotas, increasingly diverse and somewhat less prepared students, and funding reductions imposed by state legislatures and institutional boards of trustees. Student affairs administrators were viewed as members of middle management. The specific nature of their roles varied from campus to campus, depending on the background and priorities of the president they served.

These same personnel professionals found themselves involved in debates about whether their field was secondary to or complementary to the academic mission of an institution. The purpose or need for student personnel work, now referred to as student affairs, was being viewed with less certainty than ever before. Following the years of turbulence, riots, sit-ins accompanying student activism, and the burning and looting of several major cities during the Civil Rights movement, college and university administrations began to reevaluate their thinking and orientation toward students and the nature of the student-institution relationship.

Institutional perceptions of students changed as did student affairs professionals' roles. Concepts of confrontation, *in loco parentis*, and meritocracy were replaced by encounter, collaboration, and egalitarianism. The attitude of professional practice moved from reactive to proactive, from an orientation of separate student services to a view of the undergraduate years as a continuous developmental sequence. Students were now thought of as adults, albeit as young adults still experiencing a critical period of growth and development. Institutional policies, based on this new view of students, were more liberal. Students were given seats on governing boards, and student advisory committees were established in many areas of the campus.

For student personnel itself, it was also a time of upheaval, turbulence, and confusion. Annual professional conference attendees heard speeches questioning future configurations of the field or even its continued existence. In 1964, ACPA President Cowley entreated conferees to support and utilize a newly created organization, the Council of Student Personnel Associations in Higher Education (COSPA). He hoped this group would present a unified voice of student affairs to legislators and academic administrators. ACPA President Barbara Kirk described the field as experiencing an "identity crisis" (Kirk, 1965, pp. 205–206), a period of questioning, self-doubt. and concern about the role future student personnel professionals would play in higher education. Adding to this uncertainty was a reordering of priorities by some institutions that suggested that unless student affairs professionals could quantitatively document their effectiveness with students, future budget allocations would be greatly reduced or nonexistent. Accountability from the corporate world had entered higher education. Hoping to provide leadership and consistency, ACPA President Ralph Berdie responded to the question "What is student personnel work?" during his presidential address.

> (It) is the application in higher education of knowledge and principles derived from the social and behavioral sciences, particularly psychology, educational psychology, and sociology. Accepting this definition student personnel work is different but not apart from other persons in higher education. Neither is it the exclusive responsibility of any one or several groups of persons in colleges and universities. The student personnel worker is the behavioral scientist whose subject matter is the student and whose socio-psychological sphere is the college. A primary purpose . . . is to humanize higher education, to help students respond to others and to themselves as human beings and to help them formulate principles for themselves as to how people should relate to one another, and to aid them to behave accordingly. . . . Another purpose . . . is to individualize higher education. We recognize the presence and significance of individual differences and hope to structure the education of each individual accordingly (Berdie, 1966, pp. 211–212).

THE MOVE TOWARD A DEVELOPMENTAL PERSPECTIVE: COSPA

Discussions among two groups of professionals meeting independently focused on the same topic: assessing the status of student personnel work and conceptualizing its future role and mission. One group in 1968, composed of representatives of various student personnel associations, was known as the Committee on Professional Development of the Council of Student Personnel Associations in Higher Education (COSPA). Their task was to prepare a statement on guidelines for professional preparation. Committee members (Grant, Saddlemire, Jones, Bradow, Cooper, Kirkbride, Nelson, Page, and Riker) concluded that to do so required that they first revisit the SPPV documents of 1937 and 1949. Keystones emerged to direct the committee's thinking. Notice the subtle shift from the previous student personnel perspective to what would become known as student development:

1. The orientation to student personnel is developmental.
2. Self-direction of the student is the goal of the student and is facilitated by the student development specialist.
3. Students are viewed as collaborators with the faculty and administration in the process of learning and growing.
4. It is recognized that many theoretical approaches to human development have credence, and a thorough understanding of such approaches is important to the student development specialist.

5. The student development specialist prefers a proactive position in policy formulation and decision-making so that a positive impact is made on the change process (Council of Student Personnel Associations in Higher Education 1975, p. 385).

Identifying the clientele (students as individuals, groups, or organizations) and functions (administrative, instructor, and consultant) of student development specialists, the committee proposed competencies to be mastered during professional preparation programs. The former student personnel worker, a generalist, was now considered more of a specialist. This new professional role of educator implied an area of expertise that could be defined as the "process" by which growth, learning, and development occur and could be facilitated. For a more thorough description, see *Student Affairs: A Profession's Heritage* (1994).

The growing diversity of the student body suggested that previous services and programs, designed for a more homogeneous student body, be evaluated and perhaps redesigned. Additionally, new research data describing development within various minority student groups began to appear in the literature. Student personnel practitioners were being introduced to a new understanding of student growth: the developmental perspective.

Student development became a separate movement within student affairs. It had its supporters and its critics. It emerged as a reaction to a perceived negative situation, the devaluing of student personnel on many campuses: "The old approach, student personnel work, was subtly or directly denigrated as inappropriate and outmoded" (Bloland, Stamatakos, & Rogers, 1994, p. 6). Student development

> . . . quickly captured the imagination of a number of student affairs professionals as a way of adding credibility and validity to the work of administrators and practitioners responsible for organizing, guiding, and facilitating the out-of-class education and development of college students (Miller, Winston, & Mendenhall, 1983, p. 11).

Support for this new movement spread, as evidenced by the title of Burns Crookston's article published in 1976 "Student Personnel—All Hail and Farewell!"

THE T.H.E. PROJECT

A second task force chartered by ACPA in 1968 was given the title, Tomorrow's Higher Education (T.H.E.) Project. The goal of this project was described in the resulting monograph *Tomorrow's Higher Education: A Return to the Academy* by Robert Brown:

> The THE Project is an attempt to reconceptualize college student personnel in a way that will serve to provide a measure of creative input from our profession toward the shaping of higher education in the future. By reconceptu-

alization we mean the systematic reconstruction of our fundamental conceptions as to the specific roles, functions, methods and procedures that will characterize future practice. (Brown, 1972, p. i).

Reviewing the literature on the impact of the college experience on students, Brown identified five key student development concepts:

1. Student characteristics when they enter college have a significant impact on how students are affected by their college experience.
2. The collegiate years are the period for many individual students when significant developmental changes occur.
3. There are opportunities within the collegiate program for it to have a significant impact on student development.
4. The environmental factors that hold the most promise for affecting student developmental patterns include the peer group, the living unit, the faculty, and the classroom experience.
5. Developmental changes in students are the result of the interaction of initial characteristics and the press of the environment (Brown, 1972, pp. 33–35).

In addition to these concepts, three families of theories were considered germane to the foundation of the movement: (1) cognitive theories, describing intellectual and moral development; (2) psychosocial theories, describing personal and life cycle development; and (3) the person–environment interaction theories, explaining the ecology of student life (Miller et al., 1983). From these theory families, three core student development principles emerged: (1) human development is both continuous and cumulative; (2) development is a matter of movement from the simpler to the more complex; and (3) human development tends to be orderly and stage-related (Miller et al., pp. 13–14). Publication of Brown's monograph in 1972 completed Phase I of the T.H.E. Project. A second group was commissioned by ACPA to complete Phase II: model building. Completed in 1974, their process model for operationalizing student development identified three major steps or functions that should guide future practice: (1) goal setting, (2) assessment, and (3) strategies for student development. Strategies to facilitate student development, or human growth and development, were defined as teaching, consultation, and milieu management.

As discussions continued, by 1976, the concept of student development was understood as "the application of human development concepts in postsecondary settings so that everyone involved can master increasingly complex developmental tasks, achieve self-direction, and become interdependent" (Miller & Prince, 1976, p. 3). Student development educators, now the preferred term, perceived everyone on campus as members of the academic community. All individuals were also viewed as collaborators and learners in an institution-wide developmental process of growth.

This new educator emphasis was an attempt to locate student affairs professionals within the academic side of the institution. Professional practice strategies were reconceptualized and labeled intentional interventions in students' lives to promote human growth and development. "Intentionality" implied that goal setting had occurred and was a collaborative act with students rather than for students. Student development educators now had the ability to assess developmental levels (psychosocial, cognitive, moral, and so on), to design environments and interventions (experiences or programs), and to help students move through a particular developmental sequence of tasks. In addition, student development educators believed they were capable of facilitating more effective classroom learning by sharing their process ideas and strategies with faculty to improve teaching. On a broader scale, the goal of higher education was to be student development.

THE 1987 NASPA STATEMENT

The field's shift to student development was neither smooth nor quick. Depending on an institution's mission and the orientation of its president, student affairs practitioners implemented student personnel work, student development, or some combination of the two during the 1980s. As more students graduated from preparation programs that emphasized student development and professionals attended conferences emphasizing student development themes, discussions about the nature of practice surfaced again. The key issue now was student diversity. Existing theories had not been developed on data gathered from diverse student populations.

As 1987 approached, 50 years of student affairs practice had been recorded. To commemorate the anniversary of the Student Personnel Point of View, NASPA President Chambers in 1986 appointed Art Sandeen as Chair of the Plan for a New Century Committee. The product was "A Perspective on Student Affairs: A Statement Issued at the 50th Anniversary of the Student Personnel Point of View" (1987) and revealed ". . . what the higher education community can expect from student affairs. . ." (Sandeen et al., 1987, p. 635). The document served "as a stimulus for discussion and debate within higher education and student affairs . . . to foster a renewed understanding and appreciation of the contributions student affairs professionals make to institutions of higher education and the students they serve" (Sandeen et al., 1987, p. 636). Identified within its pages are the core assumptions the committee hoped would guide future student affairs practice. These were:

> The academic mission of the institution is preeminent; Each student is unique; Each person has worth and dignity; Bigotry cannot be tolerated; Feelings affect thinking and learning; Student involvement enhances learning; Personal circumstances affect learning; and Out-of-class environments affect learning (Sandeen et al., 1987, pp. 641–642).

These assumptions are reminiscent of the core values and beliefs described by pioneer student personnel practitioners decades earlier.

STUDENT DEVELOPMENT PRACTICE

Because several of the contributing authors to this book are specialists within specific areas of student affairs practice, a thorough discussion of the application of student development theory to practice is not deemed appropriate for this chapter. The reader is encouraged to consult particular pages of interest.

What is significant to note is that during this stage in the evolution of student affairs, practice stressed the assessment of developmental levels as described by theorists such as Chickering and Reisser, Perry, Kohlberg, and subsequent contributions of Helms and Cass, to name a few. The impact on student growth associated with the interaction between the student and the student's environment was not only recognized and confirmed, but also led student development educators to attempt to create positive environments that would provide the requisite ratio of challenge and support. These theories therefore were useful because they allowed practitioners the opportunity to identify specific pathways or road maps of students' movement toward maturity. Student development educators' ability to define specific goals for their programmatic efforts, or intentional interventions, was enhanced by an understanding of these theories. Viewing growth, development, and learning almost synonymously, the entire academic community was perceived as one whose goal was the personal growth and development of each of its members.

FOCUS ON STUDENT LEARNING

As with previous movements within student affairs, student development has had its supporters and its critics. An important critique of the movement by Bloland, Stamatakos, and Rogers is contained in the 1994 monograph, *Reform in Student Affairs: A Critique of Student Development*:

> Our argument is not with student development per se. It is rather with our fellow professionals . . . who failed to exercise their critical faculties to raise questions about student development, to slow down the headlong pace of its engulfment of the field of student affairs, and to examine alternatives and options as they presented themselves (Bloland et al., p. x).

Essentially, these three seasoned professionals examined, challenged, and highlighted student development as a reform movement, the application of its theories, and the problems they perceived the use of the term *student development* "has created for the field of student affairs" (Bloland et al.,

p. xi). Suggesting a new paradigm, they proposed "the student affairs profession again take its cue from the central educational mission of higher education and view the learning process as integral to the implementation of that mission" (p. 103). Included among final recommendations were:

1. Cease identifying with the student development model as the wellspring or philosophical underpinning of the field of student affairs. . . .
2. Return to the general principles so cogently expressed in the Student Personnel Point of View (ACPA, 1949), clearly placing academic and intellectual development at the center of the student affairs mission.
3. Re-emphasize the primacy of learning as the cardinal value of higher education and employ learning theory, conjointly with student development theory, as an essential tool for planning experiences and programs that will enhance the learning process.
4. Clearly identify with the institutional educational mission for unless student affairs takes its cue from the mission and goals of higher education, it has no function except the provision of support services; any educational outcomes it may claim are purely accidental (p. 104).

In 1993, ACPA President Schroeder convened a group of leaders in higher education to consider how student affairs might enhance its role relative to student learning and personal development. Members of The Student Learning Imperative Project included A. Astin, H. Astin, P. Bloland, K. P. Cross, J. Hurst, G. Kuh, T. Marchese, E. Nuss, E. Pascarella, A. Pruitt, M. Rooney, and C. Schroeder. Their deliberations produced the document, "The Student Learning Imperative: Implications for Student Affairs . . . , "intended to stimulate discussion and debate on how student affairs professionals can intentionally create the conditions that enhance student learning and personal development" (American College Personnel Association, 1995, p. 1). In addition, project members perceived the present as yet another period of major transformation precipitated in part by the continued increase in diversity in higher education, the eroded public confidence, the effects of accountability being imposed by external constituencies and the new importance attached to positive educational environments. Committee members proposed five characteristics student affairs divisions committed to student learning and personal development should exhibit:

1. The student affairs division mission complements the institution's mission, with the enhancement of student learning and personal development being the primary goal of student affairs programs and services;
2. Resources are allocated to encourage student learning and personal development;
3. Student affairs professionals collaborate with other institutional agents and agencies to promote student learning and personal development;

4. The division of student affairs includes staff who are experts on students, their environments, and teaching and learning processes; and

5. Student affairs policies and programs are based on promising practices from the research on student learning and institution-specific assessment data (American College Personnel Association, 1995, pp. 2–5).

While many professionals perceived this new emphasis on student learning, which sometimes included the concept of teaching, as a major paradigmatic shift from previous goals and values, others viewed it simply as another evolutionary stage in the dynamic development of student affairs. Certainly, teaching and learning are, and always have been, central to the mission of American higher education. In 1954, Lloyd-Jones and Smith coauthored *Student Personnel Work as Deeper Teaching*, a conceptualization of student personnel as fundamentally educative in nature. Almost 20 years later, Brown issued his call for a "return to the academy" (Brown, 1972). One must wonder about the efficacy of that return to the academy. Being so much inside its walls, student affairs professionals may find themselves looking over their shoulders at students' growth and development in areas other than intellectual. To do so would not be consistent with the core values and beliefs espoused by early pioneer deans and practitioners. In addition, members of the academic side of the institution may well perceive student learning as their prerogative and responsibility. Assuming this, future student affairs practitioners may find themselves realigned with tasks associated with the maintenance of students. The purpose of student affairs as extracurriculum or cocurriculum has been and obviously will continue to be debated into the foreseeable future. Such discussions and reassessments may lead to the ambiguous realm of noncurriculum. In the next few decades, will practice focus on services only if and when a consuming student perceives a need? Will students be viewed as young adults whose familial and emotional backgrounds require little or no attention? And which side, if sides exist in the future, will have the expertise, inclination, and time to provide such attention to aspects of growth other than intellectual? It seems we are again in the midst of a period of transition or transformation. Where will we look for the beliefs and values to guide student affairs practice in the future? Will we look to the institution and its mission, to faculty and their values, or to students and their needs? And which needs will we attend to? Should we lose sight of the individual student as our specialty and weaken our resolve to provide experiences and guidance for holistic development? Who have we become? The role, mission, and goals of student affairs have never been, and hopefully never will be, static. For it is in the dynamic tension that resides within and between the field and higher education's changing institutions that the seeds of our power and value can be found.

REFERENCES

American College Personnel Association. (1994). *The student learning imperative: Implications for student affairs.* Washington, DC: Author.

American Council on Education, (1994). The Student Personnel Point of View (1937). In A. L. Rentz (Ed.), *Student affairs: A profession's heritage* (pp. 66–78). Lanham, MD: University of America Press

American Council on Education (1994). The Student Personnel Point of View (1949). In A. L. Rentz (Ed.), *Student affairs: A profession's heritage* (pp. 108–123). Lanham, MD: University of America Press.

Berdie, R. (1966). Student personnel work: Definition and redefinition. *Journal of College Student Personnel, 7,* 131–136.

Bloland, P., Stamatakos, L. C., & Rogers, R. R. (1994). *Reform in student affairs: A critique of student development.* Greensboro, NC: ERIC Counseling and Student Services Clearinghouse.

Brown, R. W. (1926). *Dean Briggs.* New York: Harper.

Brown, R. D. (1972). *Student development in tomorrow's higher education.* Student Personnel Series, No. 16. Washington, DC: American Personnel and Guidance Association.

Brubacher, J. S., & Rudy, W. (1958). *Higher education in transition.* New York: Harper & Row.

Clothier, R. C. (1931). College personnel principles and functions. In A.L. Rentz (Ed.), *Student affairs: A profession's heritage* (pp. 9–18). Lanham, MD: University of America Press.

Commission of Professional Preparation of COSPA (1994). Student development services in post secondary education (1975). In A. L. Rentz (Ed.), *Student affairs: A profession's heritage* (pp. 428–437). Lanham, MD: University of America Press.

Cowley, W. H. (1936). The nature of student personnel work. In A. L. Rentz (Ed.), *Student affairs: A profession's heritage* (pp. 43–65). Lanham, MD: University of America Press.

Cowley, W. H. (1937, April,). A preface to the principles of student counseling. *The Educational Record, 18(1),* 217–234.

Cowley, W. H. (1949). Some history and a venture in prophecy. In E. G. Williamson (Ed.), *Trends in student personnel work.* Minneapolis, MN: University of Minnesota Press.

Cowley, W. H., & Williams, D. (1991). *International and historical roots of American higher education.* New York: Garland.

Fleming, J. (1984) *Blacks in college.* San Francisco: Jossey-Bass.

Fley, J. (1979). Student personnel pioneers: Those who developed our profession. *National Association of Student Personnel Administrators Journal, 17,* 23–39.

Goodenow, R. K. (1989). Black education. In C. R. Wilson & W. Ferris (Eds.), *Encyclopedia of southern culture.* Chapel Hill, NC: University of North Carolina Press.

Hill, S. (1984). *The traditionally black institutions of higher education: 1860 to 1982.* Washington, DC: U.S. Department of Education.

Holmes, L. (1939). *A history of the position of dean of women in a selected group of co-educational colleges and universities in the United States.* New York: Teachers College, Columbia University.

Humphreys, J. A. (1930). Techniques of college personnel work. In J. E. Walters (Ed.), *College Personnel Procedures: Proceedings of Purdue-Wabash Conference of College Personnel Officers* (pp. 11–13). Lafayette, IN: Purdue University.

Kirk, B. A. (1965). Identity crisis—1965. *Journal of College Student Personnel, 6,* 194–199.

Knock, G. H. (1985). Development of student services in higher education. In M. J. Barr, L. A. Keating, & Associates, *Developing effective student services programs.* San Francisco: Jossey-Bass.

Lloyd-Jones, E. (1994). Personnel administration (1934). In A. L. Rentz (Ed.), *Student affairs: A profession's heritage* (pp. 19–26). Lanham, MD: University of America Press.

Lloyd-Jones, E. (1949). The beginnings of our profession. In E. G. Williamson (Ed.), *Student personnel work* (pp. 260–263). Minneapolis, MN: University of Minnesota Press.

Lloyd-Jones, E., & Smith, M. R. (1954). *Student personnel as deeper teaching.* New York: Harper.

Miller, T. K., & Prince, J. S. (1976). *The future of student affairs.* San Francisco: Jossey-Bass, Inc.

Miller, T. K., Winston, R. B., Jr., & Mendenhall, W. R. (1983). *Administration and leadership in student affairs.* Muncie, IN: Accelerated Developments.

Morison, S. E. (1930). *The development of Harvard University since the inauguration of President Eliot 1869–1929.* (pp. Lxviii–lxix). Cambridge, MA: Harvard University Press.

Mueller, K. H. (1961). *Student personnel work in higher education.* Boston, MA: Houghton Mifflin.

National Advisory Committee on Black Higher Education and Black Colleges and Universities. (1979). *Black colleges and universities: An essential component of a diverse system of higher education.* Washington, DC: Department of Education.

Ranbom, S., & Lynch, J. (1987, Fall 1988, Winter). TIMELINE: The long, hard road to educational equity, *Educational Record, 46,* 16–17.

Rentz, A. L. (Ed.). (1994). *Student affairs: A profession's heritage.* Lanham, MD: University Press of America.

Roebuck, J. B., & Murty, K. S. (1993). *Historically black colleges and universities: Their place in American higher education.* Westport, CT: Praeger.

Rosenberry, L. M. (1915). *The dean of women.* Boston, MA: Houghton Mifflin.

Rudolph, F. (1990). *The American college and university: A history.* Athens, GA: University of Georgia Press.

Sandeen, A., Albright, R. L., Barr, M. J., Golseth, A. E., Kuh, G. D., Lyons, W., & Rhatigan, J. J. (1994). A perspective on student affairs: A statement issued on the fiftieth anniversary of the student personnel point of view (1987). In A. L. Rentz (Ed.), *Student affairs: A profession's heritage* (pp. 635–636). Lanham, MD: University Press of America.

Solomon, B. M. (1985). *In the company of educated women.* New Haven, CT: Yale University Press.

Stock, P. (1978). *Better than rubies: A history of women's education.* New York: G. P. Putnam's Sons.

T.H.E. Phase II Model Building Conference (1983). A student development model for student affairs in tomorrow's higher education (1975). In A. L. Rentz (Ed.),

Student affairs: A profession's heritage (pp. 410–422). Lanham, MD: University Press of America.

Thomas, G. E., & Hirsch, D. J. (1987). Black institutions in U.S. higher education: Present roles, contributions, future projections. *Journal of College Student Personnel, 27,* 496–503.

Thomas, G. E., & Hirsch, D. J. (1989). Blacks. In A. Levine (Ed.), *Blacks in higher education: Overcoming the odds.* Lanham, MD: University Press of America.

Williamson, E. G. (1949). *Trends in student personnel work.* Minneapolis, MN: University of Minnesota Press.

Chapter 3

FROM ADMISSIONS TO
ENROLLMENT MANAGEMENT

Don Hossler

OVERVIEW

It is appropriate that this chapter falls at the beginning of this book because the admissions office is usually the point of first contact between prospective students and the student affairs division as well as the entire campus. Both the 1939 Student Personnel Point of View and the subsequent revision in 1947 placed the function of the admissions office within the purview of student affairs (American Council on Education, 1994). On many campuses, however, the admissions office is not even a part of the student affairs division. This is unfortunate because student affairs divisions should be concerned about all aspects of the students' college experience from the point of initial contact to the point of graduation. Admissions offices frequently are housed in divisions of academic affairs or institutional advancement. An increasingly common organizational structure is to locate admissions offices within separate enrollment management organizations. Indeed, it is this trend that is part of the warrant for this chapter.

This chapter examines the development of the field of admissions and traces admissions into the emerging concept of enrollment management. Whereas the admissions function has primarily been interested in attracting and admitting college students, enrollment management is concerned with the entirety of the college experience. The first part of this chapter defines admissions work and presents a history of the admissions field. The second part of the chapter defines enrollment management and explores this organizational concept.

ADMISSIONS

INTRODUCTION

Swann (1998) identified the following roles for admissions officers:

58

1. Processing applications and credentials;
2. Analyzing the processing and reporting analysis to internal and external parties;
3. Distributing admissions, scholarship, and financial aid materials to the constituent schools and prospect lists, and presenting program sessions about the institutions at those feeder schools;
4. Conducting preview programs and tours at the institution; and
5. Counseling visitors to appropriate referral resources within the institution (advisors and student personnel sources such as housing, financial aid, and testing (Swann, 1998, p. 35).

The purpose of the admissions process is to help students make a successful transition from high school to college (Munger & Zucker, 1982) as well as to recruit students for specific colleges and universities (Shaffer & Martinson, 1966). Thus, it is important for admissions officers to understand the needs of traditional and nontraditional college students and to know the institution for which they are working. In this way, admissions officers can help students make the best college choice decision possible while at the same time recruiting students who will be well suited to the specific institution the admissions officer represents. Like most functional areas in student affairs divisions, the admissions function has a long history in American higher education, but its formal history is relatively short.

A HISTORY OF THE COLLEGE ADMISSIONS OFFICE

GATEKEEPER OR SALESPERSON: THE IMAGE OF THE ADMISSIONS OFFICER

The history of the field of admissions in American colleges and universities is difficult to unravel. This is because our understanding of the field has been shaped by two competing images of the admissions officer. On the one hand, the image of the admissions officer is that of the "Ivy League" admissions officer who, along with a faculty admissions committee, decides who will receive the coveted offers of admissions on "Bloody Monday"[1]

They decide who will be able to "join the club." The other image is that of the salesperson, attempting to attract prospective students to a college or university so that the institution's budget will be balanced, the doors will be open, and the faculty will be happy. Depending on the image to which you resonate, your history of the admissions function might look quite different. Thelin (1982) has described these two contrasting images of the admissions field as those of "gatekeeper" and "headhunter." Actually, both images are

---

[1] This is the term used to describe the Monday in April on which all highly selective colleges send out their notices of acceptance or rejection to new student applicants.

accurate descriptions of various time periods in American higher education, as well as of different types of institutions of higher education.

Early American colleges can trace the role of the admissions office to that of the "major beadle" in the medieval university (Smerling, 1960). The major beadle was succeeded by the office of the archivist (Lindsay & Holland, 1930) and later by the office of the registrar. The role of the faculty members or administrators in these positions was to keep track of student progress while enrolled in college and to determine whether prospective students, or new applicants, had the right background for admission to the institution. For the early American college, the right background frequently meant that the student could speak the English language with some modicum of proficiency and was of good moral character. At more selective institutions of the time, students were expected to have some knowledge of Latin and Greek (Broome, 1903; Rudolph, 1962). In any case, most early colleges also had preparatory schools attached to them so that students who did not meet the admissions requirements could acquire the necessary skills for admission (Brubacher & Rudy, 1968; Rudolph, 1962).

Not all colleges, however, were able to sit passively and wait for students to arrive for their admissions test. Part of the American dream included equal access to education and upward mobility. During the expansion westward in the nineteenth century, every town aspired to greatness. The presence of a college in a town was viewed as a clear signal to current and prospective residents that the town was going to become a major center and a good place to live. As a result, colleges were created at a rapid rate. For example, in the early 1870s, England had four universities for a population of 23,000,000. The state of Ohio had 37 colleges for a population of 3,000,000 (Rudolph, 1962). Many of these colleges consisted of one to three faculty and probably did not even have a building. Frequently, the education offered by these institutions was at the preparatory level.

In these institutions, however, we find the forerunner of the other image of the admissions officer, the salesperson. Early American colleges did not have large faculties and staff, and they frequently consisted of the president and one or two additional faculty. The president taught classes, and in addition performed all of the roles now associated with positions such as the chief fund-raiser, the academic dean, the dean of students, and the registrar. Rudolph's (1962) history of American higher education is replete with stories of college presidents traveling through the countryside trying to attract the sons (and it was only sons during most of the eighteenth and nineteenth centuries) of farmers and the emerging merchant class.

There simply were not enough potential college students to support the large number and variety of colleges that had been established in the United States. As a result, many institutions of higher education had to be creative in devising new ways to attract students. Frequently, new entrants into the college student affairs field view the current marketing efforts and financial aid strategies, such as telemarketing, prepaid tuition plans, or guaranteed cost plans, as new ideas emerging as the result of rising college costs and competition for students. However, many early American colleges also had to devise creative marketing and recruitment strategies. In the middle part of the nineteenth century, several colleges sold tuition payments in advance to families. The idea was to attract revenues that could be invested in endowments to support faculty and instruction immediately, thus reducing current as well as future instructional costs. Unfortunately, these early colleges could not afford to invest the money. They were forced to spend the money on current needs. Thus, when these new prepaid students arrived, the money was gone and in some cases the colleges were also gone, having been forced into bankruptcy. The surviving institutions such as Dickinson and DePauw lost large amounts of money ranging in excess of more than two dollars for each dollar raised (Rudolph, 1962).

Even the mass-marketing techniques of today are not entirely new. In 1893, one state university had sufficient funds and political clout to send out brochures to every school superintendent in the state describing the virtues of attending the institution. Superintendents throughout the state were fined $50 if the university brochures were not posted in their high schools (Thelin, 1982). The entrepreneurial activities of these struggling colleges to attract students are part of the history of the salesperson image of the admissions field. Although the first dean of admissions was not appointed until the early part of the twentieth century, the need for a guiding professional was certainly there.

THE EMERGENCE OF THE ADMISSIONS FIELD

The tension between the images of gatekeeper and salesperson continued into the twentieth century even as the professional admissions field began to emerge. Prior to the actual appointment of the first deans of admissions in the 1920s, two important trends emerged that would shape the role of the admissions officer. By the end of the nineteenth century, many colleges and universities had become concerned about the lack of standardization in the preparation of high school students. As a result, institutions of higher learning could make few assumptions about the skills and academic training of college applicants.

In response to this problem, in 1870 the University of Michigan sent teams of faculty out to visit high schools in order to improve the level of instruction and articulation between colleges and high schools. Other states followed suit, and in 1894 the North Central Association was formed to standardize high school curricula. Although the University of Michigan was the first university to employ this process, the precedent for regional associations had already been set by the 1880s with the creation of the New England Association of Colleges and Preparatory Schools (Brubacher & Rudy, 1968).

Along with the creation of associations to improve education at the high school level, standardized testing also emerged as a way to improve high school education and to standardize the "chaotic entrance requirements" employed by colleges and universities (Brubacher & Rudy, 1968). The Regents exam (created in 1878) was the first such effort. In the 1890s, a meeting of the Association of the Colleges and Secondary Schools of the Middle States and Maryland led to the establishment of the College Entrance Examination Board, later renamed The College Board. The creation of standardized tests by the College Entrance Examination Board caused many colleges and universities to slowly abandon their own entrance exams and rely on one standardized test.

The emergence of the accreditation associations and standardized testing had an important impact on the admissions function. It was now easier to determine who was prepared for college (although the criteria for admissions varied), and it was also easier to compare the quality of entering students. Standardization forever changed the dialogue on institutional quality and prestige and formalized the tension between the role of the gatekeeper and the salesperson. Now admissions officers could use objective criteria to compare not only the number of students enrolled but also the quality of those students enrolled.

The use of objective criteria in admissions practice did not become widespread until the 1930s even though the first deans of admission were hired in the 1920s. It was during the 1930s that the concept of selective admissions was formally articulated (Thresher, 1966). The concept of selective admissions helped to further entrench the concept of institutional prestige based on selectivity. However, the emergence of elite, highly selective institutions such as Harvard, Yale, and Stanford is still a relatively recent phenomenon.

The onset of the Depression resulted in a downturn in college applicants. As a result, the 1930s was an era of the salesperson—not the gatekeeper. The subsequent entry of the United States into World War II also depressed college applications. Thus, it was not until the end of World War II that the gatekeeper function reemerged.

With the large numbers of veterans (GIs) returning to college after World War II and the subsequent rise in enrollments because of the baby boom generation, the 1960s and 1970s are often referred to as the "Golden Age" of American higher education (Jencks & Reisman, 1969). During this era ,even some admissions officers at many well-known but less prestigious private colleges and universities as well as many public institutions were able to function as gatekeepers. Nevertheless, it would be a mistake to think of this as an era of gatekeeping for all admissions officers. The rapid growth of public four-year and two-year colleges had a major impact on admissions officers at smaller and lesser-known private institutions. As a result, many private colleges and universities had to actively market themselves and recruit students in order to maintain enrollments (Thresher, 1966).

THE ADMISSIONS OFFICER OF TODAY

By the beginning of the 1970s, colleges and universities were preparing for a predicted decrease of traditional-aged college students estimated to be as high as 42 percent before the end of the twentieth century (Hossler, 1986). Institutions began to implement for-profit business techniques to maintain or increase student enrollments as college administrators shifted from the "bullish" student enrollment market of the 1950s and 1960s to the "bear" market of the 1980s and 1990s.

This set the stage for the emergence of the admissions officer of today and for the concept of enrollment management. The admissions officers have, in many cases, become hybrids of both the gatekeeper and the salesperson. At nonselective institutions, admissions officers continue to function primarily as salespersons. However, even at the most selective institutions where gatekeeping continues to play an important role, admissions officers have also had to become salespersons in order to attract a sufficient number of high ability students who have all the other attributes desired by prestigious colleges and universities (geographic representation, minority representation, as well as music, leadership, athletic, and other special talents).

Starting in the 1970s, offices of admissions began to use marketing techniques such as improved publication materials, targeted mailing strategies, and telemarketing techniques in order to attract larger numbers of students. At the same time, senior level administrators began to utilize strategic planning techniques also borrowed from business. Strategic planning incorporates market research so that organizations can better understand their clients and the institution's position in relation to competitors. This was the impetus for the push toward marketing and the foundation for enrollment management that is discussed later in this chapter.

Marketing techniques have forced admissions officers to attend to tracking and communicating with prospective students. Targeted mailing and telemarketing and electronic communication techniques require that admissions officers be able to analyze the background and attitudinal characteristics of students in order to identify the best potential markets. Personalized communication techniques, using both print and electronic media, are also hallmarks of modern marketing. These developments required admissions officers to become more analytical than before and able to use computer-assisted technology. For admissions officers serving as salespersons, the adoption of these techniques and skills became essential for institutional well-being.

The 1990s and the new century have seen an increased emphasis on the importance of pricing and student financial aid as well as the use of sophisticated marketing techniques. Whereas 10 years ago new marketing techniques such as direct mail and telemarketing were thought to be key to successful student recruitment, many admissions directors now believe that newly developed enrollment modeling approaches to setting tuition costs and to awarding financial aid are the most important elements of successful new student recruitment. Pricing and student aid may have arguably become the most important part of student recruitment. Many admissions directors report that they now spend more time with vice presidents of business on financial aid issues than on any other aspect of their job.

The emergence of the modern admissions office, with its emphasis on marketing, electronic technology, pricing, and student financial aid, has separated admissions officers from other student affairs areas that have strong counseling or student development orientations. As a result, many professionals in the field of admissions do not think of themselves as student affairs personnel (Hossler, 1986). However, as will be seen in the next section of this chapter, while admissions and student affairs staff have become part of enrollment management efforts, the connections between admissions and student affairs work is once again becoming apparent.

ENROLLMENT MANAGEMENT

AN INTRODUCTION

As a result of the predicted declines in traditional-aged college students, college and university administrators became interested in student retention as well as student recruitment. Student attrition became a frequent topic of inquiry during the late 1970s and 1980s, and research in this area has continued (Bean, 1980; Braxton, 2000; Noel, Levitz, & Saluri, 1985; Pascarella & Terenzini, 1991; Tinto, 1993). Student affairs administrators often found themselves assigned the responsibility for developing institutional retention programs. In addition to this line of retention research, a growing body of studies of the college decision-making process and the impact of student financial aid on recruitment and retention also emerged during the 1990s (Brooks, 1996; Hossler, Braxton, & Coopersmith, 1989; McDonough, Antonio, Walpole, & Perez, 1998; Paulsen, 1991; Scannell, 1992; St. John, Paulsen, & Starkey, 1996).

The converging interests in attracting and retaining new students provided the impetus for the emergence of the enrollment management concept. Enrollment management provided an integrating framework for institutional efforts to more directly influence student enrollments than previously practiced. On some campuses, student affairs divisions began to play key roles in enrollment management activities. However enrollment management as a formal concept is relatively new and has little history to document.

A number of conceptual frameworks have been suggested for use as the organizational basis for student affairs divisions (Komives, Woodard, &

Associates, 1996). Enrollment management can be viewed as one more framework for organizing student affairs divisions. In order for this to occur, many student affairs professionals will have to become familiar with the enrollment management concept. To this end, the purposes of the second part of this chapter are to accomplish the following:

1. Define enrollment management.
2. Examine the evolution of enrollment management.
3. Discuss enrollment management as a concept.
4. Examine enrollment management as a process.
5. Present four archetypal enrollment management models.
6. Explore the role of student affairs in enrollment management.
7. Discuss ethical issues related to enrollment management.
8. Consider the professional preparation needs of enrollment managers and the future of enrollment management.

DEFINING ENROLLMENT MANAGEMENT

In order for student affairs professionals to utilize the enrollment management concept, they must first understand it. On many campuses, the term *enrollment management* has developed a potent image as a systematic institutional response to issues related to student enrollments. At most institutions, enrollment management has become associated with a diverse set of activities that are employed by colleges and universities that are attempting to exert more control over the characteristics of their enrolled student body or the size of their enrolled student body. In one sense, the images of the gatekeeper and salesperson in admissions are still relevant. However, from an enrollment management perspective, institutions are concerned not only about the characteristics and the total number of new students, but also about the characteristics and total number of all enrolled students.

Enrollment management has been defined in a number of ways, but in each case students are the fundamental unit of analysis. Enrollment management is not just an organizing concept—it is a process that involves the entire campus.

> Enrollment management is both an organizational concept as well as a systematic set of activities designed to enable educational institutions to exert more influence over their student enrollments and total net tuition revenue derived from enrolled students. Organized by strategic planning and supported by institutional research, enrollment management activities concern student college choice, transition to college, student attrition and retention, and student outcomes. These processes are studied to guide institutional practices in the areas of new student recruitment and financial aid, student support services, curriculum development and other academic areas that affect enrollments, student persistence, and student outcomes from college. (Revised in 2001 from Hossler, Bean, & Associates, 1990)

The evolution of this new concept can now be examined with this definition of enrollment management in mind. Later in this chapter, process elements of an enrollment management system are examined, followed by a discussion of organizational models. These sections further enhance our understanding of enrollment management.

THE EVOLUTION OF ENROLLMENT MANAGEMENT

The term, and perhaps the concept, of a comprehensive enrollment management system first emerged in 1976. However, as a process, enrollment management had been developing for many years. In fact, an examination of the evolution of offices of admissions and financial aid, along with other areas of student affairs, nonprofit marketing in higher education, research on student college choice and student persistence demonstrates that the enrollment management concept represented the convergence of developments in each of these areas. The convergence made possible the complex and comprehensive nature of the competitive college admissions process.

It is difficult to determine whether the competitive nature of college admissions in recent decades caused the advances in marketing techniques for higher education or whether the emergence of nonprofit marketing made possible the increasing sophistication of collegiate recruitment activities. It is equally difficult to determine whether the emergence of differentiated financial aid and pricing activities were the products of competition for students or if research on student college choice and the effects of aid and price on college choice have resulted in up-to-date, effective aid and pricing policies. Additionally, research on student attrition, the impact of college on students, and student–institution fit produced institutional retention programs that are often tailored to meet the needs of specific student populations such as nontraditional adult students, transfer students, or minority students.

It may be difficult to determine the precise genesis of the enrollment management concept. It is clear, however, that the declining numbers of traditional-aged students along with the overbuilding of colleges and universities to accommodate the veterans and baby boomers of the 1950s and 1960s created a set of internal and external constraints that required college administrators to be more attentive to student enrollments. Thus, the emergence of the concept of enrollment management has been tied to the environmental press to which institutions of higher education have been forced to respond.

When it first appeared, what made the enrollment management concept new was not the development of new marketing techniques or new retention strategies. Rather, it has been the organizational integration of functions, such as academic advising, admissions, financial aid, and orientation, into a comprehensive institutional approach designed to enable college and university administrators to exert influence over the factors that shape enrollments.

Research and scholarship in applied fields frequently lag behind new developments in these fields. Scholars and educational observers sometimes find themselves in the position of following institutional trends by describing emerging developments, thus formalizing them. In 1976, Maguire used the term *enrollment management* to describe his efforts to attract and retain students at Boston College (Maguire, 1976). One of the first times the term *enrollment management* formally appeared in the literature was in a *College Board Review* article by Kreutner and Godfrey (1981) that described a matrix approach to managing enrollments developed at California State University at Long Beach. Since these early publications, a spate of books, book chapters, monographs, and articles have been published on the topic of enrollment management.

The concept and process of enrollment management continue to evolve. As enrollment management systems mature, they continue to focus on marketing and recruitment. In addition, institutions give more attention to student retention, student learning, and college rankings (Black, 2001). Undoubtedly, enrollment management systems will continue to change and develop in response to the needs of individual institutions.

ENROLLMENT MANAGEMENT AS A CONCEPT

Although definitions and a sense of the history of enrollment management provide some perspective, they do not provide a sufficient understanding of enrollment management. Hossler and Hoezee (2001) suggested that continuous, long-term success in the field of enrollment management rests on the following theories and concepts:

1. Resource dependency theory;
2. Systems theory;
3. Revenue theory and revenue maximization;
4. Students as institutional image; and
5. Enrollment management as courtship.

Resource Dependency Theory

No theoretical construct provides a better understanding of the emergence of the field of enrollment management or provides a better focal point for enrollment managers, than resource dependency theory. Through the lens of resource dependency theory, enrollment managers are able to understand how colleges and universities respond to the demographic, budgetary, competitive, and public policy changes taking place around them (Pfeffer & Salancik, 1978; Tolbert, 1985). Pfeffer and Salancik

(1978) noted that resource dependency theory is a means for analyzing the relationships between organizations and the external environment in which they operate. Most organizations are heavily dependent on the external environment for resources because they are not self-sufficient. Organizations require resources from the external environment for their continuing survival. For-profit organizations operate under some constraints, but they can try developing new markets and new sources of support as they see fit. Nonprofit organizations, however, operate under different constraints. They have less geographic mobility, have less control over their product, and face a difficult external environment because their role in society is so distinctive (Clark, 1983; Clott, 1995).

Because there is uncertainty in the environments of universities and colleges, institutions seek to acquire additional resources by structuring their relationships to establish unique connections with the external environment. Resource dependency theory helps enrollment managers to continually ask "What are the scarce resources for my campus associated with student enrollments?" These scarce resources range from (1) the number of students enrolled, (2) the total net revenue generated by the number of students enrolled, (3) the diversity of enrolled students, to (4) the academic characteristics of the students enrolled (Breneman, 1994).

Systems Theory

For enrollment managers, an important feature of systems theory is its focus on closed and open systems. "Closed systems" are organizations that are focused inwardly and are primarily concerned with what happens within their unit. "Open systems," on the contrary, emphasize a constant interchange between the organization, or units within an organization, and the external environment.

Greater levels of collegiality and informality than found in many other organizations also distinguish institutions of higher education. The openness and decentralization characteristics of colleges and universities can minimize tendencies toward closed systems. However, these same characteristics can foster a high degree of independence among administrative units, which creates more opportunities for closed system thinking within these individual units. Senge (1990) observed that successful modern organizations require open systems and high levels of communication among units throughout the organization. In order to effectively influence student enrollments, enrollment managers and the elements comprising an enrollment management unit frequently must share information, goals, and strategies. They have to recognize their mutual dependence on each other.

Successful enrollment management efforts require open systems. A complex array of factors influences the success of enrollment management efforts. Issues (such as the mission of an institution, the types of majors, the degree of emphasis on teaching and research, location, tuition and financial aid policies, the student–faculty ratio, the demographic profile of enrolled students, the degree of admissions selectivity, the quality of student life, state and federal policies, student recruitment and retention programs, and the economy) exert pressure on student enrollments. Therefore, enrollment managers must approach their task from an open systems perspective. Enrollment management involves many organizational units on campus; it requires high degrees of collaboration and *interdependence*. An open systems approach with high levels of communication is fundamental to the profession.

Revenue Theory

The increased practice of providing campus-based financial aid to help recruit and retain students has accentuated and made visible the role of enrollment management in providing revenue to run colleges and universities. In his 1980 book, *The Costs of Higher Education*, Howard Bowen put forth a theory that continues to be just as practical today. Bowen's examination of revenue theory, along with current work in the area of revenue maximization, provides an important conceptual underpinning for enrollment management.

Bowen observed that without the profit motive of for-profit businesses, institutions spend as much money as is available from various sources to achieve their goals. Thus, costs follow revenues—an idea counter to some budgeting practices. Bowen's "rules of thumb" are: (1) the dominant goals of institutions are educational excellence, prestige, and influence; (2) in quest of excellence, prestige, and influence, there is virtually no limit to the amount of money an institution could spend for seemingly fruitful educational ends; (3) each institution raises all the money it can; (4) each institution spends all it raises; and as a result (5) the cumulative effect of the preceding four laws is toward ever-increasing expenditures. It goes beyond the scope of this chapter to discuss Bowen's laws in detail, but the primary emphasis of his revenue theory of higher education bears repeating: The goals of institutions of higher education are to use all resources available to maintain and preferably enhance prestige and influence.

These goals should not be lost on enrollment managers. At most institutions enrollment management efforts can *never do enough* to help institutions achieve these goals. If enrollments have increased, then the focus will shift to the quality factor or to student diversity so the campus can further enhance its perceived excellence. If enrollment demand curves look solid, efforts to reduce campus-based financial aid are likely to emerge in order to increase net tuition revenue, which in turn frees up more funds for laboratories, library holdings, and faculty salaries. For enrollment managers, Bowen's observations are simultaneously normative, descriptive, strategic, and frustrating: No matter how successful enrollment management efforts have been, they are never enough. Given the use of campus-based financial aid to help achieve enrollment goals, revenue theory leads naturally to its companion theory—revenue maximization.

Revenue Maximization

In colleges and universities, as in all organizations, maximizing revenue, minimizing costs, substituting inputs while monitoring the quality of the output and opportunity costs, all play into administrative practices in higher education. Like all budget administrators, enrollment managers have three options to find more funds for the activities of their organizations: (1) grow more dollars, (2) maximize the return from a budgeted dollar, and (3) minimize costs. Growing dollars can be quite difficult. To maximize dollars, strategy sessions to review the various returns on every dollar spent are common. For example, some institutions find that simple, inexpensive black-and-white brochures and reply cards sent to prospective students are nearly as effective as full-color, and more costly, brochures and reply cards.

Another way for enrollment managers to enhance resources has been found in the practice of tuition discounting. Conceptual leads for this practice can be found in Robert Cross's book, *Revenue Management* (1997). Cross was an early pioneer of financial strategy in the airline industry. Instead of charging a flat fee for each seat on an airplane, variable costs were made available, largely based on the timing of the purchase decision. The rationale behind this strategy ties into a discussion of fixed, variable, and marginal costs. The same ideas are the foundation for tuition discounting.

Breneman (1994), an economist and former college president, examined the cost structure of operating a college. As a former college president, he understood clearly that overhead and salaries were fixed costs and represented a sizable portion of the operating budget. Furthermore, he knew that some classrooms were filled to capacity and others had empty chairs. In this context, institutions may provide some students (who exhibit certain characteristics of value to the institution) a financial aid award, basically a discount, as an incentive to encourage their conversion from an admitted student to an enrolled student. As long as the financial aid award is less than the total cost of tuition, an institution can still garner additional tuition revenue that would otherwise not have been earned. This reduces the number of empty seats, or unused capacity, thus holding fixed costs constant while increasing revenue.

Revenue theory and revenue maximization are major foundations of current enrollment management practices.

Enrollment Management as Courtship

Hossler and many of his colleagues have viewed courtship as a valuable metaphor for many aspects of the enrollment management process

(Abrahamson & Hossler, 1990; Hayek & Hossler, 1999; Hossler, 2000; Hossler, Schmit, & Vesper, 1998). Recruitment and retention activities are likely to be successful if they are conceptualized in the following ways: How can we convey to prospective students, or current students, that we think this campus would be a good fit for them? How can we encourage students to spend more time with us?

If enrollment managers and their staff think of both recruitment and retention activities from the perspective of courtship, they are likely to continually develop innovative recruitment and retention strategies. Hayek and Hossler (1999) elaborated on this notion of courtship to discuss the role of timeliness and personalization. The authors noted that the best way to convey a sense of courtship is to constantly seek ways to improve the degree of personalization and timeliness in all interactions with prospective students. Indeed, they opined that timeliness and personalization might be the foundation of both the courtship and the recruitment processes. When applied to college students who continually reevaluate their decision to attend, the courtship strategy for retention is productive and transparent.

No institution of postsecondary education can compromise its academic standards just to court students. However, given the importance of student life, student services, and out-of-class contact with faculty, a welcoming and personalized style of exchanges with enrolled students can enhance student persistence. The elements of courtship—timeliness and personalization—provide a clear conceptual road map to help guide the recruitment and retention efforts of enrollment managers.

Students as Institutional Image

Although surprising to student affairs professionals who are socialized to focus their attention on students, the reality is that many college administrators and faculty fail to realize the extent to which the students who matriculate define the institutions in which they are enrolled. Nevertheless, many of the descriptors used to portray an institution are derived directly from the characteristics of the enrolled student body. Terms such as *small, large, selective, nonselective, diverse, prestigious, national,* or *regional* describe not only the institution but also the enrolled students, the high school rank or test scores of students, national or local recruitment, and so forth.

The visibility and importance of college rankings and ratings have steadily increased in the past decade. While most enrollment managers are not fond of rankings, they are aware that this level of importance is unlikely to diminish. Unfortunately, the impact of rankings is likely to become more pronounced, not less so. Increasingly, the enrollment manager knows that the impact of rankings on students, parents, college presidents, boards of trustees, and faculty governance groups is greater than ever. Thus, enrollment managers and other campus administrators can ill afford to ignore rankings publications. The students whom campuses attract and enroll play a major part in defining colleges and universities. Enrollment managers must constantly monitor their image and how it is affecting recruitment and retention efforts. In a very real sense, the students we enroll define the image of our campuses to many internal and external audiences.

ENROLLMENT MANAGEMENT AS A PROCESS

In order to develop a comprehensive enrollment management system, a diverse set of functions and activities must be formally or informally linked. Functional areas ranging from admissions, financial aid, career planning and placement, and new student orientation must be linked. Equally important are activities such as student outcome assessments and retention efforts that must be used to inform policy decisions in areas such as admissions, financial aid, or curriculum decisions.

Planning and Research

As a process, enrollment management begins with institutional planning. Planning begins with a discussion of the institutional mission statement. Following the institution's mission statement, most authors on strategic planning call for an objective assessment of the external and internal environment (Bean, 1990; Dolence, 1993). That is, colleges and universities must carefully assess external social trends (such as reductions in state and federal student financial aid or an increasing number of adults enrolling in higher education) as well as internal strengths and weaknesses (such as the need for new buildings on campus, the skills of some administrators, or the lack of an academic major that is popular among high school graduates). Following an environmental assessment, planning involves the development of goals and objectives that take into consideration both the mission of the institution, its strengths and weaknesses, and the external environment.

A planning process such as the one outlined in this chapter cannot be undertaken without institutional research and evaluation capabilities. Information provided by institutional research guides the planning process, as well as policy decisions in areas such as admissions and student retention. Not all campuses are large enough to be able to afford a full-time institutional research office, but even small campuses should have a faculty member or an administrator who conducts institutional research projects. Knowledge gained through institutional research establishes a context for decisions in areas ranging from admissions to student activities.

Attracting Applicants and Matriculants

To attract applicants who are likely to matriculate, an effective enrollment management program requires the cooperation of several campus offices. Marketing and recruitment are typically located in the admissions office. However, institutional research efforts provide needed information about student characteristics that help the admissions office determine what types of potential students are most likely to be interested in coming to the campus. Marketing research can also provide insights into the type of information in which students and parents will be most interested. Tuition levels, or the "sticker price," and targeted financial aid packages play an important role in determining whether a student will apply to an institution and matriculate (Hossler & Hoezee, 2001). Indeed, financial aid directors have become key actors in all enrollment management efforts. The financial aid and admissions offices should coordinate financial aid awards with other courtship activities in order to attract the quality and number of students the institution is seeking. The admissions and financial aid offices represent the admissions management subsystem of an enrollment management system.

Influencing the Collegiate Experience

In an enrollment management system, once students arrive on campus, attention shifts to the students' collegiate experiences. The comprehensive nature of enrollment management systems means that they are concerned with the students' experiences during their entire tenure at the institution.

An enrollment management system advocates that admissions officers be just as concerned about student–institution fit as they are about the number of students they recruit. Hossler and Bean (1990), for example, suggested that admissions officers be evaluated on the basis of how many matriculates persist rather than on the number of students who are recruited. An enrollment management system encourages student affairs officers to be responsible for creating an attractive campus environment that will help to retain students. Satin (1985) recommended that student affairs administrators strive to facilitate student involvement in all facets of the college experience. The work of Kuh and his colleagues in the areas of involving colleges and student engagement demonstrated the importance of the college experience in both in-class and out-of-class learning (Kuh, Schuh, Whitt, & Associates, 1991). Pascarella and Terenzini (1991) provided evidence that formal and informal faculty contact has a positive impact on student satisfaction and perceptions of the college environment. Both administrators and faculty have roles to play in an enrollment management system.

Orientation and Enrollment Management

Orientation is the point of transition into the college experience. Orientation programs are an important part of an enrollment management system. A comprehensive orientation should help students adjust to the intellectual norms, the social norms, and the physical layout of the campus. Pascarella (1985) recommended that orientation be viewed as an opportunity for "anticipatory socialization." Orientation should create new student expectations that closely approximate campus environment and norms. In this way, students are likely to find meaning and satisfaction in their collegiate environment (Hossler, Bean, & Associates, 1990). Perigo and Upcraft (1989) discussed the importance of orientation in improving the transition to college, enhancing the college experience, and increasing the probability of student success and persistence.

Academic Advising and Enrollment Management

In addition to orientation, academic advising is also important for new students. For many students, the first advising session takes place during orientation. Academic advising is also an excellent place to encourage student involvement with faculty. Several campuses have begun to take advantage of the linkages between orientation and advising to develop extended orientation and advising programs. "University 101," an orientation and advising course offered at the University of South Carolina, is an example of an approach linking advising and orientation (Gardner, 1989). Academic advising is an excellent place to encourage student involvement with faculty. Using faculty in these extended orientation and advising programs, or in small freshman seminars, can be used to encourage student-faculty interaction.

Course Placement and Enrollment Management

The first interactions students have with their new environment revolve around academic advising, course placement, and orientation. The diversity of today's college students has resulted in wide variations in student interests, experiences, and skills. This is especially true of two-year colleges and open-admission four-year institutions where some matriculants will enter with minimal academic skills while other new students are eligible for honors programs. This has increased the importance of academic advising and course placement. An enrollment management system should include academic assessment tests that will increase the likelihood of appropriate course placement. Helping students to select the courses that will challenge them, but not overwhelm them, is a function of orientation and advising during the critical first year. Students who do not fare well academically are less likely to persist.

Student Retention and Enrollment Management

Successful integration into the campus environment should have a positive impact on student satisfaction and persistence. Student retention research and retention programs should also be part of an enrollment management plan. Unlike functional areas such as admissions or orientation, retention is usually not the direct responsibility of one office. Retention cuts across many functional areas and divisions within the institution. Nevertheless, precisely because of the many organizational variables that can affect student attrition, student retention research and programming should be assigned to one administrative office. Retention activities are usually assigned to a committee—and that ensures that retention will not receive adequate attention. As committee assignments change and new members rotate on and off the committee, it is difficult to develop an ongoing set of retention activities. The importance of student attrition in maintaining enrollments requires that it be assigned as the responsibility of a specific office, just as admissions or student activities are the assigned task of identifiable administrators. This ensures that data will be collected and programs will be planned, implemented, and evaluated.

The retention officer should not be held personally accountable for attrition rates; the issue is too complex for one office to "control." Nevertheless, creating an administrative office to monitor student attrition and develop retention programs ensures that the institution will continue to address student persistence. The retention officer is an integral element of the enrollment management system.

Academic Support Services and Enrollment Management

Academic support offices should also be a part of retention efforts. Many colleges continue to admit underprepared students. In order to help these students succeed academically, campuses have established learning assistance offices. These offices offer a wide range of services, including study skills workshops, reading assistance, writing labs, test-taking workshops, and tutoring in specific subject areas. Professionals in this area are also part of the enrollment management staff. The admissions office usually identifies underprepared students during the admissions process. The admissions office is in the best position to inform the learning assistance office of the particular academic needs of these students.

Learning assistance offices should monitor the academic success of students, thus completing the feedback cycle. This places the office in a unique position to provide continual feedback regarding student success to the admissions office. If few underprepared students are succeeding, then the institution may not be spending recruiting and financial aid dollars wisely or it may not be providing adequate academic support services.

Career Services and Enrollment Management

A significant part of the college experience is preparation for a career. Career concerns have become one of the most important considerations for college students from the time they select an institution until the time they graduate. Students are very aware of the competitive nature of the job market. Institutions that are perceived as helping to place their graduates in good jobs after graduation will be in a position not only to attract new students, but also to retain current students. Part of the job turnover model of student attrition developed by Bean (1980; 1983) posits that the practical value of a college degree, the likelihood of getting a desirable job after graduation, has a positive effect on student persistence. A successful career planning and placement office should help students establish linkages between their academic goals and their vocational goals. In an enrollment management system, the career planning office should successfully help students secure desirable positions after graduation.

The Role of Other Student Affairs Functions in Enrollment Management

Enhancing student life on campus facilitates recruitment and retention and supports the enrollment management mission. Career services, learning assistance, and orientation are part of an array of student services found on most campuses. They are usually part of the student affairs division. Depending on whether the campus is residential, intramural and intercollegiate athletics, residence life, and Greek affairs can greatly enhance the quality of campus life.

In addition to adding to the quality of student life, student participation in intramurals, student government, or Greek affairs may also enhance student development and student persistence. Gardener (1989), Kuh, Schuh, Whitt, and Associates (1991), and Pace (1991) asserted that student involvement in cocurricular and extracurricular activities plays an important role in determining the range and quality of student outcomes, as well as influencing student persistence. The goals of facilitating student development and managing student enrollments may not be in conflict, but instead may be mutually reinforcing goals in some areas of student life. The theory of student involvement provides a theoretical basis for strategies to facilitate student development through student involvement. Student affairs officers, through careful planning and evaluation, can develop programs that encourage student involvement in order to enhance development and increase student persistence.

The Faculty Role and Enrollment Management

The faculty plays an important role and it is a mistake for any enrollment manager not to consider the role of the faculty. For example, the quality and reputation of faculty members are important factors in determining where a student will go to college (Hayek & Hossler, 1999; Hossler, Schmit, & Braxton, 1999; Litten, 1991). It is difficult, however, for administrators to speak directly to issues of faculty quality. At best, administrators are likely to be disregarded, and at worst they will alienate themselves from the faculty and reduce their effectiveness. Faculty, however, should be aware of the impact they have on student enrollments.

In the areas of marketing and student recruitment, the academic image of an institution and individual majors may determine where students decide to go to college. Marketing research can be used to create an institutional lens that lets faculty see how prospective students view them. In some cases, faculty discover that the negative image that students hold of academic programs discourages students from enrolling. Information such as this can create an impetus for changes in academic programs that would be difficult for administrators to require of the faculty.

Student–faculty interaction has a significant impact on student outcomes and student persistence. Enrollment managers should play an educative role with the faculty in this area. On many campuses, faculty already understand the connection between enrollment and institutional health. On these campuses, acquainting faculty with research that establishes the impact of faculty on students and the role of academic programs in college choice is likely to create a receptive audience for enrollment management activities. Many commuter institutions, as well as research universities, however, do not have a strong tradition of faculty involvement with students. At institutions where faculty are not concerned about student enrollments, it will be difficult to convince them to seek out opportunities for student–faculty interaction, yet students at these institutions can also benefit from contact with faculty.

Enrollment management begins with planning and research. Marketing and recruitment of students follow. The student collegiate experience leads to student retention and graduation. However, a comprehensive enrollment management plan does not stop with graduation. This is where enrollment management demonstrates its cyclical nature. Student outcome studies should include regular assessments of alumni. Alumni experiences and attitudes can provide institutions with useful information. The enrollment management systems perspective provides the imagery of the wide-angle lens that enables colleges and universities to see and understand the entire collegiate experience.

ORGANIZING FOR ENROLLMENT MANAGEMENT

One of the most commonly asked questions on most campuses is, "How should we organize to most effectively influence our student enrollments?" Many administrators who aspire to be in leadership roles in enrollment management organizations seem to intuitively assume that the establishment of a senior enrollment manager or a "czar of enrollment management" will automatically solve all of the enrollment issues on an individual campus. Organizational life is seldom that simple.

Enrollment management organizations typically include some elements of a matrix organization and some elements of a senior management role. Figure 3.1 visually captures the central elements of an enrollment management effort that are typically included within an enrollment management organization and those areas that are less likely to be within the direct purview of a senior enrollment officer. Areas outside the direct control of the enrollment manager require a matrix approach to management. Both of these elements are briefly described.

Figure 3.1: The Scope of Enrollment Management

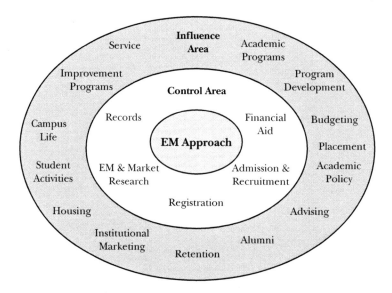

The Enrollment Management Division

In the past decade, the employment of a senior enrollment administrator has become normative in most colleges and universities. In this organizational model, the major offices connected with enrollment management efforts are brought together under the authority of one senior-level administrator. The advantages of such an organizational model are many. One vice president can direct each of the principal components of the system. Cooperation, communication, and resource allocation can be dealt with from a system-wide perspective. In addition, the vice president speaks with formal authority on enrollment issues in all policy decisions.

There can be problems, however, with establishing a comprehensive enrollment management organization. Rarely do other vice presidents gladly give up their control over offices that are part of their responsibilities. In many colleges and universities, philosophical differences make it difficult for areas such as career planning or student activities to find themselves reporting to someone who carries the title of enrollment manager. Such a title does not sound "very developmental." In addition to all of the preceding problems, Leslie and Rhoades (1995) noted that the number of administrators at colleges and universities has been increasing for several decades, while the number of faculty members has remained constant. Many faculty members are concerned about the growth of administrative "empires" and would react negatively to the creation of a new vice president. Thus, the potential benefits and liabilities of an enrollment management division should be weighed carefully before implementing this model. A discussion of the limitations of an enrollment management division leads naturally into a discussion of the matrix elements of enrollment management efforts.

The Enrollment Management Matrix

The factors that influence student matriculation and persistence decisions are too complex for any college or university administrator to control. Even the senior enrollment manager with a wide-ranging set of responsibilities is still faced with the need to coordinate the activities of units outside his or her organization and to convince other senior campus administrators of the benefits of cooperating to achieve enrollment goals. Key campus administrators who can influence recruitment and retention often are not part of a formal enrollment management organization. In such instances, it is helpful to have a formal or informal enrollment management matrix in place.

In the matrix model, key administrators, such as residence life, academic advising, career planning, or student activities, units that might not normally be part of a formal enrollment organization, are asked to participate in regular meetings to focus on student recruitment, success, and graduation. In such a situation, the senior enrollment manager functions somewhat like the enrollment management coordinator, because he or she must rely more on cooperation and persuasion and less on the organizational hierarchy.

To make the matrix model work, however, the senior enrollment manager must be regarded as an influential campus-level administrator who is empowered to make important decisions. This ensures a noticeable impact on organizational structure and resources across the campus. Cooperation and communication among the appropriate offices will increase. Finally, the head of this matrix will thus be able to become enmeshed in all elements of an enrollment management system. Such a process is also likely to help educate other campus administrators about enrollment management issues and garner support across a wide array of campus stakeholders.

The Role of Student Affairs

The specialized expertise of student affairs personnel is students, just as the expertise of a biologist is living organisms, or the professional expertise of a business officer is managing money. The unit of analysis in student affairs work and enrollment management *is* students.

In classical models of student affairs organizations, all of the administrative elements of an enrollment management system (excluding curriculum decisions and teaching) fall under the student affairs umbrella. Admissions, financial aid, orientation, career planning and placement, student activities, and alumni affairs are traditionally part of student affairs divisions. Although some offices, especially admissions and financial aid, are frequently housed in areas outside student affairs, there can be little doubt that student affairs professionals can play an important role in an enrollment management system. On some campuses, student affairs staff members may be responsible for student retention or for conducting student outcomes research. On other campuses, student affairs has very little input as a formal, direct enrollment management division.

Conversely, in other instances, student affairs divisions have included admissions, financial aid, and registration and records for many years. At times these areas have felt unwanted. Missions such as student development and student engagement as the *raison d'être* for most offices of student affairs can sometimes make enrollment related offices feel unwanted because of the lack of a developmental orientation or formal educational mission. The enrollment management concept, however, provides an administrative framework that makes these offices an important part of a student affairs division.

Student affairs professionals on some campuses may see the marketing emphasis that accompanies the enrollment management concept as incompatible with a student development perspective. However, if we believe that student development and student engagement result in increased student growth and satisfaction, then enrollment management and student development need not be in conflict. Marketing efforts grounded in sound student college choice research should help students to understand the college or university they have chosen to attend, thus enhancing student–institution fit. Increasing student development and involvement should enhance student persistence. The enrollment management concept need not replace existing philosophies for student affairs divisions. It can, in fact, be used along with other frameworks within a comprehensive student affairs division.

Ethical Issues

Although enrollment management need not conflict with or create ethical dilemmas with the traditional goals of student affairs divisions, a number of ethical issues are inherent in attempts to influence student enrollments. During the recruitment process and after students matriculate, there are opportunities for unethical practices.

Throughout the recruitment process, institutions should be careful to portray the campus accurately. Written publications must accurately describe the location of the campus, the academic offerings, and the nature of the student body. Admissions folklore is replete with stories: admissions representatives who have told prospective students that they could earn a degree in a major that the campus did not even offer, or representatives who used aerial photographs to make a campus that was 45 minutes from the ocean appear as if it were almost "on the beach." Deceptive recruitment is unfair to students and harms both the institution and the entire higher education system in the long run. Students and the public lose confidence in the mission and purpose of American higher education when representatives of colleges and universities act without integrity.

The Role of Standardized Tests in Admissions

Standardized tests such as the SAT and the ACT have been long-standing admissions requirements. By playing an important role in the admissions process at most institutions, standardized tests help to determine the composition of the student body, thereby exerting a profound influence on the first-year experience. Growing concerns about the appropriate role of standardized tests in admissions abound. For one thing, there are competing interpretations of the modest correlation between SAT scores, grades, and other measures of collegiate success. Perhaps most importantly, there are profound concerns about the persistent racial and ethnic differences in test scores and the effects of the SAT on campus diversity.

The University of California President, Richard Atkinson, has suggested that far from serving the needs of disadvantaged students, a focus on the SAT perpetuates the advantages of the already advantaged who can afford expensive tutoring and creates an unhealthy focus on test-taking, thus distracting from learning (Atkinson 2001). In his view, admissions decisions should be more appropriately based on mastery of secondary school curriculum as measured with high school grades and standardized tests. There is a wide consensus that admissions and scholarship decisions should never be based on the SAT or the ACT alone, yet Hossler (2001) indicated that the use of standardized tests increased during most of the 1990s at the expense of high school rank or grades. It is too soon to see if this trend has been reversed as a result of the recent criticisms of standardized testing.

The role of the SAT and other standardized tests in admissions is a contentious topic with no ready resolution in sight. These debates will continue to influence policies and practices in enrollment management. Enrollment managers will need to stay abreast of judicial cases and state policies as they craft institutional policies that will be legally and morally defensible and serve the needs of students and institutions.

Merit-Based Campus Financial Aid

Enrollment management has become an important role of enrollment managers, as noted earlier in this chapter. Merit-based financial aid, as opposed to need-based financial aid, is an important tool, but it is also becoming an increasingly contentious issue among enrollment managers, financial aid administrators, and higher education public and institutional policy makers. Financial aid can be a powerful tool for addressing a variety of competing institutional goals such as excellence, access, diversity, and revenue enhancement. Between 1988 and 1996, the number of non–need-based scholarship recipients at public four-year schools increased over 160 percent, while the average award amount nearly tripled. This large increase in institutional aid disproportionately went to funding middle- and upper-income students rather than those with demonstrated need (Redd, 2000a).

This use of financial aid to attract the best and the brightest without regard to need has come to be called tuition discounting (Loomis-Hubble, 1991). While conceptually similar to the academic merit and athletic scholarships that have been used for decades, the widespread use of discounting has added a new element of expensive competition to the admissions landscape. This strategic use of discounting to leverage enrollments has been supported by the emergence of a number of sophisticated analytical tools, including econometric modeling (Brooks, 1996). However as bidding wars escalate among schools all competing for the same small pool of the "best and the brightest" students, there is a danger of further concentration of resources on those who need them least, squeezing the neediest students out of the market entirely. As Baum (1998) noted, equity does not necessarily suffer from discounting. At least conceptually, it is possible to use revenue generated from discounting to fund need-based aid.

College Rankings

College rankings have formally linked the characteristics of enrolled students with the image of colleges and universities. Rankings have become an important part of the professional lives of enrollment managers. Increasingly, prospective students and their parents, college trustees, alumni, faculty, and even some public policy makers are interested in how different colleges and universities fare in the world of rankings (Hossler & Foley, 1996). Many scholars of the college student experience have argued that rankings publications primarily measure input variables such as SAT scores, institutional selectivity, or faculty characteristics rather than what students actually gain during their college experience or outcome measures (Hossler, 2001; Pascarella, 2001). Nevertheless, rankings appear to be gaining in visibility and influence.

Internal and external pressures are forcing more and more campuses to seek ways to improve their rankings. This has led some institutions to a dubious assortment of misleading strategies to make themselves look more selective than they really are. Hossler (2001) has described a number of these efforts, which include, for example, (1) encouraging students who are not admissible to apply so that they can be rejected, thus increasing the selectivity measures; (2) early decision programs that increase yields; and (3) inaccurately reporting admissions statistics. Enrollment managers must tread a fine line when dealing with rankings. They are well advised to educate key campus constituents about the problems with rankings. However, senior enrollment officers cannot simply ignore rankings and their impact upon their applicant pools.

PREPARATION AND TRAINING

Currently, there are few formal preservice training programs that are specifically designed to prepare enrollment managers. The University of Miami has started the first master's degree and certificate program in enrollment management. The University of Florida, in conjunction with the Noel-Levitz Company, has launched a web-based program in enrollment management. These efforts are too new to yet assess their success or effectiveness. The American Association of Collegiate Registrars and Admissions Officers (AACRAO), ACT, The College Board, and the National Association for Student Personnel Administrators (NASPA) have played leadership roles in offering professional development opportunities for aspiring and practicing enrollment managers.

Leadership positions in enrollment management systems typically are assigned to mid-level or senior-level administrators. These administrators may have been the chief student affairs officer or the director of admissions or financial aid. Occasionally, the position is filled by a faculty member or a director of institutional research. The enrollment management concept has gained recognition and acceptance, but it continues to be difficult to find professionals with the necessary skills and background. The career opportunities in this area, as well as in related entry-level areas such as admissions and financial aid, should continue to be strong for the foreseeable future. The demand for professionals in new student orientation and student retention is not as strong, but these areas also provide a sound background for enrollment managers. Entry-level student affairs professionals should attempt to have a range of experiences in the work areas outlined.

In 1989, when the first edition of this chapter went into print, the enrollment management concept was too novel to assertively predict the future of what was then a new organizational model. However, seven years have passed, which is sufficient time to assess the future of enrollment management. Competition among colleges and universities has not abated. Not all campuses use the term *enrollment management* as a label to describe their efforts to recruit and retain students, but the use of research and evaluation in admissions, financial aid, and retention programs is widespread and is not likely to disappear. Organizational linking, through a matrix model or a more centralized model, such offices as admissions, financial aid, career planning, and other student affairs areas, is now common. Student enrollments account for 60 to 80 percent of all revenues on most campuses, so the health and vitality of institutions of higher education are linked to the ability to attract and retain students. Enrollment management, or whatever term is used to label admissions and retention activities, is here for the foreseeable future.

Even student affairs professionals who are not attracted to the concept of enrollment management should be aware of it because so many of the functional areas within a student affairs division are potentially part of an enrollment management system. In the future, student affairs professionals may find themselves in leadership roles or in support roles on many campuses. Student affairs divisions that choose to become involved with this new concept can be an important element of any enrollment management system.

TECHNOLOGY RESOURCES

http://www.aacrao.org/: The American Association for Collegiate Registrars and Admissions Officers has emerged as one of the leading professional organizations for the field of enrollment management.

http://www/act.org/ and http://www.collegeboard.com/: Like AACRAO, ACT and The College Board provide services, issue publications, and host conferences.

http://nces.ed.gov/: Successful enrollment management relies heavily on data and analysis. The National Center for Educational Statistics is one of the best sources of data on enrollment trends, financial aid patterns, and retention statistics and studies.

http://www.postsecondary.org/: This monthly publication provides a host of interesting statistics and trend data that enrollment managers can use to understand trends they are experiencing. The information provided can also be useful in enabling enrollment managers to better explain to other senior campus administrators the regional and national trends affecting student enrollments at individual campuses.

http://www.coe.ilstu.edu/grapevine/: Many of the goals of enrollment management efforts are linked directly to campus finance issues. The Grapevine is an excellent source of higher education finance trends among the 50 states. The data reveal state financial aid trends. The Grapevine provides detailed information about funding patterns for public and private colleges and universities.

REFERENCES

Abrahamson, T. D., & Hossler, D. (1990). Applying marketing strategies in student recruitment. In D. Hossler & J. P. Bean (Eds.), *The strategic management of college enrollments*, (pp. 100–118). San Francisco: Jossey-Bass.

American Council on Education, (1994). The Student Personnel Point of View (1937). In A. L. Rentz (Ed.), *Student affairs: A profession's heritage* (pp. 66–78). Lanham, MD: University of America Press

American Council on Education (1994). The Student Personnel Point of View (1949). In A. L. Rentz (Ed.), *Student affairs: A profession's heritage* (pp. 108–123). Lanham, MD: University of America Press.

Astin, A. W. (1985). *Achieving educational excellence*. San Francisco: Jossey-Bass.

Atkinson, R. C. (2001, February 15). *Standardized tests and access to American universities*. Atwell Lecture at American Council on Education, Washington, D.C. Retrieved February 18, 2001, from http://www.ucop.edu/ucophome/pres/comments/satspch.html

Baum, S. (1998). Balancing act: Can colleges achieve equal access and survive in a competitive market? *The College Board Review, 186,* 12–17.

Bean, J. P. (1990). Using retention research in enrollment management. In D. Hossler, & J. P. Bean (Eds.), *The strategic management of college enrollments*. San Francisco: Jossey-Bass.

Bean, J. P. (1980). Dropouts and turnover: The synthesis and test of a causal model of student attrition. *Research in Higher Education, 12,* 155–182.

Bean, J. P. (1983). The application of a model of job turnover in work organizations to the student attrition process. *Review of Higher Education, 6,* 129–148.

Black, T. (2001). Garnering resources and building infrastructure. In T. Black (Ed.), *Strategic enrollment management revolution*, (pp.173–184). Washington, DC: American Association of Collegiate Registrars and Admission Officers.

Bowen, H. (1980). *The costs of higher education: How much do colleges and universities spend per student and how much should they spend?* San Francisco: Jossey-Bass.

Braxton, J. M. (2000). *Reworking the student departure puzzle*. Nashville, TN: Vanderbilt University Press.

Breneman, D. W. (1994). *Liberal arts colleges: Thriving, surviving, or endangered?* Washington, DC: The Brookings Institution.

Brooks, S. H. (1996). Econometric modeling of enrollment behavior. *Journal of Student Aid, 3,* 3–17.

Broome, E. C. (1903). *A historical and critical discussion of college admissions requirements*. New York: Macmillan.

Brubacher. J. S., & Rudy, W. (1968). H*igher education in transition: A history of American colleges and universities,1636–1976*. New York: Harper & Row.

Clott, C. B. (1995). T*he effects of environment, strategy, culture, and resource dependency on perceptions of organizational effectiveness of school of business*. Paper presented at the Annual Meeting of the Association for the Study of Higher Education (ASHE), Orlando, FL.

Clark, B. R. (1983). *The higher education system*. Berkeley, CA: The University of California Press.

Cross, R. G. (1997). *Revenue management: Hard-core tactics for market domination.* New York: Broadway Books.

Dolence, M. G. (1993). *Strategic enrollment management: A primer for campus administrators.* Washington, DC: American Association of Collegiate Registrars and Admissions Officers (BBB10774).

Hayek, J., & Hossler, D. (1999, April). *The information needs of prospective students: I want what I want when I want it.* Paper presented at the Annual Meeting of the American Association of Collegiate Registrars and Admissions Officers, Charleston, S.C.

Hossler, D. (2001). *The Enrollment Management Review, 17(3)*, 1–8.

Hossler, D. (2000). Effective admissions recruitment. In G. Gaither (Ed.), *Promising practices in recruitment, remediation, and retention* (New Directions in Institutional Research, No. 108, pp. 15–30). San Francisco: Jossey-Bass.

Hossler, D. (1986). *Creating effective enrollment management systems.* New York: College Entrance Examination Board.

Hossler, D, Bean, J. P., & Associates. (1990). *The strategic management of college enrollments.* San Francisco: Jossey-Bass.

Hossler, D., Braxton, J., & Coopersmith, G. (1989). Understanding student college choice. In J. Smart (Ed.), *Higher education: Handbook of theory and research, IV.* New York: Agathon Press.

Hossler, D., & Foley, E. M. (1996). Reducing the noise in the college choice process: The use of college guidebooks and ratings. In D. Walleri & M. Moss (Eds.), *Assessing the impact of college guide and rating books.* (New Directions in Higher Education, No. 88, pp. 21–30). San Francisco: Jossey-Bass.

Hossler. D., and Hoezee, L. D. (2001). Conceptual and theoretical thinking about enrollment management. In T. Black (Ed.), *Strategic enrollment management revolution* (pp. 57–72). Washington, DC: American Association of Collegiate Registrars and Admission Officers.

Hossler, D., Schmit, J., & Vesper, N. (1999). *Going to college: How social, economic, and educational factors influence the decisions students make.* Baltimore, MD: Johns Hopkins University Press.

Jencks, C., & Reisman, D. (1969). *The academic revolution.* Garden City, NY: Doubleday.

Kreutner, L., & Godfrey, E. S. (1981, Fall/Winter). Enrollment management: A new vehicle for institutional renewal. *The College Board Review, 6–9*, 29.

Kuh, G. K., Schuh, J., Whitt, E., and Associates. (1991). *Involving colleges: Successful approaches to fostering student learning and development outside of the classroom.* San Francisco: Jossey-Bass.

Leslie, L. L., & Rhoades, G. (1995). Rising administrative costs: Seeking explanations. *Journal of Higher Education, 66(2)*, 187–212.

Lindsay, E. E., & Holland, O. C. (1930). *College and university administration.* New York: Macmillan.

Litten, L. H. (1991). *Ivy bound: High ability students and college choice.* New York: The College Board.

Loomis-Hubble, L. (1991). *Tuition discounting: The impact of institutionally funded financial aid.* Washington, DC: National Association of College and University Business Officers.

Maguire, J. (1976, Fall). To the organized go the students. *Bridge Magazine*, 6–10.

McDonough, P. M., Antonio, A. L., Walpole, M., & Perez, L. X. (1998). College rankings: Democratized college knowledge for whom? *Research in Higher Education, 39(5)*, 513–533.

Munger, S. C., & Zucker, R. F. (1982). Discerning the basis for college counseling in the eighties. In W. Lowery and Associates, *College admissions: A handbook for the profession*. San Francisco: Jossey-Bass.

Noel, L., Levitz, R., Saluri, D., & Associates. (1985). *Increasing student retention*. San Francisco: Jossey-Bass.

Pace, C. R. (1991). *The undergraduates*. Los Angeles: Higher Education Research Institute, University of California at Los Angeles.

Pascarella, E. T. (1985). *A program for research and policy development on student persistence at the institutional level*. Paper presented at the Second Annual Chicago Conference on Enrollment Management: An Integrated Strategy for Institutional Vitality, sponsored by The Midwest Region of The College Board and Loyola University of Chicago, Chicago, IL.

Pascarella, E. T. (2001). Identifying excellence in undergraduate education: Are we even close? *Change, 33(3)*, 18–23.

Paulsen, M. B. (1990). *College choice: Understanding student enrollment behavior*. ASHE-ERIC Higher Education Reports No. 6. Washington, DC: ERIC Clearinghouse on Higher Education and The George Washington University.

Perigo, D.J, & Upcraft, M. L. (1989). Orientation. In M. L. Upcraft & J. N. Gardner, and Associates, T*he freshman year experience*. San Francisco: Jossey-Bass.

Pfeffer, J., & Salancik, G. R. (1978). *The external control of organizations: A resource dependence approach*. New York: Harper & Row.

Redd, K. E. (2000). Tuition discounting: A view from the financial aid office. *NASFAA Journal of Student Financial Aid, 30*, 27–37.

Rudolph, F. (1962). *The American college and university: A history*. New York: Vintage Books.

Senge, P. M. (1990, Fall). The leader's new work: Building learning organizations. *Sloan Management Review, 32(1)*, 7–23.

Scannell, J. J. (1992). *The effects of financial aid policies on admission and enrollment*. (Admission Practices Series). New York: The College Board.

Shaffer, R. F., & Martinson, G. (1966). *Student personnel services in higher education*. New York: Center for Applied Research in Education.

Smerling, (1960). The registrar: Changing aspects. *College and University, 35*, 180–186.

St. John, E. P., Paulsen, M. B., & Starkey, J. B. (1996). The nexus between college choice and persistence. *Research in Higher Education, 37(2)*, 455–480.

Swann, C. C. (1998). Admissions officer: A profession and training. In C. C. Swann & S. E. Henderson (Eds.). *Handbook for the college admissions profession*. Washington, DC: American Association of Collegiate Registrars and Admissions Officers.

Thelin, J. R. (1982). *Higher education and its useful past: Applied history in research and planning*. Cambridge, MA: Schenkman.

Thresher, B. A. (1966). *College admissions and the public interest*. New York: The College Entrance Examination Board.

Tinto, V. (1993). *Leaving college: Rethinking the causes and cures of student attrition* (2nd ed.). Chicago: University of Chicago Press.

Tolbert, P. S. (1985). Institutional environments and resource dependence: Sources of administrative structure in higher education. *Administrative Science Quarterly, 30(1)*, 1–13.

Upcraft, M. L., Gardner, J. N., & Associates. (1989). *The freshman year experience.* San Francisco: Jossey-Bass.

Chapter 4

ACADEMIC ADVISING

Judith J. Goetz

INTRODUCTION

Academic advising is an activity that colleges and universities provide to help students (1) identify and develop suitable programs of study; (2) seek enriching experiences while at college; and (3) expand horizons and opportunities while becoming aware of talents, skills and options. The curriculum establishes the context for the activity, the policies and procedures set the guidelines, and various personnel coordinate the delivery systems. The activity is grounded in factors such as curricular complexity, administrative configurations, institutional tradition, financial resources, and enrollment management considerations. The activity may be as involved as an intentional design of advising centers, interactive databases, faculty and staff training, and special courses for students. Or it may be as simple as having faculty interact with students each semester.

Over the years, the activity of academic advising has gained more visibility as a critical component of student development. Out-of-class interaction with faculty has been identified as an important way for students to feel connected to their institution. Professional organizations focused on academic advising have provided advisors with vehicles to converse about standards, theories, and procedures in ways that can enhance institutional programs and ways to assist students in their educational planning.

The idea of academic "guidance" began in response to the increasingly complex college curriculum that evolved at the end of the nineteenth century. Prior to this time, academic programs were highly structured, curricular choices were limited, and few persons enrolled in college. As society's need for educated people grew to meet the requirements of advancing technology, colleges and universities broadened their curricula and opened enrollment to a wider range of students. The demands placed on higher education today to be cost-effective and efficient in educating an increasingly diverse clientele has placed the activity of academic advising in a position to respond again to new challenges.

This chapter addresses the following four areas relevant to the activity of academic advising: (1) historical development, (2) institutional configurations, technology, (3) issues that guide the practice, and (4) future considerations.

HISTORICAL DEVELOPMENT

Academic advising is a fairly recent institutionalized term. Early academic guidance focused on faculty interaction with students to discuss curriculum, institutional procedures, course selection, and choosing a field of study (Brubacher & Rudy, 1968; Hardee, 1962, 1970; Kramer & Gardner, 1977; McKeachie, 1978; Moore, 1967; Rudolph, 1962).

Perhaps the first recognized systems of advising existed at Johns Hopkins University and at Harvard University in the late 1800s (Brubacher & Rudy, 1968; Rudolph, 1962). The Harvard student advising program focused on faculty helping students "to select those programs which were best suited their needs and interests" (Brubacher & Rudy, 1968, p. 432).

The Harvard advising plan developed as an outgrowth of the broad curricular experiment of the elective system instituted by President Charles Eliot in the latter part of the nineteenth century (Brubacher & Rudy, 1968). By 1895, Harvard freshmen were required to take two only English courses and a modern foreign language, with the remaining courses chosen from an array of electives. According to Rudolph (1962), "[t]he creation of a system of faculty advisors at Johns Hopkins and Harvard . . . was apparently the first formal recognition that size and the elective system required some closer attention to undergraduate guidance than was possible with an increasingly professionally oriented faculty" (p. 460).

The Harvard elective system, as well as similar curricular innovations at other colleges, was in part a reflection of the expansion of knowledge that was occurring in the latter part of the nineteenth century. This was especially true in the sciences and the newly developing professions, such as social work, education, and economics. According to Wiebe (1967), universities played an important role for the professions with the ". . . power to legitimize, for no new profession felt complete—or scientific—without its distinct academic curriculum" (p. 121).

The expansion of knowledge as embodied in the curriculum required specialists (Light, D. 1974) who became organized into departments that represented academic disciplines. These affiliations became ". . . the focus of the identity of an academic professional" (Parsons & Platt, 1973, p. 113). Differentiation into academic departments increased the complexity of programs of study and encouraged the subject matter specialization of the faculty (Brubacher & Rudy, 1968; Weaver, 1981).

As the American college and university system adapted to include expanded course offerings, more choice in programs of study, greater diversity of students, and continuing faculty specialization (Levine, 1978), the concern for educating the "whole student" resulted in the student personnel movement, which attempted to restore the concern of the "old-time college . . . for the non-intellectual side of the student's career" (Brubacher & Rudy, 1968, p. 331). Developments in psychological measurement and new approaches to viewing human behavior and learning laid the groundwork for the task of educational planning and career development. Educational counseling became one area of interest within the broader framework of the expanding area of student personnel (Brubacher & Rudy, 1968).

In addition, concern with student–institution "fit" and the institutional impact on students brought researchers to examine such issues as the effects of student–faculty interaction on persistence and satisfaction (Astin, 1977; Feldman & Newcomb, 1969; Jacob, 1957; Light, R. J., 2001; Pascarella, 1980, 1985; Pascarella & Terenzini, 1991; Terenzini, Pascarella, & Lorgan, 1982; Tinto, 1987; Vreeland & Bidwell, 1966). The issue of student retention has been a key focus for those concerned with one aspect of student–institution fit, that of academic advising (Carstensen & Silberhorn, 1979; Crockett, 1986; Ender, Winston, & Miller, 1982; Tinto, 1993). Achieving excellence through involvement, especially through a strong academic advising system, has been a key topic in national studies, such as that produced by the Study Group on the Conditions of Excellence in American Higher Education (1984) and the Carnegie Foundation's investigation of the undergraduate experience (Boyer, 1987).

Two professional associations have been developed for educators whose primary concerns include academic advising. In 1971, the Association of Academic Affairs Administrators (ACAFAD) adopted a constitution that included strengthening the quality of higher education by focusing on the individual student and the academic environment. In 1979, the National Academic Advising Association (NACADA) was established as a new organization specifically created to address issues and concerns of practitioners in academic advising. The NACADA has prepared academic advising standards that address such issues as mission, administration, resources, facilities and ethics. It also hosts regional and national meetings, and publishes a journal and occasional monographs related to the topic of academic advising.

The American College Testing Program (ACT) has addressed issues related to academic advising by providing training sessions and developing resource materials (Crockett, 1978a, 1979, 1984), as well as by conducting national studies of academic advising (Carstensen & Silberhorn, 1979; Crockett & Levitz, 1984; Habley, 1988, 1993; Habley & Morales, 1998). These efforts have proved useful to practitioners faced with establishing new academic advising programs and enriching existing ones.

In 1981, the term *academic advising* became a descriptor for the Educational Resource Information Center (ERIC) information retrieval system. This recognition of advising as an identifiable programmatic effort brings together under one rubric the varied efforts of formal and informal academic planning assistance to students.

The first "textbook," of sorts, on the topic of academic advising was published in 1984 under the title *Developmental Academic Advising* (Winston, Miller, Ender, Grites, & Associates). Three years earlier, a small monograph had been published by AAHE/ERIC entitled *Academic Advising: Getting Us Through the Eighties* (Grites). In 1992, Gordon produced an annotated work, *Handbook of Academic Advising*. In 2000, Gordon, Habley, & Associates, edited a second "textbook," *Academic Advising: A Comprehensive Handbook*. These works span about 20 years, as the activity of academic advising became more organized on college and university campuses.

INSTITUTIONAL CONFIGURATIONS

Various organizational patterns exist to provide academic advising to students (Habley and McCauley, 1987; King, 1993). As pointed out by Ender, Winston, and Miller (1984) and Grites (1979), no one form of organization exists for all institutions because the individual institutional mission must be considered for the process to be effective.

Although no single program or set of services is appropriate for all institutions, the curriculum, the students, and the structure of procedures and policies are fundamental to the way an institution defines the advising activity. The curriculum forms the basis for the programs of study, as well as for the array of general education and elective options available to students. The enrollment helps to shape academic programs and services as the institution responds to student enrichment and remediation needs, as well as to student preferences for courses and fields of study. The procedures and policies that govern requirements affect how smoothly students can accomplish their educational goals.

However, the curriculum, the students, and the policy issues do not function independently of one another. The way these factors interact is critical. How the institution responds to these interactions is fundamental to advising because it is through the advising activity that the interactions are unfolded to students.

Colleges and universities with more traditional students and curricula will find that different approaches to advising may be needed than at those institutions with very "career-oriented" students and programs. The multiversities that provide extended curricula may find that different services are required than would be true for those institutions that are smaller or that have a more restricted purpose in their curricular aims. The sheer size of the enrollment can affect advising services, as can the diversity of preparation of the students. Policies at large institutions may be far more complex and numerous than those at smaller institutions, a factor that often interacts with curricular issues. The increasing use of technology has both enhanced and detracted from more traditional advising delivery

DESCRIPTIONS

Early advising programs were developed when the college president selected a core of faculty to aid in the process of providing counsel to students about their academic programs of study (Rudolph, 1962; Brubacher & Rudy, 1968). When Mueller (1961) differentiated advising from counseling, it was to describe advising as more restricted than counseling, that ".. . the term 'faculty advising' is usually reserved specifically for aiding a student in planning his academic program" (p. 210). Hardee (1962) described faculty advising as a three-part activity of identifying institutional purpose, student purpose, and assisting the student to identify options. Levine (1978) described the purpose of advising to include those areas related to the curriculum, such as course selection, major field requirements, and the area of student performance.

Broader descriptions of academic advising are usually affected by both who does the advising and what constitutes the process. Crookston (1972) approached two relationships possible in the advising encounter: one prescriptive, based on authority, and one developmental, based on personal interaction. He viewed advising as ". . . a teaching function based on a negotiated agreement between the student and the teacher. . ." (p. 17). Borgard (1981) used ideas derived from John Dewey to discuss a philosophy of advising that rests on ". . . the principle that learning begins in experience" (p. 3). He indicated that the advisor should help students to arrange experiences and to assist them in seeing the learning process as "a constant revision through systematic inquiry" (p. 4). Such an approach encourages students to become actively engaged in the learning process, with advisors serving as ". . . the bridge between the student in his present environment and his environments to be" (p. 4). Borgard noted that the purpose of advising should be to encourage the use of skills derived through content courses as the foundation for ". . . growth both in and out of college" (p. 4).

Winston, Grites, Miller, and Ender (1984) identified four components that characterize academic advising: (1) a teaching-learning activity, (2) a way to stimulate personal and intellectual growth, (3) a support function, and (4) a record-keeping function. Crockett (1978b) associated six tasks with academic advising: (1) values clarification and goal identification; (2) understanding the institution of higher education; (3) information-giving; (4) program planning that reflects the student's abilities and interests; (5) program assessment; and (6) referral to institutional resources (p. 30). Trombley (1984) found that advising tasks could be classified as technical and informational, on the one hand, and as interpersonal and developmental on the other hand. More complex tasks, such as helping students define educational goals, result in the use of both sets of tasks. Creamer and Creamer (1994) outlined a considerably expanded definition of advising theory and practice using developmental issues that have grown in importance over the years.

Although the scope of academic advising is much broader than issues solely associated with curricular choice, the fundamental expectation is that students will decide from among alternatives the most appropriate direction to take in planning a program of study. Therefore, academic advising is intimately tied to the curriculum, which directly affects such tasks as deciding on a field of study, selecting and monitoring the proper alternatives for required and elective courses, and determining the need for remediation or acceleration in skill components of the major field. Procedures and policies that affect this decision-making process interact with the complexity of the curriculum. The institutional support for academic advising will affect how well students can interpret the academic decision-making tasks.

MODELS FOR PRACTICE

Various programmatic options exist as ways of accomplishing advising. Grites pointed out in 1979 that "few theoretical models of the complex process (of advising) exist; rather, descriptions of various advising delivery systems prevail in the literature" (p. 1). Habley and Morales (1998) describe the changing organizational structures that have occurred over the years of the ACT studies of advising models: less reliance on a faculty-only model and more emphasis on models that involve a variety of personnel.

The faculty model of advising exists at some institutions as the only model and at many institutions as part of other models. Faculty provide students with an interpretation of their disciplines and an awareness of the institution's policies and procedures that govern degree requirements. Size, and possibly the emphasis on research, may make a difference in the effectiveness of the faculty model. With advising responsibilities only part of the teaching, research, and service tasks traditionally those of college and university faculties, the institutional mission becomes important in establishing the basis for effectiveness in an all faculty advising model.

Models that incorporate faculty into a larger advising plan often have faculty advise students within the major field of study. These mixed plans may use professional advisors from academic or student affairs units to work with freshmen or special populations, such as undecided students. Colleges and schools within larger universities may have record-keeping functions within a dean's office or a departmental office or may have other personnel handle such matters.

Some institutions organize advising around a center, an idea pioneered by community colleges (Grites, 1979; O'Banion, 1971, 1972). The advising center, a centralized approach, combines a number of personnel (faculty, professional advisors, peer advisors) to provide information to students and to assist students with their academic decision making (Crockett & Levitz, 1984). The advising center may exist for the entire institution, for specific academic units, or for delivering services to special subgroups of students (Crockett & Levitz, 1984; Gerlach, 1983; Grites, 1984; Johnson & Sprandel, 1974; Pardee, 2000; Polson & Jurich, 1979; Spencer, Peterson, & Kramer, 1982).

Some academic advising models use as one component the formal course, providing to students an extended academic orientation. These courses frequently are referred to as freshman seminars, often multipurpose in intent and taught by faculty and/or staff from academic and student affairs. Orientation courses have been used for many years as mechanisms for integrating students into the institutional environment. Increased emphasis has been placed on the potential for using formal courses as an aid to understanding basic issues and strategies related to advising (Gardner, 1982; Gardner, et al., 1990; Gordon & Grites, 1984; King, 2000).

Conceptual structures that guide administrative models are important to consider. The model credited to the community college (O'Banion, 1972) emphasizes process, or sequencing of events that identify advising as a teaching-learning experience. According to Crockett (1986), advising models such as the model developed by O'Banion should acknowledge that there exists ". . . a logical and sequential set of steps to the advising process" (pp. 246–247).

Basically, this early community college model relies on the use of developmental theory as an organizing tool for advising, an idea that has remained a consistent theme for advising over the past several years (Frost, 1991). The notion of "developmental academic advising," as described by Ender, Winston, and Miller (1982) offers ". . . a systematic process based on close student-advisor relationship intended to aid students in achieving educational, career, and personal goals through the utilization of the full range of institutional and community resources" (p. 19). Using a framework that addresses the needs of students at various points in their development can provide a way to help students view educational planning as part of a life process.

Both the organizational framework and the conceptual framework for an advising program need support throughout the institution to develop goals, personnel selection, and adequate funding (Frost, 1991). The emphasis on coordination among various academic units and student service support areas are important to address, along with a ". . . systematic program of . . . advisement that involves students from matriculation through graduation" (Study Group on the Conditions of Excellence in American Higher Education, 1984, p. 31). These considerations can be highly political, affecting the very nature of the organization. For instance, faculty responsibility for advising students is a long-standing tradition in higher education. However, more complex institutions have turned to nonteaching personnel to assume increasing responsibility for advising. The degree to which an articulated system of advising, using both faculty and staff effectively, can be implemented is an issue that has educational and budgetary implications. Implementing campus-wide models for academic advising can be even more of a challenge because of the cooperation required across constituencies.

STAFFING

The major staffing patterns for college and university advising include faculty, professional staff advisors, and student advisors (Barman & Bansen, 1981; Crockett, 1986; Grites, 1979; Hardee, 1970; Kramer & Gardner, 1977; Reinarz, 2000).

Faculty usually will play the key advising role for students who have entered a major field, where the advising tasks will be carried out through the academic department or division housing the appropriate field of study. Faculty often are involved as resource persons in both general and specialized advising centers. They also may serve their academic departments as resources to students seeking information about various fields of study.

The use of professional staff advisors in conjunction with or instead of faculty has taken on increased importance over the years, in part because of the proliferation of information in large institutions, where nonteaching faculty and staff advisors are often found. Professional staff advisors whose full-time responsibility is academic advising are usually part of advising centers or specialized academic or support units. These advisors frequently work with the students who have not yet declared majors, helping to identify options and to develop basic curricular plans that can provide a structure to future decisions.

APPLICATION OF STUDENT LEARNING THEORY

The relationship of an individual to an institution can be enriched considerably through the exchange between a student and an academic advisor. An advisor can represent for the student a bridge to the often complicated and complex world of the curriculum, the academic requirements, the procedures, and the classroom. However, the bridge must be more than informational. It must be conceptual as well.

Research over the years has shown that interaction encourages learning and that learning can be enriched when the intellectual stage of the individual is acknowledged as fundamental to the meaning-making activity. The idea of approaching the student in a holistic way helps to acknowledge the stages of learning and respects the activity of how the individual comes to understand the world.

The American College Personnel Association (ACPA) Student Learning Imperative highlights in its Preamble that faculty need to consider "[creating] conditions that motivate and inspire students to devote time and energy to educationally-purposeful activities, both inside and outside the classroom" (http://www.acpa.nche.edu/sli/sli.htm). The report goes on to say, "Environments can be intentionally designed to promote student learning." Academic advising can contribute to this purposeful activity as students develop their educational plans.

The phase of educational exploration that could be identified as "indecision" often brings into focus how theory applies to academic advising. When students attempt to sort through potential choices in developing a program of study, their focus may go to previous authorities (family, the media, teachers) to help in deciding. Then the focus may be transferred to current authorities (roommate, advisor, professor) to explore possibilities. Eventually the horizon expands, multiple sources of information are captured, and increasing confidence in the new environment allows for a positioning of oneself into a more relative relationship to choices.

What is critical for advisors is the need to acknowledge how the student frames the task of educational exploration and asks the questions relating to deciding. Some students are able to accept "indecision" as a necessary part of learning and frame the educational exploration process accordingly. Other students consider "indecision" not as learning, but as incompetence. These students frame an entirely different educational exploration process.

How academic advisors, whether professional staff or disciplinary faculty, frame their relationship to the idea of "indecision," and therefore to the students who have made meaning of "indecision" in positive or negative way, is a complex advising idea. Sharing one's own learning experiences, especially those related to the embryonic stages of academic exploration, can strengthen the bridge between an advisor and a student.

ENTRY-LEVEL QUALIFICATIONS

Institutions that employ professional staff advisors in entry-level positions generally require a graduate degree or specialized experience and training in a specific field relevant to the advising area. Graduate degrees may be in a variety of areas, from general college student development or counseling to specific academic disciplines. Sometimes a degree or coursework relevant to the advising area may be a requirement.

These entry-level positions usually will require familiarity both with the institution's policies and procedures and with the general structure and philosophy of higher education. Experience working with students in a teaching, staff training, or counseling capacity is typically a criterion used for entry-level positions. Strong interpersonal skills are important in all types of institutions, and excellent organizational skills are critical in complex settings.

Institutions that use faculty models for advising incorporate academic advising into the faculty members' area of teaching, research, and service responsibilities. This advising responsibility frequently will rest within an academic department or division to determine the role advising plays in relation to promotion and tenure decisions. A beginning faculty member may or may not have assigned advisees, and an individual on a research appointment in a large institution may confine the advising responsibilities to graduate students.

ISSUES

How well an advising program works is dependent on many factors. The capacity to respond to student needs means juggling many factors with an effort to integrate the importance of advising into the institutional culture. Responsiveness to student needs is affected by the flexibility of curricular options, the programming to meet the diversified preparation levels of entering students, the availability of information retrieval systems, and the commitment to advising as part of enrollment management concerns.

In 1997, a sample of the NACADA membership was asked about critical issues in advising. This was a follow-up to previous studies (see Polson & Cashin, 1981; Polson & Gordon, 1988). As reported by McGillin (2000), the responses could be characterized as issues faced by students, advisors, and organizations.

Student issues included the relationship of advising to retention, special population advising, and developmental models of advising. Advisor issues included the faculty role, advisor workloads, recognition and reward factors, assessment of advising, and training and staff development of advisors. Organizational issues included reporting lines and structures, addressing the changing student populations, and technology in advising.

Any advising program, to be effective, should be structured using some type of organizational plan guided by a statement of purpose (Crockett & Levitz, 1984; Gordon, 1992; White, 2000). Included in such a plan is the issue of identifying, selecting, and training an advising staff (Crockett & Levitz, 1984; Goetz & White, 1986; Gordon, 1980). Building evaluation into the advising program is also an important consideration (Lynch, 2000; Polson & Cashin, 1981) and forms a key part of a reward system frequently found lacking in advising programs (Carstensen & Silberhorn, 1979; McGillin, 2000). The main issue associated with the reward system concern is the degree to which the institutional decision makers recognize and support the need for a strong advising program. Once such a commitment is made, the organizational factors associated with the development of a coordinated system must be considered, such as the degree to which the advising program will be centralized under a specific unit, or the extent of uniformity in the selection and training of the advising staff, or the mechanisms for budget control.

An issue that affects the structure of an advising program is the degree to which the needs of subgroups of students will be addressed through specialized advising. Considerable work has been reported in the literature to determine the best ways to identify and to structure academic advising programs for groups such as academic risk students, minority students, honors students, undecided students, reentry students, women students, and student-athletes (Anderson, 1995; Frost, 1991; Gordon, Habley, & Associates, 2000; Gordon, 1984; Gordon & Steele, 1992; Grites, 1982; *NACADA Journal,* 1986; Polson, 1989; Smith & Baker, 1987; Titley & Titley, 1980; Upcraft & Stephens, 2000; Ware, Steckler, & Leserman, 1985).

Although the fundamental task of identifying and developing an academic program of study is true for all students, special issues may exist in remediation for students with weak backgrounds or in support for individuals returning to school after an absence who may need careful review of previously acquired college credits. Academic enrichment experiences for honors students may blend the role of faculty mentor and academic advisor. Regulations that apply for academic progress of student-athletes may necessitate specialized training for academic advisors. Continuing research on socialization factors that have an impact on the academic progress of students previously underrepresented in college add dimensions to advising programs that attempt to meet individualized needs of students. Addressing these issues often will have budgetary implications in staffing and training. In some cases, the issue of multiple advisors for a student may result in confusion as to who is performing what function for the student. In other cases, if a student thinks that special needs are not being addressed, no advising assistance is sought from anyone.

Demands on certain curricular areas have forced some institutions to consider the population of students unable to enter the fields of study they desire because of institutional or departmental limitations on enrollment (Gordon & Polson, 1985; Steele, Kennedy, & Gordon, 1993). The implications of student consumerism on curricular demand force the issue of advising alternatives, with interaction among academic units needed to make information readily available to those students so that contingency plans can be developed and alternative program requirements met.

The way an institution constructs the activity of academic advising should reflect the needs of the students, set in the framework of the institution's mission and resources. How well the institution responds in setting forth this experience will depend on the philosophy toward student learning and the appropriation of financial and human resources. The ability of the institution to provide a multifaceted approach to helping students realize their goals means a broadly based effort to support a range of options that will help students effectively negotiate the academic experience.

TECHNOLOGY

The use of information technology in advising is a complex subject. Each year students come to our institutions with more and more technical skill and expectation that we will have available the equipment and the training to provide them with more advanced skills. The world of work expects technologically savvy graduates; indeed, future generations of advisors will come to their jobs with the expectation that the institution will support advising through technology. Online learning through distance education, virtual classrooms, e-mail exchanges, and so forth, provide an interesting challenge to what has been considered to be a face-to-face activity, that of the advising exchange.

The potential for integrating technology with advising is significant for those who have the equipment, technical support staff, and advisor training programs to make technology work. There are institutional advantages to providing easy access to information for advisors. This type of access usually results in better interactions with students.

Early use of technology on campuses was often done at a high level, in financial and administrative activities. Today technology use can be seen at all levels (Childs, 1996; Kramer, Peterson, & Spencer, 1984). An institution's registrar often will be a motivating force in the use of technology for such things as degree audits, transfer of courses and credits, online institutional documents, computer and touch-tone telephone registration, and various procedural activities. Electronic calendars and online advising records can offer more comprehensive ways to support the advising needs of students (McCaulley, 2000: Sotto, 2000).

Technology support that addresses the needs of advisors can greatly enhance an institution's program. The information-giving part of an advisor's job can be made more effective with timely and accurate material available online. The record-keeping part of an advisor's job can be more easily managed with programs written specifically to meet the needs of advisors.

Technology support that addresses the needs of students enhances the educational planning aspects of students' lives by making accessible, 24/7, institutional information about programs of study, policies affecting those programs, and procedures for implementing sound planning. As with advisors, the appropriate training is needed for students to make effective use of their alternatives.

A few institutions have mounted some particularly good integrated programs for advisors and/or students. These web sites offer a sampling of effective use of technology in advising, including some vehicles for keeping advisors up-to-date in virtual professional worlds. Here is a selection of some approaches to the use of information technology for advisors and students:

Monroe Community College [http://www.monroecc.edu/depts./counsel/AAA/homepage.htm]

Richard Stockton College of New Jersey [http://www2.stockton.edu/advising]

Weber State University OnLine [http://wsuonline.weber.edu/]

Pennsylvania State University, Division of Undergraduate Studies [http://www.psu.edu/dus/]

Western Governors University (OnLine Learning in a Competency-Based Experience) [http://www.wgu.edu/wgu/index.html]

National Academic Advising Association (Nacada) [http://ksu.edu/nacada] The NACADA web site will allow access to advising-related materials and should be bookmarked for those interested in advising topics.

NACADA Electronic Network (Acadv Listserv)—An electronic information exchange for professionals interested in advising topics. To join the listserv, send e-mail to <Listserv@Listserv.nodak.edu>, no subject, with this message on the first line: subscribe ACADV [first name, middle initial, last name].

The Mentor—An electronic journal devoted to academic advising issues [http://www.psu.edu/dus/mentor/]

FUTURE CONSIDERATIONS

For some institutions, academic advising is not an organized, well-constructed system, but either a decentralized "silo" approach to services or something that happens only when a student needs to register for classes. For other institutions, advising is so integrated that it is fundamental to the culture.

For some institutions, technology has been incorporated without careful thought from teams made up of stakeholders: the technical support staff, advisors, students, and budget managers. Sometimes, instead of enhancing advising, technology has provided a way to bypass advising interactions thorough the use of online conveniences, such as dropping courses or course registration. For other institutions, the depth of skill in and knowledge about advising is so well developed that technology has given a new tool that is truly advisor- and advisee-friendly.

Regardless of complexity or technological sophistication, the opportunity to have students interact with the institution for the specific purpose of educational planning can add to the value and substance of the academic experience. Making intellectual connections with learning in the disciplines and applying one's ways of knowing are important experiences where an academic advisor can often provide the bridge to understanding.

Six issues seem to be at the forefront for consideration.

1. One fundamental consideration is how to structure advising so that the activity is clearly defined as to purpose, programmatic options, and desired outcomes in the most efficient and cost-effective way. The degree to which academic advising differs from and is similar to other programs offered to students must be described in a cogent statement of purpose showing the relationship of the activity to the broader institutional mission. A critical part of defining the activity is establishing assessment mechanisms that are attached to institutional goals and reward systems. In 1997, as part of the standards for 24 functional areas of higher education, the Council for the Advancement of Standards (CAS) approved an update of the 1986 standards and guidelines for academic advising, which can be found at the following web site: (http://www.nacada.ksu.edu/profres/standard/htm).

2. A timely consideration facing institutions is providing adequate staff training to use computer technology to assist in advising, as both a record-keeping system and a data management system for staff and as an interactive and information retrieval tool for students. With the capacity to provide more and more academic information, some serious reflection is needed about the interpretation of this information to students and staff. A related consideration is the awareness that information put up on a web site must be monitored for accuracy and access. Mounting elaborate systems without recognizing the need to keep links live and respond to policy and program changes can doom the effectiveness of online complements to advising. Academic advisors can play a critical role in helping institutions to incorporate information technology effectively.

3. With the emphasis on assessment to justify programs and services, collecting information about students prior to entrance and throughout their college years can add significantly to the institutional usefulness of an advising program. For instance, advising tools developed for students that actively engage them in their own program planning, such as feedback of information they have contributed at various points in their academic careers, strengthens the developmental nature of an advising program. In addition, such baseline information can give the institution useful measures for assessment and program planning, such as providing trend data about student academic interests and detailing skill remediation needs for course development.

4. Factors associated with why students select different fields of study (Jackson, Holden, Locklin, & Marks, 1984) can contribute consider-

ably to the advising program. Helping students to develop a perspective of the nature of the curriculum (Ford & Pugno, 1964: Hursh, Haas, & Moore, 1983) can help them to understand better the choices they are making. Faculty can play a critical role as resources for this. Academic support areas such as career services also contribute their tools in the advising process by helping students to understand the relationships of educational and career planning (McCalla-Riggins, 2000).

5. Continuous evaluation of the academic advising program is essential to justify programs that range beyond the minimal record-keeping functions of academic advising. Establishing mechanisms that build student feedback into the evaluation process can keep advisors current to the needs of their constituencies. Demonstrating the usefulness of advising to the overall aims of the institution comes about through studying multiple measures of effectiveness using broadly designed program evaluation agendas.

6. Attempting to understand what theoretical structures apply to advising and whether a "theory" of advising can be developed is on the minds of some within the profession (see Lowenstein, 1999, as an example, as well as the work done in the mid-1980s on "developmental" advising). The idea of advising as a profession warrants a clear understanding of theoretical possibilities to underpin the practice.

REFERENCES

Anderson, V. (1995). Identifying special advising needs of women engineering students. *Journal of College Student Development, 36(4)*, 322–329.

Astin, A. W. (1977). *Four critical years: Effects of college on beliefs, attitudes, and knowledge.* San Francisco: Jossey-Bass.

Barman, C. R., & Benson, P. A. (1981). Peer advising: A working model. *National Academic Advising Association (NACADA) Journal, 1(20)*, 33–40.

Borgard, J. H. (1981). Toward a pragmatic philosophy of academic advising. *National Academic Advising Association (NACADA) Journal, 1(1)*, 1–7.

Boyer, E. L. (1987). *College: The undergraduate experience.* New York: Harper & Row.

Brubacher, J. S., & Rudy, R. (1968). *Higher education in transition.* New York: Harper & Row.

Carstensen, D. J., & Silberhorn, C. A. (1979). *A national survey of academic advising, final report.* Iowa City, IA: American College Testing program.

Childs, M. W. (1996). Enhancing academic support services through information technology. In G. L. Kramer & M. W. Childs, *Transforming academic advising through the use of information technology* (pp. 13–22). Monograph Series #4, National Academic Advising Association.

Creamer, D. G. and Creamer, E. G. (1994). Practicing developmental advising: Theoretical contexts and functional applications. *National Academic Advising Association (NACADA) Journal, 14(2)*, 17–24.

Crockett, D. S. (Ed.). (1978a). *Academic advising: A resource document.* Iowa City, IA: American College Testing Program.

Crockett, D. S. (1978b). Academic advising: A cornerstone of student retention. In L. Noel (Ed.) (New directions for student services, No. 3, Reducing the dropout rate, pp. 29–35). San Francisco: Jossey-Bass.

Crockett, D. S. (Ed.). (1979). *Academic advising: A resource document* (1979 Supplement). Iowa City: American College Testing program.

Crockett, D. S. (1984). ACT as a strategic resource in enhancing the advising process. *National Academic Advising Association (NACADA) Journal, 4(2),* 1–11.

Crockett, D. S. (1986). Academic advising. In L. Noel, R. Levitz, D. Saluri, & Associates (Eds.), *Increasing student retention.* San Francisco: Jossey-Bass.

Crockett, D. S., & Levitz, R. (1984). Current advising practices in colleges and universities. In R. B. Winston, Jr., T. K. Miller, S. C. Ender, T. J. Grites, & Associates (Eds.), *Developmental academic advising* (pp. 35–63). San Francisco: Jossey-Bass.

Crookston, B. B. (1972). A developmental view of academic advising as teaching. *Journal of College Student Personnel, 13,* 12–27.

Ender, S. C., Winston, R. B., Jr., & Miller, T. K. (1982). Academic advising as student development. In R. B. Winston, Jr., S. C. Ender, & T. K. Miller (New directions for student services, No. 17, Developmental approaches to academic advising, pp. 3–18). San Francisco: Jossey-Bass.

Feldman, K. A., & Newcomb, T. A. (1969). *The impact of college on students.* San Francisco: Jossey-Bass.

Ford, G. W., & Pugno, L. (Eds.). (1964). *The structure of knowledge and the curriculum.* Chicago: Rand McNally.

Frost, S. H. (1991). *Academic advising for student success: A system of shared responsibility* (ASHE-ERIC Higher Education Report No. 3). Washington, DC: George Washington University School of Education and Human Development.

Gardner, J. N., et.al. (1990). *Guidelines for evaluating the freshman year experience.* Columbia, SC: Center for the Study of the Freshman Year Experience. (ERIC Document Reproduction Service No. ED 334 885).

Gardner, J. N. (1982). *Proceedings of the national conference on the freshman orientation course/freshman seminar concept.* Columbia, SC: University of South Carolina.

Goetz, J. J., & White, R. E. (1986). A survey of graduate programs addressing the preparation of professional academic advisors. *National Academic Advising Association (NACADA) Journal, 6(2),* 43–47.

Gordon, V. N. (1980). Training academic advisers: Content and method. *Journal of College Student Personnel, 21,* 334–340.

Gordon, V. N. (1984). *The undecided college student: An academic and career advising challenge,* Springfield, IL: Charles C Thomas.

Gordon, V. N. (1992). *Handbook of academic advising.* Westport, CT: Greenwood Press.

Gordon, V. N., & Grites, T. J. (1984). The freshman seminar course: Helping students succeed. *Journal of College Student Personnel, 25,* 315–320.

Gordon, V. N., Habley, W. R., & Associates. (2000). *Academic advising: A comprehensive handbook.* San Francisco: Jossey-Bass.

Gordon, V. N., & Polson, C. L. (1985). Students needing academic alternative advising: A national survey. *National Academic Advising Association (NACADA) Journal, 5(2),* 77–84.

Grites, T. J. (1979). *Academic advising: Getting us through the eighties* (Report No. 7). Washington, DC: American Association for Higher Education–Educational Resource Information Center.

Grites, T. J. (1982). Advising for special populations. In R. B. Winston, Jr., S. C. Ender, & T. K. Miller (Eds.) (New directions for student services, No. 17, Developmental approaches to academic advising, pp. 67–86). San Francisco: Jossey-Bass.

Grites, T. J. (1984). Noteworthy academic advising programs. In R. B. Winston, Jr., T. K. Miller, S. C. Ender, T. J. Grites, & Associates, *Developmental academic advising* (pp. 469–537). San Francisco: Jossey-Bass.

Habley, W. R. (1988). *The status and future of academic advising: Problems and promise.* Iowa City, IA: American College Testing Program.

Habley, W. R. (1993). *Fulfilling the promise? Final report: ACT fourth national survey of academic advising.* Iowa City, IA: American College Testing Program.

Habley, W. R., & McCauley, M. E. (1987). The relationship between institutional characteristics and the organization of advising services. *National Academic Advising Association (NACADA) Journal, 7(1)*, 27–39.

Habley, W. R., & Morales, R. H. (1998). *Current practices in academic advising: Final report on ACT's fifth national survey of academic advising.* National Academic Advising Association Monograph Series, No. 6. Manhattan, KS: National Academic Advising Association.

Hardee, M. D. (1962). Faculty advising in contemporary higher education. *Educational Record, 42*, 112–116.

Hardee, M. D. (1970). *Faculty advising in colleges and universities.* Washington, DC: American College Personnel Association.

Hursch, B., Haas, P., & Moore, M. (1983). An interdisciplinary model to implement general education. *Journal of Higher Education, 54(1)*, 42–59.

Jackson, D. N., Holden, R. R., Locklin, R. H., & Marks, E. (1984). Taxonomy of vocational interests of academic major areas. *Journal of Educational Measurement, 21(3)*, 261–275.

Jacob, P. E. (1957). *Changing values in college.* New York: Harper.

Johnson, J., & Sprandel, K. (1975). Centralized academic advising at the departmental level: A model. *University College Quarterly (Michigan State University), 21(1)*, 16–20.

King, M. C. (Ed.) (1993). *Academic advising: Organizing and delivering services for student success.* New Directions for Community Colleges, No. 82. San Francisco; Jossey-Bass.

King, N. S. (2000). Advising students in groups. In Gordon, V. N., Habley, W. R., & Associates, *Academic advising: A comprehensive handbook* (pp. 228–237). San Francisco: Jossey-Bass.

Kramer, G. L., Peterson, E. D., & Spencer, R. W. (1984). Using computers in academic advising. In R. B. Winston, Jr., T. K. Miller, S.C. Ender, T. J. Grites, & Associates, *Developmental academic advising* (pp. 226–249). San Francisco: Jossey-Bass.

Kramer, H. C., & Gardner, R. E. (1977). *Advising by faculty.* Washington, DC: National Education Association.

Kuh, G. D., & Andreas, R. E. (1991). It's about time: Using qualitative methods in student life studies. *Journal of College Student Development, 32(5)*, 397–405.

Levine, A. (1978). *Handbook of undergraduate curriculum.* San Francisco: Jossey-Bass.

Light, D. (1974). Introduction: The structure of the academic professions. *Sociology of Education, 47,* 2–28.

Light, R. J. (2001). *Making the most of college: Students speak out.* Boston, MA: Harvard University Press.

Lowenstein, M. (1999). An alternative to the developmental theory of advising. *The Mentor: An Academic Advising Journal* (www.psu.edu/dus/mentor)

Lynch, M. L. (2000). Assessing the effectiveness of advising programs. In Gordon, V. N., Habley, W. R., & Associates, *Academic advising: A comprehensive handbook* (pp. 324–348). San Francisco: Jossey-Bass.

McCalla-Riggins, B. (2000). Integrating academic advising and career planning. In Gordon, V. N., Habley, W. R., & Associates, *Academic advising: A comprehensive handbook* (pp. 162–176). San Francisco: Jossey-Bass.

McCaulley, M. E. (2000). Technology resources that support advising. In Gordon, V. N., Habley, W. R., & Associates, *Academic advising: A comprehensive handbook* (pp. 238–248). San Francisco: Jossey-Bass.

McGillin, V. A. (2000). Current issues in advising research. In Gordon, V. N., Habley, W. R., & Associates, *Academic advising: A comprehensive handbook* (pp. 365–380). San Francisco: Jossey-Bass.

McKeachie, W. J. (1978). *Teaching tips: A guidebook for the beginning college teacher* (7th ed.). Lexington, MA: Heath.

Moore, K. M. (1976). Faculty advising: Panacea or placebo? *Journal of College Student Personnel, 17,* 371–375.

Mueller, K. H. (1961). *Student personnel work in higher education.* Boston, MA: Houghton Mifflin.

National Academic Advising Association (NACADA) Journal. (1986). Special issue number three: *Resources for advising student-athletes, 6(1),* 1–100.

O'Banion, T. (1971). *Student personnel monograph series: No. 15. New directions in community college student personnel programs.* Washington, DC: American College Personnel Association.

O'Banion, T. (1972). An academic advising model. *Junior College Journal, 44,* 62–69.

Pardee, C. F. (2000). Organizational models for academic advising. In Gordon, V. N., Habley, W. R. & Associates, *Academic advising: A comprehensive handbook* (pp.192–209). San Francisco: Jossey-Bass.

Parsons, T., & Platt, G. M. (1973). T*he American university.* Cambridge, MA: Harvard University Press.

Pascarella, E. T. (1980). Student-faculty informal contact and college outcomes. *Review of Educational Research, 50,* 545–595.

Pascarella, E. T., & Terenzini, P. T. (1991). *How college affects students.* San Francisco: Jossey-Bass.

Polson, C. J. (1989). Adult learners: Characteristics, concerns, and challenges to higher education—a bibliography. *National Academic Advising Association (NACADA) Journal, 9(2),* 86–112.

Polson, C. J., & Cashin, W. E. (1981). Research priorities for academic advising: Results of a survey of NACADA membership. *National Academic Advising Association (NACADA) Journal, 1(1),* 34–43.

Polson, C. J., & Gordon, V. N. (1988). *Issues affecting academic advising revisited.* National Academic Advising Association (NACADA) Journal, 8(2),49–58.

Reinarz, A. G. (2000). Delivering academic advising. In Gordon, V. N., Habley, W. R. & Associates, *Academic advising: A comprehensive handbook* (pp.210–219). San Francisco: Jossey-Bass.

Rudolph, R. (1962). *The American college and university.* New York: Random House.

Sotto, R. R. (2000). Technological delivery systems. In Gordon, V. N., Habley, W. R. & Associates, *Academic advising: A comprehensive handbook* (pp.249–257). San Francisco: Jossey-Bass.

Smith, M. A. & Baker, R. W. (1987). Freshman decidedness regarding academic major and adjustment to college. *Psychological Reports,* 61(3), 847–853.

Steele, G. E., Kennedy, G. J., & Gordon, V. N. (1993). The retention of major changers: A longitudinal Study. *Journal of College Student Development, 34,* 58–112.

Study Group on the Conditions of Excellence in American Higher Education. (1984). I*nvolvement in learning: Realizing the potential of American higher education.* Washington, D.C.: National Institute of Education.

Terenzini, P. T., Pascarella, E. T., & Lorgan, W. G. (1982). An assessment of the academic and social influences on freshman year educational outcomes. *Review of Higher Education, 5(2),* 86–109.

Thomas, R. E., & Chickering, A. W. (1984). Foundations for academic advising. In R. B. Winston, Jr., T. K. Miller, S. C. Ender, T. J. Grites, & Associates, *Developmental academic advising* (pp. 89–117). San Francisco: Jossey-Bass.

Tinto, V. (1987). *Leaving college.* Chicago: University of Chicago Press.

Tinto, V. (1993). *Leaving college: Rethinking the causes and cures of student attrition.* Chicago: University of Chicago Press.

Trombley, T. B. (1984). An analysis of the complexity of academic advising tasks. *Journal of College Student Personnel, 25(4),* 234–239.

Upcraft, M. L. & Stephens, P. S. (2000). Academic advising and today's changing students. In Gordon, V. N., Habley, W. R. & Associates, *Academic advising: A comprehensive handbook* (pp.73–83). San Francisco: Jossey-Bass.

Vreeland, R. S., & Bidwell, C. E. (1966). Classifying university departments: An approach to the analysis of their effects upon undergraduates' values and attitudes. *Sociology of Education, 39(3),* 237–254.

Ware, N. C., Steckler, N. A., & Lesterman, J. (1985). Undergraduate women: Who chooses a science major? *Journal of Higher Education, 56,* 73–84.

Weaver, F. S. (1981). Academic disciplines and undergraduate liberal arts education. *Liberal Education,* Summer, 151-165.

White, E. R. (2000). Developing mission, goals, and objectives for advising programs. In Gordon, V. N., Habley, W. R. & Associates, *Academic advising: A comprehensive handbook* (pp.180-191). San Francisco: Jossey-Bass.

Winston, R. B., Jr., Grites, T. J., Miller, T. K. Ender, S. C. (1984). Epilogue: Improving academic advising. In R. B. Winston, Jr., T. K. Miller, S. C. Ender, T. J. Grites, & Associates, *Developmental academic advising* (pp. 538-550). San Francisco: Jossey-Bass.

Wiebe, R. H. (1967). *The search for order: 1877-1920.* New York: Hill & Wang.

Chapter 5

CAREER SERVICES

Kathryn S. Hoff, Joann Kroll, Fiona J.D. MacKinnon,
and Audrey L. Rentz

INTRODUCTION

Career services carries out an important function not only in the lives of students but also in the interface between higher education and the workplace. In this fast-paced world of information, technology, and global economics, the role of career services is integral to the successful experience of students in higher education. The central developmental task demanded by society of college students is the independent choice of a career informed by the academic course of study. However, this developmental task, involving (1) an accurate assessment of the self, (2) a sophisticated understanding of the world of work, and (3) the ability to make good decisions, is not a simple one. Most students spend more time watching television or preparing to buy their next CD than immersing themselves in the career development process and preparing for decisions that may affect them for a lifetime. Students, faculty, and parents mistakenly view career services as the office that students seek out to help them find a job in their final term in college. This misconception is perpetuated by the sense that career development is essentially a simple placement operation (Rayman, 1993).

The developmental task of career choice is grounded in the cultural value system of the United States. Economic viability, the outcome of a satisfying career, is a central component of citizenship as well as societal well-being. Without economic viability in the United States citizens do not have access to the benefits of democracy and the American way of life. Economic viability evolves from appropriate career choice and is the key to social justice in a capitalist society (Merriam & Caffarella, 1999). Thus, career services is responsible for a support role that is crucial to the welfare of students as well as society.

The career services office, as part of the enrollment management team, views the college or university from a unique vantage point. Career services personnel receive a wealth of feedback about the institution from important stakeholders such as employers, alumni, and students. These stakeholders have a vested interest in (1) the efficacy of the knowledge transmitted, (2) the lifelong learning skills developed, and (3) the ability of learners to operate independently and wisely as employees and adults. Employers and alumni provide career services professionals with an external perspective of the institution and scrutinize the academic departments for the appropriateness and integrity of the curriculum (Gardner & Liu, 1997; Patterson, 1996). Employers also examine the cocurriculum for the experiences that help students develop communication, leadership, and cooperative skills (Reardon, Lenz; & Folsom, 1998). As alumni change positions or move up the career ladder, they report back to the career services office about the strengths and gaps in their in-class and out-of-class education as it relates to their career experience (Ryan, 1996). Undergraduate and graduate students provide immediate and candid feedback as learners in the process of their education. Career services staff members can share with campus personnel their understanding of the integrity and validity of academic and cocurricular programs in relationship to the world of work (Aviles, 2001).

The diversity of students on the college campus has changed the nature of career services. The standard approach to career choice does not necessarily meet the needs of first-generation college students "who have limited knowledge and experience dealing with the professional job search subculture" (Rayman, 1993, p. 6). Subpopulations of students (such as ethnic and racial minorities; students with disabilities; gay, lesbian, bisexual students; adult learners; students from low socioeconomic backgrounds; international students; and so on) may have difficulty translating the choice of major into a career field (Herr & Cramer, 1992). Career counselors are trained to help all students untangle the complexity of career choice.

Career services guides students through a four-year process model of career development focusing on self-awareness, decision-making, and providing opportunities for understanding the world of work. At the same time, the work of the career services staff contributes to social justice and social change by encouraging all students to use their talents to the fullest by selecting careers through which they can contribute to society (O'Brien, 2001).

HISTORICAL DEVELOPMENT

ORIGIN OF PLACEMENT

The increasing importance to the college or university of the placement function of career services has been sure and steady. During the colonial period, placement was the responsibility of the dons who frequently assumed responsibility for assisting male graduates to secure ministerial positions in local churches. In the newly independent United States, the earliest placement offices were established to "aid young people in choosing an occupation, preparing themselves for it, and building up a career of efficiency and success" (Brewer, 1942, p. 61). The University of Nebraska in 1892, Teachers College in 1907, and Yale University in 1919 were among the first colleges to recognize the need for employment offices or bureaus of occupation that were staffed by faculty committees (Ebel, Noll, & Bauer, 1969).

The Gilded Age of the United States was a time of great industrial change spanning the end of the nineteenth century and the beginning of the twentieth century. Careers and work were of central concern to working people, who did not want to be viewed as chattel of industry, and to the barons of industry, who were fully aware of the industrialization, immigration, technology, and urbanization that was changing the landscape (DeBell, 2001). In 1908, at the height of the Gilded Age and the progressive movement, Frank Parsons, an engineer by training and the founder of vocational psychology in the United States, established the Vocation Bureau in Boston (Zytowski, 2001). Parsons's book, which was published posthumously in 1909 and was entitled *Choosing a Vocation*, was the first major analysis of job-choice behavior. Parsons (1909) proposed a three-part model that stands today as the archetype of career decision making:

> First, a clear understanding of yourself, your aptitudes, abilities, interests, ambitions, resources, limitations, and their qualities. Second, a knowledge of the requirements and conditions of success, advantages and disadvantages, compensations, opportunities, and prospects in different lines of work. Third, true reasoning on the relations of these two groups of facts (p. 5).

The World War I years were associated with dramatic changes in the application of psychometric principles for the purpose of matching individuals to specific jobs. The Army Alpha General Classification Test assisted the military to assign draftees to leadership and training specialty programs. This new and objective method of personnel matching was soon generalized to college and university campuses. Similar surveys were developed to assess the attributes of entering college students. Several years later, the administration of assessment instruments was required during freshman orientation and registration programs. These activities helped new students select courses, preprofessional or technical curricula, and undergraduate degree programs.

During the 1920s and 1930s, the placement of graduates required minimal services on the part of many institutions. The availability of jobs following the Stock Market Crash in 1929 and during the Depression of the 1930s was lower than at any previous time in U.S. history.

World War II changed the vocational landscape. Toward the end of the war in 1944, federal funding created the Vocational Rehabilitation and

Educational Counseling Program and the Veteran's Administration. This led to a contract involving 429 institutions of higher education that agreed to provide job-related counseling services and programs for returning veterans reentering the job market (Blaska & Schmidt, 1977).

After World War II, consumer demands and new technologies created a tremendous need for employees, especially in the manufacturing sector. Industrialization resulted in an increased need for engineers, managers, educators, and professionals. By the early 1950s, 600 employers had established college recruiting programs (Korvas, 1994). As a result, placement services witnessed the largest expansion phase in its history.

Placement services initially were defined as matching graduates with employers (Heppner & Johnston, 1993). As colleges and universities examined their mission statement and realized that career placement required more initiative on the part of graduates, the mission of the placement office broadened to include the entire career planning process.

EMERGENCE OF CAREER PLANNING

The civil rights movement, the Vietnam War, the women's movement, and student activism in the 1960s had profound effects, not only on students, but also on college and university administrators. A new focus on actualizing potential as a goal of life affected basic values and attitudes toward education and the role of work. The major developmental process involved in linking education and employment became the focus of career services.

In the late 1960s, placement offices began adding career planning and counseling to their umbrella of services. The significance of this new integration of career planning with placement was characterized in Robb's (1971) statement: "A superb academic program which lacks corollary strength in placement can represent institutional failure to the student who does not receive adequate assistance in working out career plans" (p. 31). The allocation of resources shifted from an emphasis on campus recruitment toward the goals of dissemination of occupational information and development of career counseling programs. These programs were designed to help students gain an understanding of self, interests, abilities, values, and needs; determine occupational or career goals; and learn strategies to obtain employment (Stephens, 1970).

The career development paradigm involves three components: self-knowledge, knowledge of the world of work, and the decision-making skills and job-seeking skills that lead to satisfactory employment (Rayman, 1993). First, self-knowledge focuses on values, interests, abilities, and motivation. This information is obtained gradually throughout life. During the college years, though, self-understanding evolves from the undergraduate curriculum as well as from explicit career services interventions. The second component, knowledge of the world of work, comes from experiences with summer jobs, internships, cooperative education experiences, and casual conversations around the dinner table about the workday. The third component, decision making combines self-knowledge with information about the world of work. This synthesis of information moves students from the exploration phase of career choice to tentative commitment or to the establishment phase (Rayman, 1993). Throughout adult life, concerns about career development resurface time and again so that skills learned from career exploration in early adulthood become life skills that are continually revisited.

SHIFT TO INFORMATION INTEGRATION PARADIGM

The commitment of colleges and universities to career services has increased dramatically over the years. Career services, which began in the early part of the last century with a simple brokering role through the placement office, has evolved and expanded with economic and social circumstances. As the economy fluctuates and business booms come and go, so do career services modify emphases and direction to meet the demands of the times. For example, in the 1980s, the business curriculum appeared to offer students the direct path to high salaries and the "yuppie" lifestyle. Colleges of business expanded and career services responded to the demand.

The 1990s brought a different set of economic circumstances to bear on career services. Salient factors changed the economic and social context in which career services were expected to help students formulate career choices:

1. The relapse of the economic boom of the Reagan years;
2. The restructuring and downsizing of business and industry with increased competition from the global marketplace;
3. The structural change from manufacturing to a service-based economy;
4. The end of the Cold War and the impact on the defense industry;
5. The growth of small companies and their emergence as less accessible employers;
6. The change of employment from commitment to the loyal employee to "just in time" hiring, "right-sizing," and outsourcing;
7. The increasing debt load of college graduates;
8. The diversity of students attending college; and
9. The decreasing state and federal support for higher education (Rayman, 1993).

For the first time ever, the standard of living for the current generation would not surpass that of their parents.

New career service models evolve to meet current needs (Freeman, 1994). Hansen (1993) urged career professionals to design new models, theories, and methods of delivery to help students and adults prepare for the changes in their life roles:

> "What do I want to be?" may be replaced by "What kinds of life choice experiences do I want to have during my lifetime?" "Which of my potentials do I want to develop and implement at what stage and with what kind of help?" and "How can my contributions make a positive difference in this society?" (p. 19)

Career professionals have long advocated for proactive rather than reactive approaches to students' vocational development. Freeman (1994) recommended a four-year career development process model. Using this model, students would be helped to understand the transferable essence of their academic experience; gain an increased understanding of self, others, and the world of work; develop skills in listening, assessment of other's needs, relationship building, negotiation, and other relevant areas; conceptualize a broad range of career possibilities, including entrepreneurial opportunities; engage in new experiences to broaden their horizons; participate in all types of experiential learning to acquire a real-world perspective, real-world skills, contacts with future professional colleagues, and access up-to-date technology and business practices; learn how to tap visible and hidden job markets; and take personal responsibility for their lives. The developmental approach would necessitate early intervention and reframing the vocational choice process for students.

Career planning services must be carefully built on "solid philosophical and psychological bases" (Heppner & Johnston, 1993, p. 63). Policy questions arise when resources are scarce. Is it better to provide comprehensive services for first-year students or seniors, or both? Is it appropriate to provide services for alumni? Can alumni help to provide services for undergraduate students? A comprehensive and reasoned philosophy as well as a mission for the office are necessary to undergird services.

Theory can be very productively used to direct practice and to channel the functions and roles of professional and paraprofessional staff. Information about vocational choice, career readiness, career indecision, and the fit between personality type and work environments, for example, is abundant in the journals that are dedicated to vocational issues. The literature on student development and adult development provide the basis for understanding how students make meaning of the world and what interventions will serve them best. Theory and research can help answer the questions that are central to students' career planning concerns and can illuminate the services that will be effective and timely.

PURPOSE AND GOALS

In 1986, the Council for the Advancement of Standards (CAS), a consortium of 21 professional associations in higher education, attempted to standardize student affairs practice. A set of criteria was proscribed in *Guidelines for Student Services/Development Programs* for evaluating services or programs. *The Role of Career Services: CAS Standards Contextual Statement (2001),* defined the primary mission of career services:

> . . . to assist students and other designated clients through all phases of their career development. In addition, the mission of career services is
>
> • to provide leadership to the institution on career development concerns
> • to develop positive relationships with employers and external constituencies
> • to support institutional outcomes assessment and relevant research endeavors (p. 67).

As each career services office creates its own mission statement, the CAS Standards (2001) suggested inclusion of eight key components, including helping students and others: to develop self-knowledge related to career choice and work performance; to obtain educational and occupational information to aid career planning and to develop an understanding of the world of work; to select suitable academic programs and experiential opportunities; to take personal responsibility for developing job search competencies; to gain experience through student activities, community service, student employment, research or creative projects, cooperative education, internships, and other opportunities; to link with alumni, employers, professional associations, and others to provide opportunities to explore the world of work; to prepare for finding suitable employment by following established career development practices; and to seek desired employment opportunities or entry into appropriate educational, graduate, or professional programs. In addition, "because of the expertise and knowledge on career-related matters, career services should be involved in key administrative decisions related to student services, institutional development, curriculum planning, and external relations" (p. 67).

Several authors offered an expanded view of the overall mission for career services. A truly comprehensive career guidance program in higher education should provide assistance in (1) selection of a major field of study, (2) self-assessment and self-analysis, (3) understanding the world of work, (4) decision making, (5) accessing the world of work, and (6) meeting the unique needs of various subpopulations (Herr & Cramer, 1992). The *Standards and Guidelines for Career Services* recommended "career services must provide faculty, staff and administrative units with information, guidance, and support on career development and employment issues and linkages with the broader community" (Council for the Advancement of Standards, 2001, p. 70).

Freeman (1994) identified three distinct missions for the college placement center: (1) translation—helping students establish an identity based on the transferable essence of their total life experiences, synthesize and recognize patterns of strengths, and see possibilities in new ways; (2) empowerment—helping students take effective action in approaching others and building long-term relationships; and (3) facilitation—helping students identify and approach others before the search is initiated, and continue to approach others once the job search is under way.

Career services on college and university campuses were viewed and delivered very differently in the 1990s than in previous decades and will continue to change in the beginning of the twenty-first century.

The dual roles of career counseling and job placement are being replaced by a comprehensive approach to career development that seeks to be fully integrated into the traditional academic curriculum. The new comprehensive career centers have strong career development foundations, with missions explicitly tied to institutional goals. They assist students from all academic disciplines, adult learners as well as those 18- to 22-year-olds, graduate students as well as undergraduates, international and multiethnic students, alumni, and sometimes even faculty and staff. Comprehensive career centers assist with student retention efforts through early career clarification, teach the importance of networking as a lifelong career skill, increase student career awareness by disseminating career information via the World Wide Web and other technological advances, and help students see connections between their academic studies and employment or volunteer experiences through experiential learning and other curricular programs (Smith & Gast, 1998, pp. 189–190).

ADMINISTRATIVE AND ORGANIZATIONAL STRUCTURES

REPORTING STRUCTURE

Since the 1950s, administrative reporting relationships involving career services offices have changed significantly. In the late 1960s, 30 percent of career planning and placement directors reported directly to the president of their institution, 30 percent to the dean of students, and 27 percent to the chief academic officer. By 1981, most directors reported to the chief student affairs officer (Weber, 1982). This trend continued into the late 1980s as the American College Personnel Association's *Career Center Directors' National Data Bank* revealed that 79 percent of respondents from public institutions reported to the chief student affairs officer or an immediate subordinate. A reversal in this trend was identified by the *2000 Career Services Survey*. Although the number of directors reporting to student affairs decreased from 74 percent to 65 percent since the 1994 survey (Nagle & Bohovich, 2000a), the largest percentage of directors still reported to the vice president of student affairs or the dean of students. Advantages of this reporting structure include stronger communication, and thus an increased likelihood of referral between career services and other related student services areas; the opportunity for career services to compete successfully with other student services units for resources; support from the vice president for the service orientation and student development point of view; and support for the costly career counseling and programming activities that are critical to a comprehensive approach to service delivery (Herr et al., 1993).

While the majority of career services offices today are part of student affairs divisions, 13.9 percent of directors responding to the *2000 Career Services Survey* reported directly to academic affairs, 4.9 percent to the president of the institution, and 2.8 percent to enrollment management (Nagle & Bohovich, 2000a). Where career services are decentralized, the most common reporting line is to an academic dean. Being allied with academic affairs often enhances the quality of communication between career services and faculty, leads to greater credibility with and stronger support from faculty, and helps career services maintain its resource base (Herr, Rayman, & Garis, 1993).

Typically, the decision of where to locate career services was based on the historical development or unique character of the individual institution. Regardless of which reporting line is selected, the following guidelines are useful: (1) faculty support, acceptance, and understanding of, and respect for, the career center and staff are essential; (2) career services professionals need to work collaboratively with student affairs professionals and with other staff who understand and value a student development approach; (3) support for a comprehensive operation must come from the highest level of administration; (4) the career center should be funded in accordance with expectations of outcomes; (5) it is critical that there be a philosophical understanding between the comprehensive career center and the academic counseling and student development centers (Shea, 1995); and (6) the presence of a clear and designated campus leader for student career development (NACE, 1997).

ORGANIZATIONAL MODELS

The advantages and disadvantages of various organizational models for career services have been the subject of numerous publications (Ash, 2002; Babbush, Hawley, & Zeran, 1986; Boynton, 1949; Casella, 1990; Chervenik, Nord, & Aldridge, 1982; Herr et al., 1993; Robb, 1979; Shea, 1995; Shingleton, 1978; Smith & Gast, 1998; Swaim, 1968; Wrenn, 1951). To determine the appropriate structure, organizational planners must analyze the institution's physical layout, its academic offerings, a demographic profile of the student body, and the types of employment solicited by recruiters visiting the campus (Babbush, Hawley, & Zeran, 1986). The three organizational models implemented most frequently are (1) a centralized program for the entire institution, (2) a decentralized program within colleges or schools within the institution, and (3) a combination program using centralized and decentralized approaches within a single institution (Herr, Raymond, & Garis, 1993).

> Regardless of the approach taken by an institution toward developing and delivering career services for students, or toward placing its organizational home in student affairs or academic affairs, the NACE standards stress a "centralized coordinated approach" at a minimum: "There should be a designated leader who will be responsible for developing collaborative efforts and cooperative strategies" (National Association of Colleges and Employers, 1997) (Smith & Gast, 1998).

Results of the 2000 *Career Services Survey* continued to support the trend toward centralized services and away from decentralized services. Of 927 directors, 90 percent indicated that coordination of services, programs, operations, budgets, staff, and records was physically and administratively centralized on their campus. Decentralized models were used by only 10 percent of the directors surveyed. The remaining 0.3 percent of respondents described themselves as having satellite offices (Nagle & Bohovich, 2000a).

Frequently cited advantages of the centralized model include more efficient use of human resources, office space, and equipment; lower administrative overhead; convenience for students and employers; greater emphasis on career planning; and better coordination of student employment, volunteer programs, internships, and cooperative education programs. A centralized service can offer students one-stop shopping for all career needs. "Student employment, co-ops, and internship programs attract students to the center in the earlier stages of their academic careers, to their obvious benefit" (Shea, 1995, p. 31). Career counselors in a centralized model are more likely to have continuous exposure to employers and can lend their counseling expertise to employment realities.

Employers prefer a centralized service because it helps them through the *academic maze* and facilitates their interests in full college relations—recruiting through co-ops, internships, and academic contacts (Shea, 1995). They can interview all majors at one location on campus, thereby reducing recruitment costs and expediting the process. "Criticisms of centralized career services also include inadequate attention to job development, lack of sufficient staff to ensure in-depth knowledge of academic programs and faculty expertise, and the perception that services are geared only toward students whose academic majors are currently in high demand in the workplace" (Smith & Gast, 1998, p. 206).

Advocates of the decentralized model base their opinion on the value derived by each specialty area on campus having their own career services and staff readily accessible. Advantages include higher levels of faculty involvement with employers, improved job development and fund-raising efforts, and heightened staff awareness of discipline-specific career opportunities. Negative outcomes are usually related to duplication of efforts, facilities, and staff; increased recruiting costs; and the fact that compartmentalization tends to deter students from pursuing a broad-based exploration of choices across academic disciplines.

There are many variations on the combination (centralized-decentralized) approach being chosen by some institutions to capture the best of both organizational structures. For instance, a centralized career services office may have career counselors located within specific academic units or residence halls. Some institutions with decentralized centers established to serve the placement needs of both students and employers for internship, cooperative education, and career positions may refer students with career exploration or development needs to a centralized counseling center. Another variation is a centralized service for undergraduate students with decentralized services for graduate or professional programs (e.g., law or MBA). "In the current customer service environment, centralized services frequently mean better response to the majority of employers who have multidisciplinary needs, provide comprehensive and consistent services to students, and create one-stop shopping for all customers" (Smith & Gast, 1998, p. 206).

TYPES OF SERVICES

Throughout its long history, career services professionals have provided students with a variety of services to help them during the process of choosing and working toward career goals. The National Association of Colleges and Employers, surveying Career Services Directors for the past 25 years, found support for these services in their latest survey (2000):

1. Career counseling (93%);
2. Occupational and employer information library (91%);
3. Placement of graduates into positions of full-time employment (91%);
4. Campus interviewing (88%);
5. Placement of students into summer and part-time employment (83%);
6. Placement of alumni (79%);
7. Cooperative education, internship, and other experiential programs (78%);
8. Resume referral (78%);
9. Internship programs (71%);
10. Computerized candidate databases (55%);

11. Credential services (53%);
12. Resume booklets (52%);
13. Placement of undergraduates into graduate school (51%);
14. Vocational testing (50%);
15. Career planning or employment readiness courses for credit (35%);
16. Cooperative education programs (34%);
17. Academic counseling (28%);
18. Career planning or employment readiness courses, not for credit (27%);
19. Dropout prevention and counseling (16%); and
20. Transfer of associate degree students to four-year institutions (12%).

Data from the 2000 survey reflected increases in service offerings with placement of students into summer and part-time employment, resume booklets, placement of undergraduates into graduate school, and placement of graduates into full-time employment expanding by more than 10 percent The only services that decreased were credential services, academic counseling, and dropout prevention and counseling, compared with the 1997 data.

While thorough discussion of each service is beyond the scope of this chapter, the following essential areas are described: (1) career counseling including computer-assisted guidance systems, career exploration groups, and career planning courses; (2) educational programs and services; (3) occupational and employer information library; (4) campus recruiting and other placement services, including job fairs and computerized resume referrals; and (5) cooperative education, internship, and other experiential programs.

CAREER COUNSELING

Long a mainstay of services offered, individual and group career counseling is still a major service provided to college students, regardless of age, academic major, or stage in career development. Career counseling is offered by 93 percent of the career centers responding to the *NACE Career Services Survey* (Nagle & Bohovich, 2000a). According to Zunker (2002),

> . . . career counseling has expanded its role and scope to include more than just helping someone find a job. Although finding an optimal career is of utmost importance, career counseling now includes a broad spectrum of concerns such as mental health issues that restrict career choice, changes in the workplace, meeting needs of workers in a competitive global economy, and how to restructure counseling procedures to better meet the needs of multicultural groups and other special populations. These issues and more involve the career counselor today. (p. 5) *Career counseling* includes all counseling activities associated with career choices over a life span. In the career counseling process, all aspects of individual needs (including family, work, and leisure) are recognized as integral parts of career decision making and planning (p. 9).

In a follow-up to a meta-analysis, Whiston, Sexton, and Lasoff (1998) "compared the effectiveness of various career interventions (e.g., workshops, career classes, computer programs, and individual counseling) and found that individual career counseling was the most effective" (in Whiston, 2000, p. 137).

Nationally, it is estimated that 77 percent of college freshmen and sophomores are in the process of deciding on an academic major (Rayman, 1993). Career exploration programs directed primarily at these audiences are common. Multiple-session, structured career decision-making groups are also offered, which introduce basic concepts of the career planning process; help students assess their occupational interests, values, aptitudes, skills, personality, and work and lifestyle preferences; identify and explore college majors; orient them to career information resources; and instruct them in decision-making skills. Informal career counseling groups often are used to discuss these same topics.

COMPUTER-ASSISTED CAREER
GUIDANCE SYSTEMS

Computer-assisted career guidance systems (CACGSs) have been used in college and university career services offices for the past 30 years. "CACGSs are defined as software packages or other computerized tools that people use to engage in tasks that mirror or complement those inherent in the career exploration process" (Iaccarino, 2000, p. 173). Another definition, offered by Niles and Harris-Bowlsbey (2002), states that a CACGS "is a group of activities, delivered by computer, designed to help with one or more steps of the career planning process" (p. 209).

In a national survey investigating the incidence and use of CACGSs, it was found that 67.3 percent of institutions had one or more. SIGI PLUS (30.0%), DISCOVER (25.4%), and Focus/Focus II (20.5%) were the most popular, with Choices also being used by approximately 9 percent of those surveyed (Nagle & Bohovich, 2000a).

These CACGSs contain interactive modules that serve two basic functions: (1) as resources for career and occupational information, and; (2) as tools for career decision making and exploration of alternatives (Gati, 1996; in Iaccarino, 2000, p. 174). Clients using CACGSs are more likely to seek individual career counseling and consult information resources in career libraries, thus becoming more involved in the career decision process (Garis & Bowlsbey, 1984). Niles and Garis (1990), studying the separate and combined effects of a computer-assisted guidance program with a career planning course, found that students who were in the course requiring use of SIGI PLUS obtained significantly lower scores on a measure of career indecision than students in the control group and those assigned to SIGI PLUS as a stand-alone intervention.

The National Career Development Association, National Board of Certified Counselors and the American Association for Counseling and Development developed standards calling for computer applications

> . . . to be appropriate to the client, and prescribe that the client understands the purpose and operation of the computer application and that there be follow-up, both to correct possible problems, such as misconceptions and inappropriate uses, and to assess subsequent needs (Howland & Palmer, 1992).

Computer technologies demonstrate many strengths in their uses in a career planning and development context. These strengths include test and inventory administration and interpretation, database searches, crosswalking (relating one database to another with ease), standard delivery, monitoring progress of the user through the career planning process, delivering instruction, and linking resources. Although this list seems impressive, we must keep in mind that "research designed to determine the best way to deliver career planning services has consistently indicated that the optimal treatment for students/clients is the combination of human support services and computer services" (Taber & Luzzo, 1999; in Niles & Harris-Bowlsbey, 2002, p. 213). We must remember that high touch must be added to the high tech.

CAREER AND LIFE PLANNING COURSES

Career and life planning courses for credit were offered by 35 percent of the career centers surveyed in the NACE study to assist undecided students in selecting a major or career path; courses not for credit were offered by 27 percent (Nagle & Bohovich, 2000a). In a study conducted by Halasz and Kempton (2000) in the summer and fall of 1998, of 40 career services offices, "a little more than two thirds of the respondents indicated that they offered some sort of career course for students at their institution" (p. 163). Theoretical bases for these courses included the work of Holland, Super, Krumboltz, Bandura, and Jung, although several of the respondents indicated they had "no real basis" for their career course. Three primary emphases were addressed: career decision making, career exploration, and job-search skills and strategies.

Although the vast majority of career centers offering career courses used self-assessment tools with students within their courses, most "did not use a standardized assessment of the effectiveness of their career courses outside of departmental and instructor evaluations. A small percentage mentioned efforts at gauging individual student career development through pre- and posttest administrations of inventories" (Halasz & Kempton, 2000, p. 165).

In addition to courses sponsored by the career center, career services staff can partner with academic departments in offering components of senior capstone courses.

In order for seniors to fully integrate their undergraduate experience, they must see its application and relevance to their immediate future. Integration can be assisted by introducing career components into capstone courses. The Chemistry Department at the University of Maryland has done just that. Chemistry 398 has members of the profession, faculty, and career center staff visiting the classroom to address issues such as career opportunities and employment trends, requirements for admission into graduate or professional school, industry applications of chemistry, innovative research in the field being conducted by faculty and private industry, and ethical issues in the form of case studies (Smith & Gast, 1998, p. 199).

EDUCATIONAL PROGRAMS AND SERVICES

Career services offices are uniquely positioned to assist students and alumni with educational programs, services, and linkages to the world of work through their partnerships with prospective employers, parents, and with faculty and staff in academic departments. Career services staff members are often the catalysts who serve as the bridge in helping students make the transition from educational environment to work environment by helping to connect those prospective employers with faculty. In doing so, Holton (1998) suggested that a comprehensive career services program should include:

- Structured partnerships with employers to identify key competencies;
- Workshops and seminars offered to students directly and through academic departments;
- Counseling for transition to work and work entry;
- Structured partnerships with academic departments to design and implement transition programs;
- Provision of access to employers (for faculty lacking organizational experience);
- Opportunities for seniors to receive mentoring from recent graduates;
- Resources to develop professional skills; and
- Strong co-op and intern programs (p. 109).

One example of faculty and business relationships is the partnership between management and marketing faculty at Kennesaw State University in Marietta, Georgia, and business leaders in both line and staff areas of corporate organizations. They have partnered to "research and identify first those behaviors and skills demonstrated by graduates that differentiate effective from less effective job performance and second how students could be exposed to and practice effective job-performance behavior while still in college" (Lasher and Brush, 1990; in Cuseo, 1998, p. 32).

Career services offices all across America are providing creative and innovative programs and services to assist students and alumni in all aspects of the career development, implementation, and management process. The NACE In Praise of Excellence Awards, which are given annually, highlight examples of outstanding programs. The 2001 NACE/Chevron Award was presented to the University of California–Berkeley for its *Web-based Employer Profile*, which assists employers in developing "a competitive, cost-effective on-campus branding strategy while providing a customized recruiting message to the job-seeking student body" (Bohovich, 2001, p. 27). The 2000 NACE/Chevron Award recognized the *Interviewing Skills Multimedia Web Site*, which was designed and launched in 1999 by the Career Development Services staff at Loyola Marymount University in Los Angeles. Albuquerque Technical Vocational Institute Community College was recognized in 2001 with the Multimedia Programs Award, another category of the Awards of Excellence program. The "Employment Skills Interactive CD-ROM helps students and alumni of Albuquerque Technical Vocational Institute Community College (TVI) conduct a job search; begin, advance, or relaunch their careers; and/or make a job or career change" (Bohovich, 2001, p. 30). The 2001 College Winner for Educational Programs was the University of Florida, for its *Cultural Diversity Reception*. Designed to provide students with a networking opportunity, this reception is attended by representatives of forward-thinking organizations recognizing the need to diversify their workplaces. Career services offices also offer educational programs and services targeted to specific student audiences, such as adult students; gay, lesbian, or bisexual students; international students; students with disabilities; and students from various ethnic or racial groups.

The importance of conducting a comprehensive needs assessment to determine program and service needs of the various constituent groups served by career services offices cannot be stressed too strongly. Although career development professionals offer expertise regarding intent and content, there are multiple processes and techniques from which to choose when designing appropriate interventions. By asking the people being served, appropriate instructional methods can be chosen to match with individual and group learning styles. When the student employment function at Bowling Green State University was moved under the umbrella of career services, for example, student employees and supervisors participated in focus group meetings and responded to a survey designed to collect data regarding information needed by those two groups to function effectively. Included were questions regarding content of training interventions, manuals, and web-based materials, as well as the desired process for assisting student employees and supervisors in learning the required information and skill sets.

Virtually every career center offers placement-related workshops to teach students job search strategies (including effective and efficient use of online sources), resume and cover letter writing, and interviewing techniques.

Frequently, alumni and employers are invited to campus to present information about trends in the employment market, career options, and career transition and management issues. Specialized workshops are often tailored to the student group by academic major, college, or degree level. An example of a targeted program is Bowling Green State University's *Multicultural Career Institute* (the 1997 NACE Award of Excellence in Educational Programming), a two-day conference during which sophomores and juniors participate in interactive sessions on workplace communication, dining etiquette, embracing diversity, networking, and job search skills for finding internships and cooperative education experiences.

OCCUPATIONAL AND EMPLOYER INFORMATION LIBRARIES

A comprehensive career library is an essential service to support the career information needs of the students served. The collection should include "videos, journals, books, assessment instruments, and a variety of kinds of software. . . . Especially given the growing importance of websites as providers of career data, the center needs to contain computers both for the use of locally resident software and for linkage to the Internet" (Niles & Harris-Bowlsbey, 2002, p. 200). Materials important to the career development process include: descriptions of workplace trends, job duties, working conditions, required education, professional development activities, advancement opportunities, and professional associations; assessments related to self-exploration, including interests, values, aptitudes, personality strengths, desired lifestyle, as well as decision-making skills; resources related to success in an educational environment, such as study skills, test preparation, and college and graduate school admission guidelines; resume writing, interviewing, and job search resources, including salary negotiation; directories of national businesses, nonprofit organizations, health care facilities providing information about services and products, with contact information to facilitate networking with prospective cooperative education, internship, and entry career employers; and resources to assist with relocation information.

The National Career Development Association, formerly the National Vocational Guidance Association, has established *Guidelines for the Preparation and Evaluation of Career and Occupational Information Literature* recommending criteria for selecting materials for career libraries. "The Association encourages the use of these Guidelines by publishers to ensure quality control in their publications and by those who select and use career occupational literature to ensure maximum value from their purchases" (NCDA, 2000, p. 1). Two annotated bibliographies that assist staff in selecting appropriate materials for their library are the *Vocational Careers Sourcebook* (Maurer & Savage, 2000) and *Career Transitions: The Best Resources to Help You Advance* (Goodenough, 1999).

Although a universal library classification system for career -related material has not been developed, many staff members organize their materials by using one of the following schemes: (1) stages of the career development process (self-assessment, career exploration, and placement); (2) the numerical system of the *Dictionary of Occupational Titles*, and (3) the general themes of the Strong Interest Inventory. Another method of organization offered by Niles and Harris-Bowlsbey (2002) is "(1) by type (print, video, software locally used, Internet access); (2) by content (self-information, occupational information, school information, financial aid information, etc.); (3) by step of the career planning process; or (4) by life role (student, worker, parent, leisurite, citizen, etc.)" (p. 201).

Career libraries are storing business directories and college catalogs on CD-ROM as well as directing students to appropriate web sites. Interactive computer software is also popular. The two most widely used computer-aided guidance systems are the Educational Testing Service's SIGI PLUS and American College Testing's Discover.

CAMPUS RECRUITING AND OTHER PLACEMENT SERVICES

On-campus recruiting has a long tradition at many colleges and universities and is perhaps the most visible program provided by career services, particularly for students majoring in business, engineering, science, and education. It offers students opportunities to interview with prospective employers from a wide variety of businesses, industries, nonprofit organizations, human service agencies, public schools, and government agencies.

Historically, Fortune 500 companies that routinely hired large numbers of recent graduates for entry-level positions and training programs have dominated on-campus recruitment programs. Always susceptible to economic ups and downs, in recent years on-campus recruiting has changed on many college campuses due, in part, to economic recessions, major restructuring occurring in business and industry, low unemployment, and expansion of military and government agencies fighting terrorism (post September 11, 2001). In the economy of the last decade, in which small businesses predominated, Pritchard and Fidler (1993) cited fewer than a quarter of the recruiters traveling to campus to represent small organizations, and this trend seems to be continuing into the beginning of the twenty-first century.

Traditionally, on-campus recruiting has been seen as an efficient and cost-effective method of bringing recruiters and student applicants together. In recent years, however, there has been considerable discussion regarding the viability of using the Internet and other electronic media in addition to or instead of campus recruiting. Seen by some as a less expensive option than campus visits, recruiting professionals are exploring the possibilities of using other media such as videoconferencing and software such as

NetMeeting to conduct screening interviews. They are also using their organization's web sites to provide information about career opportunities and available positions, information that was previously housed in individual career centers in notebooks containing promotional and recruiting brochures, annual reports, and so on. "According to a poll conducted by kforce.com, recruiters are willing to use technology as one of their hiring tools, but recognize that electronic communication isn't a replacement for personal interaction with candidates, e.g., a campus interview or job fair" (Allen, 2000, p. 32). From the candidate's perspective, "fully 99% of the survey respondents used the Internet to research companies during their job search, and the percentage who had applied for a job online increased to 83% (from 73% in a comparable survey conducted in 2000, and 20% in 1997)" (Scott, 1998).

Many techniques and strategies are available to recruiters wishing to build relationships with faculty, career services professionals, student leaders, and other key members of college and university communities. Among the strategies cited as being most useful by college relations representatives are: hosting informational sessions, presenting to or hosting corporate site visits for student organizations, making classroom presentations, and providing scholarships. "Given their efforts to gain a foothold on campus, it's not surprising that employers said image, or branding, was one of their top concerns. Asked which techniques were most effective for image building, survey respondents cited their corporate web site, print advertising, and campus information sessions" (Nagle & Bohovich, 2000b, p. 42).

The viability of on-campus recruiting appears to ebb and flow, depending on the state of the economy. James Burke, former manager of technical recruiting and university relations for Rohm and Haas, included the following recommendations for employers on maintaining a positive image during a difficult time: maintain a presence on campus, regardless of whether you are actively hiring; conduct telephone interviews if campus visits are beyond your budget; and "make internships available at schools where you can't recruit. . . . An experiential education program also is one of the most effective ways of maintaining positive campus connections when you can't offer permanent positions" (Bohovich, 2002, p. 27).

Through interactions with human resource professionals and managers interviewing on campus, career services staff and faculty learn about the market for their graduates, emerging career opportunities, and current economic issues facing business and industry. In turn, recruiters and managers gain insight about changes in today's college students and issues facing higher education.

An established on-campus recruiting program also influences other areas of the university. Frequently, a company's past success in hiring a university's graduates is used as justification for corporate gifts and grants to the institution. Prospective students and their parents often request lists of recruiters and placement statistics from admissions officials when choosing a college or university.

Despite the discussion in recent years about the decline in on-campus recruiting and the need for alternative methods of recruiting, employer respondents to the *NACE 2000 Employer Benchmark Survey* "overwhelmingly favored . . . building relationships with key college contacts and establishing a stronger presence on campus" (Nagle & Bohovich, 2000b, p. 40). The top five techniques used to hire technical talent are (1) offering internships and co-ops, (2) offering projects using cutting-edge technology, employee referrals, (3) sourcing through college career services offices, and (4) offering higher salaries than competitors.

The most well-known aspect of college recruiting is the on-campus interview process. Career centers employ many procedures for scheduling on-campus interviews. Often, employers are permitted to prescreen resumes and select candidates for half or all of their on-campus interviews. In the last several years, the traditional walk-in or "first-come, first-served" approaches and computerized bidding or lottery systems have given way to online scheduling systems that allow students to arrange interviews through a campus computer network.

Generally 30 minutes long, the on-campus interview is designed to help the recruiter gather information about the student's career goals, academic preparation, cocurricular activities, relevant work experiences, and job-related skills. A typical on-campus interview is segmented into a three-stage process: (1) planning, (2) conducting, and (3) evaluating. During the initial stage, prior to the actual interview, the interviewer decides which information from the student's resume will be explored, which criteria will be used to evaluate the student, and which questions will be asked of the student. During the conducting stage, once the student is comfortable in the interview situation, the recruiter explains the procedure and clarifies incomplete data from the resume. One of four interviewing techniques is used to gather needed information: (1) open-ended questions designed to encourage expansive responses, (2) asking closed-ended questions to limit responses, (3) using silence to allow the student the opportunity to formulate a response before sharing it, and (4) encouraging comments to help the student feel at ease and willing to respond freely and fully. During and after the interview, the recruiter evaluates the candidate's responses based on the criteria selected in the planning stage.

The top two qualities of an effective career center, identified by participants of a roundtable discussion sponsored by NACE, were customer service and a timely response to their requests. They also indicated they "seek out practitioners who know their students and are helpful in identifying contacts on campus, opportunities for campus presentations, and effective techniques for recruiting on their individual campuses. . . . They also consider the quality, diversity, and preparedness of candidates; the number of hires from a particular campus; and the retention rate for those hires" (Nagle & Bohovich, 2000b, p. 42). Career services professionals can attract and retain recruiters by providing efficient and responsive services, training their students well for interviews, monitoring interview schedules for compliance with employer requirements, helping recruiters develop relationships with faculty and student leaders, and assisting employers with diversity recruitment efforts.

CAREER DAYS AND JOB FAIRS

A central mission of career services is to facilitate student and employer contacts. Career days and job fairs enable students to gain valuable career information in an informal setting, make initial contact with employers, and in some cases, interview directly with many employers in a single location. Twenty-one percent of the respondents to the *NACE 2000 Employer Benchmark Survey* rated career days and fairs as the most effective strategy in attracting new college hires (Nagle & Bohovich, 2000b). Bowling Green State University's Teacher Job Fair is an example of a specialized fair where education candidates and alumni interview for available or anticipated teaching openings with school systems from across the country. An example of a consortium effort is the Toledo Collegiate Employ-Net Job Fair, offered by 18 colleges and universities in northwestern Ohio and southeastern Michigan to help their students find internship, part-time, summer, and full-time employment in the region. Career services offices often design career days that focus on academic programs or colleges not usually served by on-campus recruitment. Involvement of alumni and parents as speakers in career information programs is recommended.

COOPERATIVE EDUCATION AND INTERNSHIPS

Career services offices are increasingly being charged with coordinating the efforts to provide cooperative education and internship experiences for undergraduate students. The *NACE 2000 Career Services Survey* reported that 78.3 percent of respondents coordinate cooperative education, internship, and other experiential education programs for their campuses. This is up from 68.3 percent in 1993. A survey completed by the Cooperative Education and Internship Association reported that "in 2002, 44% of the respondents indicated that they reported to the academic side of the institution, 47% report to student affairs, and 9% report to another area, most commonly enrollment management. In 1998, 51% reported to the academic area and 30% reported to student affairs" (Cooperative Education and Internship Association, 2002).

An internship is a planned educational experience, approved by university officials, that provides students with practical work experience related to their major or career interest. Internships are usually one semester in duration, and the student earns academic credit or a grade for participating in the experience. They may be paid or unpaid. "Cooperative education is a structured educational strategy integrating classroom studies through productive work experiences in a field related to a student's academic or career goals" (Hutcheson, 1999, p. 22). Cooperative education experiences can be completed either parallel (concurrently) to a student's attending classes or can be experienced in alternating terms to a student completing courses on campus. Co-op students are paid during their work assignments.

The National Commission for Cooperative Education identified key elements for the Cooperative Education Model:

- Formal recognition by the school as an educational strategy
- A structure providing for multiple work experiences in formalized sequence with study
- Work experiences that include both an appropriate learning environment and productive work
- Work experiences that are related to career or academic goals
- Pre-employment preparation for students, as well as ongoing advising
- Formal recognition of the co-op experience on student records
- Agreement among the school, employer and the student on:
  - Job description and new learning opportunities
  - Specified minimum work periods
  - Monitoring of work by the school and supervision by the employer
  - Official school enrollment during employment
  - Employer recognition of student as an employee
  - Evaluations by student, school, and employer, with guided student reflection
  - Remuneration for student work
- Provision for employer and school evaluation of the quality and relevance of the work experience and curriculum
- Program design that maximizes outcomes for students, employers and the school (Hutcheson, 1999, p. 22)

As found in the *NACE 2001 Experiential Education Survey*, of the colleges and universities that have co-op programs, 34 percent require a co-op experience for graduation in one or more field of study. Some (5%) require a co-op for all majors. Of the institutions offering internships, 64 percent require them for graduation in one or more field of study, with 8 percent reporting that internships were required for most or all majors. The most frequently cited fields were business administration (46%), health care (41 %), and education (27%). (Gold, 2001 http://www.naceweb.org/pubs/spotlight/080101fp.htm

TECHNOLOGY IN CAREER SERVICES

The use of technology within career services has been developing at an accelerated pace since the mid-1980s. In 1984, fewer than 60 percent of career services directors responding to the College Placement Council's *Computer Usage Survey* reported using computers, while nearly 90 percent reported computer use in 1988 (Stewart, 1989). By the *1993 Career Services Survey*, 94 percent of directors used computers in their departments. The largest increase was in computerized student resume production, which was up 19 percent. Other uses of computers focusing primarily on students were career guidance/counseling (59%), candidate databases (45%), career planning (42%), and interview sign-up systems (23%). In addition, directors reported using computers for many clerical and administrative tasks (College Placement Council, 1994). Several authors reported success in automating various operational functions such as interview sign-up scheduling, vacancy notification, and electronic registration (Miller, 1994; Roth & Jones, 1991; Van De Weert & Baumgartner, 1992). By 1997, 86 percent of career centers surveyed by Behrens and Altman (1998) reported providing Internet access for student use; 75 percent used career guidance systems; 68 percent computerized job banks; 62 percent resume writing programs; 60 percent resume-job matching programs; 51 percent on-campus interviewing scheduling programs; and 39 percent video-distance interviewing.

Posed in the *2000 NACE Career Services Survey* were questions to career services professionals related to technology currently applied within their offices. The most popular technological device being used is the facsimile (fax) machine, which increased in use from 64.3 percent in 1991 to 97.3 percent in the year 2000, an increase of 33 percent. Next highest usage is the personal computer, with 94.2 percent (up from 89.3% in 1991) of career services offices utilizing them in 2000, closely followed by the use of the World Wide Web at 94 percent. Also used are VCRs, modems, and mainframe computers, at 78 percent, 41 percent, and 41 percent, respectively (Nagle & Bohovich, 2000a).

Another aspect of technology usage reported in the *2000 NACE Career Services Survey* was the preferred software for various functions. Just less than 70 percent of career centers use Career Exploration software, with SIGI/SIGI Plus used by 30 percent of the respondents, Discover by 25 percent, Focus/Focus II by 21 percent, and 9 percent using Choices. For candidate/recruitment management, 42 percent of offices indicated using one of three primary commercially available products: 21 percent have chosen 1st Place/ASI, 16 percent were using Career Connections/Resume Expert, and 14 percent were using Interview TRAK/JOBTRAK.com. Although used by a significant number of career centers in 2000, 1stPlace/ASI and Career Connections/Resume Expert were no longer available by the names indicated by 2002, due to their acquisition by Experience.

Other software programs used in career centers include appointment scheduling and office management, both by 37 percent; resume writing software being used by 34 percent; publishing software by 32 percent; graphics by 29 percent; and voice-activated software by 4 percent (Nagle & Bohovich, 2000a).

It has become increasingly important for career aervices professionals to embrace emerging technologies and teach students how to use them as career planning and management tools. The use of Computer-Assisted Career Guidance Systems by 68 percent of career centers surveyed by Nagle and Bohovich (2000) indicates the prevalence of technology to support career exploration and decision making. "A computer-assisted career guidance system (often called a CACGS) is a group of activities, delivered by computer, designed to help with one or more steps of the career planning process" (Niles & Harris-Bowlsbey, 2002, p. 209). There are multiple categorical systems used in the literature to describe CACGSs. One example, offered by Zunker (2002), differentiates with this description:

> The most common types of computer-assisted career guidance systems are information systems and guidance systems. Information systems provide users with direct access to large databases on such subject areas as occupational characteristics (work tasks, required abilities, work settings, salary) and lists of occupations, educational and training institutions, military information, and financial aid. Guidance systems are typically much broader in scope. They contain a variety of available modules, such as instruction in the career decision process, assessment, prediction of future success, assistance with planning, and development of strategies for future plans. Many computer-assisted career guidance systems contain an information system as well as a guidance system (p. 257).

Niles and Harris-Bowlsbey (2002) delineate three types of CACGS: Assessment Systems, Career Information Systems, and Career Planning Systems. Examples of Assessment Systems are the Strong Interest Inventory (http://www.cpp-db.com/products/strong/index.html), the Self-Directed Search (http://www.self-directed-search.com), and the Campbell Interest and Skill SurveyTM ((http://www.profiler.com/ciss). Career Information Systems include Choices (http://www.careerware.com) and Focus II (http://www/focuscareer.com). Two of the most widely used Career Planning Systems are SIGI-PLUS (http://www.ets.org/sigi) and Discover (http://www.act.org).

Several authors offer cautions and advantages of using CACGS. The cautions include ensuring confidentiality, appropriate measurement standards, counselor involvement in the selection and interpretation of instruments and online sites, and minimization of user anxiety. Advantages include active client involvement in the career planning process, immediate feedback leading to sustained client motivation, personalized career search strategies, 24/7 access from anywhere in the world where there is an

Internet connection, and access to large databases of information (Davidson, 2001; Iaccarino, 2000; Niles & Harris-Bowlsbey, 2002; and Zunker, 2002). The Ethics Committee of the National Career Development Association developed the Guidelines for the Use of the Internet for Provision of Career Information and Planning Services, which were approved in 1997. The standards address eight specific topics: (1) qualifications of developer or provider, (2) access and understanding of the environment, (3) content of career counseling and planning services on the Internet, (4) appropriateness of client for receipt of services via the Internet, (5) appropriate support to the client, (6) clarity of the contract with the client, (7) inclusion of linkages to other web sites, and (8) use of assessment instruments (NCDA, 1997).

Creating web sites has become a common practice of career services offices (88%, according to Nagle & Bohovich, 2000a) on many college and university campuses. Students may use the web sites to access information related to self-assessment, career exploration, career planning, and job searching. The most common features of career services web sites for student use include links to career-related sites (81%), career information online (69%), job postings online (60%), registration for students (48%), internship postings online (47%), and resume bank online (42%). Similar services are provided to alumni on these web sites as well. Employers use career services web sites for job postings online (49%), registration (41%), resume bank search online (34%), on-campus visit scheduling online (30%), and career or job fair registration online (20%).

Major advantages of having career services offices using the Internet to provide information to students, alumni, and employers are convenience for students; easy sorting and searching capabilities; ease of updating information as needed; reduction in paper resources; broad variety of information—assessment, resumes, job search in one place; links to other sites; reduction of repetitive tasks and freeing of staff time; and user autonomy and independence during the career development process (Davidson, 2001). Emerging areas under development include using campus portals for online surveys, just-in-time training, self-reflection journals, and electronic portfolios.

A myriad of web sites have been designed to assist practitioners and students with the entire process of career development. Examples are:

http://icdl.uncg.edu/—The International Career Development Library (ICDL) is a free, online collection of full-text resources for counselors, educators, workforce development personnel, and others providing career development services.

http://www.collegeart.org/caa/career/—The College Art Association's web site offers information about fellowships and scholarships, suggested conventions for curriculum vitae of those in the arts, and directories of academic programs in the arts.

http://www.jobweb.com/—The National Association of Colleges and Employers (NACE) site helps students find employers, learn to job search, offers an online career fair, assists with resume writing and interviewing techniques, and has links to career development, internships/co-ops, salary information, job market research, and after college.

http://www.jobweb.com/Career_Development/Default.htm—This NACE site supports career services for college freshmen, sophomores, and juniors.

http://www.ohiocareerdev.org/—Ohio's Career Development Program provides educational services to all 612 K–12 public school districts.

http://www.rileyguide.com/—The Riley Guide provides information about employment opportunities and job resources on the Internet. Links include a "What's New," updated frequently; Prepare for a Job Search; Resumes & Cover Letters; Targeting & Research Employers, etc.; Job Listings; Salary Guides & Guidance; and Networking, Interviewing, & Negotiating.

http://www.bls.gov/opub/ooq/2000/summer/art02.htm—The Occupational Outlook Quarterly Online, sponsored by the Bureau of Labor Statistics, offers practical information on jobs and careers.

http://www.bgsu.edu/offices/sa/career/—The Bowling Green State University career services web site offers information and links to sites related all aspects of the career planning and job hunting process.

http://www.careercc.com/interv3.shtml—The Career Consulting Corner offers tips on interviewing as well as links to information related to other facets of the career development, job hunting process.

http://www.career.fsu.edu—Florida State University's web site features a section for other career services professionals who want to learn about career development theory created at the university, develop career courses, design career activities, and use the web in career services delivery.

http://www.uncwil.edu/stuaff/career/Majors/—An excellent resource for exploring academic majors and careers is available on the University of North Carolina at Wilmington web site.

QUALIFICATIONS FOR CAREER SERVICES EMPLOYMENT

The profile of the career services director has changed since 1975 when the typical director was a white male in his mid-forties (Crouch & Tolle, 1982). The *1993 Career Services Survey* revealed that women held 58 percent of office directorships (College Placement Council, 1994). More than half of the directors were between 35 and 49 years of age and the vast majority

(89%) were Caucasian. According to the 2001 Career Services Survey, women hold 63 percent of career services directorships, and these directors are aging. In 2001, 40 percent were between the ages of 35 and 40, and 45 percent were 50 to 65 years of age. Approximately 91 percent are Caucasian, 5 percent are Black, and 3 percent are Hispanic. Directors have an average of 12 years of experience in a career services position and 7 years of experience as director. They are likely to hold at least a master's degree, typically in guidance and counseling or college student personnel (Nagle, 2001).

The director's role has become increasingly complex as demands for service from various constituent groups have expanded. Greenberg (2001) identified 18 skills, qualities, and attributes sought in career services directors, and in a survey of geographically and institutionally diverse directors, asked the directors to rate them as most important (3), very important (2), or somewhat important (1). Those scoring at least 1.81 were interpersonal skills, management skills, problem solving, organizational skills, ethics, writing skills, teaching/presentation skills, computer knowledge, counseling skills, and flexibility. "The results of the survey reflect the wide range of skills, qualities, and attributes valued by and in career services directors" (p. 47). Although one might expect campus size of to account for significant differences in attributes sought in a director, an analysis of the responses revealed only minor variations:

- Directors of large programs (serving more than 15,000 students) viewed ethics, commitment to the profession, and finance skills to be of greater importance than counseling skills.
- Directors of mid-sized programs (serving 3,000 to 14,999 students) cited flexibility, creativity/imagination, and team player as more important than writing skills and computer knowledge.
- Directors of small programs (serving fewer than 3,000 students) regarded writing and counseling as more important than management and finance skills. (p. 47)

As career centers have become increasingly sophisticated in the use of computer technology, directors face complex decisions about which database management systems, hardware, local area networks, and software to purchase and/or update. To supplement shrinking budgets, many directors solicit donations from corporations and foundations and funding from other outside agencies.

Other staff members in career services are usually categorized by functional area. An associate or assistant director and placement advisors have primary responsibilities to manage placement-related services, including on-campus recruitment, referrals, workshops, seminars, career days and job fairs, placement advising, and to serve as liaisons with assigned faculty or departments. Job developers and co-op or internship coordinators advise students on experiential education opportunities, develop new sites, and maintain relationships with faculty and employers. Associate or assistant directors and career counselors often conduct individual and group counseling sessions, administer and interpret vocational assessments, teach career and life planning courses for credit, supervise graduate interns and instructors, and deliver a wide range of career decision-making programs. Many career services offices have hired information specialists and/or systems analysts to design customized programs, evaluate commercially available software, and integrate information systems as well as train staff members and users of the services in new applications and emerging technologies.

Skills used by staff include project management, marketing, counseling, public speaking, writing, program evaluation, research, teaching, and information management. According to the Greenberg (2001) survey of career services directors, career services practitioners are likely to:

- Reach far outside of their functional area to build relationships with faculty, employers, students, and others.
- Get outside the "ivory tower" to stay on top of issues that affect their clients, including the changing needs of employers who recruit new college graduates.
- Apply and enhance their technical skills to deliver services and/or communicate with their constituents.
- Teach, advise, and mentor students. . . .
- Benchmark and maintain relationships with their colleagues. . . .
- Exercise their creativity and imagination. . . .
- Manage relatively complex operations that entail hiring, evaluating, and training employees; overseeing the delivery of a wide range of services; and continually doing more despite shrinking budgets.
- Multi-task. . . .
- Face new and exciting challenges that, ultimately, contribute to long-term career satisfaction. Many practitioners hold the same positions for 20 or more years without ever feeling that they would rather have their boss' job (p. 50).

Although it is obviously a career individuals seem to enjoy, "career services remains a field that many professionals fall into, rather than plan to enter. . . . Citing the importance of actively recruiting young professionals to the field, a number of responding practitioners offered recommendations on how to fill the ranks" (Greenberg, 2001, pp. 50, 52). Included in their suggestions were using graduate assistantships as a way of bringing people into the profession, providing ample opportunities for peer mentors and interns to receive professional development and training, advising students about opportunities in this field, building relationships with student leaders on campus, educating corporate and government recruiters about career services positions, establishing relationships with graduate students in college student personnel and counseling psychology programs, hiring doctoral candidates as graduate assistants or working with them on their research, and promoting from within the career services organization as nonexempt employees complete degrees.

ENTRY-LEVEL QUALIFICATIONS

The minimum educational requirement for an entry-level career services position is usually a master's degree in college student personnel administration, guidance and counseling, clinical or counseling psychology, business, or education. Prior full-time work experience and career counseling and placement advising skills; teaching, presentation, and facilitation skills; and technological literacy are also required. New professionals responsible for career counseling, vocational assessment, and teaching career decision-making courses are advised to obtain counselor certification and licensure. Knowledge of occupational and employment trends, career information resources and systems, program design and evaluation, and process consultation are also helpful.

PROFESSIONAL ASSOCIATIONS

There are three professional associations with which many practitioners in career services are actively involved, depending on the role and mission of their particular department.

THE NATIONAL ASSOCIATION OF COLLEGES AND EMPLOYERS

The first professional association devoted to placement in the United States was established in 1924 as the National Association of Appointment Secretaries, an application of the British concept of appointment secretary to the American function of placement director (Herr; Rayman, & Garis, 1993). In 1940, President Thomas Gates of the University of Pennsylvania and chair of the Committee on Educational Cooperation of the Governor's Job Mobilization Program established the Pennsylvania Association of School and College Placement (Sinnott, Beebe, & Collins, 1990). Within a year, the state's name was dropped and the journal *School and College Placement* was published. In 1952, it became the *Journal of College Placement* and today is the *Journal of Career Planning and Employment*. The earlier national College Placement Council in 1995 became the National Association of Colleges and Employers (NACE). A report entitled the *New Organizational Structure for the Profession* (NACE, Special Report from the Presidents, April, 1994) outlined the principal roles and responsibilities for the national organization, whose primary role was to advocate for the profession and provide a national and international voice.

The current vision of NACE is to be the world's premier association linking organizations engaged in the career development and employment of the college educated. The association serves its more than 4,000 members by providing "meaningful networking opportunities; key benchmarking; relevant research; ethical guidelines and standards for best practices; state-of-the-art professional development, training, education; and value-added services and information" (NACE, 2001).

The creation of regional associations can be traced through the expansion of placement services throughout the United States and by efforts of professionals to improve the coordination of placement activities and planning. In 1926, five charter members of the Eastern College Placement Officers (ECPO) sought to facilitate "professional improvements for the members through an interchange of information on common problems" (Powell & Kirts, 1980; Stephens, 1970). The other regional associations and their dates of establishment are the Rocky Mountain and Southern College Placement Associations in 1946, the Middle Atlantic Placement Association in 1948, and the Southeast and the Midwest College Placement Associations in 1950. The last regional association to be formed was the Western College Placement Association, which was chartered in 1951. Reflecting the name change of the national association, most of the regional associations began modifying their names in 1995 to include Association of Colleges and Employers in the titles. The principal role of the regional associations is to provide professional development services to their members, which enables them to access quality workshops and seminars, attend regional conferences, obtain leadership training for association volunteers, and participate in regional networking events (NACE, Special Report: From the Presidents, April, 1994).

On September 1, 2001, a Statement of Cooperation was approved and implemented by the presidents of the seven regional professional associations. It states:

As separate and autonomous organizations, we are committed to "bridging education and the world of work" and agree to support and cooperate with each other in achieving mutual goals and objectives. With the intent to enhance relationships and increase communication across our organizations, we will cooperate in the following areas (this list is not meant to be exhaustive and will change as our organizations advance and evolve):

- Benchmarking and communicating information
- Coordinating calendar of events
- Sharing resources and talent
- Providing value-added services and professional development opportunities

(Rocky Mountain Association of Colleges and Employers, 2002)

Responding to the need for expanded member services, NACE launched JobWeb, a home page on the World Wide Web. Through JobWeb, members could access employer information and literature, search bibliographic databases, consult a calendar of professional events, participate in discussion groups, read professional journals, and order materials online (Allen, 1995). Now called NACEWEB, it also connects members to other home page sites on the Internet, enables them to place or read current job listings, taps into a virtual library of career information and job search resources, and accesses videoconferencing. Regional organizations have also developed home page sites.

The National Career Development Association

A division of the American Counseling Association, the mission of the National Career Development Association (NCDA) is to

Promote the career development of all people over the life span. To achieve this mission, NCDA provides service to the public and professionals involved with or interested in career development, including professional development activities, publications, research, public information, professional standards, advocacy, and recognition for achievement and service (NCDA, 2002).

The Cooperative Education and Internship Association

Founded in 1963, the original mission of the Cooperative Education & Internship Association (CEIA) was "To provide professional development and resources to the field of cooperative education" (CEIA, 2002b). Its members are professionals from colleges, universities, and business and industry. The CEIA currently has four key areas to which it is dedicated:

- Promoting cooperative education and internships as premier models of work-integrated learning;
- Providing professionals with opportunities to enhance skills;
- Offering state-of-the-art resources and information; and
- Advancing the field through research and programs (CEIA, 2002b).

CHALLENGES FACING PROFESSIONALS

The work of career services professionals has become increasingly complex. Much has been written about the current and future challenges facing career services (for an in-depth discussion, see Bechtel, 1993; Heppner & Johnston, 1993; Herr, Rayman, & Garis, 1993; Niles & Harris-Bowlsbey, 2002; Rayman, 1999; Stewart, 1993; Wessel, 1998; and Yerian, 1993). Numerous issues are currently of pressing concern:

1. Meeting the career development needs of diverse groups of students in a time of diminishing resources;

2. Responding to increasing demands from alumni for counseling services for midlife career and job changes;

3. Integrating new service imperatives such as student employment, internships, cooperative education, and other forms of experiential education in the design of a comprehensive career services delivery model;

4. Employing emerging technologies to achieve greater efficiency and effectiveness in operations by creating new learning systems and computerized assessment instruments, communicating the availability of job opportunities to graduates, and nominating candidates to employers;

5. Assuring that the materials designed and delivered via electronic media meet rigorous standards set by our profession through the collaboration of our professional organizations and instructional and web designers;

6. Procuring "significant funding to support research and development related to methods where counselors can effectively provide support to individuals via the Internet as they engage in career planning" (Harris-Bowlsbey, 2000);

7. Becoming more aware of the wide range of ethical issues related to the use of technology in counseling and career development environments,

8. Developing new methods to evaluate services and assess their impact on student learning;

9. Communicating more effectively the role of career services within the overall mission of the college or university;

10. Developing cooperative efforts with other internal and external groups (i.e., faculty, academic advisors, other functional areas within student affairs and employers); and

11. Becoming more integrally involved in institutional initiatives that are aligned with the academic missions of our institutions.

REFERENCES

Allen, C. (2000). Technology. *Journal of Career Planning and Employment, 60(4)*, 31–32, 35.

Allen, C. (1995). JobWeb: Welcome to our virtual office. *Journal of Career Planning and Employment, 55(3)*, 6–8, 58.

Ash, K. (2002). Team management of career services in a decentralized environment. *Journal of Career Planning and Employment, 62(4)*, 37–40.

Aviles, C. B. (2001). Survey brings together—and benefits—student and academic affairs. *Journal of Career Planning and Employment, 61(4)*, 45–48.

Babbush, H. E., Hawley, W. W., & Zeran, J. (1986). The best of both worlds. *Journal of Career Planning and Employment, 16(3)*, 48–53.

Bechtel, D. S. (1993). The organization and impact of career programs and services within higher education. In J.R. Rayman (Ed.), *The changing role of career services* (pp. 23–36). San Francisco: Jossey-Bass.

Behrens, T., & Altman, B. (1998). Technology: Impact on and implications for college career centers. *Journal of Career Planning and Employment, 58(1)*, 48–55.

Blaska, B., & Schmidt, M. R. (1977). Placement. In W. T. Packwood (Ed.), *College student personnel services* (pp. 368–421). Springfield, IL: Charles C Thomas.

Bohovich, J. (2001). 2001 awards. J*ournal of Career Planning and Employment (62)1*, 25–32.

Bohovich, J. (2002). Making a case for college relations. *Journal of Career Planning and Employment (62)1*, 25–32.

Boynton, P. W. (1949). *Selecting the new employee.* New York: Harper.

Brewer, J. (1942). *History of vocational guidance* (p. 61). New York: Harper.

Casella, D. A. (1990). Career networking: The newest career center paradigm. *Journal of Career Planning and Employment, 50(3)*, 33–39

Chervenik, E., Nord, D., & Aldridge, M. (1982). Putting career planning and placement together. *Journal of College Placement, 42*, 48–51.

College Placement Council. (1994). *1993 Career services survey.* Bethlehem, PA.

Cooperative Education and Internship Association. (2002a). *2002 Survey of Internship/Co-op Professionals in Higher Education.* Available: http://www.ceainc.org/research/CEIASurveyRpt.htm

Cooperative Education and Internship Association. (2002b). About CEIA. Available: http://www.ceainc.org/about/about.htm

Council for the Advancement of Standards in Higher Education. (2001). *The book of professional standards for higher education* (2nd rev. ed.). Washington, DC: CAS.

Crouch, L. R., & Tolle, D. J. (1982). The placement director of the '80's: A profile. *Journal of College Placement, 42*, 43–46.

Cuseo, J. B. (1998). Objectives and benefits of senior year programs. In J. N. Gardner, G. Van der Veer, & Associates, *The senior year experience: Facilitating integration, reflection, closure, and transition* (pp. 21–36). San Francisco: Jossey-Bass.

Davidson, M. M. (2001). The computerization of career services: Critical issues to consider. *Journal of Career Development, (27)3*, 217–228.

DeBell, C. (2001). Ninety years in the world of work in America. *The Career Development Quarterly, 50(1)*, 77–88.

Ebel, R. L., Noll, V. H., & Bauer, R. (1969). *Encyclopedia of educational research.* London: Macmillan.

Freeman, J. (1994). *A vision for the college placement center systems, paradigms, processes, people.* Westport, CT: Praeger.

Gardner, P. D., & Liu, W. Y. (1997). Prepared to perform? Employers rate work force readiness of new grads. *Journal of Career Planning and Employment, 57(3)*, 32–56.

Garis, J. W., & Bowlsbey, J. H. (1984). DISCOVER and the counselor: Their effects upon college student career planning progress. *ACT Research Report, 85.2* (Ed.), Student development on the small campus (pp. 92–126). National Association of Personnel Workers.

Gold, M. (2001). Colleges, Employers Report on Experiential Education. *Spotlight, (24)* 2. Bethlehem, PA: National Association of Colleges and Employers. Available: http://www.naceweb.org/pubs/spotlight/080101fp.htm

Goodenough, D. (Ed.). (1999). *Career transitions: The best resources to help you advance.* Seattle, WA: Resource Pathways.

Greenberg, R. (2001). In search of career professionals. *Journal of Career Planning and Employment, 61(3).* 45–48, 50, 52.

Halasz, T. J., & Kempton, C. B. (2000). Career planning workshops and courses. In D. A. Luzzo (Ed.). *Career counseling of college students: An empirical guide to strategies that work* (pp. 157–172). Washington, DC: American Psychological Association.

Harris-Bowlsbey, J. (2000). *Career development and the future.* Available: http://icdl.uncg.edu/ft/080800-02.html

Heppner, M. J., & Johnston, J. A. (1993). Career counseling: A call to action. In J. R. Rayman (Ed.), *The changing role of career services* (pp. 57–78). New Directions for Student Services. San Francisco: Jossey-Bass.

Herr, E. L., & Cramer, S. H. (1992). *Career guidance and counseling through the life span: Systematic approaches* (4th ed.) New York: HarperCollins.

Herr, E. L., Rayman, J. R., & Garis, J. W. (1993). *Handbook for the college and university career center.* Westport, CT: Greenwood Press.

Holton, E. F. III (1998). Preparing students for life beyond the classroom. In J. N. Gardner, G. Van der Veer, & Associates, *The senior year experience:Ffacilitating integration, reflection, closure, and transition* (pp. 95–115). San Francisco: Jossey-Bass.

Howland, P., & Palmer, R. (1992). Ethics and computer guidance: Uneasy partners? *Journal of Career Planning and Employment, 52(4),* pp. 38–45.

Hutcheson, P. (1999). *Educating a globally productive citizenry: The role of higher education in the integration of learning and work.* Boston, MA: National Commission for Cooperative Education.

Iaccarino, G. (2000). Computer-assisted career-guidance systems. In D. A. Luzzo (Ed.)., *Career counseling of college students: An empirical guide to strategies that work* (pp. 173–190). Washington, DC: American Psychological Association.

Korvas, T. F. (1994). Factors influencing program development in career planning and placement centers. Unpublished dissertation, University of Toledo.

Maurer, C., & Savage, K. M. (Eds.). (2000). *Vocational careers sourcebook : Where to find help planning careers in skilled, trade, and nontechnical vocations.* Detroit, MI: Gale Group.

Merriam, S. B., & Caffarella, R. S. (1999). *Learning in adulthood: A comprehensive guide.* San Francisco: Jossey-Bass.

Miller, S. J. (1994). Career planning and placement programs. In J. L. Baier & T. S. Strong (Eds.), *Technology in student affairs: Issues, applications and trends* (pp. 135–145). Lanham, MD: American College Personnel Association.

Nagle, R. (2001). Facilities, finances, and staffing: Key findings from NACE's 2001 Career Services Survey. *Journal of Career Planning and Employment, 61(4),* 21–26.

Nagle, R., & Bohovich, J. (2000a). Career services in the year 2000. *Journal of Career Planning and Employment, 60(4),* 41–47.

Nagle, R., & Bohovich, J. (2000b). College recruiting in the 21st century: Competitive job market has employers rethinking and retooling their hiring strategies. *Journal of Career Planning and Employment, 61(1),* 36–40, 42.

National Association of Colleges and Employers. (2002). Vision, Mission, Value, Customers. Available: http://www.naceweb.org/about/mission.html

National Association of Colleges and Employers. (2001). Statement of Cooperation: Associations of Colleges and Employers. Available: http://www.naceweb.org/about/region/cooperation.htm

National Association of Colleges and Employers. (1997, January). Professional standards for college and university career services. Working draft 3. Bethlehem, PA: National Association of Colleges and Employers.

National Association of Colleges and Employers. (1994). *Special report: From the presidents.* Bethlehem, PA: Author.

National Career Development Association. (2002). About NCDA. Available: http://ncda.org/index.html

National Career Development Association. (1997). Career counseling competencies: Revised 1997. Available: http://icdl.uncg.edu/ft/051399-04.html

National Career Development Association. (2000). Guidelines for the preparation and evaluation of career and occupational information literature. Available: http://icdl.uncg.edu/ft/061200-17.html, 12-17-01.

Niles, S., & Garis, J. W. (1990).The effects of a career planning course and a computer-assisted career guidance program (SIGI PLUS) on undecided university students. *Journal of Career Development, 17(4),* 237–247.

Niles, S. G., & Harris-Bowlsbey, J. (2002). *Career development interventions in the 21st century.* Upper Saddle River, NJ: Merrill Prentice-Hall.

O'Brien, K. M. (2001). The legacy of Parsons: Career counselors and vocational psychologists as agents of social change. *Career Development Quarterly, 50(1),* 66–76.

Parsons, E. (1909). *Choosing a vocation.* Boston, MA: Houghton Mifflin.

Patterson, V. (1996). Industry and education collaborate to shape future workers. *Journal of Career Planning and Employment, 56(2),* 28–32.

Powell, C. R., & Kirts, D. K. (1980). *Career services today.* Bethlehem, PA: College Placement Council.

Rayman, J. R. (1999). Career services imperatives for the next millennium. *Career Development Quarterly (48)2,* 175–184.

Rayman, J. R. (Ed.). (1993). *The changing role of career services.* San Francisco: Jossey-Bass.

Reardon, R., Lenz, J., & Folsom, B. (1998). Employer ratings of student participation in non-classroom-based activities: Findings from a campus survey. *Journal of Career Planning and Employment, 58(4),* 36–39.

Robb, F. C. (1971). The three P's: Preparation, placement, performance. *Journal of College Placement, 31,* 31.

Robb, W. D. (1979). Counseling—placement, must they be separate entities? *Journal of College Placement, 39,* 67–71.

Rocky Mountain Association of Colleges and Employers. (2002). Available: http://www.rmace.org/

Roth, M. J., & Jones, D. A. (1991). Expanding career services via the campus-wide computer network. *Journal of Career Planning and Employment, 51(4),* 32–45.

Ryan, R. (1996). Shaping alumni careers. *Journal of Career Planning and Employment, 56(4),* 45–48.

Scott, M. E. (1998). A case for college relations and recruitment. *Journal of Career Planning and Employment, 59(1),* 40–42, 44.

Shea, D. D. (1995). Merging career and ex ed centers: A perspective. *Journal of Career Planning and Employment, 55(2),* 29–35.

Shingleton, J. D. (1978). The three R's of placement. *Journal of College Placement, 38,* 33–38.

Sinnott, P. A., Beebe, W. B., & Collins, M. (1990). You're reading Vol. L1, No. 1 of a good, 50-year-old idea. *Journal of Career Planning and Employment, 51(1)*, 26–31.

Smith, D. D., & Gast, L. K. (1998). Comprehensive career services for seniors. In J. N. Gardner, G. Van der Veer, & Associates (Eds.), *The senior year experience: Facilitating integration, reflection, closure, and transition* (pp. 187–209). San Francisco: Jossey-Bass.

Stephens, E. W. (1970). *Career counseling and placement in higher education: A student personnel function.* Bethlehem, PA: College Placement Council.

Stewart, R. A. (1989). The use of computers in career planning, placement, and recruitment. *Journal of Career Planning and Employment, 49(3)*, 51–53.

Stewart, R. A. (1993). Placement services. In J. R. Rayman (Ed.), *The changing role of career services* (pp. 37–54). San Francisco: Jossey-Bass.

Swaim, R. (1968). Centralization or decentralization: Two approaches to placement receive an up-to-date review. *Journal of College Placement, 28(3)*, 117–128.

Van De Weert, P. K., & Baumgartner, D. (1992). Computerizing the career services office for total management. *Journal of Career Planning and Employment, 52(3)*, 25–27.

Weber, D. W. (1982). *The status of career planning and placement.* Bethlehem, PA: College Placement Council.

Wessel, R. D. (1998). Career centers and career development professionals of the 1990s. *Journal of Career Development (24)3*, 163–177.

Whiston, S. C. (2000). Individual career counseling. In D. A. Luzzo (Ed.)., *Career counseling of college students: An empirical guide to strategies that work* (pp. 137–156). Washington, DC: American Psychological Association.

Wrenn, C. G. (1951). *Student personnel work in college.* New York: Ronald.

Yerian, J. M. (1993). Career programming in a contemporary context. In J. R. Rayman (Ed.), *The changing role of career services* (pp. 79–100). San Francisco: Jossey-Bass.

Zunker, V.G. (2002). *Career counseling: Applied concepts of life planning* (6th ed.). Pacific Grove, CA: Wadsworth.

Zytowski, D. G. (2001). Frank Parsons and the progressive movement. *Career Development Quarterly, 50(1)*, 57–65.

Chapter 6

COUNSELING CENTERS

Irvin W. Brandel and Elizabeth Yarris

INTRODUCTION

Counseling centers have long been an enigmatic operation within the student affairs field. Most student affairs professionals see counseling as an important part of their professional tools, and, in fact, counseling has been identified as the generic service of student personnel work (Williamson, 1961). Many faculty members, especially those who enjoy personal contact with students, profess to counsel students. It has been this way for as long as we have had knowledge of the American college. (Hopkins, 1926, p. 27, as cited in Williamson, 1961). Even in our society at large, the term *counseling* has been applied to the practice of law, medicine, finance, and countless other fields. Additionally, although there are some basic commonalities, counseling centers can be as different in form and function as the institutions that they serve (Stone & Archer, 1990). It is not surprising, then, that the role of the counseling center may seem vague to many members of the campus community, even those in the student affairs field. This chapter is designed to reduce the mystery and illuminate the reader on the nature of counseling centers.

HISTORY

The earliest college counselors, perhaps more accurately called advisors, were college faculty members and presidents (Gibson et al., 1983). The first formal recognition that institutions of higher education had the obligation to provide a specifically designated "counseling service" for students may have been the appointments of a "Chief of Advisors" at Johns Hopkins University in 1889 and a "Dean of Student Relations" at Harvard in 1890 (Gibson et al., 1983). A variety of influences led to the need for more specialized "counselors" and these were the student personnel workers of the late nineteenth and early twentieth centuries (Davis & Humphrey, 2000).

144

Colleges and universities had expanded in both number and type. The development of land grant colleges, the elective curriculum, and a renewed emphasis on technological and scientific education presented American educators and their students with new challenges. The college and university environments were ripe for developments that addressed both the personal and the academic needs of their students.

Three major events coincided to establish the first centers of professionally trained counselors. The first of these events was the development of psychometrics during World War I (Schneider, 1977). The second event was the 1909 publication of Clifford Beers's *A Mind that Found Itself*, which is cited as the beginning of the mental hygiene movement with attention to both the prevention and the cure of less serious, as well as more serious, emotional difficulties (Tyler, 1969). The third event was Frank Parsons's 1906 publication of *Choosing a Vocation*, in which he proposed a model of counseling that focused on the need for helping young people to find suitable places in the world of work (Tyler, 1969). The convergence of these three events led to the appearance of the earliest counseling centers on a few college campuses after World War I. They also led to the rise of the counseling profession and to a counseling center specialty area within student personnel work (Berk, 1983; Hedahl, 1978; Tyler, 1969).

These three threads can be seen throughout the historical development of counseling centers, and even in the centers of today, as weaving together the fabric of three essential functions of counseling: to measure and assess, to facilitate wise choices and decisions, and to promote adjustment or mental health (Tyler, 1969). While student mental hygiene clinics were created at Princeton University, the University of Wisconsin, Washburn College, the U.S. Military Academy, Dartmouth College, Vassar College, and Yale University between 1910 and 1925 (Farnsworth, 1957, cited in Davis & Humphrey, 2000), the earliest separate unit organized to offer professional educational and vocational guidance appears to be the University Testing Bureau, which was established in 1932 at the University of Minnesota (Hedahl, 1978). The service emphases of this unit were psychometrics and facilitation of vocational choice. Most colleges had no professional counselors on campus at this time.

After World War II, the Veterans Administration (VA) funded guidance bureaus to monitor the large population of veterans who were attending college with government subsidies. These efforts were aimed primarily at vocational and psychological assessment of the returning veterans. As the numbers of veterans on campus declined, the VA left the campuses and many colleges and universities took over the budgetary and administrative support of what became the forerunners of the modern counseling center.

The years from 1945 to 1955 were ones of "transition and professionalism" (Heppner & Neal, 1983). Just as the VA was pulling out of the college counseling business, the field of psychology was experiencing the development of counseling psychology as a speciality area within the American Psychological Association. If a counseling psychology faculty existed on campus, they typically were involved in the further growth of the counseling center (McKinley, 1980). Also, in the early 1950s, counseling center directors began to meet annually to discuss mutual problems and concerns.

Some of the growth and development during this period and into the 1960s paralleled changes within the field of counseling psychology (Whitely, 1984), which is a trend that continued into the 1990s (Sprinthall, 1990; Tyler, 1992). Now the third thread, the attention to personal adjustment and mental health, began to emerge as a major emphasis in many centers during this period. The field of counseling psychology and counseling centers themselves began a trend away from exclusively vocational guidance to a broader, developmental form of personal counseling (Berk, 1983).

The decade from 1960 to 1970 was a time of social unrest, student activism and idealism, "encounter groups," and draft counseling. For college and university counseling centers, it was a time of expansion and consolidation (Heppner & Neal, 1983; Lamb et al., 1983). However, the call for universities to be more responsive to social concerns led administrators to ask counseling services to be more relevant to the goals of higher education, and to do it with lower budgets (Forman, 1977). Expectations of centers expanded to include outreach, consultation, and crisis intervention. An emphasis on preventive, developmental activities was gaining momentum in many centers. Even from within the profession (Warnath, 1971, 1973), criticism was leveled at counseling centers that were practicing in a medical model, viewing the student as "sick" and "in need of treatment," and serving only a small select group of students in long-term counseling and psychotherapy. While this perspective did have its adherents, they were being more openly questioned and challenged. The decade ended dramatically and tragically, as in May 1970, four students were killed by National Guard troops on the campus of Kent State University, and two students were killed by police on the campus of Jackson State University. These events caused everyone involved in higher education to reexamine priorities and policies, and counseling centers were no exception.

The 1970s were a period of reassessment of the role of counseling centers (Lamb et al., 1983). Fortunately for the field, groundwork had already begun for constructive change. In 1968, Morrill, Ivey, and Oetting (cited in McKinley, 1980) provided a major stimulus for change in function by proposing that the counseling center become a center for student development that would (1) move out into the campus to create programs to prevent problems, (2) mobilize community resources for mental health, and (3) redefine the counseling center role within a developmental framework (McKinley, 1980). This important work legitimized for many centers the movement to a more developmental theoretical model. A task force of counseling center directors kept the momentum in this direction by developing guidelines (Kirk et al., 1971), which distinguished between remedial services and preventive or developmental services.

This distinction among services and the concept of a human development center came into clearer focus through a conceptual scheme called the "cube" (Morrill, Oetting, & Hurst, 1974). The "cube" was a model for organizing the expanding role of counselors' specified targets (individual, primary group, associational group, and institution or community); purposes (remedial, preventive, or developmental); and methods (direct, consultation and training, or media) for intervention on a college campus (McKinley, 1980). It was also in the 1970s that the related concept of "campus ecology" emerged. This concept emphasized the interrelationship between students and their environment. College and university counselors were encouraged to see the campus environment as the client and to participate in campus environmental change (e.g., Aulepp & Delworth, 1976; Conyne et al., 1979).

Additional influences toward redesigning the role of counseling services during the 1970s were the counseling center directors themselves, external accrediting bodies, and professional organizations (Lamb et al., 1983). Finally, legal requirements for licensing or certification of psychologists, social workers, and counselors affected the changing role of counseling centers in the 1970s.

By the 1980s, counseling centers were functioning in broader and more comprehensive roles (Heppner & Neal, 1983). At most campuses, they were established as important members of the student affairs team. However, throughout the 1980s and continuing into the 1990s, many campuses were dealing with two major phenomena. The first of these was declining enrollment and the correlating decrease in resources, and the second was an increase in student demand for psychological services and an accompanying increase in the perceived severity of student problems (Gallagher et al., 1995; Gallagher et al., 2001). It was a time of "doing more with less." The centers of the 1980s and 1990s also began to vary in design from campus to campus. At some campuses, services such as testing, career counseling, and training were part of the mission of the counseling center, while at other campuses these services were shared with or assigned altogether to another office. (Stone & Archer, 1990) In particular, these decades saw many placement offices assume much of the traditional career assessment and career counseling that was once the exclusive responsibility of counseling centers.

Adding to the pressures and challenges for counseling centers in these decades were worries about managed health care, mergers, and outsourcing (Gallagher et al., 1995–2001; Whitaker, 1997; Widseth et al., 1997). The dominant theme was the growing insufficiency of funding for higher education, and college and university administrators focused considerable energy on ways to conserve resources. Managed health care represented a potential way to limit the expenses of campus health services and counseling centers. Likewise, mergers of student affairs offices were another administrative way to save resources. The concern about mergers was widespread enough that the 2000 International Association of Counseling Services, Inc. (IACS) Standards included a new section on mergers (Boyd et al., 2002). The most common mergers, proposed and/or carried out, were counseling centers with health services or with career planning and placement services, with the former being the more common. This threat of outsourcing and/or merging was taken very seriously by center leadership and numerous creative efforts were undertaken to quell such efforts. These efforts included the increased development of internships in counseling centers (Boggs & Douce, 2000) and the attainment of accreditation for centers and for internships. Training became an increasingly important aspect of centers, especially at larger institutions, since the staff size could be increased with significantly less expense than adding licensed staff. Additionally, counseling center directors became more involved in utilizing client data and evaluations in research that supported the value of counseling center services (Archer & Cooper, 1998; Bishop, 1995; Guinee & Ness, 2000; Turner & Berry, 2000; Wilson et al., 1997). They also developed, through their professional organization, The Association of University and College Counseling Center Directors (AUCCCD), the AUCCCD Research Consortium, which was designed to create a database on the impacts of university and college counseling centers (Archer & Cooper, 1998).

The concern about campus ecology of the 1970s led most centers to be concerned about their integration into and involvement within the campus community (Guinee & Ness, 2000). Now centers were more and more involved with training resident advisors, consulting with faculty and other administrators, providing outreach programs, and training. The second major concern of this time period, the increase in student demand for services and in the severity of student problems, began to put enormous and unrealistic demands on centers. They were doing more things with more people, while at the same time seeing larger caseloads with more disturbed students (Guinee & Ness, 2000). In 1990, Stone and Archer published a landmark article on the counseling centers of the 1990s. In it they recommended many steps that centers should take to address this myriad of challenges that had befallen them (Stone & Archer, 1990).

By the 1990s, centers were also increasingly involved in major campus tragedies, in effect making the campus and local communities the client (Davis & Humphrey, 2000). It became more and more common for centers to reach out to the campus community with services and support after student and faculty suicides, homicides, and major events such as accidents, severe storms, and fires (Archer & Cooper, 1998; Stone, 1993). In September 2001, the terrorist attacks on New York City and Washington, D.C., also motivated centers to provide resources to their campus communities for students, faculty, and staff who were frightened, disturbed, and confused by these world affairs. These resources and strategies were shared with one another via the Counseling Center Directors Listserv and the AUCCCD Listserv.

DEFINITION

MISSION, GOALS, AND PURPOSES

Most four-year postsecondary institutions report a counseling center on campus (Whiteley et al., 1987). The fundamental mission of counseling center work is to serve students (Corazzini, 1995). According to the Accreditation Standards of the International Association of Counseling Services, Inc. (IACS), "Counseling services are an integral part of the educational mission of the institution and support the mission in a variety of ways, such as consultation, teaching, preventive and developmental interventions, and treatment" (Boyd et al., 2002). Centers provide counseling services to address students' stress from personal, academic, and/or career pressures that may interfere with their attaining the educational opportunities available to them (Boyd et al., 2002). Counseling center staff are advocates for student needs and are involved in program development, teaching, and consultation activities that support the efforts of faculty and staff in improving the university environment. In addition, counseling service professionals work with faculty and administrators in promoting the goal of psychological and emotional development in many aspects of campus life (Boyd et al., 2002).

Most centers provide services in the three general categories of remedial, preventive, and developmental, as conceptualized by the "cube" model (Morril et al., 1974). Remedial services include solving existing problems and crisis intervention. Preventive services are designed to aid the student in avoiding difficulties. Examples of preventive services are providing study and anxiety management skills. Developmental services are designed to aid the student in his or her normal developmental tasks. Career planning, groups addressing relationship issues, and assertiveness training are examples of developmental services.

The proportion of attention that should be given to each of these purposes is a common and ongoing issue, both at individual centers and for the field at large. Few, however, would disagree with Demos's and Mead's (1983) statement:

> Personal counseling and therapy should be based on a developmental and clinical foundation—that is, counselors should be well-versed in both developmental psychology and diagnosis and assessment procedures. Since a focus on any single theoretical background is too narrow, professional staff should be diverse in their training and background. Consultation services are important, but they are supplementary to counseling services, which are the primary function of the center (p. 6).

Demos and Mead clearly state, "a direct contact of students and counselors in counseling interactions, individual or group, is the major function of the psychological counseling center" (1983, p. 7).

Many current issues, including the possible impact of health care reform, have added to the long-standing debate over the ratio of direct service to the preventive and developmental functions of outreach and consultation. In practice, it is difficult to avoid a large proportion of direct and remedial service. Many centers, however, have found that utilizing brief models of therapy (Cooper & Archer, 1999), group work, videotapes, self-help materials (Guinee & Ness, 2000), computer programs, and other creative programming efforts can create some relief from large caseloads. However, as is the case with most areas of student affairs, counseling centers experience certain times of the year when the demand for their services, particularly individual counseling, peaks. Finding the balance between developmental and clinical approaches, and viewing them as complementary rather than mutually exclusive, is the challenge for counseling centers (Davis & Humphrey, 2000).

It is becoming increasingly common for counseling centers to include some level of commitment to the advancement of multiculturism and the appreciation of human diversity (Guinee & Ness, 2000). Efforts to reach out to underserved populations such as ethnic minorities; the physically and emotionally challenged; and gay, lesbian bisexual, and transgender students have been undertaken at many centers (Archer & Cooper, 1998; Davis & Humphrey, 2000). These efforts might also include outreach presentations regarding diversity, mediation of campus conflicts related to diversity issues, and integrating diversity issues into the training that may take place at the center (Boggs & Douce, 2000).

In major statements concerning counseling services of the 1990s, Bishop (1990) and Stone and Archer (1990) recommended increased attention to the use of consultation with a renewed emphasis on the goal of prevention of problems. Stone and Archer also recommended that centers not give up the career counseling function, that outreach and consultation be continued within limits, and that centers should learn to value diversity, including seeking out diverse staff members and trainees, among other recommendations.

ADMINISTRATION AND ORGANIZATIONAL STRUCTURE

ADMINISTRATION

Counseling centers are unique in that much of the work is confidential in nature and, therefore, less obvious both to the public and to administrators (Likins, 1993). It is more complicated and time-consuming for counseling center directors to provide letters from students or parents to upper-level administrators regarding satisfaction with their services than offices less bound by confidentiality issues. Counseling services do not fit easily into the administrative bureaucracy (Schoenberg, 1992) and may have an ambiguous place in the organizational structure, with conflicts of interest that arise because of simultaneous responsibilities to institution, client, and profession (Gilbert, 1989). Autonomous is a common adjective used to describe counseling centers. Although the relationship to other units within the institution will vary based on organizational structure and individual campus needs and history, the counseling service should be administratively neutral to preserve students' perceptions that information disclosed in counseling sessions will not affect other academic or administrative decisions (Boyd et al., 2002).

Counseling services are typically housed in the student affairs unit and work closely with academic units, other student service offices, campus and community medical services, community mental health services, as well as with faculty and administrators (Boyd et al., 2002). Some college and universities have both an independent counseling center and a mental health unit that is part of student health services. Other institutions have one or more training clinics, usually aligned with the departments of counseling and/or counseling psychology, that provide some services by trainees as part of their graduate training. On most campuses, the independent counseling center is the only service-oriented center focusing on preventive and developmental services as well as on remedial services.

Many campuses have separate academic advising centers, career placement centers, sexual assault services, alcohol education and prevention offices, and learning support centers. It can become very complicated, especially for students, to determine where to go for counseling-related services on their campuses. In some institutions, a coordinator of sexual assault services reports to the counseling center (Gallagher et al., 1994). This is especially true for smaller institutions.

Gallagher et al. (1998) found 19 percent of counseling centers surveyed to be administratively linked to a student health service. Of those centers that were administratively linked to a student health service, 34 percent of the counseling center directors reported to the student health service director and 31 percent of the student health service directors reported to the counseling center director (Gallagher et al., 1998). A smaller number of mergers have connected career placement services with counseling centers.

A great deal of a counseling center director's time must be spent in developing and maintaining a strong working relationship with her or his immediate supervisor and other relevant campus administrators (Davis & Humphrey, 2000). Frequent changes in administrative personnel and administrative structure, phenomena not uncommon in student affairs, force directors to regularly feel a need to educate or reeducate supervisors to the design and work of the center. Reconfigurations of the center's model, mission, and charge add to the challenge of maintaining productive relationships with college and university administrators.

FINANCIAL SUPPORT

Although most counseling centers are funded mainly by the institution, 13 percent of 274 counseling center directors surveyed reported pressure from their institutions to be more self-supporting (Gallagher et al., 2001). This figure is down from the 19 percent who reported such pressure in 1994 (Gallagher et al., 1994). At the beginning of the decade, less than 4 percent of centers charged students a fee for personal counseling, and this figure increased to 17 percent in 1996; however, there has been a gradual decline since then, with 13 percent of centers charging such a fee in 2001 (Gallagher et al., 2001). Almost 20 percent of centers generate some income by charging for services such as specialized testing programs, consultation to external groups, and workshops (Gallagher et al., 2001). Creative financing has been a concern of counseling center directors for the last decade, and a variety of efforts, including third-party billing, requiring mandatory student health fees, and fees for longer term counseling have been and are continuing to be used by some centers (Gallagher et al., 2001). The most common emerging funding pattern seems to be implementing a mandatory fee for counseling services required of all students, either as a separate fee or as part of the student health fee (Bishop, 1995). This concern about finances has driven many of the innovations in counseling centers and is an ongoing concern for directors.

PHYSICAL FACILITIES

Counseling services should be centrally located; physically separate from administrative offices, campus police, and judicial offices; and readily accessible to all students, including those who are physically challenged (Boyd et al., 2002). IACS Standards (Boyd et al., 2002) recommend individual soundproof offices with a telephone, an interoffice communications system, audio or video recording equipment, and furnishings that create a relaxing environment for students. Today's counseling centers also require access to computers and other appropriate equipment to support record keeping, research, and publication activities; technical resources for media presentations; and other adjuncts to treatment (Boyd et al., 2002). A reception area that provides a comfortable and private waiting space and a central clerical area where all client records are kept secure are recommended for all centers (Boyd et al., 2002). Also necessary are areas to house library resources, areas suitable for individual and group testing, and areas for group counseling and staff meetings (Boyd et al., 2002). Centers with a training program will also require audio and visual recording facilities as well as facilities for direct observation (Boyd et al., 2002).

TECHNOLOGY

The use of new technology to enhance the delivery and management of services and programs is quite recent for counseling centers (Baier, 1993). In the 1990s, most counseling centers were using computers for purposes such as monthly reports and anonymous client demographic data, scheduling, billing and attendance records, and various assessment instruments. In 1998, 73 percent of centers reported keeping client information on a computer, up from only 34 percent in 1993 (Gallagher et al., 1998).

The most recent IACS Standards (2000) also address the use of technology within counseling centers. Center personnel are expected to have a basic understanding of new technology before adopting it (Boyd et al., 2002). Furthermore, it is necessary to train any nonpsychologists or noncounselors who may provide technical assistance on issues related to confidentiality (Boyd et al., 2002). All client data kept on computers must be secured to prevent unauthorized access, and clients must be informed that such information is stored on computers (Boyd et al., 2002). E-mail and the use of cordless or cellular telephones should not be used to transmit confidential information. If fax machines are used in such a way, a system must be developed to secure the faxed material from unauthorized access, and informed consent must be used (Boyd et al., 2002).

Listservs for various interest groups, including center directors, clinical directors, and training directors, are becoming essential tools in the operation of counseling centers. In 2001, most directors (90%) surveyed reported being on a director's listserv and both seeking assistance (71%), and benefiting from the assistance they received (91%) from the listserv (Gallagher et al., 2001). The creation of web sites for counseling centers is also becoming a common phenomenon, with most centers now having some form of home page.

PROGRAMS AND SERVICES

RANGE OF SERVICES

The programs and services offered by a counseling center will depend on the size and type of institution, the model of the center, the orientation of the director, and services offered elsewhere on campus. Some counseling centers will provide services to faculty, staff, and members of the community (Gallagher et al., 1994). While it is common to provide consultation and referral to nonstudents, the number of centers providing direct services to faculty, staff, and members of the community is decreasing.

IACS Standards require the following program functions:

1. Individual and group counseling and therapy services that are responsive to student needs;
2. Crisis intervention and emergency coverage either directly or through arrangements with other resources;
3. Outreach programming focusing on the developmental needs of students;
4. Consultation services with members of the university community;
5. Referral resources;
6. Research services;
7. Program evaluation of services; and
8. Training and professional development experiences for staff, interns, practicum students, and others in the university community (Boyd et al., 2002).

Centers with larger staffs, centers at public institutions, and those accredited by IACS were most likely to provide this wide range of functions (Whiteley et al., 1987).

Career counseling, historically a cornerstone of university and college counseling centers, appears to be part of the price of keeping up with the increased demand for psychological services. As recently as 1994, 67 percent of centers provided career counseling (Gallagher et al., 1994). In 1999, 61 percent of centers reported that career counseling takes place primarily in a separate office, 23 percent reported that it takes place in the counseling center, and 13 percent reported that it was shared equally by the two offices (Gallagher et al., 1999). The wisdom of such changes in counseling services delivery systems has been seriously questioned (e.g., Guinee & Ness; Stone & Archer, 1990). The debate on whether to provide career counseling in the counseling center will undoubtedly be engaged in on many fronts and for many years to come.

As a result of increased requests for individual service, many centers are limiting the number of individual sessions that are available (Gallagher et al., 1994; Magoon, 1994; Stone & Archer, 1990). In 2001, 44 percent of centers have definite limits on the number of client sessions, and an additional 38 percent encourage time-limited counseling (Gallagher et al., 2001). The trend toward establishing session limits is growing and appears to be a common response to the increase in demand for services (Bishop, 1995; Stone & McMichael, 1996). Instead of longer term counseling and therapy, a student who requests counseling services might be referred to an appropriate group program either immediately or upon completion of a prescribed number of individual counseling sessions (Stone & McMichael, 1996). Group goals might be remedial (most often called therapy groups) or preventive and developmental (most often called psychoeducational groups). Although counseling center directors report difficulty in filling them, most centers offer counseling groups (Gallagher et al., 1994).

Outreach programming can be used to reach students who are less likely to make use of traditional counseling services (Boyd et al., 2001). Outreach programs frequently have a goal of prevention of problems and focus on such issues as study skills, assertive communication, responsible decisions about the use of alcohol, and the prevention of sexual offenses. The target population of prevention programs might also be the parents of students, as it is becoming more common for representatives of the counseling center to meet with groups of parents of new students to discuss student development, typically during a student orientation period. Direct service to students (individual and group counseling, psychoeducational groups, and workshops) accounts for an average of 25 hours of a 40-hour workweek for counseling center staff, but in smaller centers direct service might fill all available time (Gallagher et al., 1994). Most centers (67%) offer some type of self-help materials such as books or audiotapes (Gallagher et al., 1994; Guinee & Ness, 2000).

Consultation refers to activities in which the counseling service interprets and advocates the needs of students to administrators, faculty, and staff of the institution (Boyd et al., 2002). Consultation frequently refers to helping others respond to a student problem, but there also is consultation activity that focuses on organizational dynamics. Consultation must be done with a commitment to protecting confidentiality, and this is not always easy. Deans and vice presidents may interpret their need to know as more important than the client's right to confidentiality (Gallagher, 2001). Centers may have ongoing consultative relationships with campus police, residence life, and academic or athletic departments. There has been an increase in the amount of time centers are spending on outreach and consultation (Guinee & Nessf 2000).

Crisis intervention usually refers to a situation that requires immediate attention for students experiencing acute emotional distress, exhibiting danger to self or others, or needing immediate hospitalization (Boyd et al., 2002). The majority (76%) of centers provide on call services for student emergencies, and 69 percent of centers consider this a part of the job responsibility and offer no additional compensation (Gallagher et al., 2001). Beepers and cell phones are being increasingly employed during on-call hours. Many centers have one or more representatives who participate on a campus crisis team.

An additional program, especially among larger counseling centers, is that of training. In addition to the training of paraprofessionals (e.g., resident advisors), many centers are involved in preprofessional training programs. These may include practicum placement for master's and doctoral level graduate students in fields such as counseling psychology, clinical psychology, counseling and guidance, and college student personnel. A more formal and structured training program exists in centers providing predoctoral and/or postdoctoral internships in professional psychology, especially if the training program is approved by the American Psychological Association. In 1997, 19 percent of centers had an APA-accredited predoctoral internship program and 64 percent reported that their training program had been increased within the past five years (Gallagher et al., 1997). While the numbers of accredited internship sites in counseling centers has increased in the past 10 years, they have not kept up with the number of applicants for internships in counseling centers, so a serious current concern is the number of applicants who are not receiving internship placements (Boggs & Douce, 2000). Counseling center staff can also be involved in a variety of training programs within the campus community.

Most counseling centers have some type of testing services available. These might include use of instruments such as interest inventories, personality assessment, or the administration of national testing programs such as the SAT, ACT, and GRE. While these can be important aspects of the center's mission and can be well integrated into the functioning of the center, it is a far cry from the centers of the 1930s and 1940s, where testing was often the most prominent service.

Many centers have a variety of learning support activities. Some centers do academic advising, many provide study skills programs and services, many center staff members teach orientation and study skill courses, and some centers provide study tables and/or tutors. Finally, ongoing evaluation and accountability research, as well as contributions to the profession, should be a part of counseling center programs (Boyd et al., 2002; Guinee & Ness, 2000; Stone et al., 2000).

TYPES OF PROBLEMS

Williamson (1939) discussed students' concerns with social maladjustments, speech adjustment, family conflicts, student discipline, educational orientation and achievement, occupational orientation, and finances. Some of these concerns are also discussed with college counselors in the twenty-first century, but some additional problems are presented as well. Many of the concerns seen in today's counseling centers are related to the expected developmental tasks of the college student:

1. Adjusting to a new environment;
2. Choosing a major and planning for a future career;
3. Establishing an identity separate from parents;
4. Learning time management and study skills appropriate to higher education
5. Establishing intimate relationships;

6. Exploring sexual identity; and
7. Values clarification.

Late adolescence and early adulthood are difficult times, and the developmental tasks enumerated here pose considerable challenge for many of today's college students. Likewise, many more nontraditional-aged students are attending colleges and universities and they are bringing new sets of problems and issues. In 2001, 85 percent of counseling center directors reported a significant increase in severe psychological problems of their students over the past five years (Gallagher et al., 2001). Some authors (Sharkin, 1997; Erickson Cornish et al., 2000) have empirically examined these perceptions, and their findings challenge the notion that the pathology is more severe; however, they do agree that some types of psychological disturbances are not uncommon in college populations, some small increases in the numbers of severely distressed students have been documented, and the perceptions of counseling center directors of an increase in pathology is long-standing and consistent.

Unexpected crisis events also happen to college students. Examples include (1) death or suicide of a friend or family member; (2) chronic illness in a family member, friend, or self; (3) parents' divorce and remarriage; (4) sexual assault; (5) legal problems an pending jail terms; (6) disability from a car accident; and (7) various types of harassment, including being stalked.

The types of problems that students experience and bring to a counseling center may vary with year in school, age, gender, academic major, ethnicity, and previous history. The fact that the college years are stressful is well documented, and it appears that stress among college students increased in the 1980s (Dunkel-Schetter & Lobel, 1990). Among the most frequently reported sources of problems are academic, career planning, social (including romantic relationships), family concerns (including a family history of alcohol abuse), and financial (e.g., Bertocci et al., 1992; Carney et al., 1990; Dunkel-Schetter & Lobel, 1990; Heppner et al., 1994). Surveys have also found an increase of student concerns with drug and alcohol use, eating and weight problems, experiences of sexual assault and harassment, various forms of violence, and AIDS (Bertocci et al., 1992; Roark, 1993; Stone et al., 2000). Hotelling (1995) also cites the number of ways in which today's students feel vulnerable: exposure to increased violence; uncertainty over functioning in a more diverse environment; fearing the loss of affirmative action; and economic pressure to choose a major or a four-year degree program that is not wanted. Surveys of graduate students find similar concerns (Bertocci at al., 1992; Hodgson & Simoni, 1995).

In addition to developmental issues, crisis situations, and environmental stressors, some students bring more chronic problems with them to college. Examples include issues such as learning disabilities; inherited biochemical imbalances that might result in major depression, compulsive behaviors, or hallucinations if not treated with the proper medications; and eating disorders, which result in either self-starvation or a habitual pattern of overeating followed by self-induced vomiting or laxative abuse. The number of students presenting at counseling centers, and those with serious psychological symptoms and emotional disorders, has increased significantly since 1990 (Gallagher et al., 1994; Guinee & Ness, 2000; Stone & Archer, 1990). In the 1980s, there was an increase in the number of students who came to counseling centers for help with eating disorders, while in the 1990s there has been an increase in problems caused by childhood physical or sexual abuse (Gallagher et al., 1994; Stone & Archer, 1990). Long-standing concerns, as well as the expected stresses of college life, can result in feelings of depression and anxiety, thoughts of suicide, substance abuse, somatic problems, interpersonal difficulties, and difficulty concentrating on academic work (Heppner et al., 1994; Miller & Rice, 1993).

PATTERNS OF USE

In the 1970s and 1980s, research indicated that between 10 percent and 25 percent of students used the counseling center (Heppner & Neal, 1983). In 1997, Magoon found that 10 percent of students at large schools and 14 percent of students at small schools were clients at counseling centers. Earlier reports indicated that students were more likely to come to the center for career planning, negotiating the system, and coping with financial and academic concerns (Carney et al., 1979), but then came to view the counseling center as an appropriate place to discuss personal and interpersonal concerns (Heppner & Neal, 1983). In the 1990s, there were numerous reports of increased requests for counseling services (Guinee & Ness, 2000). A growing demand for services was reported by 63 percent of directors surveyed in 2001, and 84 percent of those surveyed reported concerns about students with severe psychological problems (Gallagher et al., 2001).

The popular media has also addressed the growing requests for campus counseling services, with sensationalist headlines and stories about mental health issues on campuses, such as "Lost on the Campus" in *Time* magazine, a story about college students' mental illnesses and suicides (Kelly, 2001). Similar stories and headlines focus on counseling as a remedial and longer term enterprise. A more accurate reality is that centers are also continuing to see students in preventive and developmental formats; those, however, do not have the media appeal of "therapy."

In order to manage increasing caseloads, many centers have undertaken steps such as seeing more students in therapy less than once a week (73%), using a brief treatment model (76%), and making more external referrals (41%) (Gallagher et al., 2001). These patterns of use refer to students who come to a counseling center requesting counseling. Other patterns of use have not been so well described in the literature but include such activities as counseling center staff going to a residence hall to discuss with students and staff the impact of a homicide in the hall (Waldo et al., 1993) or mobilizing a community-wide support and counseling effort after a campus tragedy (Archer & Cooper, 1998; Stone, 1993).

STAFFING

The 2000 IACS Standards state, "The human resources necessary for the effective operation of a counseling service depend, to a large degree, on the size and nature of the institution and the extent to which other mental health and student support resources are available in the area" (Boyd et al., 2002, in press). IACS guidelines recommend minimum staffing ratios of one FTE professional staff member to every 1,000 to 1,500 students and require hiring practices that are consistent with the goals of equal opportunity and affirmative action (Boyd, et al., 2002). Magoon (2000) reported median ratios of professional staff to students of 1:1,608 for large institutions and 1:970 for small schools. Gallagher et al. (2001) approximate the ratio of FTE mental health professionals to FTE students to be 1:2,216 at large schools and 1:677 at small schools.

Staff may include a range of disciplines, specialties, and levels of training, including paraprofessionals, practicum students, and interns. There appears to be a growing trend at larger centers to develop multidisciplinary staffs, utilizing psychologists, social workers and/or counselors, and psychiatrists on the same staff. This is particularly beneficial if the center has a training program, because it allows the trainees exposure to several fields and the opportunity to witness the collaborative efforts across fields. Credentials for entry-level professional staff are reviewed in a subsequent section.

In 2001, the majority of counseling center directors (69%) held the doctoral degree (Gallagher et al., 2001). There was a slight rise in the number of directors with master's degrees since the early 1990s (Gallagher et al., 2001). Also in 2001, 46 percent of directors identified themselves as counseling psychologists, 28 percent as clinical psychologists, and 12 percent as professional counselors (Gallagher et al., 2001). Doctoral degrees are more likely for directors with large staffs, in public institutions and in centers accredited by IACS (Whiteley et al., 1987). IACS Standards for accreditation recommend that the director have an earned doctorate, and equivalency criteria are recommended for nondoctorate directors (Boyd et al., 2002).

There is a definite shift in the numbers of females employed as professionals in counseling centers and employed as directors. Gallagher et al. (2001) reported that 45 percent of directors responding to the annual survey were female, as compared to 19 percent in 1982. Between 1989 and

1995, newly hired doctoral female staff outnumbered newly hired doctoral males nearly 2 to 1, and at the master's degree level the ratio was nearly 3 to 1 (Affsprung, 1997). Similarly, 69 percent of all paid professional staff in counseling centers in 1999 were female, prompting 35 percent of directors to indicate that they were finding it increasingly difficult to hire qualified male staff (Gallagher et al., 1999). It appears that the majority of counseling center staff of the future will be women (Affsprung, 1997).

Although approximately half of the directors held academic rank in 1994 (Gallagher et al., 1994), since 1980 there has been a decline in the number of directors who possess academic rank in the large institutions (Magoon, 1994). IACS (2000) Standards expect "Salaries, benefits, and career advancement opportunities should be commensurate with those of others in the institution with similar qualifications and responsibilities and comparable professionals in other institutions of higher education in the region" (Boyd et al., 2002).

Those centers with a predoctoral internship training program typically designate a staff member as training director, and many larger centers delegate responsibilities to directors of clinical services, evaluation and research, career services, and outreach and consultation. Counseling centers with testing services might employ a psychometrist. There is an increasing trend, regardless of the size of the institution, to have a psychiatrist on the counseling center staff. In 2001, 30 percent of campuses reporting had a psychiatrist in the counseling center, 20 percent had a psychiatrist in the student health service, while 30 percent reported having no access to a psychiatrist except as a private referral (Gallagher et al., 2001).

Since support staff play important roles in students' impressions of the counseling service, they should be selected carefully and receive training not only in the operation of the service but also in issues regarding confidentiality and the limits of their functioning (Boyd et al., 2002). Furthermore, the 2000 IACS Standards insist, "Student-workers must not have access to client files, confidential office records, and should not do client scheduling" (Boyd et al., 2002).

MODELS

The model of a counseling center is determined in part by the types of programs and services expected from the center, the philosophy of the director, and the philosophy and practical pressures on other key administrators. Other concepts related to the model of any given center are staff size, accreditation status of the center (Whiteley et al., 1987); similar services available on campus or in the community; the professional training programs on campus and their relationship to the center; the relationship between student health services and the center; the relationship with the center and service assignments of a career placement office; the relationship with academic advisors and whether advising is centralized or decentralized; and the location and extent of services available for sexual assault and alcohol and drug abuse prevention and treatment.

The "original counseling center" followed a *vocational guidance model* (Oetting et al., 1970) in which testing and vocational choice counseling were the primary functions. Vocational guidance was the most prevalent model in the 1960s. A survey in the late 1960s (Oetting et al., 1970) also identified six other models of counseling centers: *personnel services model, academic affairs model, psychotherapy model, training model, research model,* and *traditional counseling model.* The "traditional" model was found among those centers whose directors had formed the original counseling center directors' organization and functioned as a separate campus agency, providing vocational counseling, short-term treatment of emotional problems, and some longer term counseling. Service to clients was the primary orientation, although some intern and practicum training experiences existed (Oetting et al., 1970). Among the models identified during the 1970s, this traditional model was evaluated most positively by counselors, resident assistants, faculty, students, and administrators (Gelso, et al., 1977).

Following the work of Oetting et al. (1970), the next major effort to characterize types of counseling centers was a survey conducted in the 1980s (Whiteley et al., 1987). The authors were able to identify five primary types of centers.

1. The *macrocenter* (21% of the sample) provided a broad range of services with an extensive number of both counseling and career-related services, testing, and special functions such as outreach and training.
2. The *career-oriented center* (16%) offered minimal counseling and related services and focused on career planning and placement assistance.
3. The *counseling-oriented center* (29%) was similar to the macrocenter but focused more on personal counseling functions and less on career services.
4. The *general-purpose center* (20%), which was more likely to be found at private schools, provided a more general level of services, with more responsibilities similar to those of a dean of students (e.g., responsibilities and services related to student organizations, fraternity and sorority advising).
5. The *microcenter* (15%) provided some counseling services and a minimal level of other services.

Models of counseling services in community colleges are discussed by Coll (1993).

In a rapidly changing social environment, with limited resources and increasing demands, there has been a tendency to focus on counseling center issues, functions, and/or models that address economic concerns

(Bishop, 1990; Steenbarger, 1995; Stone & Archer, 1990). Crego (1990), for example, admonished counseling center leaders to move beyond "simply adding programs, balancing programs, and . . . prioritizing programs" (p. 609) and notes that counseling centers continue to employ a model designed for the White, middle-class, full-time, traditional-aged, self-directed student. The diversity and changing needs of college students must not be ignored as new models and approaches to the design of counseling centers are explored.

One attempt to reconceptualize models of counseling center functioning suggested "rounding out the cube" (Pace et al., 1996). According to Pace et al., the original cube presented the counseling center as an independent and fixed structure with a closed unidirectional system and decision making that was primarily internal. The cube concept did not address resource allocation, and it implied a noncollaborative style. Pace et al. proposed a "global" model for counseling centers that has an "interactive" cube that focuses on the institution as a system; is interdependent with the system; is a living system rather than a fixed structure; is multidirectional; makes decisions in consultation with the campus community; strives for a homeostatic balance of resources and services; and collaborates with the university community as equals.

PROFESSIONAL DEVELOPMENT

IACS Standards identify professional development as an essential dimension of a counseling program and recommend that release time and budget resources be provided to staff for such purposes (Boyd et al., 2002). Counseling center personnel are further directed by the professional standards of IACS, to participate in professional organizations; attend local, state, and national conferences; take part in in-service training; engage in scholarship and leadership within their field; and become involved in relevant community activities (Boyd et al., 2002).

Professional organizations provide opportunities for collegial interaction, professional development, collection and dissemination of information, contributions through publications, presentations, and committees, as well as the establishment and maintenance of standards.

The Association for University and College Counseling Center Directors (AUCCCD) is the primary professional affiliation for directors of centers (Gallagher, et al., 2001). This organization is primarily concerned with the functioning of counseling centers as integral parts of collegiate institutions (Archer & Bingham, 1990). The annual AUCCCD conferences have been used to establish guidelines, review accountability issues, develop clearinghouses for the dissemination of innovative counseling programs, and formulate constructive responses to the challenges facing counseling centers.

The primary professional affiliations for counseling center staff members are the American Psychological Association (APA), with possible involvement in Division 17 (Counseling Psychology), which has a special interest group focused on counseling centers, and the American College Personnel Association (ACPA) (Magoon, 1994). Commission VII (Counseling and Psychological Services) of ACPA is a very active organization of a wide range of professionals interested in counseling and psychological services in community colleges, colleges, and universities. Affiliation with the American Counseling Association (formerly the American Personnel and Guidance Association) has declined, especially among staff of larger institutions (Magoon, 1994); however, this organization is reported to be the most popular national association for community college counselors (Coll, 1993). Some counseling center staff also are active in their state psychological or college personnel associations, and 3 percent are affiliated with the American College Health Association (Gallagher et al., 1994).

Those centers that provide pre-doctoral internship training are affiliated with the Association of Counseling Center Training Agencies (ACCTA) and the Association of Postdoctoral and Psychology Internship Centers (APPIC). In addition to their specific annual meetings, these organizations, as well as AUCCCD, frequently meet at the annual conventions of APA and ACPA. It is important to note that in these rapidly changing times, traditional methods of professional communication, such as publications and meetings, have been augmented by the use of electronic communication.

The International Association of Counseling Services, Incorporated has developed standards that are used for the formal accreditation of college and university counseling programs (Boyd et al., 2002). Approximately half of the centers from institutions of over 15,000 are accredited by IACS (Gallagher et al., 1994).

Periodicals that publish articles on issues, theory, and research relevant to counseling services include *The Counseling Psychologist*, *The Journal of Counseling Psychology*, and *Professional Psychology: Research and Practice*, which are journals of the American Psychological Association. Also relevant are the *Journal of College Student Development* (ACPA), the *Journal of Counseling and Development* (ACA), the *Journal of Multicultural Counseling and Development* (ACA), The *Journal of College Student Psychotherapy*, and the newsletters of professional organizations (Hood & Arceneaux, 1990; Stone & Lucas, 1991). Although counseling center directors report that research activities become problematic due to heavy service demands (Stone & Archer, 1990), a survey of counseling-relevant journals found that counseling center–related authors, participants, and topics were well represented in the literature (Stone & Lucas, 1991).

In addition, various data banks are available, such as the AUCCCD Data Bank collected by Dr. Thomas Magoon at the University of Maryland and the National Survey of Counseling Center Directors collected by Dr. Robert

Gallagher at the University of Pittsburgh. The Research Consortium of Counseling and Psychological Services in Higher Education was organized by Dr. David Drum at the University of Texas (Drum, 1995).

Finally, it is the responsibility of all professionals in counseling and higher education administration to continue in the development of their professional skills and understanding, especially since student culture and needs do change (Davis & Humphrey, 2000). In some states, it is a legal requirement to demonstrate continuing education in order to remain licensed in one's professional field. Such continuing education credits might come from attendance at workshops aimed at a specific issue (such as a conference on counseling persons living with HIV and AIDS) and/or from relevant presentations at conventions such as those of ACPA, APA, AUCCCD, and ACCTA.

ENTRY-LEVEL QUALIFICATIONS

Counselors were the first of the student services staff to become professional in regard to their training, and they remain highly professional because of the training necessary, their professional organizations with codes of ethics, and the movement toward accreditation and licensure (Hood & Arceneaux, 1990).

A survey (Gallagher et al., 1994) of 310 counseling center directors found that about 85 percent of the centers have a licensed psychologist on staff, while 32 percent reported staff who were licensed MSWs, and 51 percent have a certified professional counselor. For colleges and universities with an enrollment of over 15,000, almost 97 percent report having licensed psychologists on the staff. A doctoral degree in clinical or counseling psychology has been the most typical educational requirement, especially for staff of centers at larger four-year colleges and universities. In many centers, an entry-level staff member is expected to be licensed or license-eligible, which means having completed a doctoral program that is either accredited by the APA or otherwise fulfilling the state requirements to be admitted to the licensing examination. This will include a year-long predoctoral internship and at least one year of supervised postdoctoral experience. Larger centers may require or prefer a psychologist with an APA approved internship. A similar process is required to become a licensed social worker or a certified professional counselor.

IACS Accreditation Standards for University and College Counseling Centers (Boyd et al., 2002) state that professional staff should have at least a master's degree from disciplines such as counselor education, counseling psychology, clinical psychology, psychiatry, and social work. Doctoral-level staff are expected to be licensed and certified to practice within their specialty, and nondoctoral staff are encouraged to seek a similar credential. Appropriate course work and supervised experience in the counseling of

. college-aged students are required. Those who have administrative responsibilities or who supervise the clinical work of others must hold a doctorate or have an appropriate master's degree and experience in the training of other professionals. A psychiatrist holds a medical degree and has completed a residency in psychiatry. Finally, standards of practice require competence in working with human differences (American Psychological Association, 1995) and freedom from prejudice with respect to race, religion, age, sex, sexual orientation, or physical challenge (Boyd et al., 2002).

Although employment in a university or college counseling center setting has tended to increase identification with counseling psychology (Phelps, 1992), it is predicted that proportionately more master's-level counselors and social workers will be employed in college counseling centers (Baron, 1995; Hotelling, 1995; Toth, 1995). As mentioned previously, more counseling centers are moving toward multidisciplinary staffs.

ROLE AND APPLICATION OF STUDENT DEVELOPMENT THEORY AND THE STUDENT LEARNING IMPERATIVE

The history of counseling centers has paralleled that of the field of counseling psychology (Sprinthall, 1990; Tyler, 1992; Whitely, 1984). Given that the distinguishing feature of counseling psychology is its emphasis on development and life planning (Tyler, 1992), counseling centers began with an inherent focus on student development. In contrast to therapy, which is generally presumed to be a remedial service, "Counseling, as it began, was a service for everybody" as "We are all faced with the necessity of choosing how we will live our lives" (Tyler, 1992, p. 343). As Stone and McMichael (1996) point out, "Internally, mental health policy relating to counseling centers has been shaped historically by a student need–based philosophy, including the SPPV student development point of view (American Council on Education, 1937) and more recently by formulations related to college student development (e.g., Chickering, 1969) and wellness and health promotion.

In addition to the emphasis on choices throughout the life span, counseling psychology was an outgrowth of the psychological study of individual differences (Tyler, 1992). Thus, counseling center staff are prepared to work with not only the traditional-aged college student, but also adult learners and students from diverse backgrounds.

As described previously, counseling centers of the 1970s and 1980s were encouraged to become "student development centers" and to focus on student development as one of its major purposes (McKinley, 1980). As mentioned in the "Types of Problems" section, most counseling centers are designed to aid students in the major developmental tasks of late adolescence and early adulthood. Many individuals active in counseling center work were committed to student development and campus ecology (Aulepp & Delworth, 1976; Conyne et al, 1979; Hurst, 1978). Relevant research demonstrates that the counseling needs of students vary according to class level, age, sex, and race of the student (Carney et al., 1990); that minority and underrepresented students may be less likely to utilize services (Brinson & Kottler, 1995); and attention to developmental struggles and needs is a prerequisite to good counseling or therapy with college students. (Whitaker, 1992). Most counseling centers are excellent examples of the application of student development theory.

However, some who do counseling with college and university students are questioning the current meaning of "normal" developmental issues, given the evidence of more and more dysfunctional and pathological families, and traumatic childhood and adolescent experiences. Thus, as Stone and Archer (1990) conclude, "the developmental issues for many of our students include learning to overcome serious psychological problems" (p. 546). Early life experiences can complicate the resolution of the expected developmental tasks of the college student. For example, White and Strange (1993) found that an unwanted childhood sexual experience had significant effects on subsequent psychosocial tasks of intimacy and career planning in a sample of college women. Similarly, typical college students' experimentation with new behaviors, as they experience physical, sexual, psychological, identity, and moral development, can increase the risk of serious problems with substance abuse, violence, and exposure to HIV infection (Rivinus & Larimer, 1993; Triggs & McDermott, 1991).

It is also true that counseling centers are outstanding examples of the application of the Student Learning Imperative (SLI). The increased focus on student learning and personal development, the collaboration with fellow educators, the experience-based and research-based expertise of counseling center staff regarding student characteristics, and the increase in data-based outcome evaluations and assessment data are all congruent with the SLI. Efforts on many campuses have long existed and continue to exist to include counseling centers as contributors to seamless learning/second curriculum environments (Kahn et al., 1999). Another growing trend, and further evidence of counseling centers' resonance with the SLI, is the effort of centers to conduct research and evaluation that demonstrate the relationship between counseling outcomes and student learning (Schwitzer & Metzinger, 1998).

ISSUES AND TRENDS

ISSUES

The face of higher education is changing. More women, members of underrepresented groups, students with disabilities, older students, and part-time students now comprise and will continue to comprise our campuses. More institutions of higher education are being run as business corporations (Baron, 1995). Likewise, the demand for counseling services and the shortage of resources that existed in the 1980s and 1990s will continue to exist in the future. Therefore, four trends seem likely for counseling centers in the twenty-first century. These trends are (1) more students with more complex problems than in the past; (2) an increasingly diverse student body; (3) greater use of Internet-based and interactional technologies in service delivery; and (4) an increase in the demand for accountability in the face of limited resources (Davis & Humphrey, 2000).

The 1990s also brought to our awareness a new problem known as Internet addiction. Many students are spending inordinate amounts of time in internet sites, including chat rooms and sexually oriented sites. This and other problems, such as alienation and isolation related to reliance on information technology, will continue in the twenty-first century. As new technological advancements are discovered, new human problems as a result of the advancements are likely to occur. As a result of the increase in the numbers of students requesting help and the seriousness of their problems, there is great concern and debate over managing these demands in the future (Stone & Archer, 1990). Among the major concerns expressed by counseling center directors are an increased demand for services with no increase in resources; the increased severity in problems presented by students; an increase in waiting lists for counseling services; an increase in crisis counseling; an increased need to make outside referrals for long-term counseling and psychotherapy; responding to the needs of the learning disabled student; and increased pressure to do more about drug and alcohol abuse on campus (Gallagher et al., 2001). All of these concerns are likely to continue into the twenty-first century.

Attempts to cope with increased service demands, as mentioned previously, have been made and will continue to be made through the use of short-term counseling models and group modalities. Other possibilities include using some form of self-help materials, videotapes, computerized guidance programs, and a counseling center home page.

Both legal and ethical issues will continue to be a high priority for counseling centers, and they are and will continue to become increasingly complex (Archer & Cooper, 1998). Lawsuits filed by students and parents against individual practitioners, centers, and universities are becoming more common. Guidelines of professional organizations and state laws suggest or require standards for professional practice (e.g., American College Personnel Association, 1990; American Psychological Association, 1995). The legal and ethical issue that is most frequently discussed is confidentiality (e.g., Archer & Cooper, 1998; Stone & Lucas, 1990). Confidentiality is the cornerstone of the counseling relationship, and there is always an ethical obligation to keep client information confidential; however, this may not be a legal privilege in all circumstances (Archer & Cooper, 1998). In many but not all states, there is a legal privileged communication between client and psychologist, counselor, or social worker, but this is typically viewed in the legal profession as a judicial privilege rather than a legislative privilege. Therefore, psychologists, counselors, and social workers can claim privileged communication, but there is no guarantee that all courts will honor the claim. Regardless, counseling center professionals are ethically bound to protect the client confidentiality. The rare exceptions to this are those situations in which someone is potentially harmful to self or others and when there is a legal requirement to report child or elder abuse (Archer & Cooper, 1998).

Issues of confidentiality and other legal and ethical issues have also become more complex due to modern technology; HIV and AIDS; third-party payments; and a societal increase in violence and terrorism. Reimbursement by insurance or managed health care programs requires the use of psychiatric diagnoses and possible review of records by third-party payers. This presents many challenges to confidentiality as well as to adherence to a student development model (Crego, 1995; Gilbert, 1994). The need by many centers to limit the number of counseling sessions raises the question of whether it is ethical to provide any services for students who might require a consistent long-term therapy relationship, such as survivors of sexual abuse (Lilly-Weber, 1993).

As the number of students with serious emotional problems increases, so does the risk of behavioral disturbances (Dannells & Stuber, 1992). Counseling centers are being asked to intervene and make decisions about these students who come to the attention of others on campus. Conflicting loyalties and confidentiality dilemmas might arise (Amada, 1993; Gilbert, 1989). There have been increased requests for counseling centers to provide mandated counseling and assessment, and directors report ambivalence about the provision of such services (Margolis, 2000; Stone & Lucas, 1994). Other challenges to confidentiality are the increased need to notify others of potential suicidal or homicidal behavior, the need to report child and elder abuse, and questions about whether the unprotected sexual activity of a person living with HIV constitutes reportable harm to others (Gallagher, 1994). Increased use of electronic communication has resulted in IACS and many individual centers developing policy statements that inform students that counseling center staff will not respond to personal problems by e-mail.

In contrast to coping with increased service demands, there is also the challenge of meeting the needs of those who are less likely to request services, such as international students, ethnic minority students, and most students who kill themselves (e.g., Atkinson et al., 1990; Brinson & Kottler, 1995; Oropeza et al., 1991; Shea, 1995).

A major challenge to the counseling center practitioner has been response to acts of violence and hate crimes. Sixty percent of centers in the year 2000 saw obsessive pursuit cases, in which 50 persons were injured and five persons were killed; and 30 percent of schools surveyed reported a student suicide in 2000 (Gallagher, et al., 2001). Although the suicide rate among college students is less than that among Americans aged 15 to 24 who are not in college, suicide is still the second leading cause of death (after accidents) for college students (Shea, 1995). Federal legislation such as the Campus Security Act requires colleges to publish crime statistics and to actively respond to the needs of victims of campus violence (Garland & Grace, 1993). Although the numbers of homicides on and around college and university campuses are small, the impact of such disasters on the campus community is far-reaching and requires immediate and expert intervention (Allen, 1992).

There has been an increase in the number of counseling centers that evaluate their services (Magoon, 1995; Guinee & Ness, 2000). Accountability, along with strategic planning, is recommended in times of competition for resources (Guinee & Ness, 2000; Stone and Archer, 1990).

Finally, Guinee and Ness (2000), who researched how well centers have responded to Stone's and Archer's recommendations for the 1990s, conclude that centers have been very active in responding to the challenges of the 1990s and in following the recommendations of Stone and Archer (1990). Furthermore, the authors conclude, "Counseling center directors and their staff must make critical decisions on where their agency's priorities will lie and their resources and energies will be directed. We hope that some future-directed professionals will come forward, as Stone and Archer did in this (last) decade, to offer us a comprehensive agenda to help centers steer the course during the next 10 years. More important, we hope that future studies will enable counseling center staff to increasingly examine when and how counseling centers can make changes that will enhance the vitality and security of the agency in the years to come" (Guinee & Ness, 2000, p. 279).

TRENDS

In concluding their major discussion of challenges for counseling centers in the 1990s, Stone and Archer (1990) stated ". . . we have a much clearer understanding of how difficult it is to predict the future" (p. 599) . One thing appears certain: It is becoming increasingly difficult to navigate the business of living. The explosion in technological advances, the increase in acts of random violence and hate crimes, the instability of global economies, and the terrorist acts of September 11, 2001, have left many people throughout the world confused distressed, frightened, and anxious. There can be little doubt that college students will continue to experience increased stress and psychological symptoms. The continuing need for counseling centers on campuses of the future seems certain (Archer &

Cooper, 1998). How these centers will be designed, administered, and financed remains the mystery.

Current debates focus on what is necessary to survive in a rapidly changing world and uncertain economic times, while retaining a commitment to the counseling center mission of serving students. The deliberation over what proportion of counseling center activity should be focused on which goal continues. Some predict a change in the percentage of time and type of direct service activity. For example, Baron (1995) predicted that 25 percent will be spent on individual counseling, 25 percent on group counseling, and 50 percent on psychoeducational modalities for prevention, health promotion, and treatment compliance. Guinee and Ness (2000) found that there is an increase in female and minority staff and an increase in the time spent on outreach and consultation. They found that the greatest changes during the 1990s were the integration of counseling services with the campus, the high quality of training, and the variety of services provided (Guinee & Ness, 2000).

The impetus of potential outsourcing and mergers seems to be waning. In 2001, 97 percent of center directors reported that outsourcing or privatization of the counseling center had not occurred and did not seem likely (Gallagher et al., 2001). Likewise, significantly more centers reported increases in staff and budget in 2001 than decreases (Gallagher et al., 2001).

It is expected that counseling centers will continue in the trends of hiring both a multidisciplinary staff and more part-time staff members. In the mid-1990s, there were slight trends for counseling centers to merge with student health centers or to lose the career counseling function. The former trend seems to be decreasing. Both Stone and Archer (1990) and Bishop (1990) made a number of recommendations that included: the need to balance demands and resources; to continue involvement in career counseling and consultation activities; to focus on the needs of special student populations such as racial and cultural minorities, international students, adult learners, and student athletes; and to increase accountability with more active administrative styles.

It has been strongly recommended, and followed by many, that counseling centers reverse the trend of the 1980s and 1990s toward a medical model and return to a more comprehensive developmental approach (e.g., Crego, 1990; 1995). Others argue that in order to survive, counseling centers must compete in a managed care market (e.g., Drum, 1995; Steenbarger, 1995). Dr. Thomas Magoon, a former counseling center director with a long history of professional involvement, recommended that counseling centers should be seen as part of the university academy and that research is the key to building that bridge (Dressel, 1995). Magoon also recommended that counseling center staff must be active in professional organizations, especially at the state level where laws governing psychology are being made.

Despite all of the uncertainty about the future, it seems very clear that in complex times, with increased reliance on technology and staggering amounts of information available at one's fingertips, human contact will become increasingly important. Counseling centers must not lose sight of their greatest asset, the ability of staff to sit down face-to-face with students and build trusting and supportive working alliances.

TECHNOLOGY RESOURCES

The following list may prove useful as examples of counseling center and counseling center information web sites:

Positions in Counseling Centers
  http://www.tarleton.edu/~counseling/picc/
University and College Counselor Resources
  http://www.tarleton.edu/~counseling/coresour/cores.htm
At the Office
  http://www.tarleton.edu/~counseling/ccv/of ice.html
Mental Health Licensure Resources
  http://www.tarleton.edu/~counseling/coresour/lllpc.htm
The Counseling Center Village
  http://ub-counseling.buffalo.edu/ccv.html
Counseling Centers on the Internet
  http://ub-counseling.buffalo.edu/centers.html
The Virtual Pamphlet Collection
  http://uhs.bsd.uchicago.edu/scrs/vps/virtulets.html
AUCCCD Website
  http://www.aucccd.org/
IACS Website
  http://mason.gmu.edu/~iacs/
Counseling Center Listservs
  http://ub-counseling.buffalo.edu/Village/Staffdev/lists.html
Clearinghouse for Structured/Thematic Groups and Innovative Programs
  http://www.utexas.edu/student/cmhc/chindex.html
ACA collaboration to encourage students to use college counseling centers
  http://www.CampusBlues.com

REFERENCES

Affsprung, E. H. (1997). Gender demographics of college counseling center hiring 1989–1995. *Journal of College Student Psychotherapy, 11(3)*, 5–11.

Allen, R. D. (1992, November). The counseling center director's role in managing disaster response. *Commission VII Counseling Psychological Services Newsletter, 19(2)*, 4–5.

Amada, G. (1993). The role of the mental health consultant in dealing with disruptive college students. *Journal of College Student Psychotherapy, 8*, 121–137.

American College Personnel Association. (1990). Statement of ethical principles and standards. *Journal of College Student Development, 31,* 11–16.

American Psychological Association. (1995). *Ethical principles of psychologists and code of conduct.* Washington, DC: American Psychological Association.

Archer, J., & Cooper, S. (1998). *Counseling and mental health services on campus: A handbook of contemporary practices and challenges.* San Francisco: Jossey-Bass.

Archer, J., & Bingham, R. (1990). Task force on organizational structure. *Proceedings of the 39th Annual Conference of the Association of University and College Counseling Center Directors,* p. 119.

Atkinson, D. R., Jennings, R. G., & Liongson, L. (1990). Minority students' reasons for not seeking counseling and suggestions for improving services. *Journal of College Student Development, 31,* 342–350.

Aulepp, L., & Delworth, U. (1976). *Training manual for an ecosystem model: Assessing and designing campus environments.* Boulder, CO: Western Interstate Commission for Higher Education.

Baier, J. L. (1993). Technological changes in student affairs administration. In M. J. Barr and Associates, T*he handbook of student affairs administration.* San Francisco: Jossey-Bass.

Baron, A. (1995, March). *Transforming the academy: A counseling center perspective.* Paper presented at the meeting of the American College Personnel Association, Boston.

Berk, S. E. (1983). Origins and historical development of university and college counseling. In P. J. Gallagher & G. D. Demos (Eds.), *Handbook of counseling in higher education* (pp. 50–71). New York: Praeger.

Bertocci, D., Hirsch, E., Sommer, W., & Williams, A. (1992). Student mental health needs: Survey results and implications for service. *Journal of American College Health, 41,* 3–10.

Bishop, J. B. (1995). Emerging administrative strategies for college and university counseling centers. *Journal of Counseling and Development, 74,* 33–38.

Bishop, J. B. (1990). The university counseling center: An agenda for the 1990s. *Journal of Counseling and Development, 68,* 408–413.

Boggs, K. R., & Douce, L. A. (2000). Current status and anticipated changes in psychology internships: Effects on counseling psychology training. *The Counseling Psychologist, 28(5),* 672–686.

Boyd, V., Brandel, I., Buckles, N., Davidshofer, C., Deakin, S., Erskine, C., Hattauer, E., Hurley, G., Locher, L., Piorkowski, G., Simono, R., Spivack, J., & Steele, C. (2002). Accreditation standards for university and college counseling centers. *Journal of Counseling and Development, 80,* 229–248.

Brinson, J. A., & Kottler, J. A. (1995). Minorities underutilization of counseling centers' mental health services: A case for outreach and consultation. *Journal of Mental Health Counseling, 17(4),* 371–385.

Carney, C. G., Peterson, K., & Moberg, T. F. (1990). How stable are student and faculty perceptions of student concerns and of a university counseling center? *Journal of College Student Development, 31,* 423–428.

Carney, C. G., Savitz, C. J., Weiscott, G. N. (1979). Students' evaluations of a university counseling center and their intentions to use its programs. *Journal of Counseling Psychology, 26,* 242–249.

Coll, K. M. (1993). *Community college counseling: Current status and needs* (Series No. 10). Alexandria, VA: International Association of Counseling Services, Inc.

Conyne, R. K., Banning, J. H., Clack, R. J., Corazzini, J. G., Huebner, L. A., Keating, L. A., & Wrenn, R. L. (1979). The campus environment as client: A new direction for college counselors. *Journal of College Student Personnel, 20,* 437–442.

Cooper, S., & Archer, J. (1999). Brief therapy in college counseling and mental health. *Journal of American College Health, 48(1),* 21–28.

Corazzini, J. G. (1995, March). Counseling centers have a future. *Commission VII Counseling & Psychological Services Newsletter, 21(3),* 8.

Crego, C. A. (1990) . Challenges and limits in search of a model. *The Counseling Psychologist, 18,* 608–613.

Crego, C. A. (1995, March). The medicalization of counseling psychology: Managed care vs. developmental models in university and college counseling centers. *Commission VII Counseling & Psychological Services Newsletter, 21(3),* 9.

Dannells, M., & Stuber, D. (1992). Mandatory psychiatric withdrawal of severely disturbed students: A study and policy recommendations. *NASPA Journal, 29,* 163–168.

Davis, D. C., & Humphrey, K. M. (Eds.). (2000). *College counseling: Issues and strategies for a new millennium.* Alexandria, VA: American Counseling Association.

Demos, G. D., & Mead, T. M. (1983). The psychological counseling center: Models and functions. In P. J. Gallagher & G. D. Demos (Eds.), *Handbook of counseling in higher education* (pp. 1–22). New York: Praeger.

Dressel, J. L. (1995, July). Commission VII: A historical perspective. *Commission VII Counseling Psychological Services, 22(1),* 3–4.

Drum, D. J. (1995, March). Paper presented at the meeting of the American College Personnel Association, Boston.

Dunkel-Schetter, C., & Lobel, M. (1990). Stress among students. In H. L. Pruett & V. B. Brown (Eds.), *Crisis intervention and prevention* (New Directions for Student Services, No. 49, pp. 17–34).

Erickson Cornish, J. A., Riva, M. T., Cox Henderson, M., Kominars, K. D., & McIntosh, S. (2000). Perceived distress in university counseling center clients across a six-year period. *Journal of College Student Development, 41(1),* 104–109.

Forman, M. E. (1977). The changing scene in higher education and the identity of counseling psychology. *The Counseling Psychologist, 7,* 45–48.

Gallagher, R. P., Sysko, H. B., and Zhang, B. (2001). *National survey of counseling center directors* (Series No. 8K). Alexandria, VA: International Association of Counseling Services, Inc.

Gallagher, R. P., Gill, A. M., & Sysko, H. B. (2000) *National survey of counseling center directors* (Series No. 8J). Alexandria, VA.: International Association of Counseling Services, Inc.

Gallagher, R. P., Gill, A. M., Goldstrohm, S. L., & Sysko, H. B. (1999). *National survey of counseling center directors.* (Series No. 8I). Alexandria, VA: International Association of Counseling Services, Inc.

Gallagher, R. P., Gill, A. M., & Goldstrohm, A. L. (1998). *National survey of counseling center directors* (Series No. 8H). Alexandria, VA: International Association of Counseling Services, Inc.

Gallagher, R. P., Gill, A. M., & Goldstrohm, A. L. (1997). *National survey of counseling center directors* (Series No. 8G). Alexandria, VA: International Association of Counseling Services, Inc.

Gallagher, R. P., Christofidis, A., Gill, A. M., & Weaver-Graham, W. (1996). *National survey of counseling center directors* (Series No. 8F). Alexandria, VA: International Association of Counseling Services, Inc.

Gallagher, R. P., Weaver-Graham, W., Christofidis, A., & Bruner, L. A. (1995). *National survey of counseling center directors* (Series No. 8E). Alexandria, VA: International Association of Counseling Services, Inc.

Gallagher, R. P., Bruner, L. A., & Weaver-Graham, W. (1994). *National survey of counseling center directors* (Series No. 8D). Alexandria, VA: International Association of Counseling Services, Inc.

Garland, P. H., & Grace, T. W. (1993). *New perspectives for student affairs professionals: Evolving realities, responsibilities and roles.* ASHE-ERIC Higher Education Report No. 7. Washington, DC: The George Washington University, School of Education and Human Development.

Gelso, C. J., Birk, J. M., Utz, P. W., & Silver, A. E. (1977). A multigroup evaluation of the models and functions of university counseling centers. *Journal of Counseling Psychology, 24,* 338–348.

Gibson, R. L., Mitchell, M. H., & Higgins, R. E. (1983). *Development and management of counseling programs and guidance services.* New York: Macmillan.

Gilbert, S. P. (1989). The juggling act of the college counseling center: A point of view. *The Counseling Psychologist, 17,* 477–489.

Gilbert, S. P. (1994, August). Practicing ethically in managed care treatment settings. Commission VII *Counseling Psychological Services Newsletter, 21(1),* 2–4.

Guinee, J. P., & Ness, M. E. (2000). Counseling centers of the 1990s: Challenges and changes. *Counseling Psychologist, 28(2),* 267–280.

Hedahl, B. M. (1978). The professionalization of change agents: Growth and development of counseling centers as institutions. In B. M. Schoenberg (Ed.), *A handbook and guide for the college and university counseling center* (pp. 24–39). Westport, CT: Greenwood.

Heppner, P. P., Kivlighan, D. M., Good, G. E., Roehlke, H. J., Hills, H. I., & Ashby, J. S. (1994). Presenting problems of university counseling center clients: A snapshot and multivariate classification scheme. *Journal of Counseling Psychology, 41,* 315–324.

Heppner, P. P., & Neal, G. W. (1983). Holding up the mirror: Research on the roles and functions of counseling centers in higher education. *The Counseling Psychologist, 11,* 81–98.

Hodgson, C. S., & Simoni, J. M. (1995). Graduate student academic and psychological functioning. *Journal of College Student Development, 36,* 244–253.

Hood, A. B., & Arceneaux, C. (1990). *Key resources on student services: A guide to the field and its literature.* San Francisco: Jossey-Bass.

Hotelling, K. (1995, March). *Environmental change and students at risk: Implications for counseling centers.* Paper presented at the meeting of the American College Personnel Association, Boston.

Hurst, J. C. (1978). Chickering's vectors of development and student affairs programming. In C. A. Parker (Ed.), *Encouraging development in college students.* Minneapolis: University of Minnesota Press.

Kahn, J. S., Wood, A., & Wiesen, F. A. (1999). Student perceptions of college counseling center services: Programming and marketing for a seamless learning environment. *Journal of College Student Psychotherapy, 14(1),* 69–80.

Kelly, K. (2001, January 15). Lost on the campus. *Time*, 51–5 3.

Kiracofe, N. M., Donn, P. A., Grant, C. O., Podolnick, E. E., Bingham, R. P., Bolland, H. R., Carney, C. G., Clementson, J., Gallagher, R. P., Grosz, R. D., Handy, L., Hansche, J. H., Mack, J. K., Sanz, D., Walker, L. J., & Yamada, K. T. (1994). Accreditation standards for university and college counseling centers. *Journal of Counseling and Development, 73*, 38–43.

Kirk, B. A., Johnson, A. P., Redfield, J. E., Free, J. E., Michel, J., Roston, R. A., & Warman, R. E. (1971). Guidelines for university and college counseling services. *American Psychologist, 26*, 585–589.

Lamb, D. H., Garni K. F., & Gelwick, B. P. (1983). *A historical overview of university counseling centers: Changing functions and emerging trends.* Unpublished manuscript.

Likins, P. (1993). The president: Your master or your servant? In M. J. Barr & Associates, *The handbook of student affairs administration.* San Francisco: Jossey-Bass.

Lilly-Weber, J. (1993, November). Should survivors of sexual abuse be treated for this issue at college and university counseling centers? *Commission VII Counseling Psychological Services Newsletter, 20(2)*, 3, 5.

Magoon, T. M. (2000). College and university counseling center directors' data bank. Unpublished manuscript, University of Maryland, College Park.

Magoon, T. M. (1999). *College and university counseling center directors' data bank.* Unpublished manuscript, University of Maryland, College Park.

Magoon, T. M. (1998). *College and university counseling center directors' data bank.* Unpublished manuscript, University of Maryland, College Park.

Magoon, T. M. (1997). *College and university counseling center directors' data bank.* Unpublished manuscript, University of Maryland, College Park.

Magoon, T. M. (1996). *College and university counseling center directors' data bank.* Unpublished manuscript, University of Maryland, College Park.

Magoon, T. M. (1995). *College and university counseling center directors' data bank.* Unpublished manuscript, University of Maryland, College Park.

Magoon, T. M. (1994). *College and university counseling center directors' data bank.* Unpublished manuscript, University of Maryland, College Park.

Margolis, G. (2000). Late drops, deadlines and depression. *Journal of College Student Psychotherapy, 14(4)*, 3–8.

McKinley, D. (1980). Counseling. In W.H. Morrill, J.C. Hurst, with E.R. Oetting and others, *Dimensions of intervention for student development.* New York: John Wiley.

Miller, G. A., & Rice, K. G. (1993) . A factor analysis of a university counseling center problem checklist. *Journal of College Student Development, 34*, 98–102.

Morrill, W. H., Oetting, E. R., & Hurst, J. C. (1974) . Dimensions of counselor functioning. *Personnel and Guidance Journal, 52*, 354–359.

Oetting, E. R., Ivey, A. E., & Weigel, R. G. (1970). The college and university counseling center. *Student Personnel Series No. 11.* Washington, DC: American College Personnel Association.

Oropeza, B. A. C., Fitzgibbon, M., & Baron, A. (1991). Managing mental health crises of foreign college students. *Journal of Counseling and Development, 69*, 280–284.

Pace, D., Stamler, V. L., Yarris, E., & June, L. (1996). Rounding out the cube: Evolution to a global model for counseling centers. *Journal of Counseling and Development, 74(4)*, 321–325.

Rivinus, T. M., & Larimer, M. E. (1993). Violence, alcohol, other drugs and the college student. *Journal of College Student Psychotherapy, 8,* 71–119.

Roark, M. L. (1993). Conceptualizing campus violence: Definitions, underlying factors, and effects. *Journal of College Student Psychotherapy, 8,* 1–27.

Schneider, L. D. (1977). Counseling. In W. T. Packwood (Ed.), *College student personnel services* (pp. 340–367). Springfield, IL: Charles C Thomas.

Schoenberg, B. M. (Ed.). (1992). *Conceptualizations: Counseling center models* (Series No. 9). Alexandria, VA: International Association of Counseling Services, Inc.

Schwitzer, A. H., & Metzinger, T. (1998). Applying the student learning imperative to counseling center outcome evaluation. *Journal of College Student Psychotherapy, 13(2),* 71–92.

Sharkin, B. S. (1997). Increasing severity of presenting problems in college counseling centers: A closer look. *Journal of Counseling and Development, 75(4),* 275–281.

Shea, C. (1995, June 11). Suicide signals. *The Chronicle of Higher Education,* pp. A35–A36.

Sprinthall, N. A. (1990). Counseling psychology from Greystone to Atlanta: On the road to Armageddon? *The Counseling Psychologist, 18,* 455–463.

Steenbarger, B. (1995, March). Managed care and the future of university counseling centers. *Commission VII Counseling & Psychological Services Newsletter, 21(3),* 2–4.

Stone, G. L. (1993). Psychological challenges and responses to a campus tragedy: The Iowa experience. *Journal of College Student Psychotherapy, 8,* 259–271.

Stone, G. L., & Archer, J. (1990). College and university counseling centers in the 1990s: Challenges and limits. *The Counseling Psychologist, 18,* 539–607.

Stone, G. L., & Lucas, J. (1990). Knowledge and beliefs about confidentiality on a university campus. *Journal of College Student Development, 31,* 437–444.

Stone, G. L., & Lucas, J. (1991). Research and counseling centers: Assumptions and facts. *Journal of College Student Development, 32,* 497–501.

Stone, G. L., & Lucas, J. (1994). Disciplinary counseling in higher education: A neglected challenge. *Journal of Counseling and Development, 72,* 234–238.

Stone, G. L., & McMichael, J. (1996). Thinking about mental health policy in university and college counseling centers. *Journal of College Student Psychotherapy, 10(3),* 3–27.

Stone, G. L., Vespia, K. M., & Kanz, J. E. (2000). How good is mental health care on college campuses? *Journal of Counseling Psychology, 47(4),* 498–510.

Toth, M. (1995, March). *Transforming the academy: A counseling center perspective.* Paper presented at the meeting of the American College Personnel Association, Boston.

Triggs, J., & McDermott, D. (1991). Short-term counseling strategies for university students who test HIV positive: The case of John Doe. *Journal of College Student Development, 32,* 17–23.

Turner, A. L., & Berry, T. R. (2000). Counseling center contributions to student retention and graduation: A longitudinal assessment. *Journal of College Student Development, 41(6),* 627–636.

Tyler, L. E. (1992). Counseling psychology—why? *Professional Psychology: Research and Practice, 23,* 342–344.

Tyler, L. E. (1969). *The work of the counselor* (3rd ed.). Englewood Cliffs, NJ: Prentice-Hall.

Waldo, M., Harman, M. J., & O'Malley, K. (1993). Homicide in the university residence halls: One counseling center's response. *Journal of College Student Psychotherapy, 8,* 273–284.

Warnath, C. F. (1971). *New myths and old realities: College counseling in transition.* London: Jossey-Bass.

Warnath, C. F. (1973). *New directions for college counselors: A handbook for redesigning professional roles.* San Francisco: Jossey-Bass.

White, K., & Strange, C. (1993). Effects of unwanted childhood sexual experiences on psychosocial development of college women. *Journal of College Student Development, 34,* 289–294.

Whitaker, L. C. (1997). The influence of managed care. *Journal of College Student Psychotherapy, 12(2),* 23–40.

Whitaker, L. C. (1992). Psychotherapy as a developmental process. *Journal of College Student Psychotherapy, 6,* 1–23.

Whiteley, J. M. (Ed.). (1984). Counseling psychology: A historical perspective (Special issue). *The Counseling Psychologist, 12.*

Whiteley, S. M., Mahaffey, P. J., & Geer, C. A. (1987) The campus counseling center: A profile of staffing patterns and services. *Journal of College Student Personnel, 28,* 71–81.

Widseth, J. C., Webb, R. E., & John, K. B. (1997). The question of outsourcing: The roles and functions of college counseling services. *Journal of College Student Psychotherapy, 11(4),* 3–22.

Williamson, E. G. (1939). *How to counsel students.* New York: McGraw-Hill.

Williamson, E. G. (1961). *Student personnel services in colleges and universities.* New York: McGraw-Hill.

Wilson, S. B., Mason, T. W., & Ewing, M. J. M. (1997) Evaluating the impact of receiving university-based counseling services on student retention. *Journal of Counseling Psychology, 44(3),* 316–320.

Chapter 7

DISCIPLINE AND JUDICIAL AFFAIRS

MICHAEL DANNELLS AND JOHN WESLEY LOWERY

INTRODUCTION

A college or university is a *disciplined* community, a place where individuals accept their obligations to the group and where well-defined governance procedures guide behavior for the common good. (Carnegie Foundation for the Advancement of Teaching, 1990, p. 37)

Student discipline is a timely, complex, and controversial subject. It is timely because now, perhaps more than at any other time in the history of American higher education, campuses are in search of civility based on shared values while they are concerned about violence and disregard for others' rights (Carnegie Foundation, 1990). It is complex because it has many different and seemingly competing dimensions, including philosophical, legal, educational, and organizational issues. And it is controversial because it resides at the interface of community needs and individual liberties.

HISTORY

The history and evolution of college student discipline in America is reflective of the development of the institutions of higher education themselves (Smith, 1994). In colonial colleges, the president and faculty exerted total behavior control over students as part of the strict moral, ethical, and religious training that, along with the classical curriculum, was the accepted role and mission of the institution. "Discipline was *the* student affairs approach of this period . . ." (Garland & Grace, 1993, p. 3). To control and mold the character of young colonial students, most of whom were in their early to mid-teens, extensively detailed codes of behavior and harsh penalties, including public confessions and ridicule, fines, and corporal punishment, were commonly and liberally employed (Smith, 1994). The handling of more serious disciplinary matters was shared with the trustees, while the

178

president often delegated less serious offenses to faculty (Leonard, 1956; Schetlin, 1967; Smith & Kirk, 1971). But students did not accept this system completely without question. A number of institutions struggled with student riots, which President Ashbel Green of Princeton attributed to this rigid system of student discipline (Rudolph, 1990).

Discipline became less paternalistic during the late 1700s and into the 1800s with the rise of the public university, the broadening of the university's mission, the increasing secularization and pluralism of higher education in general, and increasing enrollments. Punishments became milder, with corporal punishment almost disappearing; trustee participation in conduct matters declined; and counseling of student offenders emerged. Several institutions also began to experiment with systems of student self-governance during this period (Bruce, 1920; Smith, 1994; Wagoner, 1976, 1986). As the president became increasingly occupied with an expanding curriculum, fiscal and administrative matters, and external relations, specialists were chosen from the faculty to deal with nonacademic conduct of the students (Leonard, 1956; Schetlin, 1967).

In the years following the Civil War, the introduction of the German university model, with its disregard for all but the intellectual growth of students, and the demands of the Industrial Revolution on faculty for development of their academic disciplines resulted in a major shift away from rigid behavior control to greater emphasis on self-discipline and self-governance (Brubacher & Rudy, 1968; Durst, 1969; Schetlin, 1967). More humanitarian and individualized methods of discipline were used, and more democratic systems involving student participation developed concurrent with student governments and honor systems (Smith, 1994). Student discipline encountered new challenges with the increasing attendance of women at colleges and universities; "supervising such daring activities as unmarried young men and women dining together in a campus dining hall" (Fenske, 1989, p. 30) complicated the administration of student discipline of the time.

By the turn of the century, the first deans of men and women had been appointed "to relieve administrators and faculties of problems of discipline" (ACE, 1937, p. 2); and during the early 1900s, these positions were established on most campuses. LeBaron Russell Briggs found student discipline to be a important part of his job when he was appointed Dean of Harvard College in 1891, one of the first student affairs professionals (Fley, 1974). These early deans expanded both the philosophy and the programs of discipline in higher education. Idealistic and optimistic about the kinds of students they could develop, they approached discipline with the ultimate goal of self-control or self-discipline, and they used more individualized, humanistic, and preventive methods. The concept of the student as a whole began to develop (Durst, 1969), and counseling as a form of corrective action became popular (Fley, 1964).

Discipline became an unfortunate point of separation between the early deans and the emerging student personnel specialists (Appleton, Briggs, & Rhatigan, 1978; Knock, 1985). While they had many purposes and approaches in common, the "personnel workers tended to view the deans' disciplining of students as antithetical to their developmental efforts" because they regarded the "dean's role as a disciplinarian only in the sense of punishment. This view, of course, separated the 'punishing' dean from the 'promoting' personnel worker" (Knock, 1985, pp. 32–33). As higher education expanded under the philosophies of meritocracy and egalitarianism, the campus student body became larger and more heterogeneous, resulting in increased disciplinary work for the dean, while the personnel worker "became the specialist in human development" (Knock, p. 33). Thus, the unfortunate schism widened as the dean was perceived as the "bad guy," interested more in control and punishment, while the student development specialist was viewed more positively as the true promoter of student interests and growth (Appleton et al., 1978). Rhatigan (2000) recently reminded us of the truly humanistic orientation of the early deans.

After World War II and the influx of veterans into colleges and universities, campus facilities and regulations were tested by the large number of older and more worldly students who "could not digest the traditional palliatives served up by the dean to justify student conduct regulation and discipline" (Smith & Kirk, 1971, p. 277). But a widespread crisis was avoided because veterans' overriding vocational orientation kept them preoccupied with academics. While they may have had little time for the dean's discipline, they also had little time or interest in revolting against it. However, a small number of institutions experienced protests by veterans and other students against the paternalistic rules of the period (Lowery, 1998c).

Throughout the 1950s and 1960s, disciplinary affairs became less punishment- and control-oriented, more democratic, and more focused on education and rehabilitation. Professionally trained counselors were delegated more responsibility, and disciplinary hearing boards composed of both staff and students were established (Sims, 1971). One of the factors that contributed significantly to this change was the emergence of the student protest movement on campus starting in 1964. Mario Savio, the leader of the free speech movement at Berkeley, spoke forcefully about the connection between the free speech movement and the civil rights movement as well as new student expectations regarding campus rules and policies:

> Last summer I went to Mississippi to join the struggle there for civil rights. This fall I am engaged in another phase of the same struggle, this time in Berkeley. The two battlefields may seem quite different, but this is not the case. The same rights are at stake in both places—the right to participate as citizens in a democratic society and the right to due process of law. We are asking that our actions be judged by committees of our peers. We are asking that

regulations ought to be considered as arrived at legitimately only from a consensus of the governed. (Warshaw & Leahy, 1965, p. 27)

The 1960s and 1970s were characterized by increased student input into disciplinary codes and processes, broadened legal and educational conceptions of students' rights and responsibilities, and the introduction of due process safeguards in the hearing of misconduct cases. These developments may be attributed to several factors: more older students, the lowered age of majority, an increasingly permissive society, the civil rights movement, the realization of the power of student activism and disruption on many campuses, and court intervention in the disciplinary process (Gibbs, 1992; Smith, 1994).

This court intervention, coupled with genuine concern for students' constitutional rights, led many colleges and universities in the 1960s to establish formal, legalistic "judicial systems" for the adjudication of misconduct and the determination of sanctions. This movement caused concern that such adversarial systems, borrowed from our system of criminal justice, focused primarily on the mechanism of the disciplinary process to the detriment of the educative purpose (Dannells, 1978; Gehring, 2001). The literature of the past three decades and contemporary practice of disciplinary affairs suggest a renewed and continuing interest in the reintegration of the concept and goals of student development within the framework of campus judicial systems designed to protect the legal rights of students and to educate all students involved in the process (Ardaiolo, 1983; Caruso & Travelstead, 1987; Dannells, 1997; Gehring, 2001; Greenleaf, 1978). The overzealous adoption of criminal-like proceedings seems to have faded (Dannells, 1990) in favor of a balanced approach designed to ensure fairness, protection of the educational environment, *and* learning (Bracewell, 1988). But the court intervention of the 1960s began the still ongoing tension between the student development approach and the legalistic approach to discipline (Lancaster & Cooper, 1998; Smith, 1994).

Another indication of the development of student discipline as a specialization within student affairs was the establishment of Commission XV: Campus Judicial Affairs and Legal Issues of the American College Personnel Association in the early 1970s and the founding of the Association for Student Judicial Affairs (ASJA) in 1987. The rapid expansion of ASJA in the years following its founding was a clear signal that student judicial affairs had become a distinct area of specialization in student affairs.

DEFINITION, PURPOSE, AND SCOPE
OF STUDENT DISCIPLINE

Probably no other specialty area in student affairs has engendered so much debate, disagreement, and dissension (Fley, 1964). As Appleton et al.

(1978) put it, "the subject of discipline has been one of the most pervasive and painful topics in the history of student personnel administration" (p. 21). It raises fundamental questions about the goals of higher education, the role of student personnel work within it, and our view of students.

Much of the controversy and disagreement about discipline relates to its several meanings and purposes. Within the context of college student personnel work, discipline may be variously defined as (1) *self-discipline*, or that virtue which may be regarded as the essence of education (Appleton et al., 1978; Hawkes, 1930; Mueller, 1961; Seward, 1961; Wrenn, 1949); (2) *the process of reeducation* or rehabilitation (Appleton et al., 1978); or (3) *punishment* as a means of external control of behavior (Appleton et al., 1978; Seward, 1961; Wrenn, 1949).

AUTHORITY TO DISCIPLINE AND THE
STUDENT-INSTITUTIONAL RELATIONSHIP

Closely related to the purpose of student discipline is the matter of the institution's authority to discipline. Seven different theories defining the institution's source of power to discipline its students and describing to some degree the nature of the student–institutional relationship have been identified (Dannells, 1977), but only three—the doctrine of *in loco parentis*, the contract theory, and the educational purpose theory—merit description here.

In loco parentis, literally "in the place of a parent," is a common-law doctrine that views the institution as taking the role of the parent with respect to all student conduct. In this view, the institution is presumed to know best the needs of students and is vested with great latitude in the disciplinary process (see *Gott v. Berea College*, 1913). As such, this doctrine was once used as the justification for paternalistic, informal, and sometimes arbitrary use of power to discipline (Hoekema, 1994; Ratliff, 1972), even though, according to Appleton et al. (1978), "its formalization into the law occurred long after the original relationship was abandoned in practice" (p. 25). Ever since its application to the college disciplinary situation, this doctrine has been problematic; it has been criticized as impractical, erroneous, and misleading as a viable educational concept (Penney, 1967; Ratliff, 1972; Strickland, 1965). Today, while vestiges of paternalism may still exist in the reaffirmation of concern for the whole student as reflected in student development theory and practice (Gregory & Ballou, 1986; Parr & Buchanan, 1979; Pitts, 1980), the doctrine of *in loco parentis* as a legal description of the student–institutional relationship is generally considered to be inappropriate, untenable, intolerable, or simply dead (Grossi & Edwards, 1997; Nuss, 1998).

Contract theory defines the relationship of the student and the institution as a contractual one, the terms of which are set forth in the institution's catalogue, other publications, and oral addenda. Students enter the contract by signing the registration document and paying fees, thereby accepting the conduct rules and academic regulations. Violations of the rules may then be met with those measures enumerated as sanctions in the contract. This theory was once restricted largely to private institutions and to academic affairs, but now, with the lowered age of majority, older students, increasing consumerism, and the general litigiousness in our society, it is seeing increasing acceptance and application to all student–institutional relationships (Barr, 1988; Grossi & Edwards, 1997; Hammond, 1978; Shur, 1983, 1988). By analogy, students at public institutions also have another type of contract with the institution, a contract created by the U.S. Constitution as well as the state constitutions.

Educational purpose theory views the student–institutional relationship as an educational one, thereby limiting disciplinary control to student behavior adversely affecting the institution's pursuit of its educational mission. Given that the institution's *raison d'etre* is education and that this is the reason for its relationship with students, this view is considered by many to be the only realistic and justifiable basis for student discipline (Callis, 1967, 1969; Carnegie Commission, 1971; National Education Association, 1971; Penney, 1967; Van Alstyne, 1966). It stems from the premise that the academy is a special place, with a special atmosphere in which educators attempt to fashion an environment "where dialogue, debate, and the exchange of ideas can proceed unfettered . . . [and] in which there is concern about preserving the sanctity of the classroom and protecting academic freedom" (Gehring & Bracewell, 1992, p. 90). This theory allows the institution to discipline students for the purpose of maintenance of order or in furtherance of its educational objectives vis-à-vis an individual student or group of students. It protects the institution from unwanted court intrusion by recognizing that the courts have historically adopted a policy of nonintervention or judicial restraint in matters that are legitimately part of the educational enterprise (Ardaiolo, 1983; Travelstead, 1987). Furthermore, the educational purpose theory serves to remind us of the inherent superiority of achieving student discipline through proactive means, especially in the face of a permissive society (Georgia, 1989).

For a new and creative model of the legal relationship of the institution and its students, the "facilitator university," the reader is referred to Bickel and Lake (1999).

EXTENT OF INSTITUTIONAL JURISDICTION

Two basic questions arise with respect to the extent of the institution's jurisdiction: (1) Should it apply internal sanctions, seek external (i.e., criminal) sanctions, or both where institutional rules and criminal law both apply (Stein, 1972)? (2) Should the institution concern itself with students' off-campus behavior? Concerning both questions, the recent trend, in keeping with the educational purpose theory of discipline, is that internal actions are appropriate in all cases, whether on- or off-campus behavior is involved, where the institutional mission is affected. Dannells' (1990) research on changes in the practice of disciplinary affairs over the period from 1978 to 1988 showed a significant increase in the number of institutions that concerned themselves with the off-campus behavior of their students. The question of the application of criminal law is essentially a separate matter, especially in dealing with students who are legal adults and when the criminal act is of a serious nature (Sims, 1971; Stein, 1972).

Double jeopardy is an issue related to jurisdiction. On occasion students have argued that, for the same act, to be both disciplined by their institution and tried for a criminal offense constitutes double jeopardy. However, it is well established that double jeopardy applies only to the two criminal proceedings for the same offense and not to a criminal proceeding and college disciplinary action for the same offense (Fisher, 1970; Kaplin & Lee, 1997; Rhode & Math, 1988). Nonetheless, it is recommended that the institution avoid the mere duplication of criminal punishments by emphasizing the educational approach of its proceedings and subsequent response (Ardaiolo & Walker, 1987; Fisher, 1970).

DUE PROCESS

Due process, while a flexible concept (Bracewell, 1988; Gehring, 2001; Janosik & Riehl, 2000) related to time and circumstances (Ardaiolo, 1983), may be defined as "an appropriate protection of the rights of an individual while determining his [her] liability for wrongdoing and the applicability of punishment" (Fisher, 1970, p. 1). It is a constitutional right granted by the Fifth Amendment with respect to action by the federal government and by the Fourteenth Amendment with respect to state action. The well-established standard used by the courts when questions of due process have arisen in the context of student discipline is that of *fundamental fairness* (Ardaiolo, 1983; Bakken, 1968; Buchanan, 1978; Fisher, 1970; Footer, 1996; Young, 1972). It is important to recognize that only students at public colleges and universities have a constitutional right to due process. At private institutions, the contracts that exist between the student and the institution define the rights and responsibilities of students.

Procedural due process refers to the individual's rights in the adjudication of an offense. That which is "due," or owing, to ensure fairness in any given circumstance, will vary with the seriousness of the alleged offense and with the severity of the possible sanction. Substantive due process relates to the nature, purpose, or application of a rule or law. Again, applying the standard of fairness, rules must be clear and not overly broad, they must have a fair and reasonable purpose, and they must be applied in fairness and good faith (Young, 1972).

Since 1960, there have been many court cases on due process in disciplinary proceedings, especially dismissal hearings. Prior to that time, under a combination of *in loco parentis* and contract theories, the courts generally assumed the college to be acting fairly and in the best educational interests of all concerned. But the civil rights movement, during which some students were summarily dismissed from college because of their participation in civil rights demonstrations, prompted significant legal and philosophical changes (Ardaiolo, 1983; Bakken, 1968; Dannells, 1977). In the landmark case *Dixon v. Alabama State Board of Education* (1961), the court ruled, on the basis of an analogy of education as property (thus bringing dismissal from a state college under the due process clause of the Fourteenth Amendment), that a student has a constitutional right to notice and a hearing. The Dixon court went on to recommend several procedural safeguards to ensure fairness in such cases: the notice should give specific charges; the hearing should consider both sides of the case; the accused should be informed about witnesses against them and the nature of their testimony; the student should have a chance to present a defense; the findings of the hearing should be reported to the student; and the "requirements of due process are met in dismissal hearings where the rudiments of fair play are followed" (Dannells, 1977, p. 249).

Numerous court decisions since *Dixon* established it as precedent and further specified the procedural due process safeguards for dismissal and other serious conduct hearings from public institutions. All of the procedural safeguards required in criminal proceedings are not required in student conduct hearings (Carletta, 1998; Correnti, 1988; Gehring, 2001; Gehring & Bracewell, 1992; Kaplin & Lee, 1997; Shur, 1983), and no one particular model of procedural due process is required (Bracewell, 1988; Buchanan, 1978; Travelstead, 1987). The court in *Esteban v. Central Missouri State College* (1969) observed, "School regulations are not to be measured by the standards which prevail for criminal law and for criminal procedure."

In the area of substantive due process, several principles for public institutions are well established (Arndt, 1971; Buchanan, 1978):

1. Colleges have the authority to make and enforce rules of student conduct to maintain discipline and order.
2. Behavioral standards, including rules applied to off-campus behavior, must be consistent with the institution's lawful purpose and function.
3. Rules must be constitutionally fair, reasonable, and not capricious or arbitrary.
4. The code of conduct should be written and available for all to see.
5. The constitutionally guaranteed rights of students can be limited to enable the institution to function, but blanket prohibitions are not permitted.
6. A rule must be specific enough to give adequate notice of expected behavior and to allow the student to prepare a defense against a charge under it. Vague or overly broad rules, such as general pro-

scriptions against "misconduct" or "conduct unbecoming a Siwash College student," have not been upheld (Gehring & Bracewell, 1992).

The courts have not required private institutions to meet these due process standards because they are not engaged in state action and so do not fall under the Fourteenth Amendment (Buchanan, 1978; Carletta, 1998; Kaplin & Lee, 1997; Shur, 1983, 1988). The analogy of education as a property right has not been extended to private schools, and their relationship with their students is still considered largely contractual. Thus, despite many projections in the 1970s that the courts would abolish the public-private distinction in disciplinary matters, the private institution still legally has more latitude in defining and adjudicating student misconduct (Correnti, 1988; Shur, 1983, 1988). But procedural reforms tend to become normative in higher education; many private colleges now contract with their students to provide the basic due process protections expected in public institutions and having done so, they are contractually required to follow their own rules and procedures (Carletta, 1998; Pavela, 1985, 2000; Shur, 1983; 1988; Stoner, 1998; Stoner & Cerminara, 1990). Furthermore, since the 1960s, the courts have more critically examined this contractual relationship and applied similar standards of review to those applied to other contracts between unequal parties.

The courts have generally distinguished between academic dismissal and dismissal for misconduct (Rhode, 1983; Rhode & Math, 1988), although this dichotomy "may be very difficult to apply in fact" (Ardaiolo, 1983, pp. 17–18). In the landmark case of *Board of Curators of the University of Missouri v. Horowitz* (1978), the U.S. Supreme Court placed limitations on the due process procedures required in academic dismissal situations. Instead of a hearing, the student need only be informed of the particular academic deficiencies and of the consequences of those shortcomings (e.g., dismissal) should they not be remedied. Once this warning has occurred, the decision-making person or body must then make a "careful and deliberate" decision based on "expert evaluation of cumulative information" (p. 79). The court noted that this process is "not readily adapted to the procedural tools of judicial or administrative decision making" (p. 79) and declined to enter this academic domain. It should be emphasized that this case involved the academic evaluation of a student and was not a matter of academic misconduct, such as cheating or plagiarism, where an allegation of wrongdoing is made and fact-finding is central to the disciplinary process. That distinction may be blurred and problematic in cases in which it is difficult to distinguish misconduct (e.g., plagiarism) from poor scholarship (Travelstead, 1987) or where standards of dress, personal hygiene, or interpersonal conduct are the focus of evaluation in professional or clinical training. The courts have clearly indicated that in cases involving allegations of academic dishonesty, students must be afforded the same rights as students in other disciplinary cases (Kaplin & Lee, 1995).

CONSTITUTIONAL PROTECTIONS OF STUDENT RIGHTS

Another general issue is the extent to which the institution can proscribe students' behavior. In the area of students' constitutional rights at public institutions, four principles are well established:

1. The institution cannot put a blanket restraint on students' First Amendment rights of freedom of assembly and expression, but it may restrain assembly and expression, which will substantially interfere with its educational and administrative duties (Gibbs, 1992; Kaplin & Lee, 1997; Mager, 1978; Pavela, 1985; Sherry, 1966; Young, 1970).
2. The institution cannot restrict, prohibit, or censor the content of speech, except for extraordinarily compelling reasons, such as someone's safety (Kaplin & Lee, 1997; Mager, 1978; Pavela, 1985; Sherry, 1966). The special problem of hate speech is addressed later in this chapter.
3. The college cannot apply its rules in a discriminatory manner (Sherry, 1966).
4. Students are protected by the Fourth Amendment from unreasonable searches and seizures (Bracewell, 1978; Fisher, 1970; Young, 1970).

STUDENT MISCONDUCT: SOURCES AND RESPONSES

What constitutes misconduct is a function of the goal of student discipline and of the nature and number of rules and regulations that follow (Foley, 1947; Seward, 1961; Williamson, 1956, 1961; Williamson & Foley, 1949; Wrenn, 1949). Other institutional factors that influence the frequency and nature of student misconduct include the full array of campus environmental conditions. It is understandable why residential campuses with largely traditional-aged student populations have greater disciplinary caseloads than commuter or nonresidential campuses given the significant additional time that students spend on campus and the residence hall experience.

Intrapersonal sources of student misconduct may be categorized as pathological or nonpathological. Nonpathological misbehavior may be viewed as stemming from lack of information or understanding or from inadequate or incomplete development, once referred to as immaturity or adolescent mischievousness and excess energy (Williamson, 1956). Pathological origins of student behavior have become of greater interest and concern as serious psychopathology among college students seems to be on the rise, at least insofar as it is manifest in such behaviors as sexual harassment, acquaintance rape, other forms of dating violence, alcohol abuse, and "stalking" (Gallagher, Harmon, & Lingenfelter, 1994). However, the increasing concern for behaviors that stem from pathological origins has not been accompanied by a significant increase in the frequency of the types of disciplinary cases one might expect (Dannells, 1991).

Institutional responses may be categorized as punitive, rehabilitative (educational or developmental are more popular terms today), or environmental (actions aimed at external sources of misconduct). The extent to which a given sanction is best categorized as punitive, or developmental, is a matter of philosophy and purpose. While sanctions may be viewed as punitive in the immediate—particularly by the recipient—they are a proper and effective developmental or therapeutic tool for much of the problematic behavior of traditional-aged college students, many of whom are still learning to manage impulses (Frederickson, 1992). In *Esteban v, Central Missouri State College* (1968), the court commented on the educational nature of the disciplinary process:

> The discipline of students in the educational community is, in all but the case of irrevocable expulsion, a part of the teaching process. In the case of irrevocable expulsion for misconduct, the process is not punitive or deterrent in the criminal law sense, but the process is rather the determination that the student is unqualified to continue as a member of the educational community. Even then, the disciplinary process is not equivalent to the criminal law processes of federal or state criminal law (p. 628).

Sanctions commonly employed include various forms of "informative" disciplinary communications, such as oral and written warnings or admonitions, often accompanied by a reference to more severe sanctions to follow if problems continue; disciplinary probation; denial of relevant privileges or liberties, such as restrictions on participation in extracurricular activities or the use of facilities, often used as a condition of probation; restitution, or monetary compensation for damage or injury; fines; denial of financial assistance (now thought to be rare); and actions that affect the student's status, such as suspension (the temporary dismissal of the student either for a finite period or indefinitely) and expulsion (permanent dismissal). In recent years, many campuses have added to the range of disciplinary sanctions (Bostic & Gonzalez, 1999), often by adding community service and other educational sanctions, but the actual use of disciplinary sanctions and rehabilitative actions appears to have changed little (Dannells, 1990, 1991).

Institutional responses involving rehabilitation or intentional human development include counseling, referral for medical or psychiatric care, and the assignment of a civic or public service project designed to enhance appreciation or awareness of personal responsibility. Disciplinary counseling may involve a professionally trained counselor; other professionals within the institution, such as an administrator or a faculty member associated with the campus judicial system or with the residence hall program; or extrainstitutional assistance from parents, clergy, social workers, or other helping professionals.

Actions aimed at sources of misbehavior external to the student include changing living arrangements and finding financial assistance or employment. Other possible responses are academic assistance, such as tutoring or learning skills development, and policy revision, where the "misconduct" is more a function of outmoded or unnecessarily restrictive rules.

The choice of institutional response in a disciplinary situation is affected by a number of considerations: one's views on changing human behavior, the institution's educational mission as reflected in the nature and extent of its behavioral standards, the degree of divergence between those standards and those of its students, the behavior itself, what kinds of information about the accused are judged to be important (Janosik, 1995), the array of responses established in policy, and the creativity of the decision maker(s).

Restorative community justice is a new approach to judicial sanctioning that deserves mention here. It is an alternative to punishment-oriented sanctioning that emphasizes student accountability and community healing. Students who are found responsible for code violations or criminal behavior on campus are expected to acknowledge responsibility by apologizing, making restitution, and working to restore damage done to the fabric of the community (Karp, Breslin, & Oles, n.d.; Warters, Sebok, & Goldblum, 2000).

ADMINISTRATION AND ORGANIZATION

The administration of student discipline, or campus judicial affairs systems, may be divided into three areas: (1) the roles and functions of student affairs professionals in discipline; (2) the nature and scope of campus judicial systems; and (3) the handling of disciplinary records. Research findings have been consistent in one important respect; from campus to campus there is substantial heterogeneity in approaches to student discipline (Dannells, 1978, 1990, 1997; Durst, 1969; Dutton, Smith, & Zarle, 1969; Lancaster, Cooper, & Harman, 1993; Ostroth & Hill, 1978; Steele, Johnson, & Rickard, 1984). Institutional factors influencing the nature of a campus' system include its educational philosophy or mission; its size, type of control (public or private), and residential character (Lancaster et al., 1993); the needs of the community; and the extent to which governance is shared with students (Ardaiolo & Walker, 1987).

ROLES AND FUNCTIONS OF STUDENT AFFAIRS
PROFESSIONALS IN DISCIPLINE

Student affairs professionals may be charged with a broad range of roles and functions related to the disciplinary process. At one end of the spectrum, they may function in the role of an ombudsman or mediator, independently and informally facilitating the resolution of conflicts and handling minor complaints. This approach has the advantage of brevity, keeping the problem at the lowest possible level of resolution; and it provides an educational, nonadversarial alternative for settling differences in certain situations (Hayes & Balogh, 1990; Serr & Taber, 1987; Sisson & Todd, 1995). At the other end of the spectrum, there may be a specialist—often called a hearing officer or judicial affairs officer—charged with the responsibility of the total disciplinary system, including orchestrating the workings of one or more tribunals or boards, handling all disciplinary records, and investigating and preparing cases in more serious matters. The main advantages of this model are expertise and freeing other staff from the disciplinary function. Continuity, equity, and improved management of the process are also arguments for the specialist (Steele et al., 1984). Specialized judicial affairs officers are uncommon in smaller colleges. Steele et al. found that of the 18 schools (12% of their respondents) that reported judicial affairs officers, 10 were large (more than 10,000 students) institutions. Lancaster et al. (1993) found that commuter, public, and large institutions are significantly more likely to have judicial specialists.

The most common model is that of a middle-level student affairs professional, most often associated with the dean of students office or the office of residence life, who administratively handles relatively minor violations and presents serious cases to a hearing board for final disposition. At larger institutions and those with residential student bodies, responsibility for relatively minor violations of student code by residential students in the halls may be delegated to hall directors or other residence life staff. For many years at smaller and private institutions, the dean of students had and continues to retain major responsibility for adjudicating student misconduct (Dannells, 1978, 1990; Lancaster et al., 1993; Ostroth, Armstrong, & Campbell, 1978; Steele et al., 1984).

Student affairs professionals involved in disciplinary programs may function as educators in several ways. As coordinators, advisors, and trainers of members of campus judicial boards, they have opportunities to encourage the development of students along moral, ethical, and legal lines (Boots, 1987; Cordner & Brooks, 1987). Working with students whose behavior is in question, they may, through a combination of teaching and counseling techniques, help students gain insight and understanding about their behavior and responsibilities. Furthermore, discipline officers can contribute to the intellectual climate of the institution not only by helping to preserve a safe and educationally conducive atmosphere (Boots, 1987), but also by leading the entire campus community in the process of defining and disseminating a behavioral code that represents a set of shared beliefs and values about the educational environment and the student's responsibilities within it (Dannells, 1997; Pavela, 1985).

Caruso (1978) defined the important roles of the student discipline specialist in terms of the basic student personnel functions outlined by Miller and Prince (1976). *Goal setting* is important for keeping the discipline system in accord with the broader institutional goals, for working developmentally with the individuals, and for designing outcomes-oriented training programs for student judicial boards. *Assessing student growth* can provide important, yet frequently lacking, evaluative information about the efficacy of the disciplinary process for all of the students involved. *Instruction* may take the form of teaching credit or noncredit courses as educational sanctions on topics such as anger management; may involve student leadership training and judicial board member education; or may take the form of offering "mainstream" coursework in a collaborative or team-teaching approach with another academic unit in subjects such as moral development, legal aspects of higher education, parliamentary procedure, or one of various life skills such as parent effectiveness. *Consultation* includes working with the campus policy committees, judicial boards, and paraprofessionals in the residence halls and assisting academic units with the administration of academic misconduct cases. *Environmental management* involves any response to a behavior problem that is designed to reduce or eliminate conditions that contribute to the problem, such as the placement of residence hall fire protection equipment, campus lighting, and the sale and distribution of alcoholic beverages on the campus. Last is the important function of *program evaluation* through which the discipline program may study itself for purposes of improvement and justification of resources.

Disciplinary counseling is another function basic to the educational approach to discipline. Williamson (1963, p. 13) defined it as "sympathetic but firm counseling to aid the individual to gain insight and be willing to accept restrictions on his [or her] individual autonomy and behavior." Frequently cited objectives of disciplinary counseling include rehabilitation and behavior change, insight, maturation, emotional stability, moral judgment, self-reliance, self-control, and understanding and accepting responsibility for and consequences of personal behavior (Dannells, 1977). The counseling techniques of information giving (teaching) and confrontation are central to the "helping encounter in discipline" and may be employed throughout the disciplinary process (Ostroth & Hill, 1978).

THE NATURE AND SCOPE OF CAMPUS JUDICIAL SYSTEMS

Like the roles and functions of the student affairs professional in discipline, campus judicial systems vary greatly, depending on those key institutional factors (philosophy, size, etc.) cited previously. Smaller and private institutions tend to have more informal, centralized systems, while larger and public schools tend toward the more formal, legalistic, and decentralized or specialized model (Dannells, 1978, 1990; Lancaster et al., 1993;

Steele et al., 1984). Campus judicial systems may differ on the extent of their authority and responsibility; the differentiation between criminal and campus codes and procedures and between academic and nonacademic misconduct; how specifically behavior is defined and proscribed; the due process rights accorded the student at both the prehearing and the hearing phases of the adjudicatory process; the availability and application of sanctions, conditions, appeals, and rehabilitative actions; the nature and extent of student input into the code of conduct; the level of student involvement in the process of adjudication; and the availability of alternative adjudicative mechanisms (Ardaiolo & Walker, 1987).

Research conducted during the past 30 years revealed the following trends about the administration of student discipline (Van Alstyne, 1963; Bostic & Gonzalez, 1999; Dannells, 1978, 1990; Durst, 1969; Dutton et al., 1969; Fitch & Murry, 2001; Leslie & Satryb, 1974; Ostroth et al., 1978; Steele et al., 1984; Wilson, 1996):

1. In the 1960s there was a dramatic increase in student input into conduct rules and procedures and the adjudication of misconduct (judicial boards). This trend continues to shape student judicial affairs and student involvement remains high on most campuses.
2. There has been a similar trend in the provision of both procedural and substantive due process mechanisms, starting with a major shift toward more legalistic processes and leveling in more recent years. More formal, legalistic procedures can be expected for cases that may result in dismissal, while more informal processes are used with minor cases.
3. Milder sanctions are more often employed than stiffer penalties. Warnings, both oral and written, and disciplinary probation have been and continue to be the most common responses to student misconduct.
4. Disciplinary counseling continues to be the most common rehabilitative action, but over the years it is increasingly more likely to take place in either a disciplinary specialist's office or in the counseling center, especially in larger institutions. At smaller colleges, the disciplinary function, including post-hearing counseling, continues to be performed in the dean of students' office.
5. While most institutions do not anticipate changes in their programs, those that do indicate a need for change and suggest that it should be in the direction of streamlining and simplifying their processes and making their hearings less legalistic.
6. Diversity continues to characterize the administration of disciplinary affairs.

Drawing on the Council for the Advancement of Standards (CAS) Standards for Judicial Services, the Statement of Principles of the Association of Student Judicial Affairs, and the research base on the subject,

Lancaster et al. (1993) offered the following model for organizing and administering the disciplinary function:

1. Assign, as a primary responsibility, all disciplinary administration to a single staff member, even where multiple hearing bodies exist.
2. Place this staff member in a direct reporting relationship to the president or chief student affairs officer.
3. Create a philosophy for this staff member's practice and for the disciplinary system that fosters a developmental approach to discipline.
4. Create a formal training and assessment procedure, supported by appropriate documentation, for judicial officers and other regular participants (p.118).

THE MANAGEMENT OF DISCIPLINARY RECORDS

The Family Educational Rights and Privacy Act (FERPA; also known as the Buckley Amendment) of 1974 was intended to protect the privacy of student records by limiting their release to third parties and guaranteeing students' right of access to their own education records. However, the protections of education records have never been absolute. For example, the legislation has always allowed institutions to share information with school officials who possess a legitimate educational interest or the parents of a dependent student (Gregory, 1998; Lowery, 1998a).

Prior to FERPA and the lowering of the age of majority, college students' parents were routinely notified of their sons' or daughters' disciplinary records, and student records, including disciplinary files, were available to other agencies and prospective employers. Within a few years after the passage of "Buckley," Dannells (1978) found that the great majority of respondent institutions conformed to the law by keeping students' academic and disciplinary records confidential. Eighty percent of colleges kept their disciplinary records separate from other student records, and very few made them available to outside agencies or prospective employers without the student's consent. Only 8 percent reported releasing records to parents. Parents were notified of their student's involvement in the disciplinary process by 37 percent of the respondents if the student was a minor, but 30 percent indicated they did not notify parents regardless of the student's age. Little change in these practices was found in a follow-up study conducted 10 years later (Dannells, 1990).

There was considerable debate in the 1990s about the privacy protections provided to student disciplinary records as part of a larger concern about campus crime (Gregory, 1998; Lowery, 1998a). Since the passage of the federal Higher Education Amendments (HEA) of 1998, "parental notification" has also become a significant issue in the administration of campus discipline (Lowery, 2000; Palmer, Lohman, Gehring, Carlson, & Garrett, 2001).

The HEA altered FERPA to permit, but do not require, colleges and universities to notify parents of students who are under the age of 21 at the time of the notification (Gehring, 2000; Lowery, 2000) that the student has violated institutional rules or local, state, or federal laws relating to the possession or use of alcohol or a controlled substance (Inter-Association Task Force, n.d.; 2001; Kaplin & Lee, 2000; Lowery, 2000). Institutional response to this and subsequent federal guidelines have varied, depending on size, type, nature of the student body, institutional philosophy, and state law (Palmer et al., 2001; Sluis, 2001). Palmer et al. (2001) found that the majority of the respondents to their survey had adopted (by January 2000) or were planning to adopt (by fall of 2000) a parental notification policy. Guidelines for the formulation of such policies have been developed by the ASJA and the Inter-Association Task Force on Alcohol and Other Substance Abuse Issues.

The Student Right-to-Know and Campus Security Act of 1990 amended FERPA to allow disclosure of the outcome of campus disciplinary proceeding to the victim of an alleged crime of violence or nonforcible sex offense (Lowery, 1998a, 2000). The HEA of 1998 also amended FERPA and the Campus Security Act with respect to reporting the outcome of disciplinary proceedings against a student alleged to have committed a crime of violence or a nonforcible sex offense. The outcome of such a proceeding may now be reported to the public when the student is found responsible for these charges. In such cases, state open public record laws and privacy protections will influence how much and to whom information may be released by public institutions (Gehring, 2000; Kaplin & Lee, 2000; Lowery, 1998a, 2000).

In recent years, student charges of unfairness in campus judicial proceedings and allegations that institutions are using the campus judicial system to hide campus crime have prompted considerable interest, especially among journalists, in opening such hearings to the public (Gregory, 1998; Lowery, 1998a). In January 1995, the U.S. Department of Education issued final rules that amended FERPA clarifying that disciplinary proceedings and subsequent actions are education records. The state supreme courts of Georgia and Ohio have ordered the release of student disciplinary records under state open records laws in *Red & Black Publishing Company v. Board of Regents* (1993) and *State ex rel The Miami Student v. Miami University* (1997), respectively. However, a federal court judge ruled that FERPA prevented the release of student disciplinary records as ordered by the Ohio Supreme Court in *U.S. v. Miami University and Ohio State University* (2000).

DISCIPLINE AND STUDENT DEVELOPMENT THEORY

Seemingly in reaction to the perceived excessive proceduralism following the *Dixon* case, the student affairs profession in the last two decades has shown renewed interest in the educational nature of discipline and the application of student development to the conduct of disciplinary affairs. Not only is there concern for protection of the individual's rights and of the institution itself, but also there appears to be a growing realization of the primacy of the educational value in the disciplinary function. This is not to suggest that meeting students' legal rights and fostering their development are incompatible, which they are not (Greenleaf, 1978), but rather that the increasingly adversarial nature of the process became a significant drain on and distraction to those charged with administering campuses' disciplinary system. It became more difficult to find that proper balance necessary to the survival of the Student Personnel Point of View (Caruso, 1978). With the growing body of theory, research, and literature on cognitive, moral, and ethical development, there appears to be increasing interest in its application to the disciplinary setting (Saddlemire, 1980).

Student discipline is, and always has been, an excellent opportunity for developmental efforts. The traditional dean of students knew this but operated without the benefit of formal developmental theories, especially those that emphasize moral and ethical growth and so lend themselves to the disciplinary process. Much of discipline involves teaching (Ardaiolo, 1983; Ostroth & Hill, 1978; Travelstead, 1987) and counseling (Foley, 1947; Gometz & Parker, 1968; Ostroth & Hill, 1978; Stone & Lucas, 1994; Williamson, 1963; Williamson & Foley, 1949). By the application of developmental theory, the individual may be better understood and counseling and developmental interventions may be more scientifically and accurately fashioned (Boots, 1987).

Various developmental theories have been applied to the disciplinary process and its impact on the individual student (e.g., see Boots, 1987; Greenleaf, 1978; Ostroth & Hill, 1978; Smith, 1978), and certain common elements and objectives of the different views and approaches are noted in the literature. These include:

1. Insight as a commonly stated objective and means to further growth in the individual "offender" (Dannells, 1977);
2. Self-understanding or clarification of personal identity, attitudes, and values, especially in relation to authority, both for the student whose behavior is in question and for students who sit on judicial boards (Boots, 1987; Greenleaf, 1978);
3. Goals of self-control, responsibility, and accountability (Caruso, 1978; Pavela, 1985; Travelstead, 1987);
4. The use of ethical dialogue in both confronting the impact of the individual's behavior and its moral implications and examining the fairness of rules (McBee, 1982; Pavela, 1985; Smith, 1978);
5. There appears to have been an extension of the scope and goals of student discipline to a broader objective of moral and ethical devel-

opment as it relates to contemporary social issues, such as prejudice, health and wellness, sexism, racism, and human sexuality (Baldizan, 1998; Dalton & Healy, 1984).

In a survey of counseling center directors, Stone and Lucas (1994) found the following frequencies of goals for disciplinary counseling: assessment/evaluation, 28 percent; behavior change, 27 percent; student insight, 16 percent; education, 10 percent; establishment of appropriate goals, 5 percent; and "other," 14 percent. When asked to identify "reference material that the respondent would recommend for counseling center staff in working with disciplinary referrals" (p. 235), none of the counseling center directors offered developmental theory or theorists. This lack of reference to developmental theory may be taken as evidence of the oft-bemoaned theory-to-practice gap in student affairs and may lend credence to the critiques of the usefulness of student development theory in our practice (e.g., see Bloland, Stamatakos, & Rogers, 1994).

Nonetheless, the weight of authority is clearly in keeping with Boots's (1987) assertion that developmental theory can be a "proactive part of the total educational process" (p. 67). Dannells (1991) provided an example of how that might be done:

> For example, in working with a student involved in disruptive behavior and underage drinking at a residence hall party, the student affairs professional may render an informal assessment (King, 1990) of the student's level of moral reasoning at Level I (preconventional morality), Stage 2 (relative hedonism) using Kohlherg's (1969) model. Concurrently, using Chickering's (1969) theory, the student may be viewed as struggling with developing interpersonal competence and managing emotions. This may be a common diagnosis that would lend itself to a group intervention focusing on the campus regulations about alcohol, the reasons for them, and the ways that students can be socially engaged without using alcohol (p. 170).

Developmental theory is also useful for thinking about the relative maturity level of students (Thomas, 1987) and about the positive outcomes for all students. Chickering and Reisser (1993) explained:

> Students may learn about community values and ethical principles when they either violate the conduct code or serve in judicial systems. The latter case represents an opportunity to develop integrity. In hearing cases, reviewing disciplinary procedures, and determining sanctions, students consider moral dilemmas in a concrete way. . . . By serving on hearing committees, students also benefit from watching faculty members, administrators, and staff members grapple with the arguments. The need for rules has not disappeared. . . . The challenge now is engaging students to take more responsibility for maintaining a safe and positive learning environment, becoming aware of the institution's code of conduct, and respecting the processes of enforcing and amending regulations (p. 448).

CURRENT ISSUES IN STUDENT DISCIPLINE

BALANCING LEGAL RIGHTS AND EDUCATIONAL PURPOSES

Following the *Dixon* decision in 1961, many institutions, both private and public, rushed to establish disciplinary systems affording students their "due" protections. Some overreacted, went far beyond the court's requirements, and became "mired in legalistic disputes" (Lamont, 1979, p. 85). Critics of this "creeping legalism," or proceduralism, argued that it has undermined the informal and uniquely educational aspect of the disciplinary process in higher education; it has resulted in costly, complex, and time-consuming processes; and it places the student and the institution in an unnecessarily adversarial relationship (Dannells, 1977, 1997; Gehring, 2001; Pavela, 1985; Travelstead, 1987). Gehring (2001) noted, "The 'creeping legalism' described by Dannells (1997) has gone far beyond what the courts have actually required in order to provide students with due process. Institutions have unnecessarily formalized their procedures" (p. 477). Judging from the frequency of the reminders in the literature, it would appear that student affairs administrators need to be periodically reminded that "due process" is, in fact, a flexible concept that allows for the less formal or legalistic disposition of most disciplinary cases, especially when the penalty or outcome is less than dismissal (Ardaiolo, 1983; Bracewell, 1988; Gehring, 2001; Pavela, 1985; Travelstead, 1987). As Bracewell (1988) pointed out, "[i]n less than two decades, colleges and universities have accommodated this legal concept [due process] in their regulations and disciplinary procedures" (p. 275), but "[a] strange amalgam of legalism and counseling was created" (p. 274). This "strange amalgam" and the struggle between the two opposing forces that created it continue to challenge many student affairs professionals engaged in disciplinary work (Smith, 1994), although the findings of Bostic and Gonzalez (1999) suggest that a rapprochement on the tension between legalism and developmentalism may be developing in the profession.

DEMANDS FOR MORE SUPERVISION OF STUDENTS

Some may find it ironic that not long after the celebration of the twenty-fifth anniversary of the "Joint Statement on Rights and Freedoms of Students" (see generally Bryan & Mullendore, 1992), and "[h]aving moved from strict control over student conduct to treating students as adults subject to much less control, institutions now are being pressed to take more responsibility for students' behavior" (Pavela, 1992, p. Bl). According to Pavela (1992), the same consumer protection movement that aided the progress for students' rights left students with concurrent liabilities, including taking more responsibility for themselves and making it more difficult for them to hold colleges responsible for injuries suffered at the hands of other students. He observed that student-consumer protection statutes, like the Crime Awareness and Campus Security Act,

> frequently go well beyond setting guidelines for reporting information to students; they often contain explicit or implicit requirements that specific disciplinary policies—like restrictions against underage drinking be adopted, enforced, and monitored by colleges to protect students and members of the public (pp. B1-2).

He pointed out that besides legislation, other social and economic forces have conspired to pressure colleges to take greater responsibility for their students' behavior, whether on campus or off campus, "at the worst possible time" (p. B2). He called on deans and presidents to take the creative lead in setting and enforcing standards of student behavior that will result in more responsible and civil student conduct.

Pavela's charge came at a time when concerns for campus crime and student safety may have been at an all-time high. Sloan (1994) reviewed the findings of the 1990 U.S. Congressional Hearings on Campus Crime and reported that from 1985 to 1989, campus crime steadily increased, over 80 percent of campus crime involved students as both perpetrators and victims, and 95 percent of campus crime involved the use of alcohol or other drugs. More recently, the U.S. Department of Education Office of Postsecondary Education (2001) conducted research based on the crime statistics that institutions submitted online in 2000. In compliance with the HEA of 1998, the U.S. Department of Education Office of Postsecondary Education submitted a report to Congress regarding crime on campus. The report concluded,

> The campus crime statistics collected by the U.S. Department of Education suggest that our nation's college campuses are safe. In nearly every category of crime for which data were collected, college campuses showed lower incidence of crime than comparable data for the nation as a whole (p. 13).

While "[m]ost studies of campus crime show that colleges are safer than the communities around them" (Lederman, 1995, p. A41), a *Chronicle of Higher Education* report (Lederman, 1995) showed a "continuing increase in the number of violent crimes" on campuses with enrollments over 5,000 (p. A41). With such reports, the pressure continues for institutions to respond with preventive measures, criminal prosecution, and disciplinary action.

ONGOING CONCERNS ABOUT ACADEMIC MISCONDUCT

In addressing this issue, it is important to distinguish between academic *evaluation* and academic *misconduct*. Academic evaluation refers to evaluative judgments, typically made by faculty, about the student's performance in a course or in the course of a professional training program. The courts have been reluctant to hear cases involving such professional judgments. In the determination of such decisions, including a decision to dismiss on the basis of academic deficiencies, students need not be afforded the same due process safeguards required in disciplinary cases. The landmark case in this area is *Board of Curators of the University of Missouri v. Horowitz* (1978).

Academic misconduct refers to violations of rules of academic honesty or integrity, such as cheating on tests or plagiarism "that involve students giving or receiving unauthorized assistance in an academic exercise or receiving credit for work that is not their own" (Kibler, 1993a, p. 253). The standards of due process in cases of academic misconduct are generally the same as those in nonacademic, or social, misconduct.

Academic misconduct, as it represents deviance from and erosion of the core value of academic integrity, has always been of concern in higher education; but in recent years the concern has grown even though empirical evidence of the increasing incidence of cheating is lacking (McCabe & Bowers, 1994). Estimates of the extent of cheating by college students vary widely. May and Lloyd's (1993) review of research done in the 1980s found that "between 40% and 90% of all college students cheat" (p. 125). Kibler (1993b) observed that cheating occurs on most, if not all, campuses, and that although it is difficult to prove it is actually increasing, "it is generally agreed that academic dishonesty is a serious issue for all segments of higher education" (p. 9).

The causes of academic misconduct and the many possible solutions to it are complex and beyond the scope of this chapter. However, one general approach deserves mention. As Gehring (1995) has pointed out,

> [b]oth NASPA's "Reasonable Expectations" and ACPAs "Student Learning Imperative" call for greater cooperation between student affairs and faculty affairs to enhance student learning. One area in which this can take place is that of fostering academic integrity. There are many issues involved in breaches of academic integrity—institutional environments, expectations, rules and regulations, moral reasoning and legal rights and responsibilities. Student affairs practitioners have expertise in many of these issues and could use that knowledge to assist faculty in improving the campus climate relative to academic integrity (p. 6).

For student affairs professionals to assert their expertise into what many faculty consider their exclusive domain will not be easy. Faculty tend to ignore formal academic dishonesty policies and procedures (Aaron & Georgia, 1994; Jendrek, 1989). Despite its unpleasantness, faculty have a strong sense of duty in this area and possess more expertise when poor scholarship confounds the problem. But as Gehring (1995) noted, many faculty do not understand the differences between academic judgments and misconduct decisions requiring due process, "something student affairs practitioners have been instructed in for the past 35 years" (p. 6). As Bracewell (1988) observed, the processes and procedures normally managed by student affairs professionals are ideally suited to the adjudication of academic dishonesty.

DISCIPLINARY COUNSELING

As previously defined, disciplinary counseling is one possible rehabilitative or educational response to student misconduct. It has a long history in the literature on student discipline (see, for example, ACE, 1937, 1949; Gometz & Parker, 1968; Snoxell, 1960; Williamson, 1956, 1963; Williamson & Foley, 1949; Wrenn, 1949), and was a commonly accepted practice since 1900. But with the rise of professional mental health centers on campuses, administrators charged with the responsibility for discipline began sending students for counseling as a form of rehabilitation, often as a condition of continued enrollment and often with the expectation that the counselor would make some report on the progress of the student's development of insight and perhaps forecast the student's future behavior. By definition, disciplinary counseling is mandatory, or nonvoluntary, unless one supports the argument that the student can always choose dismissal rather than accept counseling, in which case it is, at least, coercive.

Referrals for disciplinary counseling appear to be increasing, and disciplinary counseling is widely practiced (Consolvo & Dannells, 2000; Dannells, 1990, 1991; Stone & Lucas, 1994) despite being highly controversial on two main points: ethics and efficacy. Almost half (48%) of the counseling center directors surveyed by Stone and Lucas (1994) responded that counseling centers should not do disciplinary counseling citing primary reservations as ethics (involving issues of coercion, confidentiality, and role conflicts) and management and effectiveness issues. Stone and Lucas concluded that there is considerable confusion, ambivalence, and ambiguity about disciplinary counseling in the minds of counseling center directors. They called for a distinction between disciplinary *therapy* and disciplinary *education*, while admitting that such "sharply drawn conceptual differences often disappear in practice" (p. 238).

Amada (1993, 1994) strenuously objected to mandatory disciplinary psychotherapy for college students on several counts, including that it "distorts and undermines the basis for corrective disciplinary action" (1993, p. 128); it is "often motivated by fanciful and naive notions about psychotherapy" (1993, p. 129); it is "unequivocally a coercive measure that serves to instill in the student resentment toward the therapist and therapy itself" (1993, p. 129); it lacks confidentiality; it is probably in violation of the laws that protect persons with handicaps from discriminatory treatment; and it "tends to transfer the responsibility and authority for administering discipline from where it rightly belongs—the office of the designated administrator—to where it does not belong—the offices of counselors and therapists" (1993, p. 130). He concluded that disciplinary therapy is definitely unethical.

In a recent study of the policy and practice of disciplinary counseling at four-year institutions, Consolvo and Dannells (2000) confirmed that its existence as policy has increased while significant issues of policy articulation and organizational and ethical conflict surround it. For example, they determined that in almost three of ten institutions, the counseling center director and the primary judicial officer did not agree that they engaged in its practice; one in five respondents agreed that there were significant organizational conflicts; one in four agreed that it posed ethical problems; and they found considerable disagreement about the goals of disciplinary counseling. Consolvo and Dannells recommended various educational or developmental alternatives to disciplinary counseling.

HATE SPEECH

By the late 1980s, there was growing concern in higher education about the rising tide of racial incidents on campus. A number of institutions sought to address this concern by adopting policies that prohibited certain forms of racist speech that came to be commonly referred to as Hate Speech Codes. The courts rejected on First Amendment grounds the Hate Speech Codes adopted by several prominent public institutions including the University of Wisconsin (*UWM Post v. Board of Regents*, 1991) and the University of Michigan (*Doe v. University of Michigan*, 1989) (O'Neil, 1997). The fundamental constitutional defect of both of these policies lay in their vagueness and overbreadth (Paterson, 1994, 1998; O'Neil, 1997). A number of authors also charged that Hate Speech Codes were antithetical to the free exchange of ideas at any institution of higher education, either public or private (Hentoff, 1992; Kors & Silvergate, 1998).

The problems associated with Hate Speech Codes reach far beyond their mere legal implications. The People for the American Way (1991) warned,

> Schools looking for a shortcut through the First Amendment toward the difficult goal of fighting intolerance forget the obligation to foster a climate of acceptance and open debate. In fact, such a shortcut is an abdication of this responsibility, a white flag that says, muffling the worst about and among us is the best we can do (p. 25).

The more significant question raised by the People for the American Way and others was whether Hate Speech Codes actually improved the racial climate on campus. Faced with mounting concerns, some institutions developed approaches that did not involve the same constitutional problems. At the same time that Wisconsin and Michigan were developing their Hate Speech Codes, the University of South Carolina developed the Carolinian Creed as a positive expression of institutional values in response to the growing problem of intolerance and incivility (Lowery, 1998b; People for the American Way, 1991; Pruitt, 1996.)

PROFESSIONAL ASSOCIATIONS

Professionals engaged in the disciplinary process on their campuses would likely find benefit in membership in at least three professional associations: (1) the American College Personnel Association has a commission structure that includes Commission XV, Campus Judicial Affairs and Legal Issues; (2) the Association for Student Judicial Affairs exists exclusively to address issues faced by administrators of campus discipline and/or judicial systems; and (3) the National Association of Student Personnel Administrators addresses leadership and professional growth opportunities for senior student affairs officers and others who are charged with disciplinary responsibilities. In addition, there are at least two recently established organizations of interest to student judicial affairs professionals: the Center for Academic Integrity, which focuses specifically on institutional responses to academic dishonesty, and the Association for Interdisciplinary Initiatives in Higher Education Law and Policy, which was established in 2002 to bring together experts to address legal and policy issues facing institutions of higher education.

ENTRY-LEVEL QUALIFICATIONS

The Council for the Advancement of Standards (CAS, 2001), in its Standards and Guidelines for Judicial Programs, requires that professional staff members in judicial programs and services "have a graduate degree in a field relevant to the position description or must possess an appropriate combination of education and experience" (p. 159). And a "qualified member of the campus community must be designated as the person responsible for judicial programs" (p. 159). Qualifications for this designated individual are also provided:

> The designee should have an educational background in the behavioral sciences (e.g., psychology, sociology, student development including moral and ethical development, higher education administration, counseling, law, criminology, or criminal justice).
>
> The designee and any other professional staff member in the judicial programs should possess (a) a clear understanding of the legal requirements for substantive and procedural due process; (b) legal knowledge sufficient to confer with attorneys involved in student disciplinary proceedings and other aspects of the judicial services system; (c) a general interest in and commitment to the welfare and development of students who participate on boards or who are involved in cases; (d) demonstrated skills in working with decision making processes and conflict resolution; (e) teaching and consulting skills appropriate for the education, advising, and coordination of hearing bodies; (f) the ability to communicate and interact with students regardless of race, sex, disability, sexual orientation, and/or other personal characteristics; (g)

understanding of the requirements relative to confidentiality and security of judicial programs files; and (h) the ability to create an atmosphere where students feel free to ask questions and obtain assistance.

Students from graduate academic programs, particularly in areas such as counseling, student development, higher education administration, or criminology, may assist the judicial programs through practice, internships, and assistantships (pp. 159–160).

TECHNOLOGY RESOURCES

Student affairs professionals interested in student discipline and judicial affairs might find the following web sites of interest.

Association for Student Judicial Affairs (ASJA)—http://asja.tamu.edu—ASJA is the leading professional organization for student judicial affairs professionals. The web site contains valuable information for those interested in this field, including the association's Statement of Ethical Principles and Standards of Conduct. The web site includes additional resources in a members only area.

Center for Academic Integrity (CAI)—http://www.academicintegrity.org/—The Center was established to promote academic integrity and response effectively to academic dishonesty. The web site includes additional resources in a members only area.

College Administration Publications (CAP)—http://www.collegepubs.com—CAP is a leading publisher of materials on legal issues in higher education.

Council on Law in Higher Education—http://clhe.org/—The Council focuses on law and policy issues in higher education. The web site includes additional resources in a members only area.

Inter-Association Task Force on Alcohol and Other Substance Abuse Issues—http://www.iatf.org/—The Task Force is a coalition of organizations committed to address alcohol and other substance abuse issues on campus. The web site includes extensive resources related to address these issues.

Restorative Justice Online—http://www.restorativejustice.org/—The International Centre for Justice and Reconciliation sponsors this newsletter, which promotes the application of restorative justice principles to various community settings.

THOMAS: Legislative Information on the Internet—http://thomas.loc.gov/—THOMAS: Legislative Information on the Internet is a project of the Library of Congress and includes extensive legislative information, including search databases of pending legislation.

U.S. Department of Education, Campus Security—http://www.ed.gov/offices/OPE/PPI/security.html—The U.S. Department of Education's Campus Security web site contains useful legislative and regulatory information regarding the Jeanne Clery Disclosure of Campus Security Policy and Campus Crime Statistics Act.

U.S. Department of Education's Family Policy Compliance Office—http://www.ed.gov/offices/OM/fpco/—The Family Policy Compliance Office web site contains useful legislative and regulatory information regarding the Family Educational Rights and Privacy Act.

U.S. Department of Education's Higher Education Center for Alcohol and Other Drug Prevention—http://www.edc.org/hec/—The Center for Alcohol and Other Drug Prevention web site contains extensive resources related to address these issues on campus.

THE FUTURE OF JUDICIAL AFFAIRS

The future of the disciplinary function in student affairs is inextricably tied to the futures of student affairs and of higher education. Innumerable influences will come to bear on those institutions, rendering futurism a risky and perhaps foolish enterprise. But as Sandeen and Rhatigan (1990) said, the "difficulty of accurate forecasting has never deterred people from the effort" (p. 98).

It is tempting to refer the reader to the section on current issues in disciplinary affairs and forecast more of the same. In many instances, that strategy might well prove accurate, but there are some new, some different, and some continuing trends and indicators to consider in thinking about the future of disciplinary work in higher education.

THE CHANGING LEGAL AND LEGISLATIVE ENVIRONMENT

With the growing recognition and acceptance that the academy is a part of the "real world" and a microcosm of the greater society, the student–institutional relationship has become increasingly viewed as a consumer business—one subject to many of the same contractual expectations and constraints as any other seller–buyer or landlord–tenant, relationship. Society, students, and even some students' parents no longer expect institutions of higher education to act on a vague set of social or parental rules in disciplinary matters. In particular, older students have little tolerance for paternalistic policies and processes. Instead, they wish to know exactly what is expected of them as adults. This has undoubtedly influenced many institutions to carefully review catalogues and other official documents, including codes of conduct, that may be considered part of the enrollment contract. This trend will continue, and it will benefit those who administer their campus disciplinary system to closely review their rules and methods to ensure that they are treating students like the adults they legally are.

Related to this is the projection (Hodgkinson, 1985; Kuh, 1990) that in addition to the increasing average age of future students, more students will be part-time and more students will be attending commuter institutions in urban settings. Since most student misconduct involves traditional-aged students in residential settings, this would suggest that the relative incidence of student misconduct should decrease over time. Alternatively, increasing pressure to get good grades may lead to higher rates of academic dishonesty. Both hypotheses are ripe for future research.

Forecasting the future regulatory and legal issues for student affairs, Fenske and Johnson (1990) noted seven crucial issues, two of which are most directly relevant for disciplinary affairs. One is that "[s]tudent affairs professionals will be increasingly involved in balancing the constitutional rights of students with the elimination of prejudice and harassment and the promotion of tolerance" (p. 133). The second is that "[c]ourt rulings and state laws on liability will require closer monitoring of on-campus and off-campus social events where alcohol is served, as well as increased willingness to take action against illegal drug and alcohol abuse" (pp. 133–134). Both of these issues have implications for codes of conduct and their enforcement.

A third significant issue that has emerged over the course of the past decade is a rapid expansion of the federal legislation impacting student judicial affairs. In addition to the changes to FERPA included in the HEA of 1998 previously discussed, the Campus Security Act was also amended to require that institutions include statistics for students referred for disciplinary action, but not arrested, for alcohol, drug, and weapons law violations. There have also been bills proposed related to such issues as fire safety and student gambling. Significant legislation on campus and fire safety has also been passed at the state level. Student judicial affairs professionals must remain current on legislative issues and take an active role in the legislative process (Lowery, 1998a, 1999, 2000).

Over this past decade, according to Bickel and Lake (1999), there has been a fundamental shift in the way the courts have viewed liability claims against universities. After the demise of *in loco parentis*, the courts moved into an era in which colleges and universities were seen to have no duty whatsoever to students described as the "Bystander Era." However, Bickel and Lake have documented an emerging trend in which the courts are moving away from the "Bystander Era" into a new era of duty for institutions in relationship to their students.

THE CONTINUING NEED FOR PROGRAM EVALUATION

Like any other student affairs program, disciplinary programs should be periodically and systematically evaluated to ensure that they are effectively meeting their established objectives (CAS, 2001, Zacker, 1996). Those objectives should be defined in terms of measurable outcomes statements and evaluated on the basis of preestablished criteria and processes. The various components of the program (such as its publications, training program for judicial board members, consistency of sanctions, and procedures and practices, as well as the personnel involved in the execution of the program) should be included in a comprehensive review. Methods of evaluation will vary according to the nature and needs of the individual program, but they may include interviews, direct observation, written reports, surveys, community feedback, task force review, questionnaires (Emmanuel & Miser, 1987), and student portfolios (Zelna, 2002; Zelna & Cousins, 2002). It must be acknowledged, however, that scientific research in the area of student discipline has been and will continue to be problematic because of difficulties in identifying and controlling variables, in gathering data from recalcitrant program participants, and in meeting legal and ethical requirements for confidentiality and informed consent. Few outcomes studies, such as that of Mullane (1999), are found in the literature. Likewise, research on the effectiveness of judicial systems, such as that of Fitch and Murry (2001), are rare.

THE SEARCH FOR COMMON VALUES

Many institutions have recently engaged in lengthy processes to clarify institutional values as they are reflected in such documents as mission statements, codes of conduct, and academic integrity policies. Many institutions have yet to approach this formidable set of tasks, but they must, and most will do so.

The increasing diversity of the many constituents on campuses makes more challenging the task of finding and implementing common values. Cultural differences can be expected to complicate the disciplinary function; consensus about what constitutes acceptable behavior may no longer be taken for granted. Thus, it is all the more important that colleges and universities that for some time have not reviewed their codes of conduct do so, and in so doing involve students, faculty, and staff from diverse backgrounds to ensure a set of behavioral principles as widely accepted as possible.

The apparent increase in, and the new or renewed concern about, student cheating may prove an important and useful ground for the collaboration of academic affairs and student affairs leaders. Codes of conduct should include clear policy statements on academic integrity that are acceptable to faculty, understandable to students, and enforceable for faculty and the administrators who are responsible for discipline and judicial systems.

Garland and Grace (1993) listed 12 "potential focal points for collaboration between academic affairs and student affairs" (p. 62). At least four of them fall directly within the area of student discipline or have direct implications for it. They are:

- Manage disciplinary problems from a unified rather than a unilateral approach for consistency in response.
- Respond to alcohol and drugs on campus to prevent personal and academic debilitation.

- Respond to increased violence on campus.
- Respond to increased psychopathology, balancing the needs of troubled students and the community (Garland & Grace, 1993, p. 62).

THE PROFESSION AND DISCIPLINE

Student discipline has been, and perhaps should continue to be, a topic of professional concern and debate because it is such a dramatic reflection of our attitudes and assumptions about the nature of our students, our relationship to them, and our role in their development. There was a period in our profession's history when the subject was all but ignored, a source of embarrassment to be apologetically dispatched and forgotten in favor of more glamorous and "positive" functions.

After a careful analysis of the undergraduate experience at American colleges and universities, Ernest Boyer (1987), then President of the Carnegie Foundation for the Advancement of Teaching, wrote:

> What we found particularly disturbing is the ambivalence college administrators feel about their overall responsibility for student behavior. Most of the college leaders with whom we spoke had an unmistakable sense of unease—or was it anxiety? Many were not sure what standards to expect or require. Where does the responsibility of the college begin and end? Where is the balance to be struck between students' personal "rights" and institutional concerns? . . . Unclear about what standards to maintain and the principles by which student life should be judged, many administrators seek to ignore rather than confront the issues (p. 203).

Student affairs leaders, particularly those charged with the responsibility for discipline, must actively and positively embrace that responsibility and stimulate the dialogue on campus necessary to ensure that it is not ignored or dispatched halfheartedly and, ultimately, poorly.

STUDENT DISCIPLINE, THE CORE CURRICULUM, AND LIBERAL EDUCATION

Those concerned with student behavior and judicial systems should find encouragement in the widespread efforts in higher education to develop an integrated core curriculum that reaffirms the traditional principles of a liberal education and which may help create a climate on campuses where the development of the whole person, including the moral aspect, is once again paramount. This movement suggests exciting possibilities for student affairs professionals to "return to the academy" (Brown, 1972).

Many institutions are considering team-taught, interdisciplinary subject matter that will challenge an increasingly materialistic, aphilosophic, and career-oriented student body. Might there not be a place for a course entitled "Student Rights and Responsibilities in the College and the Community?" Such a course could be approached from a myriad of combinations of the different disciplines of law, political science, sociology, psychology, education, and philosophy (ethics) and could include the campus' chief disciplinary or judicial officer. In this way the subject of student conduct and moral and ethical development could be considered within the broader context of civic responsibility and community involvement. Thus, the moral dialogue inherent in a developmental approach to discipline (Pavela, 1985) could be brought to the classroom with the student affairs professional as an integral part of the teaching and learning partnership and process.

REFERENCES

Aaron, R., & Georgia, R. T (1994). Administrator perceptions of student academic dishonesty. *NASPA Journal, 31*, 83–91.

Amada, G. (1993). The role of the mental health consultant in dealing with disruptive college students. *Journal of College Student Psychotherapy, 8*, 121–137.

Amada, G. (1994). *Coping with the disruptive college student: A practical model.* Asheville, NC: College Administration Publications.

American Council on Education (ACE). (1937). *The student personnel point of view* (American Council on Education Studies, Series 1, Vol. 1, No. 3). Washington, DC: Author.

American Council on Education (ACE). (1949). *The student personnel point of view* (Rev. Ed.). (American Council on Education Studies, Series 6, Vol. 13, No. 13). Washington, DC: Author.

Appleton, J. R., Briggs, C. M., & Rhatigan, J. J. (1978). *Pieces of eight.* Portland, OR: National Association of Student Personnel Administrators.

Ardaiolo, F. P (1983). What process is due? In M. J. Barr (Ed.), *Student affairs and the law* (New Directions for Student Services, No. 22, pp. 13–25). San Francisco: Jossey-Bass.

Ardaiolo, F. P., & Walker, S. J. (1987). Models of practice. In R. Caruso & W. W. Travelstead (Eds), *Enhancing campus judicial systems* (New Directions for Student Services No. 39, pp. 43–61). San Francisco: Jossey-Bass.

Arndt, J. R. (1971). Substantive due process in public higher education: 1959–1969. *Journal of College Student Personnel, 12*, 83–94.

Bakken, C. J. (1968). *The legal basis of college student personnel work* (Student Personnel Monograph Series No. 2). Washington, DC: American Personnel and Guidance Association.

Baldizan, E. M. (1998). Development, due process, and reduction: Student conduct in the 1990s. In D.L. Cooper & J.M. Lancaster (Eds.), *Beyond law and policy: Reaffirming the role of student affairs* (New Directions for Student Services, No. 82, pp. 29–37). San Francisco: Jossey-Bass.

Barr, M. J. (1988). Conclusion: The evolving legal environment of student affairs administration. In M. J. Barr & Associates, *Student services and the law* (pp. 347–353). San Francisco: Jossey-Bass.

Bickel, R. D., & Lake, P. F. (1999). *The rights and responsibilities of the modern university: Who assumes the risks of college life?* Durham, NC: Carolina Academic Press.

Bloland, P. A., Stamatakos, L. C., & Rogers, R. R. (1994). *Reform in student affairs. A critique of student development.* Greensboro, NC: ERIC Counseling and Student Services Clearinghouse, University of North Carolina.

Board of Curators of the University of Missouri v. Horowitz, 435 U.S. 78 (1978).

Boots, C. C. (1987). Human development theory applied to judicial affairs work. In R. Caruso & W. W. Travelstead (Eds), *Enhancing campus judicial systems* (New Directions for Student Services, No. 39, pp. 63–72). San Francisco: Jossey-Bass.

Bostic, D., & Gonzalez, G. (1999). Practices, opinions, knowledge, and recommendations from judicial officers in public higher education. *NASPA Journal, 36,* 166–183.

Boyer, E. L. (1987). *College: The undergraduate experience in America.* New York: Harper & Row.

Bracewell, W. R. (1978). An application of the privacy concept to student life. In E. H. Hammond & R. H. Shaffer (Eds.), *The legal foundations of student personnel services in higher education* (pp. 24–33). Washington, DC: American College Personnel Association.

Bracewell, W. R. (1988). Student discipline. In M. J. Barr & Associates, *Student services and the law* (pp. 273–283). San Francisco: Jossey-Bass.

Brown, R. D. (1972). *Student development in tomorrow's higher education—A return to the academy.* Washington, DC: American College Personnel Association.

Brubacher, J. S., & Rudy, W. (1968). *Higher education in transition.* New York: Harper & Row.

Bruce, P. A. (1920). *History of the University of Virginia 1819–1919 (Vol. 2).* New York: Macmillan.

Bryan, W. A., & Mullendore, R. H. (Eds.). (1992). *Rights, freedoms, and responsibilities of students* (New Directions for Student Services, No. 59). San Francisco: Jossey-Bass.

Buchanan, E. T., III. (1978). Student disciplinary proceedings in collegiate institutions—Substantive and procedural due process requirements. In E. H. Hammond & R. H. Shaffer (Eds.), *The legal foundation of student personnel services in higher education* (pp. 94–115). Washington, DC: American College Personnel Association.

Callis, R. (1967). Educational aspects of in loco parentis. *Journal of College Student Personnel, 8,* 231–233.

Callis, R. (1969). The courts and the colleges: 1968. *Journal of College Student Personnel, 10,* 75–86.

Carletta, C. F. (1998). Distinctions between the criminal justice system and the campus judicial process: Implication for public and private institutions. In B. G. Paterson & W. L. Kibler (Eds.), *The administration of student discipline: Student, organizational, and community issues* (pp. 43–54). Asheville, NC: College Administration Publications.

Carnegie Commission on Higher Education. (1971). *Dissent and disruption.* New York: McGraw-Hill.

Carnegie Foundation for the Advancement of Teaching. (1990). *Campus life: In search of community.* Princeton, NJ: Author.

Caruso, R. G. (1978). The professional approach to student discipline in the years ahead. In E. H. Hammond & R. H. Shaffer (Eds.) *The legal foundations of student personnel services in higher education* (pp. 116–127). Washington, DC: American College Personnel Association.

Caruso, R., & Travelstead, W. W. (Eds.). (1987). *Enhancing campus judicial systems* (New Directions for Student Services No. 39). San Francisco: Jossey-Bass.

Chickering, A. W. (1969). *Education and identity.* San Francisco: Jossey-Bass.

Chickering, A. W., & Reisser, L. (1993). *Education and identity* (2nd ed.). San Francisco: Jossey-Bass.

Consolvo, C., & Dannells, M. (2000). *Disciplinary counseling: Implications for policy and practice, 38,* 44–57

Cordner, P., & Brooks, T. F. (1987). Training techniques for judicial systems. In R. Caruso & W. W. Travelstead (Eds.), *Enhancing campus judicial systems* (New Directions for Student Services, No. 39, pp. 31–42). San Francisco: Jossey-Bass.

Correnti, R. J. (1988). How public and private institutions differ under the law. In M. J. Barr & Associates, *Student services and the law* (pp. 25–43). San Francisco: Jossey-Bass.

Council for the Advancement of Standards in Higher Education (CAS). (2001). *The book of professional standards for higher education.* Washington, DC: Author.

Dalton, J. C., & Healy, M. A. (1984). Using values education activities to confront student conduct issues. *NASPA Journal, 22(2),* 19–25.

Dannells, M. (1977). Discipline. In W. T. Packwood (Ed.), *College student personnel services* (pp. 232–278). Springfield, IL: Charles C Thomas.

Dannells, M. (1978). *Disciplinary practices and procedures in baccalaureate-granting institutions of higher education in the United States.* Unpublished doctoral dissertation, University of Iowa, Iowa City, IA.

Dannells, M. (1990). Changes in disciplinary policies and practices over 10 years. *Journal of College Student Development, 31,* 408–414.

Dannells, M. (1991). Changes in student misconduct and institutional response over 10 years. *Journal of College Student Development, 32,* 166–170.

Dannells, M. (1997). *From discipline to development: Rethinking student conduct in higher education.* ASHE-ERIC Higher Education Report, 25(2). San Francisco: Jossey-Bass.

Dixon v. Alabama State Board of Education, 294 F.2d 150 (5th Cir. 1961).

Doe v. University of Michigan, 721 F.Supp. 852 (E.D. Mich. 1989)

Durst, R. H. (1969). *The impact of court decisions rendered in the Dixon and Knight cases on student disciplinary procedures in public institutions of hither education in the United States* (Doctoral dissertation, Purdue University, 1968). *Dissertation abstracts, 29,* 2473A–2474A. University Microfilms No. 69-2910.

Dutton, T. B., Smith, F. W., & Zarle, T. (1969). *Institutional approaches to the adjudication of student misconduct.* Washington, DC: National Association of Student Personnel Administrators.

Emmanuel, N. R., & Miser, K. M. (1987). Evaluating judicial program effectiveness. In R. Caruso, & W. W. Travelstead (Eds.), *Enhancing campus judicial systems* (New Directions for Student Services, No. 39, pp. 85–94). San Francisco: Jossey-Bass.

Esteban v. Central Missouri State College, 290 F. Supp. 622 (W.D. Mo. 1968), aff'd, 415 F.2d 1077 (8th Cir. 1969).

Family Educational Rights and Privacy Act, 20 U.S.C. §1232g (1974).

Fenske, R. H. (1989). Evolution of the student services profession. In U. Delworth, G. R. Hanson, & Associates, *Student services: A handbook for the profession* (2nd ed.) (pp. 25–56). San Francisco: Jossey-Bass.

Fenske, R. H., & Johnson, E. A. (1990). Changing regulatory and legal environments. In M. J. Barr, M. L. Upcraft, & Associates, *New futures for student affairs*
(pp. 114–137). San Francisco: Jossey-Bass.

Fisher, T. C. (1970). *Due process in the student-institutional relationship.* Washington,
DC: American Association of State Colleges and Universities.

Fitch, E. E., Jr., & Murry, J. W., Jr. (2001). Classifying and assessing the effectiveness
of student judicial systems in doctoral-granting universities. *NASPA Journal, 38,*
189–202.

Fley, J. (1964). Changing approaches to discipline in student personnel work.
*Journal of the National Association for Women Deans, Administrators, and Counselors,
27,* 105–113.

Fley, J. A. (1974). Student personnel pioneers: Those who developed our profession. *NASPA Journal, 17(1),* 23–39.

Foley, J. D. (1947). Discipline: A student counseling approach. *Educational and
Psychological Measurement, 7,* 569–582.

Footer, N. S. (1996). Achieving fundamental fairness: The code of conduct. In W.
L. Mercer (Ed.), *Critical issues in judicial affairs: Current trends in practice* (New
Directions for Student Services, No. 73, pp. 19–33). San Francisco: Jossey-Bass.

Frederickson, J. (1992). Disciplinary sanctioning of impulsive university students.
NASPA Journal, 29, 143–148.

Gallagher, R. P., Harmon, W. W., & Lingenfelter, C. O. (1994). CSAOs' perceptions
of the changing incidence of problematic college student behavior. *NASPA
Journal, 32,* 37–45.

Garland, P. H., & Grace, T. W. (1993). N*ew perspectives for student affairs professionals.
Evolving realities, responsibilities and roles* (1993 ASHE-ERIC Higher Education
Report No. 7). Washington, DC: George Washington University, School of
Education and Human Development.

Gehring, D. D. (1995, April/May). Abreast of the law: Academic and disciplinary
dismissals. N*ASPA Forum, 6.*

Gehring, D. D. (2000, September/October). New revisions clarify FERPA rules.
NASPA Forum, 22(1), 6–7.

Gehring, D. D. (2001). The objectives of student discipline and the process that's
due: Are they compatible? *NASPA Journal, 38,* 466–481.

Gehring, D. D., & Bracewell, W. R. (1992). Standards of behavior and disciplinary
proceedings. In W. A. Bryan & R. H. Mullendore (Eds.), *Rights, freedoms, and
responsibilities of students* (New Directions for Student Services, No. 59, pp.
89–99). San Francisco: Jossey- Bass.

Georgia, R. T. (1989). Permissiveness and discipline in the higher education setting: A prolegomenon. *NASPA Journal, 27,* 90–94.

Gibbs, A. (1992). *Reconciling the rights and responsibilities of colleges and students:
Offensive speech, assembly drug testing, and safety* (1992 ASHE-ERIC Higher
Education Report No. 5). Washington, DC: George Washington University,
School of Education and Human Development.

Gometz, L., & Parker, C. A. (1968). Disciplinary counseling: A contradiction?
Personnel and Guidance Journal, 46, 437–443.

Gott v. Berea College, 156 Ky 376 (1913).

Greenleaf, E. A. (1978). The relationship of legal issues and procedures to student
development. In E. H. Hammond & R. H. Shaffer (Eds.), *The legal foundations*

of student personnel services in higher education (pp. 34–46). Washington, DC: American College Personnel Association.

Gregory, D. E. (1998). Student judicial records, privacy, and the press's right to know. In B. G. Paterson & W. L. Kibler (Eds.), *The administration of student discipline: Student, organizational, and community issues* (pp. 55–73). Asheville, NC: College Administration Publications.

Gregory, D. E., & Ballou, R. A. (1986). Point of view: In loco parentis reinvents: Is there still a parenting function in higher education? *NASPA Journal, 24(2),* 28–31.

Grossi, E. L., & Edwards, D. T. (1997). Student misconduct: Historical trends in legislative and judicial decision-making in American universities. *Journal of College and University Law, 23,* 829–852

Hammond, E. H. (1978). The consumer-institutional relationship. In E. H. Hammond & R. H. Shaffer (Eds.), *The legal foundations of student personnel services in higher education* (pp. 1–11). Washington, DC: American College Personnel Association.

Hawkes, H. E. (1930). College administration. *Journal of Higher Education, 1,* 245–253.

Hayes, J. A., & Balogh, C. P. (1990). Mediation: An emerging form of dispute resolution on college campuses. *NASPA Journal, 27,* 236–240.

Hentoff, N. (1992). *Free speech for me—but not for thee: How the American Left and Right relentlessly censor each other.* New York: HarperCollins.

Higher Education Amendments of 1998, Pub. L. No. 105-244, 112 Stat. 1581 (1998).

Hoekema, D. A. (1994). *Campus rules and moral community: In place of in loco parentis.* Lanham, MD: Rowan & Littlefield.

Hodgkinson, H. L. (1985). *All one system: Demographics of education—Kindergarten through graduate school.* Washington, DC: Institute for Educational Leadership.

Inter-Association Task Force on Alcohol and Other Drug Abuse. (n.d.). *Parental notification.* Available online at www.iatf.org/parent1a.htm

Janosik, S. M. (1995). Judicial decision-making and sanctioning: Agreement among students, faculty, and administrators. *NASPA Journal, 32,* 138–144.

Janosik, S. M., & Riehl. J. (2000). Stakeholder support for flexible due process in campus disciplinary hearings. *NASPA Journal, 37,* 444–453.

Jendrek, M. P. (1989). Faculty reactions to academic dishonesty. *Journal of College Student Development, 30,* 401–406.

Kaplin, W. A., & Lee, B. A. (1995). *The law of higher education* (3rd ed.). San Francisco: Jossey-Bass.

Kaplin, W. A., & Lee, B. A. (1997). *A legal guide for student affairs professionals.* San Francisco: Jossey-Bass.

Kaplin, W. A., & Lee, B. A. (2000). *Year 2000 cumulative supplement to the law of higher education* (3rd ed.). Washington, DC: National Association of College and University Attorneys.

Karp, D. R., Breslin, B, & Oles, P. (n.d.). *Community justice in the campus setting.* Unpublished manuscript. Skidmore College, Saratoga Springs, NY.

Kibler, W. L. (1993a). Academic dishonesty: A student development dilemma. *NASPA Journal, 30,* 252–267.

Kibler, W. L. (1993b). A framework for addressing academic dishonesty from a student development perspective. *NASPA, 31,* 8–18.

King, P. M. (1990). Assessing development from a cognitive-developmental perspective. In D. G. Creamer & Associates, *College student development: Theory and practice for the 1990s* (pp. 81–98). Alexandria, VA: American College Personnel Association.

Knock, G. H. (1985). Development of student services in higher education. In M. J. Barr, L. A. Keating, & Associates, *Developing effective student services programs* (pp. 15–42). San Francisco: Jossey-Bass.

Kohlberg, L. (1969). Stage and sequence: The cognitive-developmental approach to socialization. In D. Goslin (Ed.), *Handbook of socialization theory and research* (pp. 347–380). Chicago: Rand McNally.

Kors, A. C., & Silvergate, H. A. (1998). *The shadow university: The betrayal of liberty on America's campuses.* New York: Free Press.

Kuh, G. D. (1990). The demographic juggernaut. In M. J. Barr, M. L. Upcraft., & Associates, *New futures for student affairs* (pp. 71–97). San Francisco: Jossey-Bass.

Lamont, L. (1979). *Campus shock.* New York: Dutton.

Lancaster, J. M., & Cooper, D. L. (1998). Standing at the intersection: Reconsidering the balance in administration. In D. L. Cooper & J. M. Lancaster (Eds.), *Beyond law and policy: Reaffirming the role of student affairs* (New Direction for Student Services, No. 82, pp. 95–106). San Francisco: Jossey-Bass.

Lancaster, J. M., Cooper, D. L., & Harman, A. E. (1993). Current practices in student disciplinary administration. *NASPA Journal, 30,* 108–119.

Lederman, D. (1995, February 3). Colleges report rise in violent crime. *Chronicle of Higher Education,* A31–42.

Leonard, E. A. (1956). *Origins of personnel services in American higher education.* Minneapolis: University of Minnesota Press.

Leslie, D. W., & Satryb, R. P. (1974). Due process on due process? Some observations. *Journal of College Student Personnel, 15,* 340–345.

Lowery, J. W. (1998a, Fall). Balancing students' right to privacy with the public's right to know. *Synthesis: Law and Policy in Higher Education, 10,* 713–715, 730.

Lowery, J. W. (1998b). Institutional policy and individual responsibility: Communities of justice and principle. In D. L. Cooper and J. M. Lancaster (Eds.), *Beyond law and policy: Reaffirming the role of student affairs* (New Direction for Student Services, No. 83, pp. 15–27). San Francisco: Jossey-Bass.

Lowery, J. W. (1998c). The Silent Generation makes some noise: Student protest at Bowling Green State University (October 1949 and May 1957). *Ohio College Student Development Journal, 1,* 9–26.

Lowery, J. W. (1999, Fall). Understanding and applying the Campus Security Act. *Synthesis: Law and Policy in Higher Education, 11,* 785–787, 799–800.

Lowery, J. W. (2000, Fall). FERPA and the Campus Security Act: Law and policy overview. *Synthesis: Law and Policy in Higher Education, 12,* 849–851, 864.

Mager, T. R. (1978). A new perspective for the first amendment in higher education. In E. H. Hammond & R. H. Shaffer (Eds.), *The legal foundations of student personnel services in higher education* (pp. 12–23). Washington, DC: American College Personnel Association.

May, D. L., & Lloyd, B. H. (1993). Academic dishonesty: The honor system and students' attitudes. *Journal of College Student Development, 34,* 125–129.

McBee, M. L. (1982). Moral development: From direction to dialog. *NASPA Journal, 20(1),* 30–35.

McCabe, D. L., & Bowers, W. J. (1994). Academic dishonesty among males in college: A thirty-year perspective. *Journal of College Student Development, 35*, 5–10.

Miller, T. K., & Prince, J. S. (1976). *The future of student affairs.* San Francisco: Jossey-Bass.

Mullane, S. P. (1999). Fairness, educational value, and moral development in the student disciplinary process. *NASPA Journal, 36*, 86–95.

Mueller, K. H. (1961). *Student personnel work in higher education.* Boston: Houghton Mifflin.

National Education Association Task Force on Student Involvement. (1971). *Code of student nights and responsibilities.* Washington, DC: National Education Association.

Nuss, E. (1998). Redefining college and university relationships with students. *NASPA Journal, 35*, 183–191.

O'Neil, R. M. (1997). *Free speech in the college community.* Bloomington, IN: Indiana University Press.

Ostroth, D. D., Armstrong, M. R., & Campbell, T. J., III. (1978). A nationwide survey of judicial systems in large institutions of higher education. *Journal of College Student Personnel, 19*, 21–27.

Ostroth, D. D., & Hill, D. E. (1978). The helping relationship in student discipline. *NASPA Journal, 16(2)*, 33–39.

Palmer, C. J., Lohman, G., Gehring, D. D., Carlson, S., & Garrett, O. (2001). Parental notification: A new strategy to reduce alcohol abuse on campus. *NASPA Journal, 38*, 372–385.

Parr, P., & Buchanan, F. T. (1979). Responses to the law: A word of caution. *NASPA Journal, 17(2)*, 12–15.

Paterson, B. G. (1994). Freedom of expression and campus dissent. *NASPA Journal, 31*, 186–194.

Paterson. (1998). Expression, harassment and hate speech: Free speech or conduct code violation. In B. G. Paterson & W. L. Kibler (Eds.), T*he administration of student discipline: Student, organizational, and community issues* (pp. 113–126). Asheville, NC: College Administration Publications.

Pavela, G. (1985). *The dismissal of students with mental disorders.* Asheville, NC: College Administration Publications.

Pavela, G. (1992, July 19). Today's college students need both freedom and structure. *Chronicle of Higher Education*, pp. B1–2.

Pavela, G. (2000, Spring). Applying the power of association on campus: A model code of student conduct. *Synthesis: Law and Policy in Higher Education, 11*, 817–823, 829–831.

Penney, J. F. (1967). Variations on a theme: In loco parentis. *Journal of College Student Personnel, 8*, 22–25.

People for the American Way. (1991). *Hate in the ivory tower: A survey of intolerance on college campuses and academia's response.* Washington, DC: Author.

Pitts, J. H. (1980). In loco parentis indulgentis? *NASPA Journal, 17(4)*, 20–25.

Pruitt, D. A. (1996, May–June). The Carolinian's Creed. *About Campus, 1*, 27–29.

Ratliff, R. C. (1972). *Constitutional rights of college students: A study in case law.* Metuchen, NJ: Scarecrow Press.

Red & Black Publishing Company v. Board of Regents, 427 S.E.2d 257 (Ga. 1993).

Rhatigan, J. J. (2000). The history and philosophy of student affairs. In M. J. Barr, D. K. Desler, & Associates, *The handbook of student affairs administration* (2nd ed.) pp. 3–24). San Francisco: Jossey-Bass.

Rhode, S. (1983). Use of legal counsel: Avoiding problems. In M. J. Barr (Ed.), *Student affairs and the law* (New Directions for Student Services, No. 22) (pp. 67–80). San Francisco: Jossey-Bass.

Rhode, S. R., & Math, M. G. (1988). Student conduct, discipline, and control: Understanding institutional options and limits. In M. J. Barr and Associates, *Student services and the law* (pp. 152–178). San Francisco: Jossey-Bass.

Rudolph, F. (1990). T*he American college & university: A history.* Athens, GA: The University of Georgia Press (Original work published 1962)

Saddlemire, G. L. (1980). Professional developments. In U. Delworth, G. R. Hanson, & Associates, S*tudent services: A handbook for the profession* (pp. 25–44). San Francisco: Jossey-Bass.

Sandeen, A., & Rhatigan, J. J. (1990). New pressures for social responsiveness and accountability. In M. J. Barr, M. L. Upcraft, & Associates, *New futures for student affairs* (pp. 98–113). San Francisco: Jossey-Bass.

Schetlin, E. M. (1967). Disorders, deans, and discipline: A record of change. *Journal of the National Association for Women Deans, Administrators, and Counselors, 30,* 169–173.

Serr, R. L., & Taber, R. S. (1987). Mediation: A judicial affairs alternative. In R. Caruso & W. W. Travelstead (Eds.), *Enhancing campus judicial systems* (New Directions for Student Services, No. 39, pp. 73–84). San Francisco: Jossey-Bass.

Seward, D. M. (1961). Educational discipline. J*ournal of the National Association for Women Deans, Administrators, and Counselors, 24,* 192–197.

Sherry, A. H. (1966). Governance of the university: Rules, rights, and responsibilities. *California Law Review, 54,* 23–39.

Shur, G. M. (1983). Contractual relationships. In M. J. Barr (Ed.), *Student affairs and the law* (New Directions for Student Services, No. 22, pp. 27–38). San Francisco: Jossey-Bass.

Shur, G. M. (1988). Contractual agreements: Defining relationships between students and institutions. In M. J. Barr and Associates, *Student services and the law* (pp. 74–97). San Francisco: Jossey-Bass.

Sims, O. H. (1971). Student conduct and campus law enforcement: A proposal. In O. S. Sims (Ed.), *New directions in campus law enforcement.* Athens, GA: University of Georgia, Center for Continuing Education.

Sisson, V. S., & Todd, S. R. (1995) Using mediation in response to sexual assault on college and university campuses. *NASPA Journal, 32,* 262–269.

Sloan, J. J. (1994). The correlates of campus crime: An analysis of reported crimes on college and university campuses. *Journal of Criminal Justice, 22,* 51–61.

Sluis, K. A. (2001). *An analysis of parent notification policy adoption in response to the Higher Education Amendments of 1998.* Unpublished master's thesis, Indiana University, Bloomington.

Smith, A. F. (1978). Lawrence Kohlberg's cognitive stage theory of the development of moral judgment. In L. Knefelkamp, C. Widick, & C. A. Parker (Eds.), *Applying new developmental findings.* (New Directions in Student Services, No. 4, pp. 53–67). San Francisco: Jossey-Bass.

Smith, D. B. (1994, Winter). Student discipline in American colleges and universities: A historical overview. *Educational Horizons, 78–85.*

Smith, G. P., & Kirk, H. P. (1971). Student discipline in transition. *NASPA Journal, 8,* 276–282.

Snoxell, L. F. (1960). Counseling reluctant and recalcitrant students. *Journal of College Student Personnel, 2,* 16–20.

State ex rel The Miami Student v. Miami University, 680 N.E.2d 956 (Oh. 1997).

Steele, B. H., Johnson, D. H., & Rickard, S. T. (1984). Managing the judicial function in student affairs. *Journal of College Student Personnel, 25,* 337–342.

Stein, R. H. (1972). Discipline: On campus, downtown, or both, a need for a standard. *NASPA Journal, 10,* 41–47.

Stone, G. L., & Lucas, J. (1994). Disciplinary counseling in higher education: A neglected challenge. *Journal of Counseling and Development, 72,* 234–238.

Stoner, E. N., II. (1998). A model code for student discipline. In B. G. Paterson & W. L. Kibler (Eds.), *The administration of student discipline: Student, organizational, and community issues* (pp. 3–42). Asheville, NC: College Administration Publications.

Stoner, E. N., II, & Cerminara, K. (1990). Harnessing the "spirit of insubordination:" A model student disciplinary code. *Journal of College and University Law, 17,* 89–121.

Strickland, D. A. (1965). In loco parentis—Legal mots and student morals. *Journal of College Student Personnel, 6,* 335–340.

The Student Right-to-Know and Campus Security Act of 1990, 20 U.S.C. §1092 (1990).

Thomas, R. (1987). Systems for guiding college student behavior: Growth or punishment? *NASPA Journal, 25,* 54–61.

Travelstead, W. W. (1987). Introduction and historical context. In R. Caruso & W. W. Travelstead (Eds.), *Enhancing campus judicial systems* (New Directions for Student Services, No. 39, pp. 3–16). San Francisco: Jossey-Bass.

U.S. Department of Education, Office of Postsecondary Education. (2001). *The incidence of crime on the campuses of U.S. postsecondary education institutions.* Washington, DC: Author.

United States v. Miami University and Ohio State University, 91 F. Supp. 2d 1132 (S.D. Oh. 2000).

UWM Post v. Board of Regents, 744 F.Supp. 1163 (E.D. Wisc. 1991).

Van Alstyne, W. W. (1963). Procedural due process and state university students. *UCLA Law Review, 10,* 368–389.

Van Alstyne, W. W. (1966). The prerogatives of students, the powers of universities, and the due process of law. *Journal of the National Association for Women Deans, Administrators, and Counselors, 30,* 11–16.

Wagoner, J. L. (1976). *Thomas Jefferson and the education of a new nation.* Bloomington, IN: Phi Delta Kappa Educational Foundation.

Wagoner, J. L. (1986). Honor and dishonor in Mr. Jefferson's university: The antebellum years. *History of Education Quarterly, 26,* 155–179.

Warshaw, S., & Leahy, J. W., Jr. (1965). *The trouble in Berkeley: The complete history, in text and pictures, of the great student rebellion against the "new university."* Berkeley, CA: Diablo Press.

Warters, B., Sebok, T., & Goldblum, A. (2000). Making things right: Restorative justice comes to the campuses. *Conflict Management in Higher Education, 1(1)*. http://www.culma.wayne.edu/CMHER/Articles/Restorative.html (accessed August 12, 2002)

Williamson, F. G. (1956). Preventative aspects of disciplinary counseling. *Educational and Psychological Measurement, 16*, 68–81.

Williamson, F. G. (1961). *Student personnel services in colleges and universities.* New York: McGraw-Hill.

Williamson, F. G. (1963). A new look at discipline. *Journal of Secondary Education, 38*, 10–14.

Williamson, F. G., & Foley, J. D. (1949). *Counseling and discipline.* New York: McGraw-Hill.

Wilson, J. M. (1996). Processes for resolving student disciplinary matters. In W. L. Mercer (Ed.), *Critical issues in judicial affairs: Current trends in practice* (New Directions for Student Services, No. 73, pp. 35–52). San Francisco: Jossey-Bass.

Wrenn, C. G. (1949). Student discipline in college. *Educational and Psychological Measurement, 9*, 625–633.

Young, D. P. (1970). *The legal aspects of student dissent and discipline in higher education.* Athens, GA: University of Georgia, Institute of Higher Education.

Young, D. P. (1972). The colleges and the courts. In L. J. Peterson & L. O. Garber (Eds.), *The yearbook of school law 1972* (pp. 201–260). Topeka, KS: National Organization on Legal Problems of Education.

Zacker, J. (1996). Evaluation in judicial affairs. In W. L. Mercer (Ed.), *Critical issues in judicial affairs: Current trends in practice.* (New Directions for Student Services, No. 73, pp. 99–106). San Francisco: Jossey-Bass.

Zelna, C. (2002). *Student portfolios.* Unpublished report. Office of Student Conduct, North Carolina State University, Raleigh, NC.

Zelna, C., & Cousins, P. (2002, May 30). Assessing judicial affairs at NC State University: Processes, techniques, and impact. *NASPA NetResults.* Available online at www.naspa.org/netresults

Chapter 8

MULTICULTURAL AFFAIRS

BETTINA C. SHUFORD AND CAROLYN J. PALMER

CULTURE AND MULTICULTURALISM

[We] have been entrusted with the difficult task of speaking about culture. But there is nothing in the world more elusive. . . . An attempt to encompass its meaning in words is like trying to seize the air in the hand when one finds that it is everywhere except within one's grasp (Lowell, cited in Kuh & Whitt, 1988, p. 10).

There may indeed be as many different definitions of the term *culture* as there are people attempting to define it. However, there appears to be agreement regarding the various elements constituting culture. Generally, these include (1) shared histories, (2) languages, (3) foods, (4) dress, (5) artifacts, (6) symbols, (7) traditions, customs, rites, rituals, ceremonies, and other practices or patterns of behavior, and (8) belief systems, assumptions, philosophies or ideologies, values, norms, moral standards, ethical principles, and other common understandings (Kuh & Whitt, 1988). College students have many ties that bind them to their families, friends, home communities, religious institutions, and other aspects of their precollege lives. They arrive on campus with expectations, needs, and aspirations that have, to varying degrees, been shaped by their cultural experiences.

Many students seek out others whose cultural characteristics are similar to their own. Relationships with these others provide social support and foster a sense of identity with and commitment to groups or subgroups where students feel welcome and comfortable. Depending on the extent to which broader institutional cultures support truly inclusive campus communities, within which all members feel they genuinely "belong" or "matter," students may or may not develop similar identity with and commitment to their colleges or universities. Nevertheless, cultural experiences before and during college undoubtedly provide "a frame of reference within which to interpret the meaning of events and actions on and off campus" (Kuh & Whitt, 1988, p. 13).

Given this admittedly incomplete, but hopefully sufficient, introduction to culture, what is multiculturalism and how are multicultural institutions to be defined? Multiculturalism is commonly described using a "salad bowl" versus "melting pot" analogy. The major difference between the two is that the ingredients of a salad maintain their own integrity. People generally do not want the tomato to taste like a cucumber, expect the carrot to turn into lettuce, or have any desire to use a blender (or melting pot) to ensure that every part of the salad will be exactly the same. Rather, the salad is enriched when a number of ingredients, which remain distinct, come together. Similarly, multiculturalism is based on the premise that a group of people can be enriched when they come together, yet maintain their uniqueness as individuals.

The mere presence of members of various subgroups may make a student population diverse, but it does not necessarily guarantee that an institution is providing a multicultural environment (Hill, 1991). Rather, a multicultural institution is one in which the cultures of diverse groups are not merely acknowledged or tolerated but accepted, respected, included, appreciated, and celebrated within the larger institutional culture. The cultures of many colleges and universities were historically based on rather homogeneous student, faculty, and staff populations. However, increasing diversity within these populations has inspired many campus leaders to reconcile some of the traditional elements of their institutional cultures with the more contemporary values of multiculturalism (McEwen & Roper, 1994a) in an attempt to create campus cultures that are inclusive of all subgroups within the college or university community.

THE BLESSINGS AND CHALLENGES OF DIVERSITY

Willer (1992) quoted an ancient Chinese saying, "May you be blessed with the opportunity to live in interesting times" (p. 161). Student affairs professionals have been blessed with opportunities to work with increasingly diverse student populations. Of course, this blessing is also a challenge. Simply stated, diversity often increases the potential for conflict. For example, when students of many races, religions, social backgrounds, sexual orientation, value systems, and sensibilities live together in "concentrated proximity" in residence halls, it becomes "inevitable that interpersonal tensions, misunderstandings, incivilities, and disharmonies will arise" (Amanda, 1994, p. 39). Consequently, higher education needs professionals "who are capable of solving problems, managing diverse environments, delivering effective services to a diverse student body, and working as part of interracial work groups" (McEwen & Roper, 1994b, p. 86).

Although challenging, there is also great personal reward to be gained from helping to create a campus "laboratory for learning how to live and interrelate in a complex world" (Spees & Spees, 1986, p. 5) and to prepare students to make significant contributions to that world. Pickert (1992) emphasized the need for college graduates to be "familiar with other cultures and their histories, languages, and institutions . . . [and] willing to consider perspectives held by people whose cultures differ from their own" (p. 61). Thus, opportunities for student affairs professionals to increase awareness and sensitivity, foster cross-cultural communication skills that contribute to human understanding and human development, and in other ways help make "the university experience the universal experience it should be" (Thielen & Limbird, 1992, p. 124) are perceived by many as "blessings."

Although many of the concepts addressed in this chapter apply to many diverse groups, page limitations clearly prohibit adequate discussion of issues pertaining to women (Jones, 1997; Whitt, Edison, Pascarella, Nora, & Terenzini, 1999); adult learners (Senter & Senter, 1998; Spitzer, 2000); commuter students (Likins, 1991); and students with disabilities (Hitchings, Luzzo, Retish, Horvath, & Ristow, 1998; Hodges & Keller, 1999; Jones, Kalivoda, & Higbee, 1997). Therefore, the remainder of the chapter focuses on underrepresented American ethnic groups; lesbian, gay, bisexual, and transgender (LGBT) students; international students; and students from diverse religious backgrounds.

RACIAL OR ETHNIC MINORITIES: DIVERSITY WITHIN UNDERREPRESENTED ETHNIC GROUPS

Demographic predictions on the browning of America by the year 2000 were referenced in several reports in the 1980s. For example, the One-Third of a Nation report, published by the American Council on Education and Education Commission on the States (1988), predicted that one-third of all school-age Americans would be racial or ethnic minorities by the year 2000. In the recent 2000 census report, 75.1 percent of the population listed themselves as White, 12.3 percent as Black or African American, 3.6 percent as Asian, 0.9 percent as American Indian and Alaskan Native, 0.1 percent as Native Hawaiian and other Pacific Islander, and 5.5 percent as some other race. Hispanics, who may be of any race, make up 13 percent of the total population (U.S. Census Bureau, March 2001). The diversity found in the general population is now surfacing in higher education.

Although African American, Hispanic/Latino Americans, Native Americans, and Asian Pacific Americans comprise four broad racial or ethnic groups, there is considerable diversity within each of these groups. For example, Asian Pacific and Latino Americans have cultural heritages within many different countries, represent different ethnic or religious groups, speak different languages, wear different clothing, eat different foods, share different value systems, honor different traditions, and celebrate different holidays (Chan & Wang, 1991; Chew & Ogi, 1987; Kodama, McEwen, Liang,

& Lee, 2001; O'Brien, 1993; Quevedo-Garcia, 1987). Similarly, American Indian tribes have "language differences and custom variations" (LaCounte, 1987, p. 66), and African Americans do not comprise a monolithic group within which all members share the same backgrounds, belief systems, expectations, aspirations, behavioral norms, or other cultural characteristics.

Even though many members of a specific cultural group may share certain experiences or perspectives, there are often exceptions that differentiate individual members of the group. Discussion of commonalities within and among groups may foster understanding of many group members, but should never be used to stereotype all members or to prejudge or make unfounded assumptions about a particular individual.

THE HISTORY OF UNDERREPRESENTED ETHNIC GROUPS IN AMERICAN HIGHER EDUCATION

Cultural groups are, to varying degrees, affected by their histories. What have been the histories of underrepresented racial or ethnic groups within American higher education?

AFRICAN AMERICANS

Although some African Americans were self-educated, served apprenticeships, and to a limited extent studied abroad (Thomas & Hill, 1987), only 28 African Americans received baccalaureates from American colleges prior to the Civil War (Bowles & DeCosta, 1971). Their pre–Civil War experiences with American higher education were limited to a few predominantly White institutions (PWIs) that would accept Blacks, and a few historically Black institutions (HBIs) in existence at the time. Additional HBIs were founded during the years between the Civil War and 1890 (Bowles & DeCosta, 1971), after the second Morrill Act of 1890 provided the "funds for Black education be distributed on a 'just and equitable basis'" (Ranbom & Lynch, 1987/1988, p. 17), and after the U.S. Supreme Court, in the case of *Plessey v. Ferguson*, ruled on the constitutionality of the "separate but equal" doctrine in 1896.

It was not until 1954 that the Supreme Court ruled, in *Brown v. Board of Education* and other cases, that separate but equal (or racial segregation within public education) was unconstitutional (Bowles & DeCosta, 1971). Still, some states continued to operate dual educational systems for Blacks and Whites (Williams, 1991) until Title VI of the Civil Rights Act of 1964 indicated that "no person in the United States, on the grounds of race, color, or national origin, be excluded from participation in, or be denied the benefits of, or be subjected to discrimination under any program or activity receiving federal financial assistance" (Malaney, 1987, p. 17). This legislation was largely responsible for opening the doors of PWIs to Blacks, and HBIs to whites. Although HBIs represented only about 3 percent of all colleges and universities in the United States, they enrolled approximately 14.2 percent of all African American college students in 1998 and awarded 26 percent of the total bachelors degrees that year (Harvey, 2001).

ASIAN PACIFIC AMERICANS

Asian Pacific Americans are the most recent group to immigrate to the United States in formerly unprecedented numbers. As a result of many military, economic, and political events (Wright, 1987), between 1970 and 1980, the United States received "a steady stream of Asian immigrants and refugees" (Hsia & Hirano-Nakanishi, 1989, p. 22). During this one decade, the Asian American population more than doubled, or grew at a rate "more than ten times that of the U.S. population as a whole" (Chew & Ogi, 1987). Between 1988 and 1998, enrollment among Asian Pacific Americans in higher education increased by 80 percent, with nearly 60 percent enrolled in four-year colleges (Harvey, 2001).

Poverty, unemployment, and undereducation are not uncommon in some Asian Pacific American communities (Chan & Wang, 1991). Like other minority group members, Asian Pacific Americans are strongly connected to their communities and particularly to their families. The influence of traditional values is often dependent on environmental and contextual factors (Kodama, McEwen, Liang, & Lee, 2001). Factors such as generational status, immigration experiences, and acculturation add to the diversity and complexity of the Asian Pacific student populations (Kodama, McEwen, Liang, & Lee, 2001). Like some Latinos and Native Americans, some Asian Pacific Americans have difficulties with English, in part because English may be seldom or never spoken in their homes.

Although campus racial incidents are often described in terms of Blacks and Whites, "other students of color, including those of Hispanic and Asian origins, have likewise been affected by rising racial tensions in colleges and universities" (Chan & Wang, 1991, p. 43). Asian Pacific Americans are sometimes victimized or ostracized by their non-Asian peers. A given student may be the "only" Asian Pacific American (or one of very few) in the classroom, residence hall, or other campus environment.

As a result of many commonalities, Asian Pacific Americans have often joined with other underrepresented ethnic groups to request or demand campus programs and services for students of color. For example, Asian American studies programs were developed following student protests in 1968–1969 seeking "ethnic studies programs that would highlight the history and contemporary experiences of nonwhite groups in the United States, in order to counter the existing Eurocentric curriculum that either failed to include any information about people of color, or worse, badly distorted the latter's history" (Chan & Wang, 1991, p. 46).

One rather unique challenge faced by Asian Pacific American students is that they have been characterized as the "model minority" (Chan & Wang, 1991), in part because many Asian Pacific Americans do well in school. This stereotype, however, minimizes the fact that, like many other students, they must struggle with their academic endeavors. Furthermore, it discounts the hard work many have done in order to succeed. Despite success in college, Asian Pacific students report a lower level of satisfaction with the college experience (Tan, 1994). High levels of enrollment and persistence of Asian Pacific students should not override the fact that special assistance is still needed by these students.

HISPANIC/LATINO/LATINA AMERICANS

According to Wright (1987), "the collegiate history of Hispanics had scarcely begun before World War II. Even when they were admitted, Hispanics often had to deny or restrict their cultural identity in order to matriculate" (p. 7). Not until 1968, primarily as a result of the civil rights movement, particularly the "La Raza" movement, and the civil rights legislation described earlier in this chapter, did large numbers of Latino/Latina students participate in American higher education, primarily at two-year colleges (Wright, 1987).

Hispanics/Latinos/Latinas experienced the highest growth rate for college enrollment among the four major underrepresented ethnic groups, with a gain of more than 85 percent between 1988 and 1998 (Harvey, 2001). In 1998, Latinos/Latinas received 5.6 percent of all bachelor's degrees awarded in the United States (Harvey, 2001), even though they constituted 10 percent of the nation's elementary and secondary school population (O'Brien, 1993). More than 41 percent of the bachelor's degrees received by Latinos/Latinas were from Hispanic-serving institutions (HSIs) (Harvey, 2001). Census data showing that the Latino/Latina American population is growing at a rate more than five times the national average (O'Brien, 1993) have inspired higher education to address the specific needs of Latino/Latina students.

HSIs, HBIs, and tribal colleges have been successful in recruiting, retaining, and graduating substantial numbers of underrepresented ethnic students, many of them from lower socioeconomic backgrounds and with admissions credentials suggesting that they may be academically marginal college students. This success may be related to the extent to which these colleges and universities provide academic programs, student services, and psychosocial support systems that are congruent with the cultural identities of their students.

NATIVE AMERICANS

Native American tribes undoubtedly socialized, acculturated, trained, and educated their own members throughout their history. The education of Indians by non-Indians began at least as early as 1568, when Spanish missionaries established schools to Christianize Indians in what is now Florida. For many years thereafter, European settlers made sporadic efforts to train or educate Indians (Ranbom & Lynch, 1987/1988). For example, special facilities for Indian students were provided at William and Mary in 1723, and "the Continental Congress approved $500 in 1773 for the education of Indians at Darthmouth College" (LaCounte, 1987, p. 65). Despite these early efforts, "only in very recent years have white institutions, with any fervor, sought Indian students" (Wright, 1987, p. 7).

Tribal colleges have played a significant role in the education of Indian students. The first tribal college opened in 1968. Currently, there are 27 tribal colleges, with the majority being community colleges. These colleges are located in 11 states, ranging "from California to Michigan, and from Arizona to North Dakota" (Boyer, 1997, p. 3). Like many other two-year institutions, tribal colleges are attempting to increase their communication with four-year institutions in order to enable more of the students who begin college in familiar surroundings (e.g., on their own reservations) to continue their education (LaCounte, 1987).

Native Americans continue to be underrepresented in higher education (Darden, Bagakas, Armstrong, & Payne, 1994). Their low matriculation rates, particularly at off-reservation four-year institutions, are related to a high school dropout rate of approximately 45 percent, underpreparation for college, and limited financial resources as well as inadequate assistance when applying for financial aid. Strong ties to family and community, culture shock in moving away from primarily Indian environments, low participation in orientation programs, insufficient personal and academic support systems for Indian students on campus, and lack of Indian professionals serving as role models also affect their adjustment to the college environment (LaCounte, 1987).

SUMMARY

Although HBIs and a few almost all-White institutions have provided undergraduate education for relatively small numbers of students of color over the course of many years, it was not until the 1960s and later, well over 300 years after the founding of Harvard, that substantial numbers of students of color entered American higher education. Many are currently enrolled at HBIs, HSIs, tribally controlled institutions, urban commuter institutions, and two-year community colleges. For many reasons related to both historical and current realities, racial or ethnic minorities continue to be underrepresented in higher education, particularly at predominantly White, residential, four-year, and graduate or professional institutions.

MINORITY STUDENT SERVICES AND MULTICULTURAL AFFAIRS

HISTORICAL OVERVIEW

When large numbers of minority students, particularly African Americans, began to appear on predominantly White campuses during the 1960s, little was done to address their special needs (Pounds, 1987; Young, 1986). A laissez-faire attitude on the part of faculty and administration may have been based on the naïve assumptions that underrepresented ethnic students would simply assimilate into the institutional culture with no effort by the institution to meet the needs of these students (Gibbs, 1973). According to Quevedo-Garcia (1987), assimilation requires "relinquishing one's cultural identity" (p. 52) and developing a new identity that coincides with the new or dominant culture. Underrepresented ethnic minority students, most of whom had no desire to sacrifice their cultural identities in order to "fit in" to the campus culture, felt isolated, lonely, alienated, and disenfranchised (Gibbs, 1973; Fleming, 1984; Young, 1986). They realized they were "in these universities but not of these universities" (Stennis-Williams, Terrell, & Haynes, 1988, p. 74). Many responded with apathy or anger (Young, 1986).

In response to student protests and community pressure, along with court orders enforcing new laws emanating from the civil rights movement, institutions developed offices of minority student services (Wright, 1987), which many students of color considered "safe havens in an alien environment" (Young, 1986, p. 18). At approximately the same time, in response to government mandates and with the help of government funds, "colleges witnessed the creation of such programs as the TRIO [Student Support Services, Educational Opportunity Centers, Talent Search, and the Ronald E. McNair Program for Graduate Studies] and Upward Bound programs" (Pounds, 1987, p. 33), designed to prepare students from low-income or disadvantaged families for college, recruit them to college, and assist them once they were in college. Many of the participants in theses special service programs were first-generation underrepresented ethnic students. Today some of these earlier programs, along with newer endeavors, continue to identify talented individuals; provide pre-college enrichment programs, which may include day-long or summer-long experiences on college campuses; and offer valuable services to students once they are enrolled in higher education (J. A. Taylor, Jr., personal communication, November 28, 1995).

Although some professionals within offices of minority student services assisted with or were responsible for precollege enrichment and minority student recruitment programs, most were charged with responding to the needs of already enrolled students of color. Many provided leadership development and advising for increasing numbers of minority student groups (e.g., Latino Student Union, Native American Student Associations, Black Greek Letter Organizations) and offered academic and financial aid advising, tutoring services, personal counseling, career development and placement services, student activities, and cultural programs (J. A. Taylor, Jr., personal communication, November 28, 1995). In some ways, these offices served as mini–student affairs divisions for minority students.

Gradually, over the course of several years, many offices of minority student services evolved into offices of multicultural affairs. Although most of these offices still provided many valuable services to underrepresented ethnic students, their missions began to include a number of outreach projects within the broader institutional community and to serve other underrepresented groups on campus (Sutton, 1998). For example, many staff in minority students services began to help their colleagues in other student affairs units to recognize, be sensitive to, and respond appropriately to cultural issues so that, for example, those in the academic advising center could be effective academic advisers for minority students. As the transition from minority student services to multicultural affairs offices began to take place, the mission of these offices expanded to include programs and services for lesbian, gay, bisexual, and transgender (LGBT) students, international students, and religious diversity.

Student affairs professionals who worked in offices of minority student services or multicultural affairs helped to develop major programs (e.g., those associated with Black History Month) and campus cultural centers (e.g., La Casa Latino Cultural Centers), which were designed to address the educational needs of both minority and majority students. In addition, they often assisted their faculty colleagues in developing individual courses (e.g., Asian American history), departments (e.g., Black studies), and interdepartmental programs related to ethnic studies, which emerged on many campuses in the late 1960s and 1970s and expanded during the 1980s and 1990s (Chan & Wang, 1991).

THE ROLES OF MINORITY/MULTICULTURAL AFFAIRS OFFICES TODAY

Although the titles and organizational placements of offices may focus on minority and/or multicultural affairs, the clientele served by these offices and the breadth and depth of their programs vary by institution (Wright, 1987). Professionals in these offices generally serve as educators and advisers for their colleagues across their campuses and coordinate multicultural endeavors for their institutions. At the same time, they provide valuable services, programs, and role models for underrepresented groups on campus.

Missions

The mission of a minority/multicultural affairs office should be three-fold:

1. The office should provide support to underrepresented cultural groups. This support should include assessment and other efforts designed to identify the psychosocial, academic, and other needs of underrepresented students; communication of these needs, along with recommendations for meeting them, to other units on campus; programs and services that enhance students' personal, social, educational, and cultural development; and efforts to encourage underrepresented cultural groups to participate in and contribute to the life of the campus.

2. The office should provide multicultural education for all students. Educational endeavors should assist majority and minority students to identify their commonalities and recognize, understand, accept, respect, and value their differences. Students should learn to relate to members of diverse groups, communicate effectively across racial or cultural lines, and transfer these skills to a variety of settings (Hoopes, 1979).

3. The office should promote systemic change that fosters a multicultural perspective across the campus. As change agents, minority/multicultural affairs professionals should work with various allies to incorporate diverse perspectives into every facet of the institution, including its admissions and hiring practices, administrative policies and procedures, academic curriculum, and cocurricular activities. Only when every unit on campus and the institution as a whole address multicultural issues in an optimal manner will minority/multicultural affairs offices no longer be needed.

Professional Standards

The Council for the Advancement of Standards in Higher Education (CAS) (Miller, 2001) emphasized that minority programs must include the following goals:

1. Assess the needs of minority students in selected areas, set priorities among those needs, and respond to the extent that the number of students, facilities, and resources permit;

2. Orient minority students to the culture of the institution;

3. Assist minority students to determine and assess their educational goals and academic skills;
4. Provide support services to help minority students achieve educational goals and attain or refine academic skills necessary to perform adequately in the classroom;
5. Promote the intellectual, career, social, and moral development of the students;
6. Promote and deepen each minority student's understanding of his or her own culture and heritage;
7. Promote and deepen majority students' understanding of their unique cultures and heritages;
8. Provide training in leadership skills and other personal and social skills for minority students and those seeking to assist them; and
9. Offer or identify appropriate minority mentors and role models (p. 180).

In addition, the program must provide educational efforts for both majority and minority students that focus on . . .

1. Awareness of cultural differences;
2. Self-assessment of cultural awareness and possible prejudices; and
3. Changing prejudicial attitudes or behaviors (p. 180).

EXPANSION OF SERVICES

Lesbian, Gay, Bisexual, and Transgender (LGBT) Students

On many campuses, LGBT students have added their voice to the multicultural playing field. Support for LGBT issues within colleges and universities has increased within the last decade as "more faculty, staff, and students take the risk of openly identifying as lesbian, gay, bisexual, or transgender and actively work to increase the awareness of institutions about the needs and concerns of LGBT people" (Evans & Wall, 2000, p. 390). The range of support varies from institution to institution, from recognition of a LGBT student organization, support and educational programming from multicultural affairs offices or cultural centers, to specific offices designated to address LGBT issues (Sanlo, 2000).

While some multicultural affairs offices provide support services to LGBT students, the support and services needed by these students are often different from those needed by underrepresented ethnic students (McRee & Cooper, 1998). LGBT students not only face the range of typical developmental issues of college students, but also must cope with developmental issues related to their sexual identity (Wall & Evans, 1991). While "most lesbian and gay adults acknowledge their affectional orientation to themselves during adolescence," the coming out process usually does not begin until they reach college (D'Augelli, 1991). Additionally, LGBT students must deal with harassment, homophobic attitudes, religious backlash, and complex family and social relationships (D'Augelli, 1991; Levine & Love, 2000; Rhoads, 1997).

Multicultural affairs programming should target both LGBT students and heterosexual students (Evans & Wall, 2000). Support services for LGBT students may include social networks for students struggling with identity, role models who can offer insights and share experiences on the coming out process, special interest housing, social events, and programs about coming out and LGBT identity development (Evans & Wall, 2000; Herbst & Malaney, 1999; Rhoads, 1997). The provision of programs and services for LGBT students should recognize the diversity within the LGBT community (Evans & Wall, 2000).

International Students

The presence of international students in American higher education is growing in significant numbers. There are over five hundred thousand international students studying in U.S. colleges and universities (Institute of International Education, 2001). The international exchange of students has transformed many American campuses (Ping, 1999). International students have begun to integrate into campus life and have been instrumental in educating American students about global life (Ping, 1999). International students are very open to sharing information about their countries, national histories and cultures (McIntire, 1992). The challenge is creating forums where American and international students can engage in information sharing about their cultural backgrounds. In addition to the cultural diversity that international students bring to campus, the recruitment of international students has enhanced enrollment (Dalton, 1999).

On many campuses there is a designated office or staff person to work with international students. Multicultural affairs offices are also beginning to provide support for international students and international programming. On campuses where there are large numbers of students from abroad, international student services offices serve as a mini–student affairs division (McIntire, 1992). The essential services for international students, whether in an international student services office or a multicultural affairs office, should include

> Immigration assistance and counseling; orientation, both initial and continuing, to campus and community as well as to cultural values and practices; and programs that address barriers to successful academic and personal adjustment in a foreign environment; barriers as basic as food and living arrangements; health services, religious practices, social interaction, and mores (Ping, 1999, p. 19).

Support for international student organizations should also be provided.

Religious Diversity

Throughout the history of this country, religion has played an important role in the lives of many of its citizens. Religious beliefs are an essential element of cultural diversity in America. "[The] United States has always had a number of different religions. The religions of Native Americans were in place when Europeans arrived" (Uphoff, 2001, p. 106). Continued immigration from non-European countries in recent years has further diversified the non-Christian-Judaic background in America (Uphoff, 2001).

An awareness of religious diversity on college campuses is essential because it helps students understand the human diversity that exists within our learning communities. Problems occur when religious beliefs, customs, and traditions are not understood by community members (Uphoff, 2001). Religion has influenced human behavior throughout history. Some religions influence the everyday responsibilities of such things as the handling and consumption of food, clothing worn by believers, dating patterns, and social interaction with others (Uphoff, 2001).

Intolerance springs from the lack of understanding of the beliefs, customs, and practices associated with religion. That was never more prevalent than with the events of September 11, 2001, when the World Trade Center and the Pentagon were attacked by terrorists. Immediately following the attack, people of Arabic descent and Muslims were profiled as potential terrorists. The misunderstanding of the Islamic faith led many people to believe that acts of violence were a part of the Muslim faith—when in fact Muslims stand for love and peace.

Multicultural affairs offices can play an important role in helping to educate the campus about the customs and beliefs of different religious groups on campus. Programs about religious holidays and celebrations; comparing and contrasting religions; and the influence of religion in politics, education, and health care are just a few examples of educational offerings that can be promoted on campus. Multicultural affairs offices and student affairs (1) can play an advocacy role in helping students overcome institutional barriers that might impede them from practicing their religion on campus (e.g., burning candles for religious ceremonies, access to specially prepared foods), and (2) can assist students with their spiritual development (Temkin & Evans, 1998).

CHALLENGES FACING MINORITY AND/OR MULTICULTURAL AFFAIRS IN THE FUTURE

In response to a study conducted by Moyer (1992), senior minority affairs administrators identified the following eight issues most likely to affect minority affairs in the new millennium:

1. Maximizing the institutional effectiveness of minority affairs offices;

2. Sustaining or increasing institutional commitment to addressing minority concerns and changing campus cultures;
3. Rectifying budgetary problems;
4. Increasing financial assistance to students;
5. Assisting underprepared students;
6. Developing curricula that are reflective of the diverse student population;
7. Developing retention programs for minority students; and
8. Merging racial and gender issues.

Multicultural affairs offices are also broadening the scope of their services to include support for international students; gay, lesbian, and bisexual students; and other subgroups on campus (Carreathers & Sutton, 1996). Because of the need for additional services, many directors of multicultural affairs express concern regarding insufficient resources to meet the needs of racial or ethnic minority students and other subgroups within the next decade.

MINORITY AND/OR MULTICULTURAL CENTERS

A number of multicultural centers evolved from Black houses, which had been requested by Black student organizations in the 1960s (Stennis-Williams et al., 1988). The initial purposes of these centers included helping students of color with their transition to the university community, promoting cultural self-understanding, and serving as social centers for students (Young, 1986). However, their service missions changed over time to reflect an educational orientation (Young, 1986). Some center staff have had academic status or have collaborated with faculty in offering credited courses and noncredit programs (e.g., guest lecture series) related to ethnicity and academic support services (Stennis-Williams et al., 1988). These educational efforts have helped to compensate for the omission of multicultural perspectives in the mainstream curriculum and have been instrumental in helping to retain students of color. However, in addition to meeting the needs of minority students, today's multicultural centers should "appeal to non-minority groups on the majority white campus" (Stennis-Williams et al., 1988, p. 92).

ADDRESSING MULTICULTURAL ISSUES
THROUGHOUT STUDENT AFFAIRS

In reference to international students, Thielen and Limbird (1992) emphasized that "it is inappropriate to cast them as 'experts' in all matters pertaining to their home countries" (p. 127). Similarly, it is inappropriate to expect American underrepresented groups to perform the impossible task of articulating the views or describing the cultures of very diverse racial or ethnic groups, and it is both unfair and irresponsible to delegate responsibility for assisting underrepresented students and fostering multiculturalism on campus to those in a single functional area. Consequently, the CAS Professional Standards for Higher Education (2001) stressed that the following fundamental principles should inform the work of student affairs:

1. Recognizing the ubiquitous nature of human diversity, institutions are committed to eliminating barriers that impede student learning and development, attending especially to establishing and maintaining diverse human relationships essential to survival in a global society.
2. Justice and respect for differences bond individuals to community; and thus education for multicultural awareness and positive regard for differences is essential to the development and maintenance of a health engendering society (p. 12).

As has been stated elsewhere in this chapter, student affairs professionals must have an awareness of and a sensitivity to multicultural issues. Pope and Reynolds (1997) identified a list of 33 competencies student affairs professionals should possess with regard to knowledge, skills, and awareness. Student affairs practitioners can use their knowledge of developmental tasks faced by underrepresented students to build programming models with goals and activities that are culturally sensitive to students of color and other underrepresented groups (Manning, 1994). According to Stage and Manning (1992), typical programming models for students of color have included a number of activities generally offered in piecemeal fashion, whereas a more holistic or systematic approach may be more effective in fostering the students' development. The following sections address some of these issues.

IMPLEMENTING A CULTURAL ENVIRONMENT TRANSITIONS MODEL

The Cultural Environment Transitions Model (Manning & Coleman-Boatwright, 1991) "assumes that organizational growth occurs as members of the community acquire knowledge about other cultures, gain experience with people different from themselves, and are challenged with structural and systemic change through these efforts" (p. 369). According to Manning (1994), multicultural organization models bring to light the value structures that support institutional policies and practices and that often perpetuate a cultural hierarchy of privilege. This knowledge may inspire administrators to question or eradicate the values and actions that maintain this hierarchy. Organizations implementing the Cultural Environment Transitions Model progress from:

Monoculturalism, through a period in which some college members are aware but unable to effect change in the institution, into a time of openly expressed conflict, through organizational rebirth reflective of multicultural goals, and finally, into a state of multiculturalism that is systemic and institutional (Manning & Coleman-Boatwright, 1991, p. 371).

BECOMING A CULTURAL BROKER

Stage and Manning (1992) prescribed the use of a cultural brokering approach to the creation of an educational system that empowers faculty, staff, and students to address the strengths and weaknesses of the various cultural systems on campus, with the desired outcome being a multicultural campus where there is a "seamless fabric of efforts" across the entire institution (p. 16). The components of the model include (1) learning to think contextually, (2) spanning boundaries, (3) ensuring optimal performance, and (4) taking action.

According to Stage and Manning (1992), "the task of learning to think contextually starts with an examination of one's underlying cultural assumptions. . . . This awareness then builds a realization that administrative actions and educational practices are not objective but rather reflect cultural backgrounds and assumptions" (pp. 17–18). A very simple example might involve one's recognition of programmatic attention to Christian holidays, but not to other religious holidays. When student activities staff decorate a Christmas tree in their office, sponsor a Christmas concert, or identify the break between semesters as "Christmas vacation" in their calendar of events, they should ask themselves how those who do not celebrate Christmas might respond. Furthermore, they might explore various ways in which Hanukkah and other religious holidays or holy days could be appropriately celebrated or recognized in student activities endeavors. The goal of learning to think contextually is to abolish the privileges that the perspectives of one cultural group have over others by using different cultural lenses to see that there is more than one way to view a situation or solve a problem.

In the second step, the student affairs practitioner spans the boundaries of the dominant perspective and considers other perspectives pertaining to their work with students. In determining administrative practices, professionals must ask themselves whether those practices reflect diverse opinions, experiences, and ways of learning (Stage & Manning, 1992). For example, those who teach freshman experience courses might span the boundaries of sometimes erroneous presumptions regarding the development of autonomy by acknowledging that many students do not value independence or individualism, but identify themselves as adults who are and will remain integral parts of their families, communities, and cultures.

The third step involves removing barriers to cultural expression, changing various aspects of campus life in order to welcome and include students of color and other underrepresented groups, and ensuring optimal performance (Stage & Manning, 1992). Orientation leaders who work in collaboration with their colleagues in minority and/or multicultural affairs, academic enhancement or advising, and other units to identify the unique needs of underrepresented groups and make plans to address those needs in orientation programs are examples of professionals who are attempting to remove barriers to the optimal adjustment and success of minority students.

The fourth and final step in cultural brokering involves taking action, which includes a variety of cultural perspectives in making decisions, developing policies, and implementing programs (Stage & Manning, 1992). Actions that may be taken in residence life, for example, would include not only deliberate efforts to recruit staff who represent diverse groups, but also effective inclusion of those staff in decisions regarding policies and procedures, physical facilities, food services, staffing patterns, student programs, and all other matters pertaining to residence life. Indeed, Hill (1991) warned that many subgroups of students, faculty, and staff will continue to be marginalized if all perspectives do not become central to the organization and if all voices are not heard at the decision-making table.

CONCLUSION

Increasing numbers of racial or ethnic minority students and members of other underrepresented cultural groups within higher education have not guaranteed their full involvement in the college or university experience. Student affairs professionals in multicultural affairs and all other functional areas must continue to identify the barriers that inhibit the inclusion of underrepresented group members and eradicate the barriers by addressing the specific needs of diverse students and by creating conditions that encourage communication and collaboration among diverse groups. Opportunities to create multicultural campus communities that maximize social integration and cross-cultural understanding, while honoring and celebrating individual and group differences, represent both challenges and blessings to today's student affairs professionals. This is the challenge of the multicultural affairs office.

TECHNOLOGY RESOURCES

Institute of International Education (November 13, 2001). Open doors 2001. http://www.opendoorsweb.org/press/international_students_in_the-us.htm
U.S. Census Bureau (March 12, 2001). Census 2000 shows America's diversity. Washington, DC: United States Department Commerce News. Retrieved from http://www.cenus.gov/Press-Release.www/2001/cb01cn61.html

REFERENCES

Amada, G. (1994). *Coping with the disruptive college student: A practical model.* Asheville, NC: College Administration Publications.

American Council on Education and Education Commission of the States. (1988). *One third of a nation* (A Report of The Commission on Minority Participation in Education and American Life). Washington, DC: Authors.

Bowles, F., & DeCosta, F. A. (1971). *Between two worlds: A profile of Negro education.* New York: McGraw-Hill.

Boyer, P. (1997). *Native American colleges.* Princeton, NJ: Carnegie Foundation.

Carreathers, K, & Sutton, M. (1996, November). *Exploring the need to establish professional standards for the minority affairs profession.* Paper presented at the meeting of the Southern Association of College Student Affairs, Mobile, AL.

Chan, S., & Wang, L. (1991). Racism and the model minority: Asian Americans in higher education. In P. G. Altbach & K. Lomotey (Eds.), *The racial crisis in American higher education* (pp. 43–67). Albany, NY: State University of New York Press.

Chew, C. A., & Ogi, A. Y. (1987). Asian American college student perspectives. In D. J. Wright (Ed.), *Responding to the needs of today's minority students* (New Directions for Student Services, No. 38, pp. 39–48). San Francisco: Jossey-Bass.

Dalton, J. C. (1999) The significance of international issues and responsibilities in the contemporary work of student affairs. In J. A. Dalton (Ed.), *Beyond borders: How international developments are changing student affairs practice* (New Direction for Student Services, No. 8, pp. 3–11). San Francisco: Jossey Bass.

Darden, J. T., Bagakas, J. G., Armstrong, T., & Payne, T. (1994). Segregation of American Indian undergraduate students in institutions of higher education. *Equity & Excellence in Education, 27(3),* 61–68.

D'Augelli, A. R. (1991). Gay men in college: Identity processes and adaptations. *Journal of College Student Development, 32,* 140–146.

Evans, N. J., & Wall, V. A. (Eds.). (1991). *Beyond tolerance: Gays, lesbians, and bisexuals on campus.* Alexandria, VA: American College Personnel Association.

Evans, N. J., & Wall, V. A. (2000). Parting thoughts: An agenda for addressing sexual orientation issues on campus. In N. J. Evans & V. A. Wall (Eds.), *Toward acceptance: Sexual orientation issues on campus* (pp. 389–403). Alexandria, VA: American College Personnel Association.

Fleming, J. (1984). *Blacks in college.* San Francisco: Jossey-Bass.

Gibbs, J. T. (1973). Black students/white university: Different expectation. *Personnel and Guidance Journal, 51(7),* 465–469.

Harvey, W. B. (2001). *Minorities in higher education 2000–2001: Eighteenth annual status report.* Washington, DC: American Council on Education.

Herbst, S., & Malaney, G. D. (1999). Perceived value of a special interest residential program for gay, lesbian, bisexual, and transgender students. *NASPA Journal, 36,* 47–54.

Hill, P. J. (1991, July/August). Multi-culturalism: The crucial philosophical and organizational issues. *Change,* 38–47.

Hitchings, W. E., Luzzo, D. A., Retish, P., Horvath, M., & Ristow, R. S. (1998). Identifying the career development needs of college students with disabilities. *Journal of College Student Development, 39,* 23–32.

Hodges, J. S., & Keller, M. J. (1999). Perceived influences on social integration by students with physical disabilities. *Journal of College Student Development, 40,* 678–686.

Hoopes, D. S. (1979). Intercultural communication concepts and the psychology of intercultural experience. In M. D. Pusch (Ed.), *Multicultural education: A cross cultural training approach* (pp. 10–38). La Grange Park, IL: Intercultural Network.

Hsia, J., & Hirano-Nakanishi, M. (1989, November/December). The demographics of diversity: Asian Americans and higher education. *Change, 21(6),* 39–47.

Jones, S. R. (1997). Voices of identity and difference: A qualitative exploration of the multiple dimensions of identity development in women college students. *NASPA Journal, 38,* 376–385.

Jones, G. C., Kalivoda, K. S., & Higbee, J. L. (1997). College students with attention deficit disorder. *NASPA Journal, 34,* 262–274.

Kodama, C. M., McEwen, M. K., Liang, C. T. H., & Lee, S. (2001). A theoretical examination of psychosocial issues for Asian Pacific American students. *NASPA Journal, 38,* 411–437.

Kuh, G. D., & Whitt, E. J. (1988). *The invisible tapestry: Culture in American colleges and universities* (ASHE-ERIC Higher Education Report, No. 1). Washington, DC: Association for the Study of Higher Education.

LaCounte, D. W. (1987). American Indian students in college. In D. J. Wright (Ed.). *Responding to the needs of today's minority students* (New Directions for Student Services, No. 38, pp. 65–79). San Francisco: Jossey-Bass.

Levine, H., & Love, P. G. (2000). Religiously affiliated institutions and sexual orientation. In N. J. Evans & V. A. Wall (Eds.), *Toward acceptance: Sexual orientation issues on campus* (pp. 89–108). Alexandria, VA: American College Personnel Association.

Likins, J. M. (1991). Research refutes a myth: Commuter students do want to be involved. *NASPA Journal, 29(1),* 68–74.

Malaney, G. D. (1987). A review of early decisions in Adams v. Richardson. In A. S. Pruitt (Ed.), *In pursuit of equality in higher education* (pp. 17–22). Dix Hills, NY: General Hall.

Manning, K. (1994). Multicultural theories for multicultural practices. *NASPA Journal, 31(3),* 176–185.

Manning, K., & Coleman-Boatwright, F. (1991). Student affairs initiatives toward a multicultural university. *Journal of College Student Development, 32(4),* 367–374.

McEwen, M. K., & Roper, L. D. (1994a). Incorporating multiculturalism into student affairs preparation programs: Suggestions from the literature. *Journal of College Student Development, 35(1),* 46-53.

McEwen, M. K., & Roper, L. D. (1994b). Interracial experiences, knowledge, and skills of master's degree students in graduate programs in student affairs. *Journal of College Student Development, 35(2),* 81–87.

McIntire, D. (1992). Introduction. In D. McIntire & P. Willer (Eds.), *Working with international students and scholars on American campuses* (pp. xi–xx). Washington, DC: National Association of Student Personnel Administrators.

McRee, T. K., & Cooper, D. L. (1998). Campus environments for gay, lesbian, and bisexual students at southeastern institutions of higher education. *NASPA Journal, 36,* 65–73.

Miller, T. K. (2001). *The book of professional standards for higher education 2001.* Washington, DC: Council for the Advancement of Standards in Higher Education.

Moyer, R. A. (1992). *A conceptual analysis of the status, role and function of chief minority affairs administrators on state assisted universities in Ohio.* Unpublished doctoral dissertation, Kent State University.

O'Brien, E. M. (1993). *Latinos in higher education* (Research Briefs, Vol. 4, No. 4). Washington, DC: American Council on Education, Division of Policy Analysis and Research.

Pickert, S. M. (1992). *Preparing for a global community: Achieving an international perspective in higher education* (ASHE-ERIC Higher Education Report, No. 2). Washington, DC: The George Washington University, School of Education and Human Development.

Ping, C. J (1999). An expanded international role for student affairs. In J. A. Dalton (Ed.), *Beyond borders: How international developments are changing student affairs practice* (New Direction for Student Services, No. 8, pp. 13–21). San Francisco: Jossey-Bass.

Pope, R. L., & Reynolds, A. L. (1977). Student affairs core competencies: Integrating multicultural awareness, knowledge, and skills. *Journal of College Student Development, 38,* 266–277.

Pounds, A. W. (1987). Black students' needs on predominantly white campuses. In D. J. Wright (Ed.), *Responding to the needs of today's minority students* (New Directions for Students Services, No. 38, pp. 23–38). San Francisco: Jossey-Bass.

Quevedo-Garcia, E. L. (1987). Facilitating the development of Hispanic college students. In D. J. Wright (Ed.), *Responding to the needs of today's minority students* (New Directions for Students Services, No. 38, pp. 49–63). San Francisco: Jossey-Bass.

Ranbom, S., & Lynch, J. (1987/1988). Timeline: The long hard road to educational equality. *Educational Record, 68(4)/69(1),* 16–22.

Rhoads, R. A. (1997). Implications of the growing visibility of gay and bisexual male students on campus. *NASPA Journal, 34,* 79–87.

Sanlo, R. L. (2000). The LGBT campus resource center director: The new profession in students affairs. *NASPA Journal, 37,* 41–53.

Senter, M. S., & Senter, R. (1998). A comparative study of traditional and nontraditional students' identities and needs. *NASPA Journal, 35,* 270–280.

Spees, E. C., & Spees, E. R. (1986). Internationalizing the campus: Questions and concerns. In K. R. Pyle (Ed.), *Guiding the development of foreign students* (New Directions for Student Services, No. 36, pp. 5–18). San Francisco: Jossey-Bass.

Spitzer, T. M. (2000). Predictors of college success: A comparison of traditional and nontraditional age students. *NASPA Journal, 38,* 82–98.

Stage, F. K., & Manning, K. (1992). *Enhancing the multicultural campus environment: A cultural brokering approach* (New Directions for Student Services, No. 60). San Francisco: Jossey-Bass.

Stennis-Williams, S., Terrell, M. C., & Haynes, A. W. (1988). The emergent role of multicultural education centers on predominantly white campuses. In M. C. Terrell & D. J. Wright (Eds.), *From survival to success: Promoting minority student retention* (NASPA Monograph Series No. 9, pp. 73–98). Washington, D.C.: NASPA.

Sutton, M. E. (1998). The role of the office of minority affairs in fostering cultural diversity. *College Student Affairs Journal, 18,* 33–39.

Tan, D. L. (1994). Uniqueness of the Asian American experience in higher education. *College Student Journal, 28,* 412–421.

Temkin, L., & Evans, N. J. (1998). Religion on campus: Suggestions for cooperation between student affairs and campus based religious organizations. *NASPA Journal, 36,* 61–69.

Thielen, T., & Limbird, M. (1992). Integrating foreign students into the university community. In D. McIntire & P. Willer (Eds.), *Working with international students and scholars on American campuses* (pp. 119–135). Washington, DC: National Association of Student Personnel Administrators.

Thomas, G. E., & Hill, S. (1987). Black institutions in U.S. higher education: Present roles, contributions, future projections. *Journal of College Student Personnel, 28(6),* 496–503.

Uphoff, J. K. (2001). Religious diversity and education. In J. A. Banks & C. S. McGee Banks (Eds.), *Multicultural education: Issues and perspectives* (pp. 103–121). New York: John Wiley.

U.S. Census Bureau (March 12, 2001). Census 2000 shows America's diversity. Washington, DC: United States Department Commerce News. Retrieved from http://www.cenus.gov/Press-Release.www/2001/cb01cn61.html

Wall, V. A., & Evans, N. J. (1991). Using psychosocial development theories to understand and work with gay and lesbian person. In N. J. Evans & V. A. Wall (Eds.), *Beyond tolerance: Gays, lesbians and bisexuals on campus* (pp. 25–38). Alexandria, VA: American College Personnel Association.

Whitt, E. J., Edison, M. I., Pascarella, E. T., Nora, A., & Terenzini, P. T. (1999). Women's perceptions of a "chilly climate" and cognitive outcomes in college: Additional evidence. *Journal of College Student Development, 40,* 163–177.

Willer, P. (1992). Student affairs professionals as international educators: A challenge for the next century. In D. McIntire & P. Willer (Eds.), *Working with international students and scholars on American campuses* (pp. 161–167). Washington, DC: National Association of Student Personnel Administrators.

Williams, J. B. (1991). Systemwide Title VI regulation of higher education, 1968–88: Implications for increased minority participation. In C. V. Willie, A. M. Garibaldi, & W. L. Reed (Eds.), *The education of African-Americans* (pp. 110–118). New York: Auburn House.

Wright, D. J. (1987). Minority students: Developmental beginnings. In D. J. Wright (Ed.), *Responding to the needs of today's minority students* (New Directions for Student Services, No. 38, pp. 5–21). San Francisco: Jossey-Bass.

Young, L. W. (1986). The role minority student centers play on predominantly white campuses. In C. A. Taylor (Ed.), *The handbook of minority student services* (pp. 15–22). Madison, WI: National Minority Campus Chronicle.

Gratitude is expressed to Dr. Jack A. Taylor, Jr., Assistant Vice President for Student Affairs/Director of Multicultural Affairs and Student Services at Bowling Green State University, for information cited as "personal communication."

Chapter 9

ORIENTATION

WANDA I. OVERLAND AND AUDREY L. RENTZ

The objectives of orientation are the objectives of the whole student personnel program in miniature. . . . The objective is to persuade the freshman to assume responsibility for himself [sic]as soon as possible; therefore the greatest problem is exactly how much help to give the freshman, neither too little nor too much. A second objective is to find out all about the student at the same time that the student is informing himself [sic] about the college (Mueller, 1961, pp. 223–224).

INTRODUCTION

For as long as new students have experienced a period of transition to the educational environment, orientation programs have been a part of American higher education. Whether formally or informally organized, their purpose has been to assist entering students during that initial adjustment period. Young men starting classes at Harvard in the 1640s were assisted by the shared efforts of dons and a graduate student or tutor whose job was "to counsel and befriend the young lads" (Morison, 1936, p. 253).

While orientation's presence within the academic community has remained constant, its popularity has not. Periodically, both faculty and students have criticized orientation programs because the needs they were designed to meet were needs perceived by institutions rather than those identified by students. The national focus on creating integrated student learning experiences has brought a greater sense of purpose to orientation programs. As the population continues to change in growth rate, demographics, socioeconomic status, and service delivery expectations, higher education institutions will need to continue to become more sophisticated and intentional with recruitment, retention, and student success initiatives (Murdock & Hoque, 1999). Today, orientation programs are recognized as effective retention strategies and viewed as pivotal institution programs in the enrollment management process (Hadlock, 2000; Penn, 1999). Research has been able to demonstrate a positive relationship between assessed educational outcomes of participation in orientation with student satisfaction with the institutional environment and student persistence.

Competition for college applicants and the increasing diversity in today's student population has provided orientation professionals with opportunities and challenges never before encountered. Viewed as one of the most significant campus forces capable of influencing student retention, as well as students' educational and personal development, many orientation directors are now members of their college's or university's enrollment management team. This innovative team concept has allowed orientation professionals to draw upon their rich and broad history of activities and program successes to help an institution foster a holistic and developmental view of the collegiate experience. Student affairs specialists in orientation must be advocates for a holistic student experience. Programs should be responsive to new student populations and subgroup needs as well as institutional research and assessment results.

In the 1920s, undergraduate students were viewed as a homogeneous group. On most campuses today, the undergraduate student body is recognized as being diverse. The college students of the late 1990s are more racially and ethnically diverse, have higher grades than previous generations of students, and enter college with academic credits that count toward graduation (U.S. Department of Education, 1998). There are an increasing number of students who are not traditional-aged, 18 to 24 years old, and who attend college part-time. The majority of students have jobs and family responsibilities (Levine & Cureton, 1998). To be effective, orientation professionals no longer can assume that a single, general, broad-based program can meet the needs of all entering students.

To help the reader understand the dynamic nature of orientation, this chapter examines eight major themes of this specialty within student affairs. These themes are (1) history; (2) definition, purpose, and goals; (3) changing student needs; (4) program models; (5) staffing; (6) effective programs; (7) serving students; and (8) trends and recommendations for practice. In each section, whenever possible, the material is presented in chronological sequence to allow the reader to become familiar with the changes in response to shifts in philosophy and societal events.

HISTORY

Two distinct programmatic emphases have been identified within orientation's history. The first emerged in 1888 at Boston University, when an orientation day for new students was offered. These one-day programs had as their focus students' personal adjustment to college rather than an introduction to specific academic disciplines or the world of higher education (Butts, 1971; Drake, 1966). As faculty responsibilities expanded outside the classroom, they also were expected to orient students to the academic environment. This shift of responsibility from parent to faculty served as the impetus for *in loco parentis* (Johnson, 1998).

The second programmatic emphasis was developed at Reed College in 1911, with the introduction of a freshman course for credit entitled *The College Life Course* (Brubacher & Rudy, 1958). Within several months, both the University of Washington and the University of Michigan sponsored weekly meetings for entering students and rewarded attendance with academic credit (Butts, 1971). These early courses, usually scheduled in a series of 25 sessions, were designed to teach students how to succeed academically, including how to use the library, study tips and career counseling, and campus involvement (Fitts & Swift, 1928). National acceptance of these structured for-credit courses was quickly achieved. Interest in this program format grew dramatically, from six institutions in 1915-1916 to 82 sponsoring institutions only a decade later (Brubacher & Rudy, 1958).

In *Advice to Freshmen by Freshmen,* University of Michigan President M. L. Burton described expectations for this time of transition:

> Remember that the change from high school to college is tremendous. You are no longer a high school boy or girl. You are a college man or woman. The University is a place of freedom. You are thrown upon your own resources. You are independent. But do not forget, I beg of you, that independence and freedom do not mean anarchy and license. Obedience to law is liberty (Crocker, 1921, p. 1).

The dramatic rise in college enrollments after World War I changed who attended college and shifted responsibility for orientation from faculty to staff. Student personnel professionals accepted the orientation function as a specialized responsibility within their administrative domain shortly after World War I. By 1930, nearly one-third of all higher education institutions offered credit courses (Mueller, 1961). During the 1930s, under the direction of E. G. Williamson, the University of Minnesota sponsored an orientation program for entering students that addressed the following areas of perceived student concern: personal living, home life, vocational orientation, and sociocivic orientation (Bennett, 1938). By the beginning of the 1940s, these credit courses were required for 90 percent of all new students (Mueller, 1961). Studies completed by the late 1940s revealed that 43 percent of higher education institutions had implemented orientation courses. While the majority of the courses focused on transitional and adjustment issues, some courses focused on the academic experience (Bookman, 1948; Strang, 1951). The courses typically were lecture style and often included a convocation program. The convocation program served as the formal induction into the academic community.

Although these two models played a crucial role in the development of contemporary orientation programs, they were not without their critics. Some argued about their proper length. For example, since the mid-1920s, the most effective length of an orientation program has been the subject of intense debate: ". . . some personnel workers have recommended that a really effective program will continue through the subsequent years to help students avoid difficulties—scholastic, health, social, economic, vocational and emotional" (Doermann, 1926, p. 162). Thirty years later, Strang (1951) and subsequently Mueller (1961) expressed their belief that an orientation program should not be a one- or two-day event, but rather should be a continuous and dynamic process beginning in high school and ending after college graduation. According to this belief, orientation is viewed as a developmental process assisting entering students with specific tasks associated with their transition and the subsequent goals of self-direction and interdependence.

As the number of orientation professionals on campuses increased, they sensed a need to come together to share ideas and discuss common problems. Twenty-four orientation directors met in Columbus, Ohio, in 1948 and convened the first conference of the professional association now known as the National Orientation Directors Association (NODA). However, official charter approval was not achieved until 1974 (Dannells, 1986). The association goals are to provide services for orientation professionals and institutions and to encourage dialogue and discussions on orientation related topics. As the association grew, regional networking structures were created to support the exchange of ideas through newsletters, conferences, and drive-in workshops.

Formal recognition and widespread support for orientation was achieved in 1943, when the Council of Guidance and Personnel Associations recommended that orientation programs be sponsored at the high school level as well as by higher education institutions. The Council recommended three major program goals: (1) increasing the understanding of occupational and social problems; (2) personal adjustment; and (3) increasing the awareness of the importance of physical fitness, including social hygiene (Council of Guidance and Personnel Associations, 1943). Responses from all 123 institutional members of the North Central Association of Colleges and Secondary Schools verified commitments to offer orientation programs that would include general lectures, testing, social activities, campus tours, religious activities, counseling, details of registration, establishment of faculty–student relationships, and "enabling courses" (voice, math, and reading improvement) (Bookman, 1948; Kamm & Wrenn, 1947). The relevance of these topics has not changed, and many continue to be part of an orientation program.

In the 1960s, in the midst of student activism and a new wave of accountability in higher education, orientation programs once again became the subject of scrutiny and criticism. Freshman Week was labeled "disorientation week" (Riesman, 1961). Orientation courses would no longer be included in the institution's curriculum unless documentation could be provided that these programs served a utilitarian and meaningful purpose on campus (Caple, 1964). Few research studies had been undertaken that could identify and assess the specific educational outcomes associated with participation in orientation activities. Involvement, let alone its relationship to student satisfaction and retention, had not yet appeared in the professional literature. Additionally, the lack of a theoretical foundation underpinning orientation programs led to the criticism that these activities were "made of hopes, good will, educated guesses and what we fondly believe to be the needs of new students" (Grier, 1966, p. 37). Nevertheless, orientation programs became more prevalent and eventually became recognized as effective retention initiatives (Mann, 1998).

From 1966 to 1976, modifications in programs included the creation of two- or three-day, overnight programs not only for new students, but also for their parents and family members. Some small institutions developed mini-courses taught by freshman faculty advisors during the 5- to 10-day period before classes to provide a brief preview of academic life. Other campuses used small group sessions to teach T-group and other human relations skills, and Friendship Days emerged with a focus on social needs (Cohen & Jody, 1978; Foxley, 1969; Hall, 1982; Klosterman & Merseal, 1978). During the 1960s, upper-class students were selected to participate in the orientation program as student orientation leaders. They served in a variety of capacities, including helping new students become familiar with the institution, facilitating the transition into the academic environment, and serving as peer mentors.

A projected decline in the number of college applicants provided additional value and significance to the efforts of orientation professionals in the 1960s and 1970s. Added to this was the shift in the 1970s from a homogeneous student population to a diverse population that necessitated changes in orientation programs (Barefoot & Gardner, 1993). Student satisfaction and retention became issues of major importance to many administrators in higher education. Consequently, orientation programs came to be viewed as contributing significantly to the economic stability of many colleges and universities. Support for the relationship between participation in orientation programs, student satisfaction, and persistence appeared with greater and greater frequency in the research literature (Beal & Noel, 1980; Feldman & Newcomb, 1969; Hossler, 1999; Pascarella & Terenzini, 1991; Ramist, 1981).

The number of orientation programs grew significantly during the 1980s. The greatest increase was seen in first-semester courses. Two-thirds of four-year institutions provided a freshman course by the beginning of 1990 (Pascarella & Terenzini, 1991). The current trend on campuses is to provide an orientation program, as well as a semester or academic year freshman course. It is common practice today for institutions to provide a number of specialized programs for targeted populations as well as welcome programs at the beginning for an institution. The need for congruence between student and institutional "fit" and the necessity of balancing competing forces of support and challenge were recognized. Previously hypothesized relationships were now no longer viewed as tentative, but confirmed.

Studies conducted on first year courses documented that students were better prepared academically and socially than students who were not enrolled in first-year courses or involved in another first-year program initiative (Rice, 1992). Additionally, studies documented that effective orientation programs had a significant influence on students' ability to socially and academically integrate into the institution. "The single most important move an institution can make to increase student persistence to graduation is to ensure that students receive the guidance they need at the beginning of the journey" (Forrest, 1982, p. 385). Within the past two decades, orientation programs have emerged as important components of a formalized enrollment management plan (Gardner & Hansen, 1993). Today, orientation professionals serve as essential members of institutional enrollment management teams.

Enrollment management is a systematic approach and institutional concept that is designed to "exert more influence over student enrollments. . . . It is organized by strategic planning and supported by institutional research. . . . It concerns student college choice, transition to college, student attrition and retention, and student outcomes" (Hossler, Bean, & Associates, 1990, p. 5). The four goals of enrollment management are (1) to define and market the institution's mission, values, characteristics; (2) to utilize the entire campus community in developing plans, initiatives, and activities; (3) to strategically plan and implement financial aid programs that enroll and retain students; and (4) to create structures and financial resources to support a comprehensive enrollment management plan (Dixon, 1995).

The enrollment management model used by higher education institutions for the past three decades began to change in the early 1990s as a result of growing government intervention, public expectations and scrutiny, and the complexities of an increasingly diverse student population. Today, enrollment management plans place a significant focus on student learning and campus wide collaboration. Both orientation programs and first year courses are recognized as opportunities for such collaboration, particularly between faculty and academic affairs units (Hirsch & Burack, 2001).

The focus on new students is documented by the emergence of numerous first-year initiatives within higher education. While the First Year Experience movement began in the 1970s at the University of South Carolina, programs have become more visible and dominant in the 1990s. Convocation and living-learning communities are examples of initiatives that are being implemented to foster student learning and to integrate the out-of-class and in-class collegiate experience. The focus can be attributed to shifts in enrollment patterns, public accountability, retention initiatives, and a philosophical shift from teaching to the creation of holistic learning environments (Cutright, 2002).

Beginning in the 1990s, growing attention and resources were placed on incorporating technological advancements and opportunities into orientation programs. These advancements included computerized databases, videoconferencing, and data management systems (Bryant & Crockett, 1993). For many students, the online, "virtual" campus is a reality. As this movement grows, it will require resources and creativity in envisioning orientation programs in a "virtual" campus or online.

A number of publications and resources have been developed or reintroduced during the last decade (Ritchie, 2001). *The Journal of College Orientation and Transition* was reestablished during the late 1990s and is published twice a year. A monograph, *Designing Successful Transitions: A Guide for Orienting Students to College*, was published jointly with The Freshman Year Experience. A listserv was created in 1996 to provide association members with an electronic vehicle to share ideas and information. In early 2000, the Parent Services Network was created to provide information on parent and family initiatives as well as a publication entitled *Helping Your First-Year College Student Succeed—A Guide for Parents.*

Mention the term *orientation* to most individuals and, depending on their age, one or more images appear in their mind's eye. Raccoon coats, yellow pompoms, football banners, and the swallowing of goldfish were prevalent in the 1920s and 1930s; the freshman "beanie" was a symbol for a rite of passage during the 1950s; and college blazers, T-shirts, and buttons were mandatory in the 1960s. All of these helped entering students maintain a visible profile on campus. Such adornments differ dramatically from the distinguishing lengths of the black academic robes worn by faculty and students at Harvard to denote the levels of status within the academic community; ankle-length for faculty, knee-length for upperclassmen, and mid-thigh for freshmen. Throughout the years, specific wardrobe items, customs, and rituals helped identify entering students to others on campus and were required elements of a process of both adjustment and socialization. While these traditions are part of the history of higher education, new traditions have been built into first year programs that are symbolic or affirm the mission and values of the institution.

DEFINITION, PURPOSE, AND GOALS

In its broadest sense, orientation has been described as "any effort on the part of the institution to help entering students make the transitions from their previous environment to the college environment and to enhance success in college" (Upcraft & Farnsworth, 1984, p. 27). Creating opportunities for new students to interact formally and informally with faculty, staff, and

current students is viewed as one of the most important contributions of orientation programs (Anderson, 1985). Contemporary student affairs professionals, with practice guided by the theoretical approaches of Chickering &
Reisser (1993) and others, view the goal of human development as a series
of sequential tasks that students accomplish by being involved in intentionally (and unintentionally) planned and structured activities. While orientation's purpose has remained constant, support for it and related activities,
discussions of goal statements, and the degree of institutional commitment
afforded to it have varied greatly during the past century. At times it has
been seen as an essential and required experience, while during other periods its activities were viewed as frivolous and extraneous.

Orientation's programmatic emphases change in response to changes
both in higher education's mission and in student affairs professionals' perceptions of undergraduate students. Consider the following representative
goal statements gathered from a review of 30 years of literature:

1. To gain perspective, a sense of purpose and balance between the
   demands and opportunities of college life (Strang, 1951);
2. To increase the student's receptivity to the total higher education
   experience (McCann, 1967);
3. To complete enrollment procedures in a humane manner (Butts,
   1971);
4. To develop cognitive, behavioral, and communication skills to facilitate assimilation into the campus environment;
5. To foster development of a peer group, creating an atmosphere of
   comfortableness and reduced anxiety (Krall, 1981);
6. To gather information that provides the institution with a better
   understanding of its student population (Smith & Brackin, 1993);
7. To provide opportunities for informal interaction and discussions
   with faculty (Mullendore, 1998a); and
8. To acclimate students to the facilities, services, and members of the
   institution's community (Hadlock, 2000).

Responding to a perceived exaggerated emphasis on students' social and
personal needs in orientation programs of the 1950s, subsequent writers
argued persuasively for a return to a focus on academic disciplines and the
mission of higher education (Drake, 1966). Orientation should be defined
as "an induction into or at least consistent with, college intellectual life
rather than" an attempt to "meet freshmen and institutional needs" (Drake,
1966). In 1960, the American Council of Education provided an authoritative definition of orientation, viewing it as the process of integrating students into the community of learning (Brown, 1972). During the past
decade, a greater emphasis has been placed on formalizing a stronger academic focus in orientation programs. However, Levitz and Noel (1989)
believed that orientation programs must help students make the transition

to college both socially and intellectually. The goals of orientation programs have been expanded to include the integration of student learning and critical thinking of values across the curriculum both in and outside the classroom. This perspective recognizes the opportunity to integrate all of the aspirations that the institution holds for its students. Programs should take a holistic perspective of student learning: "orientation should give newcomers the impression that they are about to start an important, qualitatively different chapter in their lives" (Kuh, 1996, p. 142).

Four goals for orientation program planners, echoing past practice, were proposed in an attempt to respond to different institutional missions and the growing variety of programs offered. All programs should (1) aid students in their academic adjustment; (2) provide assistance with personal adjustment; (3) help entering students' families understand the collegiate experience; and (4) assist the institution in gathering data about its entering students (Perigo & Upcraft, 1989; Upcraft & Farnsworth, 1984).

As program goals multiplied, Sagaria (1979) suggested a framework for classifying programs: *interdisciplinary,* offered through liberal arts or general education departments and focusing on student as learner; *developmental,* affiliated with counseling services or general education areas and emphasizing the student as a person as well as his or her self-perceptions and relationships with others; and *utilitarian,* aligned with student affairs divisions emphasizing the mastery of a defined knowledge base and resources as basic skills.

Attempts were made to develop a generic mission or purpose statement as well as a set of common goals that might apply to all programs regardless of the institution. The most recent effort is documented in the 2001 edition of *The Book of Professional Standards for Higher Education* produced by the Council for the Advancement of Standards in Higher Education (CAS). In this document, the council defined orientation as

> . . . an ongoing process that begins when a student decides to attend a particular institution. The process should aid students in understanding the nature and purpose of the institution, their membership in the academic community, and their relationship to the intellectual, cultural, and social climate of the institution (CAS, 2001, p. 222).

The CAS Standards and Guidelines suggested that this can be accomplished through credit and noncredit courses as well as through specialized programs. "Student orientation programs must be (a) intentional; (b) coherent; (c) based on theories and knowledge of learning and human development; (d) reflective of developmental and demographic profiles of the student population; and (e) responsive to special needs of individuals" (2001, p. 222).

In addition, CAS recommended a list of 11 goals to help orientation professionals design programs and activities. The list implies a broad institutional role for orientation. The student orientation program must:

1. Be based on stated goals and objectives;
2. Be coordinated with the relevant programs and activities of other institutional units;
3. Be available to all new students to the institution;
4. Assist new students in understanding the purposes of higher education and the mission of the institution;
5. Assist new students in understanding their responsibilities within the education setting;
6. Provide new students with information about academic policies, procedures, requirements, and programs sufficient to make well-reasoned and well-informed choices;
7. Inform new students about the availability of services and programs;
8. Assist new students in becoming familiar with the campus and local environment;
9. Provide intentional opportunities for new students to interact with faculty, staff, and continuing students;
10. Provide new students with information and opportunities for self-assessment;
11. Provide relevant orientation information and activities to new students and their primary support groups (e.g., parents, guardians, spouses, children) (CAS, 2001, pp. 222–223).

The freshman orientation transition is complex:

Anthropologists see the campus as a strange new culture to which students must become acculturated. While freshmen orient to the social environment of a campus, they must channel their enthusiasm to the challenges of academic life as they explore and cope with the new culture. Sociologists view the campus as an interlocking configuration of social systems where success in mastering one subsystem may depend on careful adaptation to another. They believe that in order for freshmen to succeed academically, they must become integrated into the campus environment. Social psychologists see the campus as an arena of human interaction and encounter that affects the self-esteem and self-actualizing qualities of each developing human. In fact, while freshmen acclimate to subsystems within the total system, they form and modify their attitudes, self-concept, and their self-awareness within their new situation. Finally, the educator is concerned with the manner and method of communication by which these cultural and social messages are transmitted and retained. By establishing a system of information motivators and encouraging participation in various activities, orientation can arouse loyalties, inspire self-exploration, and bind a diverse group of students to a campus (Twale, 1989, p. 161).

CHANGING STUDENT NEEDS

Program emphases change not only in relation to our understanding of the students to be served, but also in response to societal and world events.

Consider the following profile of the typical student of past decades compared with that of the typical student of today. From 1920 until the 1950s, entering students' needs were defined in terms describing the characteristics of the typical 18-year-old, middle-class, Caucasian undergraduate student. For these first-generation college students, the move to the collegiate environment was usually their first experience in living away from their family, friends, and hometown. Their needs were described most often in terms of perceived levels of their development.

The student personnel literature of the time reflected four concerns believed to be common to all new students: (1) breaking away from the family; (2) choosing a vocation; (3) establishing satisfactory relationships with members of the opposite sex; and (4) integrating the personality. Mueller (1961) later recast these concerns into three developmental tasks using a somewhat more psychosocial perspective: (1) ego integration (the process of achieving physical control, emotional development, and integration values); (2) identification of different roles for the self (sex roles, dating, and new identities); and (3) practice in future roles (social responsibilities, occupational roles, civic competence, and family life). Each of these bears a striking resemblance to the developmental tasks that would be found in the professional literature and attributed to Chickering and others more than 10 years later.

Student affairs professionals conducted formal assessments of entering students during the 1950s as they responded to the need to provide data not only evaluating but also supporting the continued existence of orientation programs. Entering students reported fears they had about their entrance into a new educational community, among them their inability to do college work, to select the right major, to make friends, and to find a desirable roommate. The friendliness or anticipated lack of friendliness of college and university faculty was also frequently mentioned as an area of concern (Drake, 1966). Issues more directly related to the academic arena soon were replaced by concerns about social and personal adjustment among entering students, as evidenced by Purdue's students' rankings of their orientation needs: (1) inform them of academic responsibilities, (2) assist them with academic program planning, and (3) familiarize them with the campus (Tautfest, 1961). During the next 10 years, the role of personal and social orientation to the academic community was viewed as less important to students than issues tied to their future academic achievement (Keil, 1966).

Many of the views expressed by student activists during the 1960s reflected criticisms directed toward social institutions such as the federal government and higher education. Students labeled these institutions "the Establishment" and believed that these bureaucratic organizations needed to be reorganized around a more humanistic philosophy. Among the changes demanded by student activists was a greater value to be assigned to the individual within complex bureaucracies. Related to this was their demand that the individual be allowed to assume a greater role within organizations promoting or creating change. Characteristic of their lack of acceptance of institutionalized authority, student activists argued that anyone over 30 years of age was not to be trusted. Their opposition to American involvement in the Vietnam War was expressed by the slogan, "Make love, not war!" They yelled "Do not fold, staple, or mutilate" in response to the perceived impersonal environment of higher education created by the swelling number of students and the use of technology to assist in class registration. These attitudes significantly changed the roles performed by student affairs professionals and altered the nature of their interactions with students. The traditional student personnel role of surrogate parent was recast as that of advisor, advocate, facilitator, counselor, and/or educator. Students were now viewed as responsible adults capable of assuming responsibility for their own development. No longer were they perceived as passive adolescents. The value previously linked to *in loco parentis* disappeared.

Increasingly, students questioned the relevance of their college courses and the extent to which their academic preparation would help them solve the problems they perceived outside the campus walls in American society. As a result, general education or core curriculum requirements were changed to permit students to pursue a wider range of interdisciplinary and individually designed topic-oriented seminars and degree programs.

Research on student satisfaction emerged during the 1960s and 1970s, a problematic period in American higher education. Several studies focused on measuring student satisfaction in purely academic terms by assessing when majors were chosen or by looking at students' years in school (Schmidt & Sedlacek, 1972; Sturtz, 1971). During this same period, students' responses to orientation need assessments reflected yet another change: Interest in vocational preparation now ranked equally with concern for academic issues.

As enrollments in the late 1970s began to decline at some colleges and universities, the retention of students became even more critical. A new significance was attached to the freshman year, particularly the initial months during which new students' attitudes, values, and adjustment to higher education were influenced the most (Butts, 1971; Chickering & Havinghurst, 1981; Feldman & Newcomb, 1969; Lowe, 1980). Administrators became aware of the link between the freshman year, student satisfaction, and student retention.

Early retention research efforts identified factors contributing to student attrition. One such conclusion was that attrition was most severe during or at the end of the freshman year (Sagaria, 1979). At four-year institutions, factors related to attrition were gleaned from student questionnaires: (1) course work requiring study habits many students did not possess; (2) large classes; (3) an impersonal, uncomfortable campus environment; and (4) academic and social regulations (Beal & Noel, 1980; Hall, 1982). This information justified a new role for orientation as an aid to student persistence. Retention became so strongly linked with orientation programs that it was almost viewed as the primary reason for their existence. However, Tinto (1985), a respected author of retention literature, suggested that the most important goal of new student orientation experiences should be education and not simply retention.

High school students became the subject of considerable research in attempts to identify personal characteristics thought to be associated with a successful transition to higher education. Entering students who later completed their transition more effectively were found to share a set of characteristics: (1) a competent self-image, (2) motivation to pursue activities to simulate growth and development, and (3) willingness to take risks (Knott & Daher, 1978). As a result, programs were designed to develop or enhance these attitudes and behaviors among new students.

Studies of retention and attrition identified several issues linked with high rates of student withdrawal: (1) academic boredom, (2) lack of academic preparedness, (3) uncertainty regarding academic major or career choice, (4) transition and adjustment difficulties, (5) dissonance or incompatibility, and (6) irrelevancy of education (Dannells, 1986). While high school students are better prepared for college than previous generations, they remain academically disengaged, unprepared, in need of remediation courses, and emotionally stressed and overwhelmed with life (Higher Education Research Institute, 1999). Orientation programs will need to find a way to address these findings.

Higher education institutions nowadays attract not only traditional-aged students, but also diverse student populations, including a growing number of women students, older students, part-time students, and racially or ethnically diverse students (Edmondson, 1997; U.S. Department of Education, 1998). Societal trends require higher education institutions to examine their orientation programs and services for students who come from complicated family units, disparate socioeconomic income and educational levels, and at risk populations (Edmondson, 1997).

The changing demographic profile of students provides a challenge for orientation professionals. How will the induction process be modified for today's students? Students come to college with diverse needs:

1. A consumer orientation and expectations that their investment in higher education will produce a return;
2. Growing racial and ethnic diversity, including multiracial and multi-ethnic backgrounds;
3. Intentional selectivity in their choice of higher education institutions;
4. Interest in healthy lifestyles;
5. Sophisticated knowledge of technology in all aspects of their lives;
6. Better academic preparation and likelihood of pursuing an advanced degree;

7. Great concern about salary when selecting a career;
8. Increased financial debt; and
9. The need for part-time jobs to defray rising tuition and fees (Alch, 2000; Brownstein, 2000; Fenske, Rund, and Contento, 2000).

PROGRAM MODELS

Three prototypes or models of programs serve as the foundation from which many of today's orientation programs evolved: the preenrollment or orientation model, offered during the summer months; the freshman day or week model, scheduled during the first semester of academic classes; and the credit course model, scheduled during the first semester or the entire year (Bergman, 1978; Herron, 1974; McCann, 1967; Strang, 1951; Upcraft, Gardner, & Associates, 1989).

In addition, two philosophical viewpoints emerged during the 1960s that influenced the content of orientation programs. The first viewpoint was known as "microcosmic" and stressed testing, campus tours, informational meetings, and course registration activities. The second viewpoint, called "macrocosmic," emphasized issues associated with the intellectual challenges of academic life, cognitive development, and the mission of higher education (Fitzgerald & Evans, 1963). Elements of these two viewpoints continue to dictate most orientation programs offered today.

Three other less common program models can be found in the literature reflecting additional changes in program emphases: (1) the emerging leaders model, (2) the institutional integration model, and (3) the holistic model (Murrary & Apilado, 1989; Striffolino & Saunders, 1989; Upcraft, Gardner, & Associates, 1989, Wolfe, 1993). Because they are less customary, these models are not addressed in this chapter.

The orientation structure adopted by colleges and universities should complement the mission and values of the institution, reflect the needs of the entering student body, and comprise aspects of the collegiate environment that enhance student success (Smith & Brackin, 1993). Today, many campuses incorporate a variety of models to address the diverse needs of the community. It is not uncommon for a campus to have preenrollment programs, extended orientation programs, freshman or orientation courses, and specialized programs for targeted populations, including summer bridge programs.

THE PREENROLLMENT OR ORIENTATION MODEL

The Pre-College Clinic, established in 1949 at Michigan State University, was a summer program, two to four days in length, that included testing, counseling, information dissemination, and social events (Goodrich &

Pierson, 1959). Its value as a public relations tool quickly became apparent as an aid to personalizing large university environments and as a means of improving students' initial adjustment and grades.

Preadmissions or preenrollment programs typically are coordinated by the admissions office and involve particular aspects of the campus community. As part of the strategic enrollment plan, these programs are designed to market the institution and attract students to campus. Programs can vary from large campus visitation events to small group sessions that include visits with faculty, campus tours, and presentations (Upcraft, Gardner, & Associates, 1989).

Preenrollment or orientation programs may also be designed for students who have applied and been admitted. Common components of such programs serve (1) to introduce students and family members to services on campus; (2) to assist students with their academic and social adjustment and integration; (3) to provide opportunities for formal and informal conversations and discussions with faculty, staff, and current students; and (4) to advise students in choosing a major and their academic courses for the first semester or quarter system (Rode, 2000).

The type of program implemented is dependent on the type of institution and its mission. For example, some large institutions with significant numbers of students from out-of-state will hold orientation sessions in central locations around the country. Colleges and universities with commuter or older student populations create programs, such as evening programs, that accommodate their needs. Regardless of the nature of the program, orientation programs are campus-wide recruitment and retention initiatives.

THE FRESHMAN DAY OR WEEK MODEL

The University of Maine is credited with developing the first Freshman Week in 1923. Large meetings were the preferred format, and the agendas emphasized sharing information, testing, counseling, registration, campus tours, recreational activities, and social events (Drake, 1966). As was true of other elements in the history of orientation, the popularity attached to this program model varied widely. By 1938, 83 percent of all higher education institutions offered programs based on this model. Support declined during the 1940s, when this initial model was replaced by the structured, for academic credit, orientation course. Twenty years later, however, in the mid-1960s, the Freshman Week model regained its earlier stature.

Freshman or welcome week programs are designed to build community, to create a sense of belonging, and to acquaint students with the collegiate environment (Upcraft, Gardner, & Associates, 1989). Activities often include convocation programs, picnics, residence hall tours, and college events. Programming at the beginning of the academic year provides opportunities to acquaint students with the expectations of the academic community and to meet faculty, staff, and returning students. The needs of specialized populations, such as international students, graduate students, scholarship athletes, commuter students, returning adults, students of color, transfer students, honor students, and students with disabilities, may also be met with activities at the beginning of the school year. Some programs extend throughout the year or are separate components of the overall program (Gonzales, Hill-Traynham, & Jacobs, 2000).

THE FRESHMAN COURSE MODEL

The traditional Freshman Course model was developed to introduce new students to available fields of study and to assist them in coping with problems associated with their freshman status (Drake, 1966). These courses sprung from the counseling movement in higher education and were motivated by the perceived need to help entering students during their initial adjustment to a new institutional setting. Prior to 1960, slightly more than half of all institutions sponsored programs of this type, with an emphasis on freshman adjustment issues. However, by the mid-1960s, in the midst of student activism, this model was viewed as obsolete (Drake, 1966). Faculty voiced strong opposition to its perceived emphasis on "fun and games," social events, and personal adjustment. They argued strongly and persuasively for a return to an orientation program that focused on academic concerns and the mission of general education (Dannells & Kuh, 1977). Orientation directors responded by designing an academic course to meet students' academic and personal or social needs (O'Banion, 1969).

During the 1960s and the 1970s, three forces merged, causing administrators to seek new programs that would teach entering students about the institution's system and how to deal with it effectively. First, campuses were faced with many first-generation students who knew little about "the skills of studenthood" (Cohen & Jody, 1978, p. 2). Second, because of revisions in curricula and changes in regulations on campus, the choices for freshmen became more complex. Finally, peer culture, with its great potential for assistance to freshmen, "seemed to have lost much of its potency in helping students to adapt" (Cohen & Jody, 1978, p. 2). It was less likely that an administrator would observe among freshmen, as Kingman Brewster had done at Yale in the 1960s, a single year's "progress from arrogance to self-doubt, to self-pity, to rediscovery, and finally to mature ambition" (Brewster, 1968, p. viii). Out of this context, John Gardner established the influential *Freshman Seminar* program at the University of South Carolina.

The Freshman Seminar meshes two major elements in a small class format cotaught by a faculty member and an upper-class student: (1) shared information to help students understand their initial transition period, and (2) establishment of an environment that is socially supportive (Gordon & Grites, 1984). The Freshman Seminar model is probably the most popular model in use on large and small campuses today. The nature and content of the courses vary, depending on the institution. However, the overarching purpose of the seminar or course is to help students make necessary academic and social adjustments as well as to assist them in developing their critical thinking skills (Upcraft, Gardner, & Associates, 1989). The courses are designed to provide a broad view of the institution as well as focus on personal and academic skill development. More recent developments include theme or academic discipline seminars or courses that focus on similar topics, but from a specific discipline or interdisciplinary perspective.

STAFFING

Staffing patterns also reflect changing times and perspectives. Traditionally, orientation activities have been the sole responsibility of student affairs professionals. During the years when the value ascribed to academic concerns was high, faculty members shared in planning and staffing programs. Others were added to the implementation team when, in the mid-1960s, the student affairs community's perception of students changed and undergraduates assumed new roles as coparticipants and collaborators in planning and as peer facilitators. This type of student involvement was studied in 1989, and student paraprofessionals reported significantly higher gain scores on the developmental tasks of interdependence and tolerance than their control group peers (Holland & Huba, 1989). In addition to the economic benefits of student paraprofessionals, these student leaders gained significantly from the experience themselves (Holland & Huba, 1989).

Generally, programs are the responsibility of a director of orientation, of first year experience, or of new students. Program implementation is made possible by a largely volunteer staff comprised of university constituents, including students. Most often, the director or the person responsible for orientation reports to the Senior Student Affairs Officer (SSAO) or to an individual who reports to the SSAO. The director of orientation may have other duties as well. To facilitate the collaborative nature of orientation, university-wide orientation committees provide assistance in shaping the program goals, learning outcomes, and program components.

As with several other specialties within student affairs (i.e., residence halls and student activities), many professionals gained their initial experience as undergraduate student participants or leaders. Many graduate students hold assistantships in departments that house orientation or first year programs that are comparable to entry-level positions while pursuing graduate work. Full-time directors generally possess a master's degree. Some positions, particularly on smaller campuses, place responsibilities for orientation programs under a full-time professional staff member who may also supervise student activities or other areas within student affairs.

Student affairs professionals specializing in orientation need to have a skill base that allows them to plan and implement programs that are educationally purposeful. Obviously, communication skills, programming abilities, and leadership or administrative skills are needed in addition to sensitivity to the complex issues associated with students' growth and development. The professional who directs orientation must have the ability to work with a variety of constituents; have credibility and respect across the institution; juggle multiple tasks, projects, and decisions; and remain calm and enthusiastic (Mullendore and Abraham, 1993). Given the changing dynamics of the campus, the professional staff must have a strong understanding of the diversity of today's students.

EFFECTIVE PROGRAMS

Research from the 1980s pinpointed five characteristics of successful orientation programs: (1) concern for the student as an individual, (2) opportunities for students to establish relationships with faculty, (3) programmatic emphasis on the academic concerns, (4) small group meetings to ease the adjustment of new students, and (5) recognition of the stressful transition experienced by entering students (Engstrom & Tinto, 2000; Kramer & Washburn, 1983).

In a similar review, Upcraft and Farnsworth (1984) found seven trait characteristics of successful orientation programs. Such a program must "(1) be a sustained and coordinated effort; (2) have the support and involvement of the entire campus community; (3) be based on sound concepts of student development and on what is known about the influence of the collegiate environment . . . and "on all available information concerning entering students" (p. 30). Other traits identified were that "(4) the program be subject to evaluation; (5) use a wide variety of interventions including media approaches, group programming, academic courses, and individual tutoring, advising and counseling; (6) be appropriately timed; and (7) be coordinated by a central office of personnel" (p. 30).

A landmark student affairs publication, *Student Learning Imperative* (SLI), refocused discussions among student affairs professionals on the importance of student learning in all functional areas (ACPA, 1996). The SLI identified the following four characteristics of learning-centered divisions and programs: (1) the focus is on the achievement of identified learning outcomes that complement the mission of the institution; (2) collaboration across campus and functions is central to the achievement of student success and learning; (3) resources are allocated based on the desired learning outcomes; and (4) effectiveness of programs is measured by what students have learned. This philosophical shift necessitates intentional focus on learning outcomes in the design of orientation programs.

The *Principles of Good Practice for Student Affairs* (ACPA, 1997; Blimling, Whitt, and Associates, 1999) were developed to assist in developing programs and services that engage students in active learning. The principles elaborate on the centrality of student learning:

1. Engage students in active learning;
2. Build coherent values and ethical standards;
3. Set and communicate high expectations for student learning;
4. Use systematic inquiry to improve student and institutional performance;
5. Use resources effectively to help achieve the institutional mission and goals;
6. Forge educational partnerships that advance student learning; and
7. Build supportive and inclusive communities.

Each of these principles should be considered in the design, implementation, and evaluation of orientation programs.

To achieve these principles, the utilization of institutional research data and orientation assessment results can be beneficial in obtaining knowledge about the institution and emerging student trends and concerns. Data that should be examined include basic demographic trends as well as specific information such as full- or part-time employment, whether they are full- or part-time students, and characteristics that distinguish them from other students. Additional data on retention, class registration, persistence and attrition, as well as housing information, can be helpful in making decisions about orientation program components. Historically, orientation programs were fine-tuned or modified to reflect results from previous year evaluations. Zis (2002) suggested that changing student demographics and trends in higher education call for a different approach. Staff will need to be more aggressive in evaluating and assessing program effectiveness and learning outcomes as well as involving campus constituents in decision-making processes.

Program evaluation is key. All aspects of orientation should be regularly evaluated, including the timing of the program, the duration of the program, program components, philosophy under girding the program, staff involvement, balance of challenge and support for parents and for students, developmental focus, balance of academic and social activities, information disseminated, and so on. The program design should be carefully scrutinized, and questions should be raised about issues such as "retention, the technical aspects of course registration and campus life, and social integration. First and foremost, orientation programs . . . will benefit greatly from basic planning, and thinking about what the intended outcomes of their experience should be" (Zis, 2002, p. 67).

The growing participation of parents and family members in orientation programs, family programs, and the admissions process necessitates attention to significant others in students' lives. Comprehensive programs for parents and family members are important for a number of reasons. First, students who feel supported by their families and the institution are more likely to be successful and satisfied with their academic experience (Hatch, 2000; Cabrera, Nora, Terenzini, Pascarella, & Hagedorn, 1999; Sandeen, 2000). Second, parents and family members are important partners in the education of their students. "Long before and long after attachments are made to new classmates, friends, roommates, faculty and staff, students rely on family/extended family members for feedback, reassurance, and guidance" (Austin, 1993, p. 97). Third, comprehensive orientation programs acknowledge the role that parents and family members play and convey the message that they are important and valued partners in the educational process.

Comprehensive parent and family orientation programs should focus on both the academic experience and the emotional transitions that will occur for both students and family members (Jacobs & With, 2002; Mullendore, 1998b). Parent and family members who are familiar with institutional services and programs are better equipped to assist when students encounter personal and academic challenges. Because parents can influence student success and persistence, their understanding of the institution and college transitions is critical.

Orientation programs must incorporate new technologies to remain effective and relevant given the comfort, familiarity, and expectations of today's students. Campus web sites; online registration for admission, housing, orientation, and classes; and web portals are commonly utilized to provide parents and students with information and services. The use of technology should be maximized to facilitate effective programs that meet the needs of students and to communicate to students the importance of technology (Zis, 2002). Some institutions have created virtual orientations and advising experiences online (Turner, 2000). As with all aspects of orientation, the technological aspects incorporated into the process should be carefully evaluated to ensure that all students and their parents have access. Demonstrating the institution's technological capabilities is important, but it is also critical that the audience not be overwhelmed by the technology. Consideration must be given to the balance between high-tech and high-touch.

The consumer orientation of prospective students requires that orientation programs be recognized institutionally as recruitment initiatives. Prospective students, particularly high school graduates, apply to multiple institutions and often attend more than one orientation program. Consumer-oriented students and their families have carefully researched institutions through print materials and the Internet. As colleges and universities compete for students, effective outreach materials and publications, both online and in print, become very important (Hossler, 1999; Upcraft & Goldsmith, 2000). High school graduates who are technologically savvy have high expectations regarding the quality of technological resources and materials available. Following the work of the admissions office, the orientation program probably is the next contact to reach students and parents, and technology can serve as a tool to enhance and communicate the mission and learning outcomes of the orientation program and the institution.

SERVING STUDENTS

As the diversity among entering students increases, orientation professionals must be able to design programs that meet specific needs of various student populations (Harbin, 1997; Johnson & Miller, 2000). This requires professional staff to be familiar with the needs of student subgroups and enrollment patterns (Eimers & Mullen, 1997). A variety of methods can be used to deliver orientation programs for particular student populations—create separate programs within a comprehensive program, extend programs, and target sessions or programs for special populations (Jacobs, 1993). The type of program offered should be informed by desired learning outcomes, an analysis of institutional research, assessment results, and institutional resources.

"Orientation professionals often find themselves faced with choices in which the best solution or answer is unclear. It is for these occasions that assessment and evaluation are necessary" (Wiese, 2000, p. 52). "Assessment is any effort to gather, analyze, and interpret evidence which describes institutional, departmental, divisional, or agency effectiveness" (Upcraft & Schuh, 1996, p. 21). Assessment results can assist in strategic program planning for special student groups and for evaluating program effectiveness. Successful assessment practices require clearly defined program learning outcomes as well as strong linkages to the educational mission of the institution (Pascarella & Whitt, 1999; Upcraft & Schuh, 1996).

Orientation programs may be targeted to particular student groups. According to the 1996, 1997, and 2000 National Orientation Directors Association (NODA) Data Bank, international students, graduate students, returning students, academically disadvantaged students, and scholarship athletes at large institutions are frequently provided with separate orientation programs (Gonzales, Hill-Traynham, & Jacobs, 2000). Breakout sessions or workshops within the comprehensive orientation program have made available an alternative programming option for international students and returning students. Workshop sessions were most frequently offered for academically disadvantaged students, minority students, and honor students. Students with disabilities, however, frequently were not served by orientation programming according to Gonzales, Hill-Traynham, and Jacobs (2000). Clearly, the choice of programming is based on the needs of the students and the mission of the particular institution.

TRENDS AND RECOMMENDATIONS FOR PRACTICE

As one of the initial student affairs specialty areas experienced by new students, the orientation program has the opportunity and the potential to significantly affect student adjustment and future success. Participation in orientation activities is linked to student satisfaction and persistence. A review of the higher education literature documents the value of orientation programs in welcoming new students into the collegiate experience and providing students with tools to be successful academically and socially.

Now more than ever, professionals must have their practice grounded in student development theory and a familiarity with the research literature that describes the new student. Committed to student development and assisted by paraprofessionals, members of an institution's orientation team comprise one of the more influential groups on campus because of their ability to foster student growth and development through intentional interventions. The following trends or issues will be a part of the orientation professional's agenda for the next few years:

- With the emphasis on student learning and new attempts to reintegrate the cocurriculum, more and more institutions will require entering students to participate in orientation programs, whether one- or two-day, ongoing orientation programs, or freshman seminar and class models.

- Given the rising costs of higher education for students and the diminishing support for higher education, retention and student success initiatives will be critical in all programs, beginning with orientation programs.

- The changing nature of the student body and the diversity of the population will require orientation staff to examine programmatic and institutional practices to facilitate campus environments that are responsive.

- The increased involvement of parents and families in the education of family members will require attention to programs that meet their needs.

- Growing concern regarding the funding of higher education will require intentional collaboration and funding models to support orientation programs. Collaboration across campus and sophisticated enrollment management models and initiatives will become standard and expected practices.

- While the increasing use of technology helps to make procedures such as registration easier for students, its use removes the opportunity for personal interaction within institutions. Professionals will need to put great emphasis on the concepts of mattering and belonging as cornerstones of future programs.

- The need for extended programs of support through small groups facilitated by peers and staff and/or faculty beyond the first few weeks seems to be evident. Such programs may be needed beyond the first year.
- With increased attention on assessment, accountability, and learning, institutions will expect that orientation professionals utilize skills to design and complete more evaluation research activities than ever before.
- Identified learning outcomes will be critical components of strong orientation programs. These outcomes will be used to measure learning and identify subsequent programmatic opportunities to enhance student reflection and academic integration.
- Fewer students residing on campuses in the future will create new challenges for orientation professionals. New methods of communication will be necessary to assist new students in building a sense of identity and a commitment to learning.
- Technology will increase the opportunity to incorporate electronic tools for communication, online programs, and create new ways to deliver orientation programs, including videoconferencing.

TECHNOLOGY RESOURCES

http://www.nodaweb.org—The web site of the National Orientation Directors Association provides helpful links and resources for orientation programs. The resource web page provides outlines of successful orientation skits from other colleges, links to the web sites of orientation programs at colleges and universities across the country, summer reading selections, and so forth.

http://www.bsu.edu/orientation/—The Ball State University orientation web site is a good example of providing needed information to students and parents along with pictures of "happy people doing happy things."

REFERENCES

Anderson, E. (1985). Forces influencing student persistence and achievement. In L. Noel, R. S. Levitz, D. Saluri, and Associates (Eds.). *Increasing student retention* (pp. 44–61). San Francisco: Jossey-Bass.

Austin, D. M. (1993). Orientation activities for the families of new students. In M. L. Upcraft, R. H. Mullendore, B. O. Barefoot, & D. S. Fidler (Eds.). *The freshman year experience. Designing successful transitions: A guide for orienting students to college.* (Monograph Series No. 13). Columbia, SC: National Resource Center for The Freshman Year Experience.

Alch, M. L. (2000). Get ready for the net generation. *Training & Development, 54 (2),* 32–34.

American College Personnel Association (ACPA), National Association of Student Personnel Administrators (NASPA). (1997). *Principles of good practice for student affairs*. Washington, DC: Authors.

Barefoot, B. O., & Gardner, J. N. (1993). The freshman orientation seminar: Extending the benefits of traditional orientation. In M. L. Upcraft, R. H. Mullendore, B. O. Barefoot, & D. S. Fidler (Eds.). *The freshman year experience. Designing successful transitions: A guide for orienting students to college.* (Monograph Series No. 13). Columbia, SC: National Resource Center for The Freshman Year Experience.

Beal, P. E., & Noel, L. (1980). *What works in student retention.* The American College Testing Program and the National Center for Higher Education Management Systems. Iowa City, IA: ACT.

Bennett, M. E. (1938). *The orientation of students in educational institutions.* Thirty-seventh Yearbook (pp. 163–166). NSSE, Part I, Public-School.

Blimling, G. S., Whitt, E. J., & Associates. (1999). *Good practices in student affairs: Principles to foster student learning.* San Francisco: Jossey-Bass.

Bookman, G. (1948). Freshman orientation techniques in colleges and universities. *Occupations, 27,* 163–166.

Brownstein, A. (2000, October 13). The next great generation? *The Chronicle of Higher Education,* A71–72.

Brewster, K. J. (1968). Introduction. In O. Johnson (Ed.). *Stover at Yale.* New York: Collier Books.

Brown, R. (1972). *Tomorrow's higher education: A return to the academy.* Washington, DC: The American College Personnel Association.

Brubacher, J. S., & Rudy, W. (1958). *Education in transition.* New York: Harper.

Bryant, P., & Crockett, K. (1993, Fall). The admissions office goes scientific. *Planning for Higher Education, 22(1),* 1–8.

Butts, T. H. (1971). *Personnel service review: New practices in student orientation.* Ann Arbor, MI. (ERIC Document Reproduction Service No. ED 0570416).

Cabrera, A., Nora, A., Terenzini, P., Pascarella, E., & Hagedorn, L. (1999). Campus racial climate and the adjustment of students to college: A comparison between white students and African-American students. *Journal of Higher Education, 70(2),* 134–150.

Caple, R. B. (1964). A rationale for the orientation course. *Journal of College Student Personnel, 6,* 42–46.

Chickering, A., & Havighurst, R. J. (1981). The life cycle. In A. Chickering & Associates (Eds.). *The modern American college* (pp. 16–50). San Francisco: Jossey-Bass.

Chickering, A., & Reisser, L. (1993). *Education and identity.* San Francisco: Jossey-Bass.

Cohen, R. D., & Jody, R. (1978). *Freshman seminar: A new orientation.* Boulder, CO: Westview.

Council for the Advancement of Standards in Higher Education (CAS). (2001). *The book of professional standards for higher education.* Washington, DC: Author.

Council of Guidance and Personnel Associations. (1943). Recommendations, *Occupations, 21,* 46–48.

Crocker, L. G. (Ed.) (1921). *Advice to freshmen by freshmen.* Ann Arbor, MI: G. Wahr.

Cutright, M. (2002, September–October). What are research universities doing for first-year students. *About Campus, 7(4),* 16–20.

Dannells, M. (1986). Orientation director's manual, NODA.

Dannells, M., & Kuh. G. D. (1977). Orientation. In W.T. Packwood (Ed.). *College student personnel services.* Springfield, IL: Charles C Thomas.

Dixon, R. R. (Ed.). (1995). *Making enrollment management work.* (New Directions for Student Services, No. 71). San Francisco: Jossey-Bass.

Doermann, H. J. (1926). *Orientation of college freshmen.* Baltimore: Williams & Wilkins.

Drake, R. W. (1966). Review of the literature for freshman orientation practices in the United States. Fort Collins, CO: Colorado State University. (ERIC Document Reproduction Service No. ED030 920).

Edmondson, B. (1997, March). Demographics: Keeping up with change. *College Board Review, 180,* 25–30.

Eimers, M., & Mullen, R. (1997). Transfer students: Who are they and how successful are they at the University of Missouri? *College and University, 72 (3),* 9–19.

Engstrom, C. M., & Tinto, V. (2000). Developing partnerships with academic affairs to enhance student learning. In M. J. Barr, M. K. Desler, & Associates (Eds.). *The handbook of student affairs* (2nd ed.). San Francisco: Jossey-Bass.

Feldman, K. A., & Newcomb, T. M. (1969). *The impact of college on students.* San Francisco: Jossey-Bass.

Fenske, R. H., Rund, J. A., & Contento, J. M. (2000). Who are the new students? In M. J. Barr, M. K. Desler, & Associates (Eds.). *The handbook of student affairs* (2nd ed.). San Francisco: Jossey-Bass.

Fitts, C. T., & Swift, F. H. (1928). *The construction of orientation courses for freshmen, 1888–1926.* Berkeley, CA: University of California Press.

Fitzgerald, L. E., & Evans, S. B. (1963). Orientation programs: Foundations and framework. *College and University, 38,* 270–275.

Forrest, A. (1982). Increasing student competence and persistence. The best case for general education. In E. T. Pascarella, & P. T. Terenzini, (Eds.). *How college affects students.* San Francisco: Jossey-Bass.

Foxley, C. H. (1969). Orientation or dis-orientation. *Personnel and Guidance Journal, 48,* 218–221.

Gardner, J. N., & Hansen, D. A. (1993). Perspectives on the future of orientation. In M. L. Upcraft, R.H. Mullendore, B. O. Barefoot, & D. S. Fidler (Eds.). *The freshman year experience. Designing successful transitions: A guide for orienting students to college.* (Monograph Series No. 13). Columbia, SC: National Resource Center for The Freshman Year Experience.

Gonzales, T. V., Hill-Traynham, P. S., & Jacobs, B. C. (2000). Developing effective orientation programs for special populations. In M. J. Fabich (Ed.). *Orientation planning manual 2000.* Pullman, WA: National Orientation Directors Association.

Goodrich, T. A., & Pierson, R. R. (1959). Pre-college counseling at Michigan State University. *Personnel and Guidance Journal, 37,* 595–597.

Gordon, V., & Grites, T. (1991). Adjustment outcomes of a freshmen seminar: A utilization-focused approach. *Journal of College Student Development, 32,* 484–489.

Grier, D. G. (1966). Orientation—Tradition or reality? *NASPA Journal, 3,* 37–41.

Hadlock, H. L. (2000, Spring). Orientation programs: A synopsis of their significance. *The Journal of College Orientation and Transition, 7 (2),* 27–31.

Hall, B. (1982). College warm-up: Easing the transition to college. *Journal of College Student Personnel, 23(3),* 280–281.

Harbin, C. E. (1997). A survey of transfer students at four-year insitutions serving a California community college. *Community College Review, 25 (2),* 21–40.

Hatch, C. (2000). Parent and family orientation. In M. J. Fabich (Ed.). *Orientation planning manual 2000.* Pullman, WA: National Orientation Directors Association.

Higher Education Research Institute. (1999). *The American freshman: National norms for Fall 1988.* Los Angeles: UCLA Graduate School of Education and Information Studies.

Hirsch, D. J., & Burack, C. (2001). Finding points of contact for collaborative work. In A. Kezar, D. J. Hirsch, & C. Burack (Eds.). *Understanding the role of academic and student affairs collaboration in creating a successful learning environment.* (New Directions for Higher Education, No. 116, pp. 53–62). San Francisco: Jossey-Bass.

Holland, A., & Huba, M. E. (1989). Psychosocial development among student para-professionals in a college orientation program. *Journal of College Student Development, 30,* 100–105.

Hossler, D. (1999, Winter). Effective admissions recruitment. In G. H. Gaither (Ed.). *Promising practices in recruitment, remediation, and retention* (New Directions in Higher Education, No. 108, pp. 15–30). San Francisco: Jossey-Bass.

Hossler, D., Bean, J. P., & Associates (Eds.). (1990). *The strategic management of college enrollments.* San Francisco: Jossey-Bass.

Jacobs, B. C. (1993). Orienting diverse populations. In M. L. Upcraft, R. H. Mullendore, B. O. Barefoot, & D. S. Fidler (Eds.). *The freshman year experience. Designing successful transitions: A guide for orienting students to college.* (Monograph Series No. 13). Columbia, SC: National Resource Center for The Freshman Year Experience.

Jacobs. B. C., & With, E. A. (2002). Orientation's role in addressing the developmental stages of parents. *The Journal of College Orientation and Transition, 9 (2),* 37–42.

Johnson, M. J. (1998, Spring). First year orientation programs at four-year public institutions: A brief history. *The Journal of College Orientation and Transition, 5(2),* 25–31.

Johnson, N. T. (1987). Academic factors that affect transfer student persistence. *Journal of College Student Personnel, 28 (4),* 323–329.

Johnson, D. B., & Miller, M. T. (2000). Redesigning traditional programs to meet the needs of generation Y. *The Journal of College Orientation and Transition, 7(2),* 15–20.

Kamm, R. B., & Wrenn, C. G. (1947). Currrent developments in student-personnel programs and the needs of the veteran. *School and Society, 65,* 89–92.

Keller, G. (2001). The new demographics of higher education—Shifts in family life. *About Campus, 6(3),* 2–5.

Keil, E. C. (1966). College orientation: A disciplinary approach. *Liberal Education, 52,* 172–180.

Klostermann, L. R., & Merseal, J. (1978) Another view of orientation. *Journal of College Student Personnel, 19(3),* 86–87.

Knott, J. E., & Daher, D. M. (1978). A structured group program for new students. *Journal of College Student Personnel, 19(5),* 456–461.

Krall, J. K. (1981). New student welcome day program. *Journal of College and University Housing, 11(2),* 320–333.

Kuh, G. D. (1996). Guiding principles for creating seamless learning environments for undergraduates. *Journal of College Student Development, 37 (2)*, 135–148.

Kramer, G. L., & Washburn, R. (1983). The perceived orientation needs of new students. *Journal of College Student Personnel, 24(4)*, 311–319.

Levine, A., & Cureton, J. S. (1998). *When hope and fear collide.* San Francisco: Jossey-Bass.

Levitz, R., & Noel, L. (1989). Connecting students to institutions: Keys to retention and success. In M. L. Upcraft, J. N. Gardner, & Associates (Eds.). *The freshman year experience* (pp. 65–81). San Francisco: Jossey-Bass.

Lowe, I. (1980, April). Preregistration counseling: A comparative study. Paper presented at the California College Association Conference, Monterey, CA.

Mann, B. A. (1998). Retention principles for new student orientation programs. *The Journal of College Orientation and Transition, 6(1)*, 15–20.

McCann, J. C. (1967). Trends in orienting college students. *Journal of the National Association of Women Deans, Administrators and Counselors, 30(2)*, 855–889.

Morison, S. E. (1936). "The histories of the universities." Lectures delivered at the Rice Institute, April 3–4, 1935. The Rice Institute Pamphlet, 1936(b), 23, 211–282.

Mueller, K. H. (1961). *Student personnel work in higher education.* Boston: Houghton Mifflin.

Mullendore, R. H. (1998a). Orientation as a component of institutional retention efforts. In R. H. Mullendore (Ed.). *Orientation planning manual.* Bloomington, IN: National Orientation Directors Association.

Mullendore, R. H. (1998b). Including parents and families in the orientation process. In R. H. Mullendore (Ed.). *Orientation planning manual.* Bloomington, IN: National Orientation Directors Association.

Mullendore, R. H., & Abrahamn, J. (1993). Organization and administration of orientation programs. In M. L. Upcraft, J. N. Gardner, & Associates (Eds.). *The freshman year experience* (pp. 61–77). San Francisco: Jossey-Bass

Murdock, S. H., & Hoque, M. N. (1999, Winter). Demographic factors affecting higher education in the United States in the twenty-first century. In G. H. Gaither (Ed.). *Promising practices in recruitment, remediation, and retention* (New Directions for Higher Education, No. 108, pp. 5–14). San Francisco: Jossey-Bass.

Murray, J. L., & Apilado, M. (1989). Design and implementation of a holistic orientation program for small colleges. *NASPA Journal, 26(4)*, 308–312.

Pascarella, E. T., & Terenzini, P. T. (1991). *How college affects students: Findings and insights from twenty years of research.* San Francisco: Jossey-Bass.

Pascarella, E. T., & Whitt, E. J. (1999). Using systematic inquiry to improve performance. In G. S. Blimling, E. J. Whitt, & Associates (Eds.). *Good Practice in Student Affairs: Principles to Foster Student Learning.* San Francisco: Jossey-Bass.

Pascarella, E. T., & Terenzini, P. T. (1991). *How college affects students: Findings and insights from twenty years of research.* San Fancisco, CA: Jossey-Bass.

Penn, G, (1999). *Enrollment management for the 21st century: Institutional goals, accountability, and fiscal responsibility.* ASHE-ERIC Higher Education Report, 26(7). Washington, DC: The George Washington University.

Perigo, D., & Upcraft, L. (1989). Orientation programs. In M. L. Upcraft, R. H. Mullendore, B. O. Barefoot, & D. S. Fidler (Eds.). *The freshman year experience. Designing successful transitions: A guide for orienting students to college.* (Monograph

Series No. 13). Columbia, SC: National Resource Center for The Freshman Year Experience.

Ramist, L. (1981). College student attrition and retention. College Board Report, No. 80–81. Princeton, NJ: College Entrance Examination Board.

Rice, R. (1992). Reaction of participants to either pre-college orientation or freshman seminar courses. *Journal of the Freshman Year Experience, 4 (2)*, 85–100.

Riesman, D. (1961). Changing colleges and changing students. *National Catholic Education Association Bulletin, 58*, 104–115.

Ritchie, J. (Ed.). (2001). *New member handbook.* Pullman, WA: National Orientation Directors Assocation.

Rode, D. (2000). {Au: title?} In M. J. Fabich (Ed.). *Orientation planning manual 2000.* Pullman, WA: National Orientation Directors Association.

Sagaria, M. A. (1979). Freshman orientation courses: A framework. *Journal of the National Association of Women Deans, Administrators, and Counselors, 43(1)*, 3–7.

Sandeen, C. A. (2000). Developing effective campus and community relationships. In M. J. Barr, M. K. Desler, & Associates (Eds.). *The handbook of student affairs.* San Francisco: Jossey-Bass.

Schmidt, D. K., & Sedlacek, W. E. (1972). Variables related to university student satisfaction. *Journal of College Student Personnel, 13*, 233–237.

Smith, B. F., & Brackin, R. (1993). Components of a comprehensive orientation program. In M. L. Upcraft, R. H. Mullendore, B. O. Barefoot, & D. S. Fidler (Eds.). *The freshman year experience. Designing successful transitions: A guide for orienting students to college.* (Monograph Series No. 13). Columbia, SC: National Resource Center for The Freshman Year Experience.

Strang, R. (1951). Orientation of new students. In C. G. Wrenn (Ed.), *Student personnel work in college* (pp. 274–292). New York: Ronald.

Striffolino, P., & Saunders, S. A. (1989). Emerging leaders: Students in need of development. *NASPA Journal, 27(1)*, 51–58.

Sturtz, S. A. (1971). Age differences in college student satisfaction. *Journal of College Student Personnel, 12*, 220–222.

Tautfest, P. B. (1961). An evaluation technique for orientation programs. *Journal of College Student Personnel, 3(32)*, 5–28.

Twale, E. J. (1989). Social and academic development in freshman orientation: A time frame. *NASPA Journal, 27(2)*, 160–167.

Tinto, V. (1985). Dropping out and other forms of withdrawal from college. In L. Noel, R. Levitz, D. Saluri, & Associates (Eds.), *Increasing student retention* (pp. 28–43). San Francisco: Jossey-Bass.

Tinto, V. (1997). Universities as learning communities. *About Campus, 1(6)*, 2–4.

Turner, D. J. (2000). In M. J. Fabich (Ed.). *Orientation planning manual 2000.* Pullman, WA: National Orientation Directors Association.

Upcraft, M. L., Gardner, J. N., & Associates. (1989). *The freshman year experience.* San Francisco: Jossey-Bass.

Upcraft, M. L., & Goldsmith, H. (2000). Technological changes in student affairs administration. In M. J. Barr, M. K. Desler, & Associates (Eds.). *The handbook of student affairs* (2nd ed.). San Francisco: Jossey-Bass.

Upcraft, M. L., & Farnsworth, W. M. (1984). Orientation programs and activities. In M. L. Upcraft (Ed.). *Orienting students to college.* (New Directions For Student Services, No. 25, pp. 27–39). San Francisco: Jossey-Bass.

Upcraft, M. L., & Schuh, J. H. (1996). *Assessment in student affairs.* San Francisco: Jossey-Bass.

U.S. Department of Education. National Center for Education Statistics. (1997). *Projections of education statistics to 2007.* (NCES 97-382). Washington, DC: U.S. Government Printing Office.

U.S. Department of Education. National Center for Education Statistics. (1998). *Descriptive summary of 1995–96, Beginning postsecondary students.* (NCES 1999-030). Washington, DC: U.S. Government Printing Office.

Wiese, D. (2000). The assessment and evaluation of orientation programs: A practical approach. In M. J. Fabich (Ed.). *Orientation planning manual 2000.* Pullman, WA: National Orientation Directors Association.

Wolfe, J. S. (1993). Institutional integration, academic success, and persistence of first-year commuter and resident students. *Journal of College Student Development, 34,* 321–326.

Zis, S. L. (2002, Fall). Changing student characteristics: Implications for new student orientation. *The Journal of College Orientation and Transition, 10(1),* 64–68.

Chapter 10

RESIDENCE HALLS

Joʜɴ H. Scʜuʜ

On residential college campuses that primarily serve traditional students (aged 18–24), student housing plays an integral role in the experiences of students. As Blimling (1993) observed,

> At the core of any established student affairs organization at a residential college is a strong residence hall program. Life outside the classroom is amplified here. It provides more opportunities to influence student growth and development in the first year or two of college than almost any other program in student affairs. Although educational opportunities are offered through a variety of student affairs programs and departments, none are as pervasive in scope or have the potential to influence as many students as residence halls do. (p. 1)

Residence halls play an important role in American higher education and "were rooted in the English universities on which American higher education was modeled" (Schroeder & Mable, 1994b, p. 5). Looking to the future, residence halls have the potential to contribute substantially to the educational experiences of students. As Schroeder and Mable (1994a) pointed out, "By focusing on student learning, residential hall programs can become interwoven with the fabric of the academy, bringing integration and coherence to a traditionally fragmented, compartmentalized, and often random approach to achieving important educational outcomes" (p. 302).

This chapter discusses selected topics concerning residence halls, including the history and purpose of residence halls, organizational patterns and staffing, residence hall programming, the influence of residence halls on students, selected legal issues, and the future of residence halls at colleges and universities. The reader should note that the administration of residence halls is a very complex matter, and a number of very important issues are not described because they are beyond the scope of this chapter. Among them are marketing facilities and programs, financing and construction of residence halls, and maintenance and renovation of facilities. Additionally, many excellent reference sources not mentioned in this chapter are available through the Association of College and University Housing Officers-International (ACUHO-I), the American College Personnel

Association (ACPA), and the National Association of Student Personnel Administrators (NASPA).

HISTORY

Three influences affected the development of student housing in the United States. The first influence (adapted from colleges in England) tried to bring students, faculty, and tutors together in a residential environment. This approach attempted to integrate learning inside and outside the classroom—efforts were made to provide an environment that fostered learning.

The second influence took place as the nineteenth century progressed and the Germanic influence on American higher education, and on housing and campus life, provided a striking contrast to the English residential system as modified in the United States. The German approach did not provide for student housing and, in fact, was not concerned with students' lives outside the classroom.

The third influence, shortly before the turn of the twentieth century, was a rekindled interest in residence halls. While a few institutions attempted to implement the English model, U.S. colleges and universities more commonly emphasized the housing, feeding, and social life of students. The goal of integrating the curriculum with residential living was not achieved and may have been impossible (Brubacher & Rudy, 1958) given the differences in the types of facilities and students who attended American colleges compared with their English counterparts.

Follow the evolution of housing philosophy through this brief discussion of the history of the American student housing movement.

THE COLONIAL PERIOD

Like the legal system, the language, and many other aspects of American culture, the initial model of "early American higher education was patterned after the colleges of Oxford and Cambridge" (Frederiksen, 1993, p. 168). Certain factors, however, made the higher education scene in the colonies different from the English model. Residential colleges in England contributed formally and informally to students' education, while the early American dormitories were viewed as places to eat and sleep. "The sparseness of the resultant barracks-like dormitories was not designed to foster the characteristic close and well-built social life of the English college" (Brubacher & Rudy, 1976, p. 41).

Colonial students were perceived as young men with souls to be saved, and therefore a profound religious influence permeated the colleges (Fenske, 1980a) and "religion dominated student life" (Brubacher & Rudy, 1976, p. 42). These early colleges were directed by presidents who were "almost without exception gentlemen of the cloth. Governing boards, too, abounded with clerics" (Fenske, 1980, p. 8). "College life was designed as a system for controlling the often exuberant youth and for inculcating within them discipline, morals, and character" (Cohen, 1998, p. 23). Parents supported having their students closely supervised by the college, giving rise to the concept of *in loco parentis*, having the college serve as surrogate parents to carefully supervise all the activities of the students, both inside and outside the classroom (Frederiksen, 1993).

> The family sent its youngster to the college and expected that the institution would take charge of the boy's life. . . . Youngsters who could not accept the form of discipline that the college imposed might be sent home (Cohen, 1998, p. 23).

Despite stringent rules governing student conduct (e.g., Statutes of Harvard, 1646), the problems created by students that emerged in early residence facilities were thievery, gambling, drunkenness, vandalism, and debauchery (Moore, 1997). Discipline was a recurring problem.

> The tendency was to house students together in a residential dormitory of one sort or another whenever possible. The aim was to foster among all students a common social, moral and intellectual life. Early experiments met with decidedly mixed results (Lucas, 1994, p. 111).

Because of poor living conditions, disciplinary problems, and the like, relationships between American students and their faculty were never as close as those in England. In fact, students' relationships with faculty were often adversarial rather than tutorial. This modified English residential concept framed the American approach to campus housing until about the Civil War (Frederiksen, 1993).

MIDDLE TO LATE NINETEENTH CENTURY DEVELOPMENTS

Two developments occurred in the 1800s that negatively influenced the development of student housing in the United States. The first of these was the Germanic influence on American higher education. "The international hegemony of German academic learning and the concrete examples of German university practices presented compelling precedents, not just for American reformers, but for scientists and scholars everywhere" (Geiger, 1997, p. 273). From about 1850 to 1890, many faculty from American colleges and universities pursued graduate education in Germany. They were exposed to a philosophy of higher education that was characterized by intellectual impersonalism (Appleton, Briggs, & Rhatigan, 1978) and viewed students as responsible for managing their own housing, food, and social life. "A number of educators returned from German universities in the mid-nineteenth century and popularized the German belief that housing students was not the responsibility of the institution" (Frederiksen, 1993, p.

169). Among these were President Francis Wayland of Brown and President Henry Tappan of Michigan. Wayland "argued an enforced residential pattern encouraged the spread of disease, fostered unsanitary habits, reinforced the disinclination of students to exercise . . . [and] diverted funds needed for building up libraries and classrooms" (Lucas, 1994, p. 126).

Recurring financial problems, the second development that hindered the development of student housing, plagued higher education; resources were not readily available to support residential construction and operations. As a result, "Dormitories built in the early nineteenth century continued in operation, but many of them had been allowed to fall into semi-decay" (Cowley, 1934, p. 712).

While Harvard and Yale continued their house systems during this time of disinterest and disfavor toward student housing, the rest of the country exhibited much less interest in the idea of housing students. Toward the end of the nineteenth century, a countervailing trend developed concerning student housing with the result that colleges and universities revived their interest in student housing. The founding of the University of Chicago dramatically contributed to the rebirth of interest in student housing (Brubacher & Rudy, 1958). William Rainey Harper, the first president of the University of Chicago, based on his experience as a faculty member at Yale, insisted that housing for students be an integral part of the Chicago campus. As the University of Chicago became an outstanding educational institution, it served as a model for others.

Two other factors led to a revitalization of student housing toward the end of the nineteenth century. The first was that several private colleges were founded for women, and these institutions valued student housing. Their rationale for housing focused primarily on providing close supervision of these young women. Alumnae of women's colleges attended graduate school at larger universities and carried with them the traditions of their residential undergraduate experiences. As larger universities began to admit women, concern for women's housing became an important agenda item for administrators. Ultimately, separate residential facilities were developed to accommodate men and women.

The second contributing factor to the attractiveness of student housing was the development of campus life outside the classroom. Intercollegiate sports, debating societies, and student publications encouraged students to spend their out-of-classroom time on campus in various extracurricular activities (Brubacher & Rudy, 1958). Living in campus housing became more convenient for those students who wished to participate in such activities, and consequently the demand for housing increased.

EARLY TWENTIETH CENTURY

While Harper organized residence halls at Chicago, Woodrow Wilson unveiled his quadrangle system for housing students at Princeton. Although this plan ultimately failed because of alumni opposition (Brubacher & Rudy, 1976), Wilson was highly regarded as a leader in higher education, and his approach influenced many of his presidential colleagues (Brubacher & Rudy, 1958).

Fueled by private funds, construction of residence halls was undertaken at perhaps the fastest rate in the American history up to this time (Frederiksen, 1993, citing Cowley). The Great Depression decreased residence hall construction in the 1930s. Such diverse institutions as the University of Idaho, Michigan State College, and Virginia Polytechnic Institute constructed housing with state assistance (Frederiksen, 1993). Similarly, the development of the Public Works Administration allowed colleges to borrow funds from the federal government to construct housing on their campuses (Frederiksen, 1993). By 1939, three-fourths of institutions examined for accreditation by the North Central Association reported making efforts to enhance their student housing facilities (Brubacher & Rudy, 1976).

POST WORLD WAR II

Campus life changed dramatically during the years following World War II since so many young people who might have gone to college were involved with the war effort. Many veterans returned to complete their education, and housing, especially for married students, was in short supply. Apartment style housing was constructed to accommodate married students (Schneider, 1977). This in itself was an oddity, because previously most of those who attended college as undergraduates had been single students, 18 to 22 years old. Institutions of higher education needed to exercise great flexibility in meeting the needs of these new and older students.

During the late 1960s, student housing increasingly was criticized for its restrictive rules governing student life. Institutional policies did not permit students to entertain guests of the opposite sex in their living quarters, and women generally had to return to their residence hall by a certain time each evening or face disciplinary action. Students vigorously questioned these policies and, where possible, left the residence halls or brought legal challenges against institutions. As a result, institutions relaxed parietal rules, often dropping regulations that required students to live on campus and making it possible for students to live under conditions similar to those of their peers who lived off campus.

Toward the middle and latter part of the 1970s, students began to return to campus residence halls because of economic conditions and the widespread indifference of students to any cause except earning a degree and finding a job (Fenske, 1980b). Inflation hindered the American economy, and on-campus living became particularly convenient and economical for students. Students returned to residence halls in large numbers, and as the

1980s unfolded, a number of campuses experienced shortages in the number of available spaces for student housing.

Moving into the 1990s, student housing faced yet another set of challenges related to the student as consumer. Students in this environment expected more services than ever before, including such former "luxuries" as cable television, access to computers in their rooms, a wide variety of meal plans, and a cornucopia of choices at each meal. Increasingly, security became a vexing issue as students expected a maximum of freedom with a minimum of supervision while being guaranteed assurance for their personal safety. As Frederiksen concluded, "The administration of student residential facilities and residence life policies presents a real challenge to housing professionals in colleges and universities throughout the United States" (1993, p. 174).

Looking forward in the new century, several trends related to student housing seem undeniable. First, as colleges and universities increasingly rely on technology for the delivery of services and programs, indeed even courses, residence halls need to provide the kind of technological infrastructure to make them attractive places for students to live. This infrastructure will include a technological environment that will help students "manage their own learning" (Engstrom & Kruger, 1997, p. 1). Second, the relationship students have with their institution will be more like that which they have with "their bank, the telephone company, and the supermarket" (Levine & Cureton, 1998, p. 50). As a consequence, institutions will have to respond to student needs or they will take their business elsewhere. Research suggests that for upper-class students this is true already (Levine & Cureton, 1998, p. 103). Finally, residence hall administrators increasingly will be held accountable for the programs, services, and activities that are offered in campus housing. The age of accountability has reached our campuses (Upcraft & Schuh, 1996) and residence halls are not immune from this trend.

MISSION AND PURPOSE

Ask a number of student affairs administrators what they think the purposes of residence halls are and you may well might receive a variety of answers. Among these might be (1) to provide a sound fiscal operation, (2) to keep physical facilities contemporary and in good repair, (3) to provide activities for students to participate in outside of class, (4) to keep order, and perhaps (5) to provide for student growth. This section describes different perspectives on the purposes of student housing.

When reviewing the purpose of student housing or any unit within student affairs, the best place to start is to examine the mission of the institution within which student housing operates. Lyons (1993) reminds us, "The most important factor that determines the shape and substance of student affairs is the mission of the institution" (p. 14). Consequently, the institutional mission will determine not only the role of student housing, but also its relative importance and the amount of attention and resources it receives from senior administration and faculty. The Council for the Advancement of Standards (CAS) described the contribution and role of student housing to the institution's mission: "The housing and residential life program is an integral part of the educational purpose of the institution. Its mission must include provision for educational programs and services, residential facilities, management services, and, where appropriate, food services" (CAS, 2001, p. 143).

In practical terms, at a small liberal arts college where virtually every student lives on campus, housing will be inextricably linked to the educational experiences of virtually all students. At a residential college, the mission would include language that describes the living-learning environment for all students enrolled in the college.

Quite the opposite would be true of a commuter university with a small residential population. In this situation, the residence halls will assume a far less central role in the life of the university, and the institution's mission statement may not describe the campus as providing a residential learning environment for students. The purposes of student housing have evolved over the past 40 years, as the following illustrate.

In 1961, three objectives for student housing were suggested: (1) accommodating the physical needs of students—that is, a place where students could eat and sleep that would be convenient to classrooms and the library; (2) promoting academic learning; and (3) aiding in the personal development of students (Mueller, 1961). In addition, two minor objectives of residence halls were (1) good public relations, especially with parents, and (2) the supervision and control of student conduct.

Riker and DeCoster (1971) identified five general objectives for student housing in building block fashion. These ranged from providing satisfactory physical facilities to developing opportunities for individual growth and development. They concluded, "the overall objectives of student housing are interrelated and interdependent" (p. 5).

Over time, educational or developmental objectives for the residential living experience have received even more emphasis. In the 1990s, Schroeder and Mable proposed that "the challenge for residence halls is to place a renewed emphasis on promoting student learning through integrating residence hall learning opportunities with the goals and priorities of undergraduate education" (1994b, p. 15). To complement this overarching goal, Winston and Anchors (1993) recommended that residence halls address the following objectives:

1. Assisting students in becoming literate, liberally educated persons;
2. Promoting students' development in becoming responsible, contributing members of multiple communities;

3. Advocating commitment to the ideals of altruism and social justice;
4. Endorsing the cultivation of a healthy lifestyle, both physically and psychologically;
5. Encouraging students to examine their spiritual life; and
6. Challenging students to confront moral and ethical issues (pp. 40–41).

While there has been considerable debate over the years about which functions of student housing are more important than others, in the final analysis the consensus of opinion probably reflects an integrated approach. The physical environment and programmatic offerings are interrelated, and each contributes substantially to the advancement of the residence hall system. Students cannot be expected to be interested in learning opportunities unless they live in adequate physical facilities. If guidelines for community living are not established, it is possible that facilities will not be respected and, in fact, may be abused. All members of the housing staff contribute to the vitality of the system, including the residence hall director, the custodian, the food service worker, the resident assistant, and the senior administrator. Most importantly, it should be remembered that housing exists within the framework of an institution's mission, and that mission will define the role of housing. "Failure to understand the institutional mission statement can result in program failure and inappropriate services for students" (Barr, 2000, p. 35).

ADMINISTRATION AND ORGANIZATION

Six contextual factors have been identified as influencing the organizational structure of a student housing department (Upcraft, 1993). They are (1) the size of the institution, (2) its mission, (3) the characteristics of the student body, (4) the class mix of resident students, (5) the institution's position on requiring students to live in campus housing, and (6) the racial and ethnic mix of resident students. To these might be added the institution's philosophy regarding the extent to which housing is regarded as an auxiliary service, a student service, or both.

The most common organizational arrangement is for student housing to report to the senior student affairs officer (Stoner, 1992). Other patterns include having housing report to the senior business officer, or having typical residential life functions report to student affairs, and the business functions report to the senior business officer (Sandeen, 2001). Michigan State University, an institution with a large residential population, is an example of the latter arrangement. Still another arrangement is for the director of housing to report to both the senior student affairs and the senior business affairs officer.

According to Upcraft (1993), having housing report to the senior student affairs officer is desirable. In the final analysis, however, the reporting arrangement depends "on the values of the leadership of the institution" (Upcraft, 1993, p. 194). In addition, the organizational structure and reporting relationship will depend on whether an institution is state-assisted or independent. Typically, housing at a state-assisted institution will function as an auxiliary service, where, in theory, the housing operation receives no support from the institution and has to achieve fiscal solvency on the basis of the revenues it receives for various services. In this approach, the housing department is an independent enterprise and operates on a self-sustaining basis (Mills & Barr, 1990).

At an independent institution (i.e., private college or university), housing may be a cost center but revenues generated for services rendered may be part of the general operating fund of the institution, and funds are allocated to operate student housing much as they would for other units on campus. Housing may be expected to contribute a surplus of funds, that is, generating more revenue than expenses for the institution so that the additional monies can be put to other uses. This distinction is important to remember when comparing the organization and purposes of residence halls on independent campuses with state-assisted colleges and universities.

STAFFING PATTERNS

While titles of various residence hall staff positions may vary from campus to campus, the functions performed remain fairly consistent across most campuses. As the size of the housing department increases, additional staff will be added at the administrative level. Consequently, housing departments on large campuses will have a variety of services provided by a large number of highly specialized staff.

The undergraduate student living on a residence hall floor and providing direct service to students usually is called a resident assistant or resident advisor (RA). At times, this person has the title of resident counselor, although providing advice and referral are more typical of this person's responsibilities than actually entering into counseling relationships with residents. Commonly an upper-class student, the RA is responsible for working with students individually and in small groups, assessing student needs and planning programs, advising the floor government, handling certain administrative matters, and enforcing university rules and regulations.

There probably is no more difficult position in student affairs work than that of the RA, because, quite literally, RAs are expected to live where they work. They are always on call and deal with many problems that can be very challenging. Additionally, since RAs are paraprofessionals, they need a great deal of support in terms of training and supervision. Winston and Fitch concluded, "effective RA programs require the commitment of substantial resources by the housing program" (1993, p. 340). Many senior student affairs officers began their careers as these frontline members of the student affairs team.

Generally, larger residence halls will employ assistant residence hall directors who are graduate students at the master's level. They supervise RAs, handle student conduct problems, organize more complex programs, and offer general supervision and staff training in the absence of full-time professional staff. Since these staff often are enrolled on a full-time basis in a graduate program, they provide assistance and support to the resident assistant staff while at the same time managing their own academic work. The professional staff person in charge of the residence hall often is called a head resident, resident director, hall director, or building manager. Typically, this person has a master's degree in student affairs, counseling, or a related field, and the position is considered entry-level in the student affairs field. Some residential systems hire graduate students to supervise buildings. This works best when the buildings are small and substantial supervisory resources are available to provide leadership for hall directors.

Beyond the individual residence hall, a variety of administrative positions may exist to provide overall direction for the housing department. In larger housing systems, it is common to find an area director responsible for a group of residence halls. Hall directors report directly to the area director, who frequently has several years of full-time experience in addition to a master's degree. In a smaller system, hall directors may report to an assistant director of housing or an assistant dean for residential life.

The assistant dean for residential life has the responsibility of overseeing residence life programs on campus including such activities as (1) coordinating the RA selection and training program, (2) advising the residence hall student government and judicial board, and (3) selecting, training, and supervising the hall directors. These tasks are particularly crucial in ensuring that a high quality experience is provided for students. Winston and Creamer (1997) asserted,

> One of the best assurances of quality in student affairs is to guarantee the quality of staff members, which is accomplished by a combination tactics including hiring the right people and then carefully and deliberately nurturing them through the division's staffing practices. (p. 273)

A person at this level of responsibility (which often requires a master's degree and, in the case of a larger system, a doctorate) usually has held several positions before coordinating an entire campus residence life program.

Particularly in larger institutions, other central office administrators may include an assistant director for operations who is concerned with the managerial aspects of student housing including room assignments, budget preparation and management, as well as the various business elements of student housing such as purchasing, personnel and summer conferences. There also may be an assistant director working with physical facilities, supervising maintenance and housekeeping, working with the campus physical plant, preparing long-range repair and rehabilitation plans, and serving as project administrator for major construction projects.

While this chapter is not designed specifically to discuss facility issues in depth, it is important to remember that "the facility and its furnishings are a vehicle for the delivery of services provided" (McClellan & Barr, 2000, p. 214). As a consequence, those who work with facilities must coordinate their activities with those who plan programs and work with students so that the overarching goals of the residential life department can be achieved.

Food service, more appropriately termed "dining services," usually is provided in one of two ways. Smaller campuses frequently contract with a private company to provide food service. Other campuses, particularly those with a larger resident population, tend to have a food service that is provided by the campus or by the housing department itself. Traditionally, campus philosophy, resources, and facilities are factors to be considered when determining whether the campus provides its own food service or contracts with a private vendor. Regardless of how food service is provided (self-operated or contracted), the contribution of this segment of the operation is crucial to student satisfaction. Underscoring this observation, Fairbrook (1993) noted, "Today's college or university food service directors are not merely cafeteria managers. They can be vital members of the student affairs team . . . dedicated to furthering students' overall development into educated, well-adjusted, and well-informed citizens" (p. 246).

The typical entry-level professional position for a person contemplating a career in student housing is as the director of a fairly large building, 500 students or more, or a director of a complex of smaller buildings. Entry-level positions require a master's degree in student affairs, counseling, higher education, or a related field. Some experience as a graduate assistant or resident assistant is highly desirable since there are subtleties to this work that are difficult to understand without direct operating experience in a student residence hall. Entry-level positions frequently require that the staff person "live in," meaning that they have an apartment in the building or complex for which they are responsible. While this living arrangement is not always highly desirable from the perspective of privacy, it does provide an excellent opportunity to work directly with students and paraprofessional staff in meaningful ways.

PROGRAMS AND SERVICES

The number and variety of programs available to the typical residence hall student are virtually limitless. On any given campus, programs can range from social to recreational, from cultural to academic. Providing sufficient programming, in a quantitative sense, rarely is a problem in a residence hall environment. Making programming meaningful to students by linking residence hall programs to student needs is another matter.

A number of conceptual frameworks are available from which one may plan residence hall programs. Among these are student development theories, intervention models, and campus ecology models. One of the best frameworks is the "dimensions of intervention for student development model" developed by Morrill and Hurst (1980). This model identified three specific types of programming: (1) remedial programming, (2) preventive programming, and (3) developmental programming.

Remedial programming refers to those programs that emphasize issues where something has gone wrong and the problem needs to be addressed. For example, if international students have experienced subtle forms of discrimination within the residence hall because of their religious customs, then educational workshops might be designed for all students where the specific customs are explained. Moreover, some emphasis might be placed on the religious discrimination that, in part, was responsible for many people leaving their homelands to come to the United States in the first place.

Preventive programming includes programs that are implemented because student problems or issues are predictable. Morrill, Hurst, and Oetting (1980), for example, identified programs that help ease the transition from home to the university setting as preventive. Such programs are designed to minimize homesickness, roommate conflicts, and academic adjustment problems.

Developmental programming sessions are designed to foster student growth. These programs include leadership development, volunteer opportunities, and social programs. The goal is to promote the growth and development of students desiring to enhance their skills and abilities.

Most educational programs can be fit into one of the three categories (remedial, preventive, or developmental programming) in the preceding taxonomy. Using this framework as a guide, program planning can be undertaken to meet the needs of students, assuming that their interests and needs have been assessed appropriately.

However, other program development models also would be appropriate to consider in providing a framework for programming: the campus ecology manager model (Banning, 1989), a health and wellness model (Mosier, 1989), program planning models (Barr & Cuyjet, 1991; Claar & Cuyjet, 2000), and the student service program development model (Moore and Delworth, 1976). The model that is chosen is less important than the logical framework that provides the desired results consistently (Schuh and Triponey, 1993).

Claar and Cuyjet (2000) provide a list of helpful recommendations for programming. Their abridged suggestions include:

1. Do not underestimate the importance of timing;
2. Involve students in planning programs and listen to them;
3. Communicate with other concerned constituents while in the planning process;
4. Identify the individual with the responsibility for leading the initiative and provide support for that person;
5. Do everything possible to succeed, but be willing to fail;
6. Be prepared to make adjustments in the plan as needed;
7. Try to engage as many people as possible in the planning and implementation of programs;
8. Enjoy the process of planning and implementing programs and use the process as an opportunity to teach students and staff; and
9. Remember that the context, goal and plan are important, but that the most important element is a committed and interested staff member (p. 325).

PROGRAM EXAMPLES

The number and range of programs that one might find in residence halls on a particular campus is extensive. Rather than provide an exhaustive listing of programs, suggestions about program development and illustrations of contemporary programming efforts are provided.

First, residence hall programming may focus on student development using psychosocial theory. Chickering and Reisser (1993) made several recommendations to enhance student development using the seven vector psychosocial theory. Among their suggestions are:

1. Incorporate learning activities into living units;
2. Adapt existing halls to allow for a balance of interaction and privacy and to permit a more personalized environment;
3. Enhance community by building new units that are small enough to allow maximum participation but large enough to allow more experienced students to induct newer ones into the culture;
4. Improve the "fit" and diversity by placing students carefully; and
5. Use regulations, policies, and hall management strategies as tools for fostering autonomy, interdependence, and integrity (p. 402).

Second, programming may enhance new student retention. "There is very clear evidence that residence halls and campus activities have a positive impact on retention and personal development, but only if institutions support and structure student participation to positive ends" (Upcraft, 1989, p. 154). Toward that end, a number of programs have been developed that address the needs of first-year students, such as the programs at Miami University (Kuh, Schuh, & Whitt, 1991). Zeller and Mosier (1993) recommended that programs be designed to (1) help new students develop skills;

(2) provide a sense of connectedness to the university; and (3) balance students' needs for autonomy, security, and interdependence. One way to accomplish these objectives is through the use of a four-phase model that includes recruitment, orientation, involvement, and academic support and involves "complementary partnerships among academic affairs, student affairs, and residential life staff" (Zeller, Kanz, & Schneiter, 1990, p. 14). What is particularly useful to remember about this program is that it symbolizes the vanguard of contemporary educational programming, with such features as collaboration across institutional divisions (student and academic affairs), clearly articulated goals, careful attention to entering students, and outcomes related to student learning. Programming in the future will continue to emphasize such features.

Third, a particularly important programming initiative that has occurred widely in the past decade or so has been the development of learning communities (Lenning & Ebbers, 1999). Learning communities attempt to create a seamless learning environment for students (Kuh, 1996; Schroeder, 1999) and provide an environment where learning in the classroom extends to the residence hall. Typical features of a learning community include students who live in close proximity to one another in a residence hall, who enroll in the same sections of two or three courses, and who form study groups. An enrichment dimension is often an aspect of the learning community (Meyer & Schuh, 2001); students may take field trips together, engage in volunteer service, or have other experiences that supplement what they have learned in class. Research (e.g., Huba, McFadden, & Epperson, n.d.; Meyer & Schuh, 2000; Pike, Schroeder, & Berry, 1997) has suggested that learning communities and other structured, intentional interventions that are residentially based enhance the education potential of residence halls. This kind of programming likely will continue in the future because of its powerful positive influence on the learning and development of students.

A fourth example of a programming trend is illustrated by the collaboration between counseling centers and residence life departments (Black, 1993; Schuh & Shipton, 1985). These departments work together to deliver programs to students and to provide support and assistance for the residence hall staff. This kind of programming represents another contemporary approach to program development in that in an era of shrinking resources, collaboration and sharing are very common, highly desirable (Schuh & Whitt, 1999), and urged by leading professional organizations (American Association for Higher Education, American College Personnel Association, & National Association of Student Personnel Administrators, 1998). It is unlikely that higher education in the foreseeable future will receive large infusions of additional resources. Consequently, sharing of assets and resources is one way that new programs can be developed to meet students' needs.

The common elements of these programming initiatives illustrate contemporary approaches to programming. Programs are most effective when a conceptual framework related to the growth of students is utilized and careful attention is paid to needs assessment. Program development in the future will feature these elements.

APPLYING STUDENT DEVELOPMENT

Before leaving the topic of programming, it is useful to provide some illustrations of how specific programs can be incorporated into an overall plan for fostering student development in the residential environment. In this case, student development refers to "specific outcome goals resulting from attending college and living in college residential facilities" (Winston & Anchors, 1993, p. 40). As was the case with having a model for program planning, what is crucial here is that a theory of student growth and development serves as the basis for plan programming. In this case, a programmatic framework described by Winston and Anchors (1993) provides the structure for these examples.

Cognitive Learning. Verbal skills: residence hall newsletter, radio station, library. Rationality: hall government and judicial board. Esthetic appreciation: art collection or contest, painting of murals, talent show, photo contest, darkroom. Intellectual tolerance: speakers' series, international living learning center.

Emotional and Moral Discipline. Psychological well-being: counselor in residence, structured group experiences. Religious interests: consultation with campus ministers; Citizenship: student government, community volunteer projects, fund raising projects for charities. Personal self-discovery: assessments conducted and interpreted by counselors in residence.

Practical Competence. Health: wellness programs, exercise and dance facilities, diet and nutrition workshops. Leisure skills: various workshops and programs, outdoor recreation programs, clubs. Practical affairs: cooperative residence hall, service projects, volunteer programs.

By no means is this list of categories or programs complete, but it provides ideas of how student development can be fostered through residential programs. Every example has been implemented in residence halls under the supervision of the author. By tying the goals of programs to developmental outcomes, a richness of meaning is given to the residential living experience. This meaning, in turn, differentiates living in campus residence halls from living in off campus facilities.

A Practical Example. Tom is a freshman who lives in Greene Hall. He has chosen a major in finance but has no practical experience handling the funds of an organization. Sally, the Greene Hall director, knows that the hall council's former treasurer resigned because she took an RA job at the last minute and is aware of Tom's concern about having no practical experience in handling an organization's funds. Sally suggests to Tom that he apply to the Hall Executive Council to become the treasurer. At the next meeting, the Hall Executive Council interviews the candidates and selects Tom. Tom spends the balance of the year as the Hall Council Treasurer gaining the practical experience he lacked.

In this example, Sally works with Tom in identifying an area where he needs to improve his skills. This can be framed by applying Chickering and Reisser's theory of psychosocial development. The first vector, Developing Competence, has three elements: (1) intellectual competence, (2) physical and manual competence, and (3) interpersonal competence (Chickering & Reisser, 1993). Tom's work as treasurer will improve his intellectual competence by engaging in active learning as the treasurer.

Other more complex examples of applying student development theory occur virtually on a daily basis in the residential setting. Student development theory helps residence hall staff understand how students change and grow, and serves as a guide in structuring interventions. Whether the presenting circumstance is simple or complex, student development theory can be extremely useful in framing educational responses in helping students learn.

THE INFLUENCE OF RESIDENCE HALLS ON STUDENTS

Numerous studies have been conducted to determine the influence of residence hall living on students. Evidence reported in these studies and published over a 25-year period concluded that students benefit substantially from living in campus residence halls.

Chickering (1974) compared commuting students with resident students and found that while resident students start from a favored position compared to commuters, the residential experience accelerates the differences between these two groups. Such factors as family background, finances, and high school academic record distinguish resident students from commuters. "Commuters and residents begin their college careers with an unequal start which strongly favors the residents. The gap between them grows. Residents have access to, find and are forced to encounter diverse experience and persons who spurt them on their way" (Chickering, 1974, p. 85).

Another example of research on this question is found in the work of Astin. In 1985, he concluded, "simply by virtue of eating, sleeping, and spending their waking hours in the college campus, residential students stand a better chance than do commuter students of developing a strong identification with and attachment to undergraduate life" (1985, p. 145).

More recent studies reiterate the benefits of residential living to students. Pascarella and Terenzini (1991) concluded,

Residential living is positively, if modestly, linked to increases in aesthetic, cultural, and intellectual values; a liberalizing of social, political, and religious values and attitudes; increases in self-concept, intellectual orientation, autonomy, and independence; gains in tolerance, empathy, and ability to relate to others; persistence in college; and bachelor's degree attainment. (p. 611)

Astin pointed to other benefits of living on campus, including "the attainment of the bachelor's degree, satisfaction with faculty, and willingness to re-enroll in the same college" (1993, p. 367).

Pascarella, Terenzini, & Blimling (1994) published what may be the most conclusive work that addresses the effect of living in residence halls on students. They asserted, "the evidence is clear that college and university residence halls, through the intellectual and interpersonal climate they foster, play a substantial role in the growth and development of students who live in them" (p. 43). More specifically, they pointed out that compared with their colleagues who lived at home and commuted to college, students who lived in residence halls:

1. Participate in a greater number of extracurricular, social, and cultural events on campus.
2. Interact more frequently with faculty and peers in informal settings.
3. Are significantly more satisfied with college and are more positive about the social and interpersonal environment of their campus.
4. Are more likely to persist and graduate from college.
5. Show significantly greater gains in such areas of psychosocial development as autonomy and inner-directedness, intellectual orientation and self-concept.
6. Demonstrate significantly greater increases in aesthetic, cultural, and intellectual values, social and political liberalism, and secularism (p. 39).

Why does the preponderance of evidence suggest that living on campus, be it in a residence hall, fraternity, or sorority house, has such a positive influence on students? There are several reasons. Applying Astin's theory of involvement as an interpretive framework, it is clear that by residing on campus, students have greater opportunities to become involved in campus life through leadership opportunities, recreational sports, and cultural activities. These opportunities ultimately are translated into greater student growth and development.

Additionally, the environment created in a campus residence contributes to student learning by providing opportunities for students to experience diversity, to be challenged by their peers, and to learn from one another. The responsibility of residence educators is to maximize the learning opportunities available and intentionally develop experiences designed to enrich students' experiences. That means finding ways of encouraging students to become involved with faculty, assume leadership positions, and participate in the myriad of activities and programs available both not only in the residence hall but also on the campus at-large. Chickering and Reisser summarized the effects of residential living on students this way: "By applying developmental principles in programming, governance, architectural design, size of units, and matching of students, college administrators can amplify the positive aspects of residential living" (1993, p. 276).

SELECTED LEGAL ISSUES

Early in a career in student affairs, one finds that the work environment is full of challenges, some of which may not be settled anywhere other than in a court of law. Students, parents, and others will hold staff legally responsible for their decisions and actions (Owens, 1984). In light of the preceding, a brief introduction to several legal issues follows.

Staff must understand that they should not function as their own attorney. When legal advice is needed, it should be sought through appropriate channels on campus (Barr, 1996). The campus may have an office of legal counsel, or it may have an attorney on retainer. Regardless, when it is concluded that legal advice is needed, do not hesitate to use your campus protocol for seeking advice!

It is also important to realize the difference in working in a public institution or a private/independent institution. Public institutions are more fully regulated than private institutions, and those working in public institutions are more fully constrained by the federal constitution than those employed in private institutions (Kaplin & Lee, 1995). The Fourteenth Amendment to the U.S. Constitution prescribes that states must respect all the rights of citizens outlined in the Constitution; this amendment does not apply to private citizens or institutions (Young, 1984). Consequently, private institutions have more latitude in promulgating rules and regulations, and while due process in disciplinary situations is absolutely guaranteed in public institutions, private institutions are not held to the same standard (Kaplin & Lee, 1995).

FIRE AND SAFETY PROCEDURES

Perhaps the greatest danger to the safety of students living in a residence hall is fire (Schuh, 1984). Most states have laws and regulations regarding firefighting equipment, smoke detectors, fire drills, and the like, so it is critical that residence life staff become conversant with these laws and regulations—and follow them explicitly. Routine inspections should be held and staff should work closely with physical plant personnel to ensure that all equipment is functional. Failure to engage in these safety procedures will result in tremendous legal exposure to the campus.

Additionally, if the campus is located in a high-crime area or there is concern that students' physical safety may be threatened, resident students should be informed of ways to minimize such risks as soon as they move into a residence hall. As criminal acts occur on the campus or in the residence halls, "schools are required to provide timely warning of the occurrences of crimes that are reported to campus security authorities and local police agencies" (Office of Postsecondary Education, n.d.).

PHYSICAL FACILITIES

Usually at inopportune times (late at night or during the weekend), something will happen to render physical facilities inoperable or dangerous. This could be anything from an elevator breaking down to a violent act of weather resulting in making the physical facility unusable. No one can predict with absolute certainty when a snowstorm, heavy rain, or lightning strike will ravage the campus. During times such as these, resident staff will need to take steps to make sure that students are protected from injury or possibly death.

When a resident staff person becomes aware of a problem, it should be reported to the appropriate individual and repairs be made. To protect staff and the institution, make sure that potential problems such as icy sidewalks or slippery hallways are addressed immediately. Anticipate problems that might arise such as an elevator that has been balky for the past day or two, and report any problems as soon as they are discovered. To protect the institution, "Documented, periodic inspections with follow-up maintenance requests are essential in avoiding negligence" (Gehring, 1993, p. 363).

DUTY TO WARN THE VICTIM OF A THREAT

One must accept the duty to warn a potential victim of a threat. A landmark case that addresses this point is *Tarasoff v. Regents of the University of California* (1976), which involved an individual threatening to do harm to a student who was away from the campus. When the student returned, she was murdered. The court found that the person receiving the information concerning the threat had an obligation to warn the potential victim. If this kind of information is received, even if the information is supposed to be confidential, the intended victim should be notified as well as campus or local police departments. The concept of privileged communication rarely is extended to student affairs practitioners, and staff are held responsible if a potential victim is not warned and becomes a victim.

PROGRAM SUPERVISION

A wide variety of programs occur in or are sponsored by the residence halls. Most require little or no risk on the part of participants. Some programs, however, require a certain amount of participant skill or involve the consumption of alcoholic beverages. In these two instances, the risk of problems occurring increases.

For programs requiring participants to master certain skills or the use of complicated equipment, the most successful strategy for the program planner is to consult a person on campus who has expertise in the skill area, or in the use of the equipment, and to follow industry standards scrupulously (Dunkel & Schuh, 1998). For example, when developing an excursion program involving mountain climbing, someone in the physical education department should be contacted to learn how best to prepare participants for the activity. An expert consultant might be hired to help with the supervision of the activity as well. Activities involving trampolines, skateboards, amateur boxing, or tugs-of-war need to be planned with great care since serious injuries might result (Miller & Schuh, 1981). Additionally, any activity involving water sports should be supervised by an individual holding a current Red Cross certification as a lifeguard.

Activities involving alcohol can result in tragedy, especially if automobiles are involved in transporting students to and from an event where alcohol will be consumed. A prudent strategy is to hire licensed, public carriers to provide transportation whenever alcohol is part of an event off campus.

To minimize risk, be knowledgeable about state laws. If students are under the legal drinking age, they should not be allowed to consume alcoholic beverages. The institution should never be a part of sponsoring illegal activities. As mentioned previously, transportation should be provided through common carriers such as buses. The amount of alcohol purchased should be realistic. Planners should purchase an amount that will be commensurate with the number of participants anticipated. Food and alternative beverages should be provided. Before planning an event at which alcoholic beverages will be available, the campus alcohol information center or health center should be consulted for information about program planning with alcohol.

Simply getting up in the morning and going to work involves some risks. The key to protecting oneself, students, and the institution is to employ risk management strategies that minimize the likelihood of potential risks becoming real disasters.

PROFESSIONAL ASSOCIATIONS

Several professional organizations extend membership to residence hall staff. Among the objectives of professional organizations are

> To advance understanding, recognition, and knowledge in the field; to develop and promulgate standards for professional practice; to inform the public on key issues; to simulate and organize volunteerism; and to serve the public

interest; and to provide professionals with a peer group that promotes a sense of identity. (Nuss, 2000, p. 493)

The primary professional association comprised of housing officers, defined as any person who works with student housing on campus, and in some cases off campus, is the Association of College and University Housing Officers-International (ACUHO-I). ACUHO-I was organized in 1949 at the University of Illinois and membership is by institution. Thus, all members of a housing department that holds membership in ACUHO-I are eligible to participate in the organization's activities and use ACUHO-I's services. Ten regional associations sponsor conferences in addition to the annual ACUHO-I conference and the association has expanded its presence in Europe and Asia. The ACUHO-I annual conference is held in the summer, typically in either June or July.

The American College Personnel Association (ACPA) is another professional organization that has a direct interest in student housing through its Commission III. Commission III is comprised of ACPA members responsible for student housing, residence hall programs, staffing issues, and so on. Membership in ACPA is on an individual basis and no additional fees are charged for commission affiliation.

In addition, professional development opportunities are offered by state groups or associations affiliated with ACPA. Typically, they will offer an annual statewide conference or drive-in workshops for members. ACPA's annual conference is held in March.

Housing officers also may hold membership in the National Association of Student Personnel Administrators (NASPA). Membership in NASPA is both individual and by institution. Although sometimes perceived as an organization for senior student affairs officers, NASPA welcomes members regardless of their professional responsibilities. Its annual conference is held in March, and conferences within the seven NASPA regional associations also are scheduled throughout the year.

One other organization worthy of note, the National Association of College and University Residence Halls, Inc. (NACURH), is a student association designed to promote student involvement in college residence halls. NACURH holds national and regional conventions that are attended by students to improve their skills in student government and programming, and to strengthen networks with their colleagues regionally and nationally. Founded in 1954 at Iowa State University (NACURH, n.d.), NACURH's central office is located on the campus of the University of Florida in Gainesville.

THE FUTURE

What does the future hold for residence halls? Planning for developments as we move past the beginning of the twenty-first century is a challenge. The residence life staff of the future will be kept very busy dealing with evolving issues centering on community development; technology and academic support; program development and student learning; financial challenges; provision of services and facility development; and identifying staffing in the future and leadership challenges.

COMMUNITY DEVELOPMENT

More than likely, future students will view privacy as the norm, requesting and expecting to live in situations where they do not have roommates. The roommate model was adopted at a time in history when families included more children and sharing one's bedroom was the usual condition. Future students may not be willing to live in a situation where their privacy is limited.

When resident students live alone, more efforts will be required on the part of residence staff to encourage students to interact with each other. Isolation and alienation are possible consequences without programs and activities that encourage students to socialize and work together. The residence hall environment, in such a situation, could promote depression. Community building will be more difficult. Thus, strategies will have to be devised that motivate students to leave their individual living spaces and to spend time with others.

TECHNOLOGY AND ACADEMIC SUPPORT

The use of computers and cable television will continue to increase as teaching media. Necessary equipment should be provided to make it possible for students to learn in their rooms. Access to computing networks, libraries, and learning resource centers should be part of every student room. Cable television hookups in a student's room will be required and therein lies a danger. As each room becomes more of a locus of learning, the possibility of isolation and depression increases. Staff will need to bring students together in meaningful ways in an effort to fight depression, isolation, and boredom, plus encourage them to engage in collaborative learning experiences (Bosworth & Hamilton, 1994).

Obviously residence halls are expected to provide more academic support facilities. Libraries, computer labs, offices for academic advisers, and classroom space will all be very much a part of future residence halls. As more classes are offered in residence halls, students should be encouraged to form study groups and may be assigned to specific residence halls based on their prospective major or area of career interest. Clearly, the continuing development of learning communities is an element of the future of residence halls. Some of these activities are already a part of residence hall responsibilities; however, it is clear that increasingly they will also be part of the future.

PROGRAM DEVELOPMENT AND STUDENT LEARNING EXPERIENCES

Linked with greater academic opportunities will be a strong emphasis on providing programs to allow faculty and students to interact in the residential situation. As concerns about greater isolation of students are defined, one way to respond to these feelings is to design programs that facilitate more faculty and student interaction. This may require increasing or expanding faculty fellow programs, faculty/student research projects, learning communities, and perhaps additional faculty-in-residence or guests-in-residence positions.

Demonstrating student learning also will be a challenge for the future. The Student Learning Imperative (ACPA, 1994) reminds us "Student affairs professionals must seize the moment by affirming student learning and personal development as the primary goals of undergraduate education" (p. 4). It is highly likely that future residence halls will be full partners in enriching the learning environment on campus and that administrators will be called upon routinely to demonstrate the influence of the residential experience on student growth (Upcraft & Schuh, 1996).

Participation in residence hall student government is becoming more complicated. Student government budgets are now larger and the demands placed on student government leaders by their constituents and university administrators make service in student government less appealing. Moreover, substantial numbers of students work to pay their college bills and may not have time for student government responsibilities. In fact, the percentage of students who worked increased from 71 percent in 1995–1996 to 74 percent in 1999–2000 (King & Bannon, 2002). Incentives must be developed to attract students to become involved in student government leadership positions. Combining a room assignment and providing an office may be one arrangement. Perhaps a scholarship program could be established to assist those student government leaders who must forgo part-time work because of their responsibilities. The point is, student government service is becoming a burden to students, and mechanisms should be found to make involvement in this type of activity more attractive.

FINANCIAL CHALLENGES, SERVICES, AND FACILITIES

On some campuses, occupancy rates of residence halls and associated financial concerns will be a problem for administrators. Many residence hall systems were designed to resolve a housing shortage caused by the attendance of the baby boom generation, creating a current oversupply of capacity. Competition with off-campus housing developments is causing problems at some institutions, especially when off-campus accommodations are newer and more luxurious. As a result, we may be very close to rather difficult financial times for many housing departments. Austere budget management will be the normal operating procedure for many institutions in the foreseeable future.

One solution to financial problems may lie in the privatization of residence halls, or at least in forming partnerships with private developers. On many campuses, partnerships have been formed with private companies to construct residence halls, or in some situations they may construct and manage residence halls. Generally, this approach removes some of the financial exposure of the residence hall operations from the campus, but it also means that the institution loses control other than what the contract with the company provides. Nonetheless, privatization may be a trend that becomes increasingly more common in future years.

It is entirely possible that students of the future will demand more services. Academic support activities have been identified earlier in this section, but we may also be moving into a closer relationship with off-campus vendors to provide services to our students. These might include convenience markets and coffee shops (if the students do not operate them as a student government or service project), barbershops and beauty salons, and dry cleaning, for example. As these kinds of services are added to the auxiliary enterprises portfolio, administrators will need to be careful not to create problems for the institution in its relationships with local businesses. One approach is to operate the new service as a concession under contract to a private firm rather than the institution operating the business by itself. A number of colleges and universities already use this approach in providing food services, bookstores, and banking services. Students will expect more recreational facilities, including aerobics rooms, exercise areas, and weight rooms. Instead of regarding these as amenities or luxuries, administrators might be better served by considering them essential to the well-equipped residence hall.

Many residence halls were built to provide housing to accommodate the baby boom generation, now the parents of incoming students. As a result, these facilities in many cases are old, tired, and perhaps obsolete. Renovation is a tremendous financial challenge facing housing officers. Blimling (1993) characterized it this way,

> After thirty years or more of service, even with good maintenance, most buildings should be renovated. . . . To find the funds, room rental charges have to be increased, fund reserves depleted, or money appropriated from educational programming funds. None of these are appealing options (pp. 11–12).

Of course, one other option is to raze residence halls that have no debt service and construct new facilities. As challenging as it was for residence hall administrators in 1965 to predict the needs of entering students in 2000, consider the challenges of predicting residence hall plans today to meet students' technological needs in 2035!

While students demand an environment free of regulations and supervision, they also expect to be safe and secure in their residence facility. It is difficult to provide these dimensions simultaneously since a natural tension exists between a lack of supervision and the presence of safety. In the final analysis, issues related to crime and security will continue to become more difficult in the future. "Residence life professionals must move campus security issues to a higher priority within their organizations and attack the problem aggressively" (Janosik, 1993, p. 514). Palmer (1998, p. 121) warns, however, "no single strategy or set of strategies for addressing violence in student residences will be effective at all institutions." While technology can be used to deal with this issue in some respects, such as installing keyless door locks and television cameras to monitor hallways, institutions often have chosen not to address safety and security issues as forthrightly as they should.

STAFFING AND LEADERSHIP CHALLENGES

Staffing itself might be a problem in the future. Anecdotal evidence suggests that live-in positions increasingly are unattractive to individuals who have completed their master's degrees for a variety of reasons, including lack of privacy and inability to have a normal work routine. Finding individuals to fill professional staff positions in residence halls is likely to be a continuing challenge for senior residence hall administrators and may require the development of alternative staffing models.

Finally, residence hall staff of the future will be faced with a variety of challenges. On the one hand, they will have to carefully market their facilities because of the competition created by off-campus housing developments for traditional college students. On the other hand, they will have to be prepared to work with students who are not accustomed to sharing living space. These students may see little value in leaving the relative comfort of their single rooms with their computer and television and thus may be less likely to participate in student activities. Special skills will be necessary for residence staff members to handle their responsibilities effectively. The challenge, then, seems to be to identify ways that staff can stay current, facilities can remain attractive, and students can find the living experience satisfying. Residence hall systems meeting these challenges will be recognized as pacesetters in the twenty-first century.

TECHNOLOGY RESOURCES

The following web sites provide useful information related to residence halls:

1. The web site for the National Association of College and University Residence Halls is www.nacurh.org.
2. The web site for ACUHO-I is www.acuho.ohio-state.edu.
3. ACPA's web site is www.acpa.nche.edu.
4. NASPA's web site is located at www.naspa.org.

REFERENCES

American College Personnel Association (ACPA). (1994). *The student learning imperative: Implications for student affairs.* Washington, DC: Author.

American Association for Higher Education, American College Personnel Association, & National Association of Student Personnel Administrators. (1998). *Powerful partnerships: A shared responsibility for learning.* Washington, DC: Authors.

Appleton, J. R., Briggs, C. M., & Rhatigan, J. J. (1978). *Pieces of eight.* Portland, OR: NASPA.

Astin, A. W. (1985). *Achieving educational excellence.* San Francisco: Jossey-Bass.

Astin, A. W. (1993). *What matters in college.* San Francisco: Jossey-Bass.

Banning, J. H. (1989). Creating a climate for successful student development: The campus ecology manager role. In U. Delworth, G. R. Hanson, & Associates, *Student services: A handbook for the profession* (2nd ed.) (pp. 304–322). San Francisco: Jossey-Bass.

Barr, M. J. (1996). Legal foundations of student affairs practice. In S. R. Komives, D. B. Woodard Jr., & Associates, *Student services: A handbook for the profession* (3rd ed.) (pp. 126–144). San Francisco: Jossey-Bass.

Barr, M. J. (2000). *The importance of institutional mission.* In M. J. Barr, M. K. Desler, & Associates, *The handbook of student affairs administration* (2nd ed.) (pp. 25–36). San Francisco: Jossey-Bass.

Barr, M. J., & Cuyjet, M. J. (1991). Program development and implementation. In T. K. Miller, R. B. Winston Jr., & Associates, *Administration and leadership in student affairs* (pp. 707–733). Muncie, IN: Accelerated Development.

Black, R. J. (1993). Facilitating a positive relationship between housing and counseling center staff. *Journal of College Student Development, 34,* 441–442.

Blimling, G. S. (1993). New challenges and goals for residential life programs. In R. B. Winston, Jr., S. Anchors, & Associates, *Student housing and residential life* (pp. 1–20). San Francisco: Jossey-Bass.

Bosworth, K., & Hamilton, S. J. (1994). Editor's notes. In Authors (Eds.), *Collaborative learning: Underlying processes and technologies.* (New Directions for Teaching and Learning Sourcebook, No. 59, pp. 1–3). San Francisco: Jossey-Bass.

Brubacher, J. S., & Rudy, W. (1958). *Higher education in transition.* New York: Harper.

Brubacher, J. S., & Rudy, W. (1976). *Higher education in transition* (3rd ed.). New York: Harper.

Chickering, A. W. (1974). *Commuting versus resident students.* San Francisco: Jossey-Bass.

Chickering, A. W., & Reisser, L. (1993). *Education and identity* (2nd ed.). San Francisco: Jossey-Bass.

Claar, J., & Cuyjet, M. (2000). Program planning and implementation. In M. J. Barr, M. K. Desler, & Associates, *The handbook of student affairs administration* (2nd ed.) (pp. 197–215). San Francisco: Jossey-Bass.

Cohen, A. M. (1998). *The shaping of American higher education: Emergence and growth of the contemporary system.* San Francisco: Jossey-Bass.

Council for the Advancement of Standards in Higher Education. (2001). *The book of professional standards for higher education.* Washington, DC: Author.

Cowley, W. H. (1934). The history of student residential housing. *School and Society, 40(1040, 1041),* 705–712, 758–764.

Dunkel, N. W., & Schuh, J. H. (1998). *Advising student groups and organizations.* San Francisco: Jossey-Bass.

Engstrom, C. M., & Kruger, K. W. (1997). Editors' notes. In Authors (Eds.), Using technology to promote student learning: Opportunities today and tomorrow. (New Directions for Student Services Sourcebook, No. 78, pp. 1–3). San Francisco: Jossey-Bass.

Fairbrook, P. (1993). Food services and programs. In R. B. Winston, Jr., S. Anchors, & Associates. *Student housing and residential life* (pp. 232–247). San Francisco: Jossey-Bass.

Fenske, R. H. (1980a). Historical foundations. In U. Delworth & G. R. Hanson (Eds.), *Student services: A handbook for the profession* (pp. 3–24). San Francisco: Jossey-Bass.

Fenske, R. H. (1980b). Current trends. In U. Delworth & G. R. Hanson (Eds.), *Student services: A handbook for the profession* (pp. 45–72). San Francisco: Jossey-Bass.

Frederiksen, C. F. (1993). A brief history of collegiate housing. In R. B. Winston, Jr., S. Anchors, & Associates, *Student housing and residential life* (pp. 167–183). San Francisco: Jossey-Bass.

Geiger, R. L. (1997). Research, graduate education, and the ecology of American universities: An interpretive history. In L. F. Goodchild & H. S. Wechsler (Eds.), *The history of higher education* (2nd ed.) (pp. 273–289). Boston, MA: Pearson.

Gehring, D. D. (1993). Legal and regulatory concerns. In R. B. Winston, Jr., S. Anchors, & Associates, *Student housing and residential life* (pp. 344–369). San Francisco: Jossey-Bass.

Huba, M., McFadden, M., & Epperson. (n.d.). *Final Report of ISU Undergraduate Education Survey 2000: A Comparison of Learning Community Participants and Non-participants.* Ames, IA: Iowa State University, Office of the Vice Provost for Undergraduate Programs. Downloaded May 29, 2002. http://www.vpundergraduate.iastate.edu/new.html

James, E. J. (1917). College residence halls. *The Journal of Home Economics, IX(3),* 101–108.

Janosik, S. M. (1993). Dealing with criminal conduct and other deleterious behaviors. In R. B. Winston Jr., S. Anchors, & Associates, *Student housing and residential life* (pp. 501–516). San Francisco: Jossey-Bass.

Kaplin, W. A., & Lee, B. A. (1995). *The law of higher education* (3rd ed.). San Francisco: Jossey-Bass.

King, T., & Bannon, E. (2002). *At what cost? The price working students pay for a college education.* Washington, DC: The State PIRGs' Higher Education Project.

Kuh, G. D., Schuh, J. H., & Whitt, E. J. (1991). *Involving colleges.* San Francisco: Jossey-Bass.

Kuh, G. D. (1996). Guiding principles for creating seamless learning environments for undergraduates. *Journal of College Student Development, 37,* 135–148.

Lenning, O. T., & Ebbers, L. H. (1999). *The powerful potential of learning communities: Improve education for the future.* ASHE-ERIC Report (Vol. 26, No. 6.) Washington, DC: The George Washington University, Graduate School of Education and Human Development.

Levine, A., & Cureton, J. S. (1998). *When hope and fear collide.* San Francisco: Jossey-Bass.

Lucas, C. J. (1994). *American higher education: A history.* New York: St. Martin's.

Lyons, J. W. (1993). The importance of institutional mission. In M. J. Barr & Associates, *The handbook of student affairs administration* (pp. 1 – 15). San Francisco: Jossey-Bass.

McClellan, G. S., & Barr, M. J. (2000). Planning, managing, and financing facilities and services. In M. J. Barr, M. K. Desler, & Associates, *The handbook of student affairs administration* (2nd ed.) (pp. 197–215). San Francisco: Jossey-Bass.

Meyer, L. D., & Schuh, J. H. (2001). Evaluating a learning community: The story of ACES. *The Journal of College and University Student Housing, 29(2),* 45–51.

Miller, T. E., & Schuh, J. H. (1981). Managing the liability risks of residence hall administrators. *Journal of College Student Personnel, 23,* 136–139.

Mills, D. B., & Barr, M. J. (1990). Private versus public institutions: How do financial issues compare? In J. S. Schuh (Ed.), *Financial management for student affairs administrators* (pp. 21–38). Alexandria, VA: ACPA.

Moore, K. M. (1997). Freedom and constraint in eighteenth century Harvard. In L. S. Goodchild & H. S. Wechsler (Eds.), *The history of higher education* (2nd ed.) (pp. 108–114). ASHE Reader Series. Boston, MA: Pearson.

Moore, M., & Delworth, U. (1976). *Training manual for student services program development.* Boulder, CO: WICHE.

Morrill, W. H., & Hurst, J. C. (1980). Preface. In W. H. Morrill & J. C. Hurst (Eds.), *Dimensions of intervention for student development,* (pp. ix–x). New York: John Wiley.

Morrill, W. H., Hurst, J. C., & Oetting, E. R. (1980). A conceptual model of intervention strategies. In W. H. Morrill & J. C. Hurst (Eds.), *Dimensions of intervention for student development* (pp. 85–95). New York: John Wiley.

Mosier, R. (1989). Health and wellness programs. In J. H. Schuh (Ed.), *Educational programming in college and university residence halls* (pp. 122–138). Columbus, OH: ACUHO-I.

Mueller, K. H. (1961). *Student personnel work in higher education.* Boston: Houghton Mifflin.

NACURH. (n.d.). History of NACURH, Inc. Downloaded May 29, 2002. http://www.nacurh.org/Guest/guests_purpose.html

Nuss, E. M. (2000). The role of professional associations. In M. J. Barr, M. K. Desler, & Associates, *The handbook of student affairs administration* (2nd ed.) (pp. 492–507). San Francisco: Jossey-Bass.

Office of Postsecondary Education. (n.d.). Campus crime and security at postsecondary education institutions homepage. Downloaded May 29, 2002, http://ope.ed.gov/security/

Owens, H. F. (1984). Preface. In H. F Owens (Ed.), *Risk management and the student affairs professional.* NASPA Monograph (No. 2, n.p.). NP: NASPA.

Palmer, C. J. (1998). Violence at home on campus. In A. M. Hoffman, J. H. Schuh, & R. H. Fenske (Eds.), *Violence on campus* (pp. 111–122). Gaithersburg, MD: Aspen.

Pascarella, E. T., & Terenzini, P. T. (199 1). *How college affects students.* San Francisco: Jossey-Bass.

Pascarella, E. T., Terenzini, P. T., & Blimling, G. S. (1994). The impact of residential life on students. In C. C. Schroeder, P. Mable, & Associates, *Realizing the educational potential of residence-halls* (pp. 22–52). San Francisco: Jossey-Bass.

Pike, G. R., Schroeder, C. C., & Berry, T. R. (1997). Enhancing the educational impact of residence halls: The relationship between residential learning communities and first-year college experiences and persistence. *Journal of College Student Development, 38*, 609–621.

Riker, H. C., & DeCoster, D. A. (1971). The educational role in student housing. *The Journal of College and University Student Housing, (1)*, 3–6.

Sandeen, A. (2001). Organizing student affairs divisions. In R. B. Winston Jr., D. G. Creamer, T. K. Miller, & Associates, *The professional student affairs administrator* (pp. 181–209). New York: Brunner-Routledge.

Schneider, L. D. (1977). Housing. In W. T Packwood (Ed.), *College student personnel services* (pp. 125–145). Springfield, IL: Charles C Thomas.

Schroeder, C. C. (1999). Forging educational partnerships that advance student learning. In G. S. Blimling, E. J. Whitt, & Associates, *Good practice in student affairs* (pp. 133–156). San Francisco: Jossey-Bass.

Schroeder, C. C., & Mable, P. (1994a). Realizing the educational potential of residence halls: A mandate for action. In C. C. Schroeder, P. Mable, & Associates, *Realizing the educational potential of residence-halls* (pp. 298–319). San Francisco: Jossey-Bass

Schroeder, C. C., & Mable, P. (1994b). Residence halls and the college experience: Past and Present. In C. C. Schroeder, P. Mable, & Associates, *Realizing the educational potential of residence-halls* (pp. 3–21). San Francisco: Jossey-Bass.

Schuh, J. H. (1984). The residential campus—high risk territory! In H. F. Owens (Ed.), *Risk management and the student affairs professional.* NASPA Monograph (No. 2, pp. 57–82). NP: NASPA.

Schuh, J. H., & Shipton, W. C. (1985). The residence hall resource team: Collaboration in counseling activities. *Journal of Counseling and Development, 63*, 380–381

Schuh, J. H., & Triponey, V. L. (1993). Fundamentals of program design. In R. B. Winston Jr., S. Anchors, & Associates, *Student housing and residential life* (pp. 423–442). San Francisco: Jossey-Bass.

Schuh , J. H., & Whitt, E. J. (Eds.). (1999). *Creating successful partnerships between academic and student affairs.* (New Directions for Student Services Sourcebook, No. 87). San Francisco: Jossey-Bass.

Statutes of Harvard, 1646. In L. S. Goodchild & H. S. Wechsler (Eds.), *The history of higher education* (2nd ed.) (pp. 125–126). ASHE Reader Series. Boston, MA: Pearson.

Stoner, K. L. (1992). Housing as an auxiliary enterprise. *The Journal of College and University Student Housing, 22(1)*, 16–21.

Tarasoff v. Regents of the University of California, 7, 551 P. 2d 3 34 (Cal. Sup. Ct., 1976).

Upcraft, M. L. (1989). Residence halls and campus activities. In M. L. Upcraft, J. N. Gardner, & Associates, *The freshman year experience* (pp. 142–155). San Francisco: Jossey-Bass.

Upcraft, M. L. (1993). Organizational and administrative approaches. In R. B. Winston, S. Anchors, & Associates, *Student housing and residential life* (pp. 189–202). San Francisco: Jossey-Bass.

Upcraft, M. L., & Schuh, J. H. (1996). *Assessment in student affairs.* San Francisco: Jossey-Bass.

Winston, R. B., Jr., & Anchors, S. (1993). Student development in the residential environment. In R. B. Winston Jr., S. Anchors, & Associates, *Student housing and residential life* (pp. 25–64). San Francisco: Jossey-Bass.

Winston, R. B. Jr., & Creamer, D. G. (1997). *Improving staffing practices in student affairs.* San Francisco: Jossey-Bass.

Winston, R. B. Jr., & Fitch, R. T. (1993). Paraprofessional staffing. In R. B. Winston Jr., S. Anchors, & Associates, *Student housing and residential life* (pp. 315–343). San Francisco: Jossey-Bass.

Young, D. P. (1984). The student/institutional relationship: A legal update. In H. F. Owens (Ed.), *Risk management and the student affairs professional.* NASPA Monograph (No. 2, pp. 15–31). NP: NASPA

Zeller, W. J., Kanz, K., & Schneiter, K. (1990). Creating partnerships with academic affairs to enhance the freshman year experience. *The Journal of College and University Student Housing, 20(l),* 14–17.

Zeller, W. J., & Mosier, R. (1993). Culture shock and the first-year experience. *The Journal of College and University Student Housing, 23(2),* 19–23.

Chapter 11

STUDENT ACTIVITIES

EDWARD G. WHIPPLE AND RENA K. MURPHY

HISTORY

Student activities have always been a part of college life; however, what constitutes "student activities" has taken different forms since the beginning of America's system of higher education history. Presently, students are able to choose from a variety of activities: lectures, films, social events, fraternity and sorority life, student organization involvement, student government participation, cultural programs, and artist series. From this assortment of activities, most students can find something to inspire their interests.

Early American higher education, however, did not offer students such an array of extracurricular activities. In colonial colleges, which focused on religion as the foundation of student life, student activities were driven by regular prayer, church attendance on the Sabbath, and activities influenced by the study of religion. As early as 1719 at Harvard University, groups of youths gathered to read poetry, discuss issues of life, and enjoy beer and tobacco. A movement away from more "pious" activities was attributed to the academic class system, a unique feature of American higher education, which perpetuated competition among students and led to hazing within certain types of student activities.

Horowitz (1987) described the beginning of college life, which originated in the late eighteenth and early nineteenth centuries as follows:

> All over the new nation, colleges experienced a wave of collective student uprising, led by the wealthier and worldlier undergraduates. College discipline conflicted with the genteel upbringing of the elite sons of Southern gentry and Northern merchants. Pleasure-seeking young men who valued style and openly pursued ambition rioted against college presidents and faculty determined to put them in their place. In every case, the outbreaks were forcibly suppressed; but the conflict went underground. Collegians withdrew from open confrontation to turn to covert forms of expression. They forged a peer consciousness sharply at odds with that of the faculty and of serious students and gave it institutional expression in the fraternity and club system (p. 11).

Among early student activities, the literary society played a major role in campus life until the latter part of the nineteenth century. The original purpose of these societies was to provide opportunities for public speaking and discussions of literature (particularly modern literature), political science, and history. These groups soon became competitive in nature and developed strong student loyalty. As literary societies grew, they took on different characteristics, depending on the students' family social status and rank. As more students joined these societies, college and university administrators recognized their importance to student life. Societies were correctly recognized as being more than a mere extracurricular phenomenon. They came to be the center of interest on the campus, a powerful student-financed and student-controlled educational enterprise that paralleled, some feared even threatened, the narrow and traditional classical academic program of the old-time college (Sack, 1961).

Literary societies eventually evolved into Greek letter organizations. The first national Greek letter organization, Phi Beta Kappa, was founded in 1776 at the College of William and Mary as essentially a literary society. Greek letter social organizations (fraternities) began with the Union Triad—Kappa Alpha Society (1825), Sigma Phi (1827), and Delta Phi Society (1827) (Anson & Marchesani, 1991). With increasing numbers of Greek letter social organizations appearing on college campuses, antagonism appeared on the part of many members of the campus communities. This antagonism and strife lessened after the Civil War. The period immediately preceding the Civil War and after saw the rise of women's Greek letter social organizations (sororities) as well as the rise of professional fraternities in fields such as medicine, law, and engineering.

Student government associations and boards began during the days of early Greek letter social organizations in the early nineteenth century. At the University of Virginia, Thomas Jefferson believed that students needed to be motivated by pride and ambition rather than by fear. He supported a student governing board to enforce university regulations, a function that had previously been a faculty responsibility. His plan was not successful because of the state legislature's failure to establish the proposed governing board, the inability of the Virginia students to handle the responsibility, and the honor code that bound many of the students from providing evidence against each other (Brubacher & Rudy, 1976; 1997).

After the Civil War, literary societies declined in importance as other forms of student organizations and athletics grew in popularity. Literary societies finally declined as institutions' curricula were expanding. More pronounced after the Civil War was the emergence of a "different" America:

> Students came to represent a broader group than heretofore and some of them were lacking in any serious intellectual or preprofessional interest. Others were coming to college mainly as a prelude to an active career in business and finance. This was the era of the emergence of modern America,

when strong-willed entrepreneurs were constructing a vast industrial plant and creating the economic basis for a complex urban society. The goals that were being pursued by the ambitious young men of the country were, more than in ante-bellum times, predominantly materialist, tangible, pragmatic ones. The attitude of such young people was very often likely to be one of profound anti-intellectualism (Brubacher & Rudy, 1976, p. 120).

This anti-intellectualism quickly provided an atmosphere on campus for the emergence of clubs, fraternities, intercollegiate athletics, and publications. In many cases, these activities were based on a philosophy antithetical to the institution's academic mission. In addition, a more radical student government movement was emerging at various campuses. At Vanderbilt, Pennsylvania, and Chicago, student committees were set up to maintain order in the dormitories. At Princeton, Vermont, Virginia, Wesleyan, and Bates, groups of student advisors were formed to consult with the faculty on a variety of matters. The Universities of Illinois and Maine even delegated responsibilities for disciplinary concerns to a body of students. These events served as the catalyst for the student council movement of the twentieth century (Brubacher & Rudy, 1976; 1997).

Also after the Civil War, faculty tended to "pull in" and not be as concerned with student life outside the classroom. With faculty hesitant to become involved with students, the fraternity became a natural place for socializing. These organizations tended to meet developmental needs not being met by the literary societies and toward the end of the nineteenth century, also provided living accommodations. For students who attended strict religious institutions, Greek letter social organizations provided a release from rules and regulations pertaining to behavior. Also, the fact that fraternities and sororities were secret in nature was appealing to students who sought to challenge college authorities (Brubacher & Rudy, 1976, p. 128).

As the country moved into the twentieth century, students not interested in fraternity or sorority life, or who could not afford it, established other types of student organizations. Thus, campus life took on a different focus with the emergence of non-secret organizations. These included clubs, which were academic in nature—English, foreign language, and history— and included faculty membership. Other clubs governed solely by students such as religious groups, music interest clubs, and special sports clubs, were also started.

The first student union facility was constructed at the University of Pennsylvania in 1896. As the campus community saw the importance of the student union and the activities associated with it, the number of unions built after World War I increased rapidly (Stevens, 1969). Along with the buildings came various programming efforts designed to meet the needs of the institution and surrounding community. Campus unions attempted to develop activities, which were tied to the academic mission of the institution. These activities included cultural events, speakers' series, lectures, and music events. The union truly became, on many campuses, the "living room" or "hearthstone" of the institution (Packwood, 1977).

After World War I, administrators were concerned about the lack of connection between the extracurricular aspect of student life and the academic mission of the particular institution. There was a concerted effort on the part of the administration and faculty to integrate the two:

> As administrators shifted from confrontation to accommodation, they officially recognized student organizations . . . as deans of men and women cooperated with leaders of student societies in planning events and enforcing codes of conduct, the apparent distinctions between institutional goals and those of college life faded (Horowitz, 1987, p. 119).

Prior to World War II, administrators worked to more clearly define the goals of students' activities. The importance of the college environment, particularly as it impacted the students' education, was being recognized. With the return of the GIs from World War II, the complexion of college and university campuses changed dramatically. Increases in the number of women and older men provided new opportunities for student activities. Fraternity and sorority life was dominant as it retained its commitment to achievement in college life (Horowitz, 1987). During the 1960s, with the decline of *in loco parentis*, institutional priorities changed the relationship between the institution and its students. Extreme cultural currents, the civil rights movement, and new left radical groups all influenced the college campus. These movements provided an air of student independence on campuses. Thus, students became more autonomous in choosing their programs, both in and out of the classroom. For example, the need to associate in traditional student activities, such as a fraternity, sorority, or student government, became unpopular. Consequently, membership nationally declined in traditional student activities programs, particularly the Greek letter social organizations.

The evolution of graduate student personnel preparation programs in the late 1960s and early 1970s also influenced student activities. Professionally prepared student affairs practitioners worked with students to promote campus environments with more positive working relationships among faculty, staff, and students. During this period of change, faculty became involved in student organization advising, special interest clubs flourished, residence halls became more attuned to the living-learning environment, and student unions provided well-designed programs covering a variety of extracurricular areas. Leadership and volunteerism also emerged as popular out-of-class activities for students.

During the 1980s, the college campus became much more diverse than ever before. Numbers of older students, international students, minorities, women, and veterans caused changes in how student affairs professionals provide student activities. Since the 1990s and into the twenty-first century, higher education is still facing the challenges of changing student demographics that were apparent in the 1980s. After the conservative movement of the 1980s and the students' focus on a career and salary, it appears that more students are attempting to balance their collegiate experience with their noncareer involvement. Higher education is also experiencing a shift in focus in the classroom from teaching toward student learning. This new focus has also spread into the planning of cocurricular activities as evidenced by American College Personnel Association's publication of the Student Learning Imperative (1994) and National Association for Student Personnel Administrator's production of its Reasonable Expectations (Kuh et al., 1995). Both documents were fashioned as guides for student affairs professionals in creating conditions to improve student learning. Student affairs professionals and academicians are currently looking at collaborative ways to enhance the overall educational experience for this increasingly diverse student population (Komives, Woodard, & Associates, 1996).

Today, as in the past, the opportunity for participation in extracurricular activities is seen by many employers as important to future success in the job market. For whatever reason, many students are seeking ways through student activities to enhance their academic experience.

DEFINITION

Student activities traditionally encompass out-of-class programs, including student organization advising, leadership development, student union programming, Greek letter social organizations, student government, and special institutional events (e.g., homecoming and family weekend). In addition, many campuses have a student programming organization, often connected with the student union, to plan events such as cultural programs, concerts, or a speakers' series. The array of opportunities for programs is great and varies from campus to campus. Higher education literature, however, does not provide for a definition of student activities. Instead it identifies specific objectives for a student activities program. For example, Mueller (1961) stated that a student's development is enhanced by activities that are successful in "complementing classroom instruction or enhancing academic learning; developing social interaction; providing for a profitable use of leisure time; and encouraging better values and higher standards" (p. 275). Miller (1982) suggested that the primary responsibility of student affairs professionals is to assist students in their personal growth, development, and education. Much of this education includes learning how "to learn, cope, lead, follow, solve problems, make decisions, relate to others, handle stress, and otherwise effectively function in an increasingly complex world" (pp. 10–11). Successful student activities programs today still encompass these objectives, which enhance learning outside the classroom, facilitate relationship and community building, encourage social interaction, and promote a value-based developmental experience.

Traditional student activities programs are not in demand as they once were. Today's college students are more focused on careers and financial concerns than ever before. Student participation in personal activities and special interest groups continues to grow at the expense of more traditional, organized activities such as student government, Greek letter social organizations, and student union programming. More students are engaged in activities that have a direct impact on their job opportunities and future careers.

Given the magnitude and variety of today's campus programming, a more comprehensive definition of student activities and student life is in order. Pike's (2000) updated definition adds a slightly different spin with the following: "Student life focuses on all students and is committed to having them learn, among other things, university traditions through which they develop a sense of community and commitment to the university" (p. 16). Pike suggested that institutions enhance student learning by making connections between what students learn and the community (including campus, local, national, and international) in which they live. Programs such as these help to ground student learning into something tangible that students experience each and every day. Such programs can be both student-sponsored and sponsored in conjunction with faculty, administration, and community members. During the last decade, students' interests have turned more toward service and volunteer work, both on the campus and in the community.

NEED

Involvement in student activities is crucial to the development and growth of students. Student activities, according to Miller and Jones (1981), are an essential part of students' educational development. By participating in student organizations, students acquire a variety of skills that are transferable from one setting to another. Dunkel and Schuh (1988) defined transferable skills as being "related to people, data, and things in a generalizable or transferable fashion (e.g., from one field, profession, occupation, or job to another)" (p. 119). Pascarella and Terenzini (1991) concluded that personal development and learning are enhanced when students are involved in educationally purposeful extracurricular activities. These might include situations in which students utilize their conflict mediation and time management skills to effectively complete a task.

Chickering and Reisser (1993) stressed the development of the whole student and the importance of educating the intellectual, social, emotional, and physical aspects of college students. A thorough understanding of students, their developmental needs, and the value of involvement is crucial.

Staff must be directed toward students' needs and development in order to provide meaningful programs. They must have the resources to assess and enhance programs. In addition, an identified educational philosophy should define the thematic rationale of activities, not a single activity or program. Within that rationale, activities should be designed to meet the programming goals of a variety of populations (Mills, 1989).

PURPOSES

The Council for the Advancement of Standards (CAS) for Campus Activities (2001) stated, "the campus activities program must complement the institution's academic programs. . . . [It] must enhance the overall educational experiences of students through development of, exposure to, and participation in social, cultural, multicultural, intellectual, recreational, community service, and campus governance programs" (p. 50). The mission of the CAS Standards encourages student activities programs to operate in an environment that focuses on development in areas that expand to the campus community and society; to provide for individual growth, both cognitively and affectively; to experience diversity in its many forms; to be informed about the institutional spirit; and to work toward providing leadership learning opportunities.

Research has focused on the "learning purpose" of involvement in student activities. For example, student activities can aid in values development. Programming strategies can be designed to provide students with values and growth opportunities (Brock, 1991). Student activities can also assist students in clarifying ethical decision making. Ethical systems that reflect different leadership values and contents may be integrated into leadership training modules and used as a basis for what students need to learn while practicing ethical leadership (Boatman & Adams, 1992).

Thus, student activities are not merely a respite from the classroom. Effective activities programming provides its own classroom through building a comprehensive campus community. "When we talk about community in higher education, we usually are referring to a broad vision for campus life that allows students to learn, grow, and develop to their best potential in a challenging yet safe environment" (Maul, 1993, p. 2). Student learning, leadership development, and campus and community involvement are all enhanced when the purposes of student activities are understood and incorporated into a comprehensive program.

ADMINISTRATION OF STUDENT ACTIVITIES

Student activities administration takes different forms, depending on an institution's mission, history, size, student demographics, funding levels, and public or private status. Common emphases, however, are found in many activities programs. These include student organization advising, leadership education, student union activities and programming, concerts, speakers' series, Greek affairs, and all campus special events. Also, on many campuses student government advising functions are found in the student activities administrative organization.

There is no common or preferred model for administering student activities (McKaig & Policello, 1979). What is crucial, however, in determining the administrative organization is the assurance that it meets the needs of a particular campus student population. An activities program, broad in scope and with a variety of offerings, enhances student retention and increases student satisfaction (Upcraft, 1985). The key to providing programs that aid in retention is the ability to effectively administer the programs.

Student activities program planners must offer programs that reflect the priorities of the student affairs organization and the institution. Styles (1985) indicated that effective program planners should pay particular attention to specific areas that impact effective programming: research, assessing special populations' needs, balancing bureaucracies, managing power and influence, internal evaluation, and accountability.

A major factor that determines the focus of a student activities program is whether the program is tied to the institution's student union. If there is a link, the administration of the student activities program most likely would be handled using a central staffing pattern. If a link does not exist, specific programs may be the responsibility of other student affairs offices, such as a dean of students office or office of student life. Depending on the size of the institution, the staff member responsible for directing student activities may report to the senior student affairs officer, or in cases where the activities program is part of the union operation, may report to the director of the union. Four sample organization models follow.

PRIVATE LIBERAL ARTS INSTITUTION OF 1,600 STUDENTS

The administrator responsible for student activities carries the title of director of student activities and the union, and reports to the senior student affairs officer (SSAO). The director has an assistant director who serves in a support capacity for all responsibilities under the director. Given the size of the campus and its liberal arts focus, the activities program is comprehensive, including all student union programming, cultural events, concerts, speakers' series, leadership training, student organization advising and services, and Greek affairs.

TWO-YEAR AND COMMUNITY COLLEGES

At this institution, student activities fall under the responsibility of a general student services professional. This person may or may not have a student affairs background and may report to the SSAO or to the dean of the college, the senior academic officer. Given the size of the campus and its unique student population, the activities program is a one-stop-shop including all student programming, cultural events and speaker series, and student organization advising and services. Traditionally, two-year and community colleges do not support fraternity and sorority systems.

PUBLIC URBAN INSTITUTION
OF 4,000 STUDENTS

At this institution, the director of student activities also carries the title of director of the union. The director reports to the dean of students, who reports to the vice president for student affairs. Staff support typically includes an assistant director, who has the primary responsibility for the student union operations. The programming responsibilities are primarily the director's. These responsibilities include student union programming and all campus events (e.g., concerts, homecoming, major speakers). Additional staff support is provided by graduate assistants. Greek affairs, student organization advising, and leadership training are the responsibilities of staff in the dean of students office.

PUBLIC INSTITUTION
OF 20,000 STUDENTS

At this institution, the director of student activities reports to an associate vice president for student affairs who is also director of the student union. The director of student activities has distinct programming areas, each administered by an assistant director of student activities. Programming areas include student union programs, Greek affairs, leadership and student organizations, and multicultural programs.

Sandeen (1989) wrote about the issue of administrative responsibility for activities programming and the student affairs staff's need to seek a balance between control and freedom. He advised program planners to be sensitive to issues of important campus constituencies, including the president, students, faculty, external groups, and other student affairs staff. In formulating policy for campus activities, administrators should consider the following:

- The educational mission of the institution;
- The priorities of the president;
- The social and educational needs of the students;
- Legal considerations pertinent to the institution;
- The willingness of faculty to participate;
- The support of the student affairs staff;

- Student participation in establishing and revising the policy;
- The establishment of a faculty-student policy council to review the policy and its application, and
- The needs (e.g., concerts, child care, cooperative living groups) of special student groups (Sandeen, p. 67).

The key to successful administration of a student activities program is dependent on the student activities staff's ability to work with different constituencies, particularly students. In addition, successful student activities staff need to understand clearly the context in which the activities programs lie at a particular institution. They must be cognizant of the "larger picture" and sensitive to the many variables that affect the student environment. Also, successful staff work collaboratively with other student affairs staff members to ensure a comprehensive student activities program. According to Newell (1999), "If students get consistent, reinforcing messages from classroom, residence hall, collaborative learning groups, service-learning and the like, they validate one another" (p. 19). Once the campus community identifies the learning initiatives of highest priority, students can receive a consistent message from a variety of sources.

STUDENT DEVELOPMENT AND STUDENT ACTIVITIES

IMPORTANCE

Why is it important for the student activities administrator to have knowledge of student development theory? Student development theory provides insight into the importance of providing both educational activities in and out of the classroom to assist in the development of the whole student. If one of the purposes of higher education is to prepare students to be informed and responsible citizens, then not only the academic experience, but also the extracurricular experience, is important.

The need for student affairs staff to be grounded in student development theory is increasingly important as research shows the tremendous impact of the extracurricular experience. Because students spend the vast majority of their waking day out of the classroom, the emotional, social, moral, physical, and mental impacts of campus activities are significant (Astin, 1993; Chickering and Reisser, 1993; Feldman and Newcomb, 1969; Pascarella and Terenzini, 1991). In addition, the influence of the peer group is significant. Astin (1993) stated that

> Perhaps the most compelling generalization from the myriad of findings summarized . . . is the pervasive effect of the peer group on the individual's development. Every aspect of the student's development—cognitive and affective, psychological and behavioral—is affected in some way by peer group characteristics, and usually by several peer characteristics. Generally, students tend

to change their values, behavior, and academic plans in the directions of the dominant orient of their peer group (p. 363).

Astin's (1993) research also indicated that satisfaction with campus is influenced directly by the degree of involvement. For example, students who were involved in activities with other students (e.g., sports, student organizations, attending campus events, socializing) were more pleased with their collegiate experience. Furthermore, the impact of association makes a dramatic difference regarding students' success in college and their retention. "There is considerable evidence, however, that active participation in the extracurricular life of campus can enhance retention" (Upcraft, 1985, pp. 330–331). Types of student activities that have a positive impact on retention include establishing close friends, participating in orientation programs and activities, belonging to student organizations, involving oneself in social and cultural activities, attending lectures, using campus facilities, and generally participating in extracurricular activities (Upcraft, 1985).

According to the 2001 National Survey on Student Engagement, almost 48 percent of senior students indicated they had engaged in "enriching educational experiences." These experiences included participating in cocurricular activities (organizations, publications, student government, sports, etc.), community service or volunteer work, and conversations with students of a different race or ethnicity. Kuh, Schuh, Whitt, and Associates (1991) posed the question, "What do students learn from these extracurricular activities?" The answer to the question and the importance of participation in student activities are central to their research reported in the book *Involving Colleges.* They concluded:

1. Orientation participation positively impacts social integration and institutional commitment and indirectly impacts the student's satisfaction with the institution and his or her desire to persist;
2. Involved students are more positive about their undergraduate experience, including their social life, living environment, and academic major. College participation, according to the research, is important to the student's job success after graduation;
3. Participation in extracurricular activities allows for the opportunity to gain leadership, decision-making, and planning skills, which are transferable to the job market;
4. Involvement allows for learning about mature, intimate interpersonal relationships;
5. The opportunity for leadership work in activities translated to more active community and civic leaders after graduation; and
6. The research indicates that the only factor that predicts adult success is participation in extracurricular activities (Kuh, Schuh, Whitt, & Associates, 1991, pp. 8–9).

The importance of student activities to promote association and involvement cannot be emphasized enough. The challenge for the student activities professional is to provide the experience necessary for positive growth and development. Therefore, activities based on an understanding of student development theory are crucial.

USING STUDENT DEVELOPMENT THEORY

How can students' development be utilized effectively in programming? To facilitate learning and development, program planners must be aware of different theories and how they can translate these theories into practice. Learning and development are dependent on the type of environment in which an activity takes place (e.g., workshop, meeting, program, policy) and the type of outcomes desired.

As leaders in higher education, we accept the challenge and the responsibility to create learning environments that encourage student development. "Student development in higher education is not accidental. Intentional student development is an achievable goal" (Komives, 1987, p. 23). These intentional interventions take place through a variety of activities both in and out of the classroom. The interactions among students potentially represent "labs for learning to communicate, empathize, argue, and reflect" (Chickering & Reisser, 1993, p. 392). Many of these interactions that encourage student development are fostered through active participation in various student organizations and activities intentionally created by student affairs professionals. These activities encourage students to create connections between learning that takes place in the classroom setting with experiences, events, and individuals that affect their lives every day.

In discussing the relationship between involvement, retention and student learning, Tinto (1987) commented,

> Though the research is far from complete, it is apparent that the more students are involved in the social and intellectual life of a college, the more frequently they make contact with faculty and other students about learning issues, especially outside the class, the more students are likely to learn (p. 69).

Involvement with various components of campus life can increase students' probability of learning, both in and out of the classroom (Tinto).

Astin (1993) provided a comprehensive analysis of the effects of involvement on student learning in his book, *What Matters in College: Four Critical Years Revisited.* Living in a campus residence hall had direct positive effects on self-reported growth in leadership and interpersonal skills (Astin). Student-faculty interaction had a positive correlation with all self-reported areas of intellectual and personal growth. Student–student interaction correlated positively with self-reported growth in leadership ability, public speaking, interpersonal skills, analytical and problem-solving skills, and critical thinking skills.

Historically, student affairs has been criticized for not basing program development on student development theory. The lack of a theoretical or conceptual foundation may be due to the personal interests of professional staff, the skill or knowledge of professional staff, emerging crises, professional fads, political expediency, special interest groups, and tradition (Hurst & Jacobson, 1985).

Given the importance of student's extracurricular experience and the time devoted to it, it is critical that student affairs staff use student development theory to facilitate learning and development. Those involved in student activities programming must be knowledgeable of appropriate theories and related issues that pertain to student development. These include learning theory, group dynamics, student demographics, educational philosophy, institutional governance, supervision, and organizational development (Marin, 1985). An understanding of different student developmental theories provides for more effective program design and delivery. Student development theory is "particularly helpful, especially when it comes to understanding why students do the things they do; without some theory, this would often be incomprehensible" (McIntosh & Swartwout, 2001, p. 25). So never underestimate the power and purpose of theory in certain situations.

A central question still remains: How do student activities programs meet the needs of the 45-year-old, divorced mother of three who is returning to college to complete a degree while at the same time attempting to provide for the 18-year-old, first-time, college freshman? Student activities practitioners must be cognizant of the developmental needs of both the 45-year-old and the 18-year-old. These two types of students are very different in what they expect from an extracurricular program. An institution can become responsive to the different needs of students. Student development theory can aid program planning in areas such as self-direction, social relations, leadership, volunteer services, and cultural preparation (Miller & Jones, 1981).

PROGRAMS

In a 1996 survey of senior student affairs officers (Ender, Newton, & Caple), 97 percent of the respondents reported having an office of student activities within their division. The activities programming provided to students was varied:

- 72 percent of the campuses sponsored programs that focused on the arts and the aesthetic development of students;

- 71 percent sponsored a lecture series that brought external speakers to campus;
- 87 percent sponsored programs to enhance race relations;
- 81 percent offered experiences designed to reinforce service learning and community service opportunities; and
- 95 percent sponsored programs in leadership development.

Certain programs tend to be common to most college and university campuses: student government advising, student organization services, Greek letter social organizations (fraternity and sorority) programming, student union activities, multicultural programs, leadership development, and volunteer activities.

STUDENT GOVERNMENT

Student government is an important part of campus life. For many student affairs staff, student government poses a problem. Most often, this problem centers on the relationship between the institution and the student government organization. If student affairs staff do not understand this important relationship, which is different from the relationship between any other student organization, serious problems can occur. In many cases, the student government president has direct access to the institution president; thus, it is crucial that the Senior Student Affairs Officer and the administrator who is the liaison to the student government be aware of this relationship. Student affairs staff should act in a strong supportive capacity with student government, ensuring that appropriate educational opportunities are available, such as leadership training and special workshops, to assist student government members' development. In addition, staff should continually keep the student government leadership aware of its role as "the voice of the students" and its legal, moral, and ethical responsibilities to represent students to the administration in a constructive and mature manner.

In a survey of student government advisors, Boatman (1988) found six characteristics of a strong student government:

1. Student leaders' understanding of the institution's structure and the relationship of student groups to student government;
2. The direct and regular access of student government leaders to top administrators and faculty in both a professional and social setting;
3. A mutual respect and common view of the institution by student government leaders, their advisors, and institutional representatives;
4. A positive working relationship between the student government and the student press;
5. A high degree of student participation and retention in student government elections, activities, and meetings; and

6. Training student government leaders to analyze the institution's structure and implementing needed change as well as being appointed to institutional committees.

Boatman (1988) also noted that the qualities of a student government advisor should include those of honesty, openness, strong interpersonal communication skills, and the ability to deal with a range of opinions and feelings. In addition, advisors should be resources to students with respect to the institution's history, culture, policies, politics, and current issues, as well as have credibility with, and access to, top administrators. While student government participation may advance student opinions and concerns on campus, at least one study indicated that involvement in student government activities had no short-term or long-term impact, either positive or negative, on students' postcollege lives (Downey, Bosco, & Silver, 1984). This same study did show, however, that those involved in student government reported greater satisfaction with their lives during their college years.

STUDENT ORGANIZATION SERVICES

On many campuses, a student affairs practitioner works with student organization registration, advising, and educational programming. With the ever-changing membership of student organizations, and at times the lack of consistent advising, staff support is important to help students become more stable and less threatened by leadership changes. Other than student governing bodies and Greek letter social organizations, most student groups on campus do not receive much attention. Such groups include honor societies, religious organizations, academic clubs, sports clubs, and special interest groups. For many students who belong to these organizations, membership is their link to student life. According to Terenzini and Pascarella (1997), "If individual effort or involvement is the linchpin for college impact, then a key matter becomes how a campus can shape its intellectual and interpersonal environments in ways that do indeed encourage student involvement" (p. 178). Student organizations provide a myriad of opportunities for student involvement regardless of the individual student's interests.

Campuses should provide their student organizations with meeting and workspace and, depending on the size of the institution and the goals of the particular student organization, office space. Mail boxes, in a central location, can aid in communication efforts and provide important community building among student groups.

Staff should be instrumental in providing educational programs for student organization leaders and their members. These may include sessions on resources available at the institution, financial management, membership recruitment, publicity, motivating members, and fund-raising techniques. Many campuses, either during new student orientation or early in the school year, sponsor a student organizations' fair, which allows for new and current students to learn more about the opportunities for campus involvement outside class.

Because of the wealth of talent among campus faculty, student affairs staff should be encouraged to utilize faculty to provide programs. Besides using their expertise, it allows faculty members to work with students in a setting outside the classroom and helps to strengthen the ties between academic and student affairs. The student activities practitioner should take any opportunity to involve faculty in their programming endeavors.

Cooper and Porter (1991) recommended that student organizations cosponsor various programs with the institution's general student programming board, if the institution has one. Cosponsorship may include sharing funds, personnel, and communication resources to plan or implement a program. Advantages of cosponsorship are that the potential for multicultural programming is enhanced, student leadership and programming skills are developed, publicity for both groups can be favorable, and synergy develops between the two organizations.

GREEK LETTER SOCIAL ORGANIZATIONS (GREEK AFFAIRS)

For campuses with Greek letter social organizations, administrative support may come from a Student Activities Office, Dean of Students Office, Office of Student Life, or Housing Office.

The Greek affairs area is undoubtedly one of the most controversial student activities programs. There has been continual debate, almost since the start of Greek letter social systems in the late nineteenth century, about the value of fraternities and sororities on college campuses. Critics have claimed that fraternities and sororities are exclusionary, sexist, and gender-specific and that their existence is contrary to the values colleges and universities hope to convey to students (Maisel, 1990). Administrators have questioned their relevance to campus life as well as the relationship between the Greek system and the institution.

Institutional emphasis on and influence of fraternity and sorority life varies from campus to campus. Fraternities and sororities tend to be less divisive at institutions where there are also strong residence life programs and other involvement opportunities for students (Kuh & Lyons,1990). In urban institutions, fraternity and sorority members are the key to maintaining campus traditions and hold many of the student leadership roles. At larger institutions, Greek letter social organization members tend to provide important community service, but at the same time they promote activities that could be construed as demeaning and even dangerous.

On a number of campuses today, the value of fraternity and sorority life remains the subject of debate and research. Institutions have established "blue ribbon" committees to review Greek life, with these committees recommending either elimination of Greeks from campus or a significant change in the relationship between the host campus and the fraternities and sororities. Campuses such as the University of Southern California, the University of Alabama, Denison University, and Gettysburg College have studied the role fraternities and sororities play on campus.

In particular, faculty have been critical as to what they perceive as anti-intellectualism among fraternity and sorority members. While a chapter may have some of the most outstanding scholars on campus, they also may have some members experiencing grave academic difficulty (Winston and Saunders, 1987).

Values and attitudes of students impact their view of learning. Baier and Whipple (1990), in a study of Greek values and attitudes, found that the Greek system appears to provide a "safe harbor" for those who seek conformity, family dependence, social apathy, and extensive involvement in extracurricular activities. The Greek system also "provides a 'legitimate' campus subculture for students to associate with others who are affluent, have relatively undefined academic and vocational goals, and place a higher priority on social life than intellectual pursuits" (p. 52).

Because of the debate on many campuses regarding the value of fraternities and sororities, it is important that staff have a well-defined plan for working with students affiliated with these organizations. "Colleges and universities must ensure that fraternity members live up to the standards expected of all students and the standards that fraternities themselves espouse" (Kuh, Pascarella, & Wechsler, 1996, p. A68). When groups fail to meet these goals, actions must be taken on the part of university officials and the national fraternity leadership to realign students' actions with their standards (Maloney, 1998). A thorough understanding of the value of fraternity and sorority life as it relates to an institution's academic mission is crucial for students to realize if Greek letter social organizations are to succeed.

The Council for the Advancement of Standards in Higher Education (2001) specified the following nine goals of a fraternity and sorority advising program:

1. Promoting the intellectual, vocational, recreational, spiritual, moral, and career development of students;
2. Providing training in leadership and other personal and social skills;
3. Promoting student involvement in cocurricular activities;
4. Promoting sponsorship of and participation in community service projects;
5. Providing training in group processes;
6. Promoting loyalty to the organization and the institution;
7. Promoting positive educational outcomes;
8. Promoting an appreciation for different lifestyles and cultural heritages; and

9. Recognizing the positive cultural traditions in a diversity of Greek organizations (p. 135).

Challenges for student affairs professionals who advise fraternities and sororities are many. Anderson (1987) stated that the advisor must fulfill certain roles to meet the challenges of Greek affairs: (1) programmer, (2) institutional representative, (3) counselor, (4) administrator and manager, (5) researcher and evaluator, (6) organization development consultant, (7) public relations person, (8) conflict mediator and manager, and (9) role model. In addition, knowledge of a variety of management techniques to deal with the many issues associated with Greek life is also necessary for a Greek advisor. Cufaude (1990) suggested eight management strategies for Greek advisors:

1. Maintain a high level of visibility by attending Greek meetings and workshops;
2. Establish regular lines of communication with all involved constituencies, such as parents, alumni, and faculty members;
3. Focus efforts where results are likely to be best, such as upon new members;
4. Establish clear expectations of behavior;
5. Incorporate fraternity and sorority members into campus leadership development programs;
6. Establish a university advisory board for Greek-letter organizations;
7. Create assistantship or paraprofessional positions to aid in advising fraternities and sororities; and
8. Set clear, attainable goals.

To be effective, student affairs staff must help students understand their role on campus and the responsibilities that role entails (Whipple & Sullivan, 1998). Programs should be designed to encourage a sense of community between the Greek system and the rest of the institution. In addition, it is critical that the Greek advisor work to establish effective lines of communication among the chapter leadership, alumni, campus administration, and the international and national Greek organizations. The communication linkage with these constituencies can prove invaluable in working with different issues that arise.

Current issues involving Greek organizations provide continual challenges. These issues include substance abuse, hazing, poor community relations, a lack of sensitivity to diversity issues, and the development of learning communities.

Substance abuse problems are an issue for both the institution and Greek members. Arnold and Kuh (1992) found that alcohol was an integral element of group life for fraternities, regardless of institutional size. In addition, alcohol and hazing were identified as key elements in socializing new members to the group. They concluded that neither international staff nor campus officials were as effective in addressing these issues and effecting positive changes as were the members themselves.

Hazing continues to be a problem for both men's and women's groups (Kuh et al., 1996; Whipple & Sullivan, 1998). National and international organizations and institutions have aggressively provided educational programs and intervention techniques to combat the mentality that promotes hazing. Unfortunately, the problem continues within many chapters. Alcohol abuse frequently serves as the precursor to hazing incidents. The challenge for staff working with fraternities and sororities is to continue to focus on substance abuse and hazing education without alienating students who are tired of hearing about it.

With many fraternity and sorority chapter houses off campus, community relationships are often strained. Good relations with neighbors and the surrounding community are important for the success of any Greek system. Many Greek letter social organizations are attempting to nurture those relationships through programs that educate chapter members about the responsibilities inherent in living in a community. In some communities, Interfraternity and Panhellenic Councils have worked with local governments to address issues and concerns.

Fraternity and sorority members have been criticized for a lack of tolerance for minority differences, religious choice, and sexual preference (Boschini & Thompson, 1998). Programs should be encouraged that promote diversity in membership and a realization of the importance of valuing differences. Some Greek governing boards have established human relations committees that work to promote, through programming, more sensitive and tolerant committees. Students need to understand that the acceptance of others can lead to the strengthening of their own group. Student affairs staff should continually look for educational opportunities to create a sensitivity and understanding among all students.

The term, *learning community* describes the environment that many colleges and universities seek to create for their faculty, staff, and students (Whipple & Sullivan, 1998). It is important that institutions expect all programs, both in and out of the classroom, to contribute to student learning in some form or fashion. Fraternities and sororities provide excellent opportunities to cultivate seamless learning, where students are active participants in the learning process and assume a large part of the responsibility for their learning (Kuh, 1996).

Fraternity and sorority life can add much to a campus and provide a positive experience for many students. It is, however, important that staff work to establish procedures whereby the institution can evaluate the positive campus contributions Greek letter social organizations can make. Evaluation of support services provided by the institution and national or international organization is also necessary.

STUDENT UNION ACTIVITIES

On many campuses, the student union is the "community center of the college, for all members of the college family—students, faculty, administration, alumni and guests" (Packwood, 1977, p. 180). Depending on the student affairs administrative organization, much of the student activities advising for campus programming may come from the union staff. In any case, the student union should be an important gathering place for students and afford an array of activities. Both social activities and academic activities should be promoted with a goal of contributing to the overall campus community.

The CAS Standards for College Unions (2001) stated that the primary goals of the college union must be ". . . to provide facilities and services, and promote programs that are responsive to student developmental needs and to the physical, social, recreational, and continuing education needs of the campus community" (p. 88). In addition, the CAS Standards indicate that campus unions must offer students "opportunities for active learning experiences in citizenship, leadership, individual and group responsibility, as well as a place for increased interaction and understanding among individuals from diverse backgrounds" (p. 88). These activities can offer an important link to all facets of student life and strengthen the ties to academic pursuit.

Student activities have played an important role in student development since the first student union was built. Fagan (1989) emphasized the need for varied programming if student growth is to occur. For example, passive programming efforts, including posters and videotapes, can introduce topics such as substance abuse, acquaintance rape, AIDS, and racism. Other types of programs, such as a speaker's series, social events, or festivals, can engage students in a more active learning process.

Union activities programming must meet the needs of today's student. Levitan and Osteen (1992) addressed changes in programming that are affected by the ever-changing media world, technology, leadership programs, need for interpersonal and relationship skill building, an increased emphasis on volunteerism and service, and changing student demographics. Trends of importance to student union activities include:

- Changing demographics and the need to incorporate and embrace opportunities those changes bring;
- Changing student involvement patterns, impacted by demands of work, family life, study, and the need to be involved;
- Defining the role of the college union in the twenty-first century;
- Emerging leadership programs which must include cross-cultural understanding and global perspectives, ethical decision making, and handling change in organizations;
- Working to help students learn healthy interpersonal relationship skills;
- Assisting and supporting students in volunteer and community service opportunities; and

- Managing the technological changes impacting institutions (Levitan & Osteen, p. 25).

MULTICULTURAL PROGRAMMING

As the student population on campuses becomes more diverse, the need for multicultural programming increases. Multiculturalism may be the most unresolved issue on campuses today (Levine & Cureton, 1998). Students, faculty and staff are demanding programs that meet the diverse needs of all members of the campus community. Student Affairs staff increasingly will be called upon to provide the expertise to promote multicultural programming. They must be able to define multiculturalism for their programs and widen their views of acceptable student leadership behaviors. Kuh and Schuh (1991) wrote,

> If college and universities are to be modes of interactive pluralism, at least three conditions must be met: institutions must change in fundamental ways to accommodate and take advantage of the contributions of students from historically underrepresented groups; opportunities must be available for students to live in and learn about their subcommunity of choice, whether it be based on race, ethnicity, gender, academic interests, or lifestyle orientation; and boundaries between students subcommunities must be permeable, allowing and encouraging positive interaction and learning (pp. 300–301).

Student activities programs have an opportunity, through the variety of interactions with students and the learning that occurs within a group, to promote multiculturalism. Students can be provided with the opportunity, structure, and reinforcement for replacing stereotypes with personal knowledge for learning to view differences for their qualities, importance, and potential to create growth. Staff should avoid the common mistakes of (1) trying to program for diverse constituencies without including input from the target groups, (2) assuming that all students within a particular culture are alike, (3) making multicultural programming the responsibility of one committee only, and (4) assuming that ethnic artists hold the greatest appeal for that particular ethnic group.

Student affairs staff must look at ways to redefine campus norms that have served as barriers to the integration of minority students into campus life. Sardo (1990) encouraged reexamining institution rules and student organization bylaws, coprogramming, bringing minority student leaders into all-White organizations, cross-grouping advertising in publications, and posting of activities notices where minority students will see them. In addition, faculty and staff need to develop their understanding of the verbal communication styles of minority students.

Intercultural learning is becoming increasingly important on the college campus. As students become more familiar with each other's cultures, the ability to program and participate becomes much easier for them. Leppo

(1987) provided strategies for the student affairs practitioner to assist students in working through the different stages of awareness. He encouraged staff to step in when cultural differences create conflict within student organizations or when student groups plan activities that could be construed as offensive to other cultures. He believed the goal should be to move beyond simple awareness to the point where differences are celebrated. Arminio et al. (2000) warned that student affairs professionals must "continue to seek means by which the racial identity of students of color is not sacrificed when students of color participate in predominately White groups" (p. 506). No one should have to sacrifice aspects of their identity in order to be involved in campus life.

To develop effective multicultural programming, student affairs staff, in conjunction with student organizations, must work to change organizational structures to (1) eliminate barriers to inclusion, (2) modify hierarchies that perpetuate majority viewpoints, and (3) recreate programming and advisory boards to encourage diverse representation. Padilla, Trevino, Gonzalez, and Trevino (1997) identified four categories of barriers that successful minority students have to overcome: (1) discontinuity barriers, (2) lack-of-nurturing barriers, (3) lack-of-presence barriers, and (4) resource barriers. It is interesting to note that in this study, students identified that three of the four barriers could be overcome through participation in student organizations and programs. Only resource barriers (financial) were not significantly affected by involvement.

LEADERSHIP DEVELOPMENT

Leadership development directly impacts the quality of student life on a campus. When student leaders are well versed in the basics of leadership, student activities will be more organized and developed, and in many cases, the process of that development will impact positively an organization's members. A student's effectiveness to lead an organization depends, in many cases, on the success of the student organization. Miller and Jones (1981) emphasized the need for leadership development:

> What is needed beyond participation . . . is some type of leadership training that does away with much of the trial-and-error learning so common in student leadership activities. Systematic training, supervision, and consultation are necessary components to be added to student leadership programs if effective leadership development is to result. It is fine to give students the opportunity to become involved, but it is essential to aid them in developing the skills and competencies necessary to become socially responsible leaders (p. 663).

Leadership is a long-studied and complex phenomenon. Over 11,000 books and articles have been written about leaders and leadership (Bass, 1990). A shift in the leadership paradigm has taken place in the past 10 years. Most existing research related to leadership is centered on the individual as leader rather than on the process of leadership (Komives, Lucas, & McMahon, 1998). Educators must redefine their definition and view of leadership to understand that "leadership is not something a leader possesses so much as a process involving followership" (Hollander, 1993, p. 29). When devising future programs and activities to foster leadership, the concept of followership (both recruiting and maintaining qualified followers) should be a major component of the discussion.

Current definitions of leadership describe a relational process with a level of interaction between leaders and followers who work together to accomplish the same goal (Komives et al., 1998). Leadership also includes a socially responsible component defined as "purposeful and intentional . . . practiced in such a way as to be socially responsible" (Komives et al., 1998, p. 14). The role of change is also prevalent in current definitions of leadership. Matusak (1996) defined leadership as "initiating and guiding and working with a group to accomplish change" (p. 5). Rost (1993) defined leadership as an "influence relationship among leaders and their collaborators who intend real changes that reflect their mutual purposes" (p. 99). The shift in definitions of leadership affects how leadership development activities are designed, promoted and implemented in the college setting.

Some institutions employ a staff member devoted solely to leadership development activities. Other institutions incorporate leadership training into the various program offerings, with the staff member responsible for each program handling the leadership education aspect.

Leadership development can take place in different environments. Seminars and workshops can be offered on specific topics. For example, a session on how to recruit members may be offered to all student organizations, or a program on improving communication skills could be provided for fraternity and sorority executive officers. Leadership development programs should highlight training, education, development, and experiential learning (Nolfi, 1993). A leadership advisory committee frequently is beneficial to assist in assessing students' needs and available resources (Nolfi, 1993).

On some campuses, a student affairs office will sponsor credit and non-credit courses. For example, specific leadership training courses offered for credit may be available to fraternity and sorority presidents and student government leaders. Credit courses are often available for freshmen and sophomores focused on beginning leadership skill building, with the purpose of preparing them to assume campus student leadership roles in the future.

Recognizing the changing demographics of campuses, leadership training should be viewed from a variety of viewpoints, in addition to the traditional-aged student's point of view. Rather than campus-focused programs, professionals may develop student leadership programs that recognize students' on-campus involvement and reflect the beliefs that the needs of traditional students and nontraditional students overlap, that leadership comes in many styles, and that leadership development is a future-oriented process (Fisher & Sartoelli (1992). Maturity and personal development play an important role, in place of skills normally associated with leadership (Fisher & Sartoelli, 1992).

VOLUNTEER ACTIVITIES

Volunteer activities are a vital part of a student activities program. Participation in a service organization helps prepare students for volunteerism in their community after graduation. "Many institutions of higher education have become active members of their local communities in a variety of ways, with both sharing their human, educational, technical, and fiscal resources" (Gugerty & Swezey, 1996, p. 92). Student affairs staff can aid in supporting volunteerism by explaining the civic responsibility it supports. These activities are also valuable because they help students learn about themselves and the world around them.

Many student organizations exist on our college campuses with the sole mission of service. In addition, many student organizations have "service" as part of their mission. These organizations include fraternities and sororities, honor societies, and student government. Examples of service activities might include fund-raising for the Heart Association, Cancer Society, or AIDS Awareness, or spending a day working with disadvantaged youth or cleaning up a city park. Given the nature of volunteer or service organizations, it is important that staff work to help members understand the group's mission to establish clear goals and expectations for participation. Also, they should communicate continually the goals and benefits of the organization to the campus community. It is easy for these groups to lose focus if strong student leadership and committed advising are not present. The rewards of a volunteer group's efforts are sometimes not readily seen, and members who desire "quick gratification" may lose interest in participation.

Volunteer organizations or service clubs are valuable to a campus culture because of the positive impact participation makes. Astin (1993) found that "participation in volunteer work also has a positive correlation with a variety of attitudinal outcomes: commitment to developing a meaningful philosophy of life, promoting racial understanding, and participating in programs to clean up the environment" (p. 392). Research on student development also supports the importance of peer influence on college students (Astin, 1993; Chickering & Reisser, 1993; Pascarella & Terenzini, 1991). Peers helping peers, in a volunteer or service setting, can be extremely beneficial for students.

Higher education is being called to renew its historic commitment to service and the learning that takes place as a result of service (Jacoby, 1996). Not only should students be encouraged to volunteer and serve others, but also initiatives should be in place to use service as a "teachable moment" for students. Jacoby defined this new relationship between service and learning as, "a form of experiential education in which students engage in activities that address human and community needs together with structured opportunities intentionally designed to promote student learning and development. Reflection and reciprocity are key concepts of service-learning" (p. 5).

Service learning can also be integrated into leadership and campus activities. Administrators can include community service opportunities for student organizations with the goal of emphasizing the advantages of different leadership models (Delve & Rice, 1990). Linking community service and leadership development opportunities helps student organization members to develop as "servant-leaders."

> Moving a student from an understanding of charity to an understanding of justice often requires a parallel move from the group to a sense of individualism that then translates back to the group and community. It is through this movement that students mature and develop as "whole people" committed to the betterment of the society of which they are a part (Delve & Rice, 1990, p. 64).

The integration of leadership and campus activities may occur through retreats and workshops, credit and noncredit leadership courses, orientation programs, and recognition.

Rubin (1990) discussed 10 principles that should characterize effective service learning programs:

1. Engage people in responsible and challenging actions for the common good;
2. Provide structured opportunities for people to reflect critically on their service experience;
3. Articulate clear service and learning goals for everyone involved;
4. Allow those with needs to define those needs;
5. Clarify the responsibilities of each person and organization involved;
6. Match service providers and service needs through a process that recognizes changing circumstances;
7. Expect genuine, active, and sustained organization commitment;
8. Include training, supervision, monitoring, support, recognition, and evaluation to meet service-learning goals;
9. Ensure that the time commitment for service learning is flexible, appropriate, and in the best interests of all involved; and,
10. Are committed to program participation by and with diverse populations (pp. 117–120).

STUDENT ACTIVITIES ISSUES AND TRENDS

The issues of the 1990s are now the trends of the twenty-first century. Changing demographics, legal concerns, and funding problems will all be on higher education agenda, including student activities, well into this century.

CHANGING STUDENT DEMOGRAPHICS

Adult Learners

At many institutions across the country, the impact of changing demographics is affecting the focus of student activities programs. "Nontraditional" students are fast becoming "traditional" students. According the U.S. Department of Education (1996), by 1994, 44 percent of all college students were over the age of 25, 55 percent were female, 54 percent were working, and 43 percent were attending part-time. Indeed, fewer than one in six of all college students fit the traditional stereotype of the American college student: 18 to 22 years of age, attending college full-time and living in a campus residential unit. The increase of adult learners, particularly women, is changing the makeup of student affairs programs and services. As a result, it is crucial for the student affairs staff to be aware of adult learners' needs and motivations. Ringgenberg (1989) submitted that

> Returning students and women students need child-care facilities, support groups for themselves and their families, a common gathering ground, and social, recreation, cultural, and educational programs that meet their interests. Programming for a family is a great deal different from programming for the traditional age student. For example, tastes in music and comedy can be extremely different. However, failure to provide family programming could isolate these students from campus (pp. 33–34).

Most adults returning to college, or attending for the first time, matriculate to accomplish specific objectives, to develop social contacts and relationships with others, or to learn for the pleasure of acquiring knowledge. Their developmental needs are different according to whether they are in early or middle adulthood, in midlife transition phase, or in later life. Within these phases are different levels of ego development, intellectual development, and moral development. The adult learner moves through three phases: moving in, moving through, and moving on (Bennett, 1992). Student affairs staff should provide appropriate support for each phase. The moving in phase is an opportunity for staff to provide a supportive atmosphere as the adult student makes the transition to college life. During the moving through phase, the support should be provided to help the student succeed (i.e., programs to meet social needs and efforts made available for involvement in student organizations). Finally, the moving on phase should provide students with support for programs dealing with finding a job, such as resume writing and interviewing techniques, and researching graduate programs.

The challenge for student affairs staff is to provide student activities for adult learners that meet developmental needs. There are two important roles for student affairs staff in working with adult learners and student activities: advocate and programmer (Moore, Miller, & Spina, 1989). The advocate helps returning adults make the transition to college life by bringing them together through organizational activities, providing a common meeting place, and encouraging that office hours be made available after the normal workday hours. Programmers can provide events for students, such as informal "return to learn" seminars focusing on transition to college issues and the distribution of communication, such as a newsletter, to help students be aware of campus events.

Gay, Lesbian, Bisexual, and Transgender Students

On many campuses, a student organization exists for gay, lesbian, bisexual, and transgender students. Unfortunately, given many campus climates, these students do not feel a part of the mainstream of student life. Student affairs staff can improve the quality of life for these students by developing programs to meet their needs. Scott (1988) wrote that institutional policies should be responsive to the needs of these students by including sexual orientation in the institution's statement of nondiscrimination; training student activities staff to work with gay, lesbian, bisexual, and transgender students; and taking steps to handle verbal and physical harassment.

Campus environments are different in their acceptance of gay, lesbian, and bisexual students. Good (1993) provided five programming stages for the student affairs staff, depending on the institution's level of readiness. The first stage is programming focused on reducing hate crimes and teaching students to appreciate diversity. The second stage develops programs to promote a positive self-identity for gay, lesbian, and bisexual students. The third stage aggressively establishes a place for students on campus and allows them to share their experiences with the college community. Stage four moves from the external environment faced by the students to personal adjustment issues. Finally, the fifth stage should provide for an environment where students can feel comfortable within the campus community and that helps them affirm who they are.

Students with Disabilities

The number of disabled students entering postsecondary education is rising (Weeks, 2001). A 1998 survey of entering freshman found that 9 percent reported having at least one disability, with 41 percent claiming a learning disability. This is an increase from a 1978 survey where only 3 percent of freshmen claimed a disability (Weeks).

Section 504 of the Rehabilitation Act of 1973 states, ". . . no otherwise qualified handicapped individual in the U.S. . . . shall solely, by reason of his handicap, be excluded from participation in, be denied the benefits of, or be subjected to discrimination under any program or activity receiving federal financial assistance." Under Section 504, provisions must be made for handicapped students when planning and executing university programs and activities. These programs include any "physical education, athletics, recreation, transportation, other extracurricular, or other postsecondary education program or activity." This means that colleges and universities are obligated to not only provide interpreters for lectures and wheelchair access to facilities, but also to create programs (e.g., recreational and educational) that cater to the special needs of students with disabilities.

International Students

As more international students arrive at institutions across the country, it is important that they are accommodated not only academically, but also socially. It is not solely the responsibility of the international student services office on a campus to care for international students (Willer, 1992). It is everyone's responsibility to ensure that international students are successfully being integrated into the campus community.

International students provide a great benefit to American institutions through their efforts to educate all students for living in a global society.

> International students contribute in several ways: by providing cultural diversity; by sharing their values, life experience and world views; by serving as resources in the creation of a more cosmopolitan learning environment; and, of course, by achieving laudatory scholarships and study in classrooms, laboratories, and libraries (Willer, 1992, p. 194).

Student affairs professionals should work closely with the staff responsible for administering the international students' program on the campus. Activities can be planned not only for international students, but also for American students, as well those that promote common goals. The benefits that result from the interactions and relationships formed are important to the personal development of all students. The challenge for staff is to acknowledge and balance the activities that are important to promoting international students' cultural, ethnic, or religious backgrounds with those activities that help assimilate them into the culture of the campus. The dilemma for the activities staff is how to create an environment where students share a sense of purpose and unity while still accepting and appreciating diversity.

Legal Issues

Like the university at-large, those in student activities are faced with a myriad of legal issues when developing student programs outside the classroom. While it is clearly not possible to discuss all the legal relationships and implications in depth here, college officials should be aware of the potential legal ramifications that may exist when implementing certain decisions relating to student activities.

Four primary legal relationships exist between students and their respective institutions. These four relationships are (1) constitutional, (2) torts, (3) statutory, and (4) contractual (Gehring, 1993). All four relationships can and will likely be formed between students who are involved with student activities and the institution as a result of decisions made by both college officials and student leaders.

For public institutions and those private institutions where state action is involved, the First Amendment must be taken into account before planning an activity or denying a student organization the opportunity to hold an event on campus. A decision to invite a controversial speaker to lecture on campus, to show an X-rated movie at the university theater, to deny a student group the opportunity to march on campus, or to hold a meeting at a campus building will typically force the institution to balance the interests of the First Amendment with college officials' and students' desires to have a campus free of obnoxious and disrespectful speech. The First Amendment protects most speech, including controversial, offensive, or obnoxious speech. All speech, however, is not protected. If speech is obscene, represents a clear and present danger, constitutes fighting words, or will incite others to imminent, lawless action, the institution may be able to restrict the person's speech. While restrictions on student's freedom of expression may be considered under only the most extraordinary of circumstances, student leaders and college officials should provide outlets to contrary opinions or activities when certain controversial events occur on campus.

As for tort liability and statutory concerns, universities will often find that such a relationship will exist with students, employees, and guests of the university. A tort is broadly defined "as a civil wrong, other than a breach of contract, for which the courts will allow a damage remedy" (Kaplin & Lee, 1995, p. 89). In the collegiate setting, tort law has been most often applied in negligent cases relating to personal injuries sustained while attending an activity sponsored by a student group or the institution, while transiting university property, or while on a class field trip (Fenske & Johnson, 1990). Higher education institutions have a duty to protect their students and other invited guests from known or reasonable foreseeable dangers.

Fraternity and sorority problems, associated with hazing, alcohol, and physical defects of university premises, have continually resulted in civil lawsuits being brought by students or their families for tortuous behavior. Thus, colleges should regularly check to see that (1) hazing or violent rivalries among fraternities are not occurring; (2) university premises (e.g., fraternity and sorority houses and residence halls) are safe from physical defects; and (3) no near-misses have occurred that forewarn the university of possible future injuries (Gulland & Powell, 1989).

Criminal statutes relating to uses of alcohol (e.g., social host liability and underage drinking) and proscribing hazing will create legal relationships not only between the students and the institution, but also between students and the state. Thus, college officials and students need to be cognizant of the criminal and civil statutes that may apply to them.

In addition, federal mandates, such as the Student Right to Know and Campus Security Act (CSA), create special relationships between students and particular employees of the university. The CSA requires "campus authorities" to report all occurrences of crime specified in the legislation (murder, sexual offenses, robbery, aggravated assault, burglary, and motor vehicle theft). The CSA defines a campus authority as "any official of the institution who has significant responsibility for student and campus activities, but does not have significant counseling responsibilities" (1998). While many leaders in the higher education community voiced their opinions that this definition was too broad, as it is written, administrators whose direct responsibilities include working with student and campus activities are considered campus authorities and are mandated by law to report all instances of crime. While this responsibility sounds positive in theory, it may create difficult situations in which confidentiality cannot be maintained. Student and campus activities advisors are urged to consult their campus legal counsel for additional information and questions about a particular situation.

Finally, it is axiomatic that the relationship between an institution and a student is contractual in nature. Contracts may be explicit or implicit, written or oral. As such, institutions should be careful as to how they draft their student handbooks, brochures, and catalogues, since courts, depending on the circumstances, may view these documents as creating a contractual relationship between the institution and the student. As is clearly evident, the law pervades the entire college campus, including action relating to student activities. Thus, when appropriate and possible, competent legal counsel should be sought to advise college officials and students on how best to stay clear of liability.

Funding Issues

On most campuses, funding of student activities programs is derived from non-state dollars. The most common terms for the funding source are a "student activity fee" or "general fee." On some campuses, student activities may be funded from both state dollars and non-state dollars, depending on which administrative office is coordinating the programs. With the increasing scrutiny of state budgets and the continual evaluation of what many institutions are doing regarding expenditures, it is important that student affairs staff be aware of the ever-changing budget situation. One of the benefits for students in extracurricular involvement is the opportunity to work with budgets. Staff should educate students about federal and state budget issues and the impact these issues have on student activity programs.

Working with volatile budgets is a problem for all higher education programs, including student activities. However Floerchinger and Young (1992) provided creative suggestions for stretching budgets:

1. Cosponsoring programs with other on-campus or off-campus organizations;
2. Using local student, staff, and faculty talent in developing low-cost programs as opposed to hiring outside speakers or consults;
3. Using computer linkages and videos for training rather than bringing in expensive outside trainers;
4. Increasing emphasis on cooperative buying and cost sharing with other campuses;
5. Improving professional and student skills in negotiating contracts and analyzing student interests;
6. Developing grant-writing skills for student activities professionals;
7. Analyzing office functions and expediters for waste;
8. Encouraging volunteerism;
9. Enhancing the prospect of students becoming supportive alumni; and
10. Gaining a better understanding of the lobbying process before the state and federal government.

PROFESSIONAL ORGANIZATIONS

Student affairs staff who work in student activities have the opportunity to join several national and/or international organizations that promote activities programming. These include the Association of College Unions-International (ACU-I) and the National Association of Campus Activities (NACA). Both provide professional development and student activities programming ideas.

The ACU-I was founded in 1914. The purpose of ACU-I is to help college unions and student activities improve their programs and services and to contribute to student growth and development. There are approximately 850 member institutions from urban and rural campuses, four-year and two-year schools, large universities, small colleges, and historically Black colleges and universities. Association members are also located in Canada, Australia, Great Britain, New Zealand, and Japan. The association is divided into 16 geographic regions. At the regional level, there are opportunities for student participation as well as opportunities for union and activities staff to participate in ACU-I programs, activities, and leadership positions. Besides regional activities, including conferences, ACU-I sponsors an international conference, and national workshops and seminars.

ACU-I publishes a magazine, *The Bulletin,* six times a year and provides updated information on the union and the student activities areas. An online newsletter, the *Union Wire,* is also published six times a year, alternating in opposite months with the magazine. ACU-I's headquarters are in Bloomington, Indiana. Additional information about ACU-I may be obtained from http://www.acuiweb.org.

The National Association of Campus Activities (NACA) was founded in 1960. NACA provides its members with educational and informational benefits related to activities programming: cooperative buying, educational programs and services, talent showcases, trade publications, as well as national and regional conferences and workshops. Over 1,200 institutions and 600 firms representing all 50 states and Canada are members. NACA features a national convention, regional conferences, summer and winter workshops, state meetings, educational projects, a resource library, numerous publications, and professional development opportunities.

Eight times a year NACA publishes a magazine, *Programming,* containing educational articles, news, reports, evaluations, and advertising of interest. The Membership Directory & Buyers' Guide, a desktop reference, contains information for campus and associate members. Headquarters for NACA are located in Columbia, South Carolina. Additional information about NACA may be obtained from http://www.naca.org.

TECHNOLOGY RESOURCES

Great strides have been made in the past 10 years by providing programs and services to students via technology. With the increase of computer labs and the number of students who bring personal computers to campus with them, the opportunities to utilize technology continue to grow.

One of the many versatile software applications, Blackboard, provides a portal mechanism through which student organizations can send messages and post announcements to communicate with other students. Blackboard also makes available links to web sites pertinent to the group membership as well as a discussion board where students can pose questions and engage each other in the learning process outside the classroom. Additional information about the many possibilities of utilizing Blackboard for student organizations may be obtained from http://www.blackboard.com.

Technology can also be helpful when maintaining records regarding membership and involvement within student organizations. Several examples are listed here:

- Most student organizations are asked to submit membership rosters annually. When this information is entered into a database, demographics about what students are involved in which organizations may be obtained. Students' involvement, as leaders and members, may also be collected for an individual leadership transcript.

- Listservs may be used for organization-wide communication. Listservs allow the membership to share information quickly and gather input with little effort exerted.

Additional web sites of interest to professionals in activities programming follow:

http://www.fraternityadvisors.org—The Association for Fraternity Advisors is located in Indianapolis, Indiana and serves as a clearinghouse of information for fraternity and sorority advisors nationwide. The organization holds an annual conference each fall, which serves to provide avenues for discussion between Greek advisors, other campus administrators, and representatives from the international fraternity and sorority headquarters.

http://www.diversityweb.org/Leadersguide—This web site, sponsored by the American Association of Colleges and Universities, provides resources regarding diversity initiatives and education. The link Student Involvement and Development, provides specific ideas for student affairs professionals.

http://www.acpa.nche.edu—The American for College Personnel Association and http://www.naspa.org—the National Association for Student Personnel Administrators, are both located in Washington, D.C. and serve as the two national umbrella groups for student affairs professionals.

http://www.studentaffairs.com—This web site identifies itself as the "online guide to college student affairs." This site serves as a clearinghouse for a broad spectrum of information about higher education, including listings for additional web sites of interest to student affairs professionals.

ENTRY-LEVEL EMPLOYMENT QUALIFICATIONS

While there are no set qualifications for student affairs staff who work in student activities, there are preferred qualifications. An active, undergraduate experience in student activities, including leadership positions, is important. This may include holding membership in a fraternity or sorority, serving as a representative on student government, planning concerts for events such as homecoming, or participating in special interest organizations. Past experience with faculty and administrators on a regular basis is also beneficial.

Many institutions, when seeking student activities staff, prefer individuals with credentials from a graduate preparation program. At the master's level, a generalist background is important. Potential staff should take advantage of the breadth of courses available to them in their graduate work. Assistantships in a student activities area, such as student union activities, student activities programming, Greek affairs, or student organization advising, can be valuable. In addition, a prospective student activities practitioner should take the opportunity to participate in practica that offer experiences in a variety of student activities settings. Preferred qualifications also include excellent organizational skills, verbal and written communication skills, and the ability to relate well with a variety of populations (students, faculty, staff, community, alumni, and parents).

Throughout the history of American higher education, student activities have been a powerful tool through which professionals enhance the learning environment for students. The knowledge, skills, and dispositions of student affairs practitioners combined with the emerging development and potential of all students on campus create the truly seamless learning environment. Indeed, student activities may be viewed as

> A viable vehicle for transmitting knowledge, affecting skills development, changing attitudes, and helping students reach their potential. This may be the heart of student affairs work and, indeed, the soul of the student affairs educator (Liddell, Hubbard, & Werner, 2000, p. 21).

REFERENCES

American College Personnel Association. (1994). *The student learning imperative: Implications for student affairs.* Alexandria, VA: Author.

Anderson, J. W. (1987). Roles and responsibilities of Greek advisors. In R. B. Winston, W. R. Nettles, & J. H. Opper. (Eds.), *Fraternities and sororities on the contemporary college campus* (pp. 75–86). San Francisco: Jossey-Bass.

Anson, J. L., & Marchesani, R. F. (Eds.). (1991). *Baird's manual of American college fraternities.* Indianapolis, IN: Baird's Manual Foundation.

Arminio, J. I., Carter, S., Jones, S. E., Kruger, K., Lucus, N., Washington, J., Young, N., & Scott, A. (2000). Leadership experiences of students of color. *NASPA Journal, 37,* 496–510.

Arnold, J. C., & Kuh, G. D. (1992). *Brotherhood and the bottle: A cultural analysis of the role of alcohol in fraternities.* Bloomington, IN: Indiana University, Center for the College Fraternity.

Astin, A. W. (1993). *What matters in college?* San Francisco: Jossey-Bass.

Baier, J. L., & Whipple, E. G. (1990). Greek values and attitudes: A comparison with independents. *NASPA Journal, 28,* 43–53.

Bass, B. M. (1990). *Bass and Stogdill's handbook of leadership theory, research, and managerial applications* (3rd ed.). New York: The Free Press.

Bennett, L. G. (1992, September). Keeping adult students on the move. *ACU-I Bulletin, 60,* 4 ff.

Boatman, S. (1988, April). Strong student governments and their advisement. *Campus Activities Programming, 20,* 58.

Boatman, S., & Adams, T. C. (1992, April). The ethical dimension of leadership. *Campus Activities Programming, 24,* 62–67.

Boschini, V., & Thompson, C. (1998). The future of Greek experience: Greeks and diversity. In E. G. Whipple (Ed.), *New challenges for Greek letter organizations: Transforming fraternities and sororities into learning communities* (pp. 19–28). San Francisco: Jossey-Bass.

Brock, C. S. (1991, December). Ethical development through student activities programming. *Campus Activities Programming, 24,* 54–59.

Brubacher, J. S., & Rudy, W. (1976). *Higher education in transition.* New York: Harper & Row.

Brubacher, J. S., & Rudy, W. (1997). *Higher education in transition: A history of American colleges and universities.* New Brunswick, NJ: Transaction Publishers.

Chickering, A. W., & Reisser, L. (1993). *Education and identity* (2nd ed.) San Francisco: Jossey-Bass.

Cooper, J. E., & Porter, B. E. (1991, April). Co-sponsorships: Bridging the gap among student organizations. *Campus Activities Programming, 23,* 42–46.

Council for the Advancement of Standards in Higher Education (2001). *The book of professional standards for higher education.* Washington, DC: Author.

Cufaude, J. (1990). Strategies from a Greek advisor: Maximizing the Greek's co-curriculum's potential. *NASPA Journal, 28,* 82–90.

Devle, C. I., & Rice, K. L. (1990, Summer). The integration of service learning into leadership and campus activities. In C. I. Delve, S. D. Mintz, & G. M. Stewart (Eds.), *Community service as values education.* San Francisco: Jossey-Bass.

Downey, R. G., Bosco, P. J., & Silver, E. M. (1984). Long-term outcomes of participation in student government. *Journal of College Student Personnel, 25,* 245–250.

Dunkel, N. W., & Schuh, J. H. (1998). *Advising student groups and organizations.* San Francisco: Jossey-Bass.

Ender S.C., Newton F.B., & Caple R.B. (1996). *Contributing to learning: the role of student affairs.* (New Directions for Student Servies, No. 75). San Francisco: Jossey-Bass.

Fagan, A. F. (1989, January). The college union: The living room of the campus. *ACU-I Bulletin, 57,* 35–37.

Feldman, K. A., & Newcomb, T. M. (1969). *The impact of college on students.* San Francisco: Jossey-Bass.

Fenske, R. H., & Johnson, E. A. (1990). Changing regulatory and legal environments. In M. J. Barr, M. L. Upcraft, & Associates (Eds.), *New futures for student affairs: Building a vision for professional leadership and practice* (pp. 114–137). San Francisco: Jossey-Bass.

Fisher, V. D., & Sartorelli, M. B. (1992, March). Leadership programs: Building bridges between non-traditional and traditional students. *Campus Activities Programming, 24,* 42 ff.

Floerchinger, D., & Yound, K. E. (1992, Summer). The money crunch: Is it killing campus activities? *Campus Activities Programming, 25,* 29–36.

Gehring, D. D. (1993). Understanding legal constraints on practice. In M. J. Barr and Associates (Eds.), *The handbook of student affairs administrators* (pp. 274–299). San Francisco: Jossey-Bass.

Good, R. T. (1993, Summer). Programming to meet the needs of the lesbian-gay community. *Campus Activities Programming, 26,* 40–44.

Gulland, E. D., & Powell, M. E. (1989, May). Colleges, fraternities and sororities: A white paper on tort liability issues. Research Report, Covington & Burling.

Gugerty, C. R., & Swezey, E. D. (1996). Developing campus-community relationships. In B. Jacoby and Associates (Eds.), *Service-learning in higher education: Concepts and practices* (pp. 92–108). San Francisco: Jossey-Bass.

Hollander, E. P. (1993). Legitimacy, power, and influence: A perspective on relational features of leadership. In M. M. Chemers & R. Ayman (Eds.), *Leadership theory and research: Perspectives and directions* (pp. 29–47). San Diego, CA: Academic Press.

Horowitz, H. L. (1987). *Campus life.* Chicago: The University of Chicago Press.

Hurst, J. C,. & Jacobson, J. K. (1985). Theories underlying students' need for programs. In M. J. Barr, L. A. Keating, and Associates (Eds.), *Developing effective student services programs* (pp. 113–136). San Francisco: Jossey-Bass.

Jacoby, B., & Associates (1996). *Service learning in higher education: Concepts and practices.* San Francisco: Jossey Bass.

Kaplin, W. A., & Lee, B. (1995). *The law of higher education: A comprehensive guide to legal implications of administrative decision making* (3rd ed.). San Francisco: Jossey-Bass.

Kirkland, R. (1987, September). Moving from philosophy to practical: Student development theories can help in the transition. *ACU-I Bulletin, 55,* 23–27.

Komives, S. R. (1987). Applying theory to practice: Understanding student and organization development. In J. H. Schuh (Ed.), *Handbook for student group advisors* (pp. 23–44). Alexandria, VA: American College Personnel Association.

Komives, S. R., Lucas, N., & McMahon, T. R. (1998). *Exploring leadership for college students who want to make a difference.* San Francisco: Jossey-Bass.

Komives, S. R., Woodard, D. B., & Associates. (1996). *Student services: A handbook for the profession* (3rd ed.). San Francisco: Jossey-Bass.

Kuh, G. D. (1996). Guiding principles for creating seamless learning environments for undergraduates. *Journal of College Student Development, 37(2),* 135–148.

Kuh, G. D., Schuh, J. H., Whitt, E. J., & Associates (1991). *Involving colleges.* San Francisco: Jossey-Bass.

Kuh, G. D., & Lyons, J. W. (1990). Fraternities and sororities: Lessons from the college experiences study. *NASPA Journal, 28,* 20–29.

Kuh, G. D., Lyons, J., Miller, T. K., & Trow, J. (1995). Reasonable expectations. Washington, DC: National Association of Student Personnel Administrators.

Kuh, G. D., Pascarella, E. T., & Wechsler, H. (1996). The questionable value of fraternities. *Chronicle of Higher Education, 43(4),* A68.

Leppo, J. (1987, April). Multicultural programming: A conceptual framework and model for implementation. *Campus Activities Programming, 19,* 56–60.

Levine, A., & Cureton, J.S. (1998). *When hope and fear collide.* San Francisco: Jossey-Bass.

Levitan, T., & Osteen, J. M. (1992). College union activities and programs. In T. E. Milani & J. W. Johnston (Eds.), *The college union in the year 2000* (pp. 11–25). San Francisco: Jossey-Bass.

Liddell, D. L., Hubbard, S., & Werner R. (2000). Developing interventions that focus on learning. In D. L. Liddell & J. P. Lund (Eds.), *Powerful programming for student learning: Approaches that make a difference,* 90, pp. 21–33.

Maloney, G. W. (1998). Disciplining student organizations. In B. G. Paterson & W. L. Kibler (Eds.), *The administration of campus discipline: Student organizational and community issue* (pp. 129–148). Asheville, NC: College Administration Publications.

Marin, J. (1985, February). The college union's role in student development. *ACU-I Bulletin, 53,* 22–23.

Masiel, J. M. (1990, Fall). Social fraternities and sororities are not conducive to the educational process. *NASPA Journal, 28,* 8–12.

Matusak, L. R. (1996). *Finding your voice: Learning to lead . . . anywhere you want to make a difference.* San Francisco: Jossey-Bass.

Maul, S. Y. (1993). *Building community on campus: A compendium of practical ideas.* Bloomington, IN: Association of College Unions-International.

McIntosh, J. G., & Swartwout, D. (2001). Lights on, lights off. *About Campus, 6(3),* 25–27.

McKaig, R. N., & Policello, S. M. (1979). Student activities. In G. D. Kuh (Ed.), *Evaluation in student affairs* (pp. 95–103). Washington: American College Personnel Association.

Miller, T. K., & Jones, J. D. (1981). Out-of-class activities. In A. W. Chickering & Associates (Eds.), *The modern American college* (pp. 657–671). San Francisco: Jossey-Bass.

Miller, T. K. (1982). Student development assessment: A rationale. In G. R. Hanson (Ed.), *Measuring student development* (pp. 5–15). San Francisco: Jossey-Bass.

Mills, D. B. (1989). In D. C. Roberts (Ed.), Designing campus activities to foster a sense of community (pp. 39–48). San Francisco: Jossey-Bass.

Moore, L. V., Miller, D., & Spina, D. (1989, May). Returning adult students need staff to serve as advocates, programmers. *ACU-I Bulletin, 57,* 27–28.

Mueller, K. (1961). *Student personnel work in higher education.* Boston: Houghton Mifflin.

Newell, W. H. (1999). The promise of integrative learning. *About Campus, 4(2),* 17–23.

Nolfi, T. (1993, November). Designing a student leadership program. *ACU-I Bulletin, 61,* 4–10.

Packwood, W. T. (Ed.). (1977). *College student personnel services.* Springfield, IL: Charles C Thomas.

Padilla, R. V., Trevino, J., Gonzalez, K., & Trevino, J. (1997). Developing local models of minority student success in college. *Journal of College Student Development, 38(2),* 125–135.

Pascarella, E. T., & Terenzini, P. T. (1991). *How college affects students.* San Francisco: Jossey-Bass.

Pike, G. R. (2000). Rethinking the role of assessment. *About Campus, 5(1),* 11–19.

Rehabilitation Act of 1973, § Section 504, as amended U.S.C.A. § 794.

Ringgenberg, L. J. (1989). Expanding participation of student subgroups in campus activities. In D.C. Roberts (Ed.), *Designing campus activities to foster a sense of community* (pp. 27–37). San Francisco: Jossey-Bass.

Rost, J. C. (1991). *Leadership for the twenty-first century.* New York: Praeger.

Rubin, S. G. (1990). Transforming the university through service learning. In C. I. Delve, S. D. Mintz, & G. M. Stewart (Eds.), *Community service as values education* (pp. 111–124). San Francisco: Jossey-Bass.

Sack, S. (1961). Student life in the nineteenth century. *Pennsylvania Magazine of History and Biography,* 270–273.

Sandeen, A. (1989). Freedom and control in campus activities: Who's in charge? In D. C. Roberts (Ed.), *Designing campus activities to foster a sense of community* (pp. 61–68). San Francisco: Jossey-Bass.

Sardo, R. C. (1990, December). Redefining the norms: A campus activities approach to multiculturalism. *Campus Activities Programming, 23,* 36–40.

Scott, D. (1988, March). Working with gay and lesbian students. *ACU-I Bulletin, 56,* 22–25.

Stevens, G. (1969). The college union—Past, present, future. *NASPA Journal, 7,* 16–21.

Student Right to Know and Campus Security Act, 20 U.S.C. § 1092.

Styles, M. (1985). Effective models of systematic program planning. In M. J. Barr, L. A. Keating, & Associates (Eds.), *Developing effective student services programs* (pp. 181–211). San Francisco: Jossey-Bass.

Terenzini, P. T., & Pascarella, E. T. (1997). Living with myths: Undergraduate education in America. In E. J. Whitt (Ed.), *College student affairs administration* (pp. 173–179). Needham Heights, MA: Simon & Schuster.

Tinto, V. (1987). *Leaving college: Rethinking the causes and cures of student attrition* (2nd ed.). Chicago: The University of Chicago Press.

Upcraft, L. (1985). Residence halls and student activities. In L. Noel, R. Levitz, D. Saluri, & Associates (Eds.), *Increasing student retention: Effective programs and practices for reducing the dropout rate* (pp. 319–344). San Francisco: Jossey-Bass.

U.S. Department of Education, National Center for Educational Statistics (1996). D*igest of educational statistics 1996.* Washington, DC: U.S. Government Printing Office.

Weeks, K. M. (2001). *Managing student disability compliance.* Nashville, TN: College Legal Information.

Whipple, E. G., & Sullivan, E. G. (1998). Greek letter organizations: Communities of learners? In E. G. Whipple (Ed.), *New challenges for Greek letter organizations: Transforming fraternities and sororities into learning communities* (pp. 7–18). San Francisco: Jossey-Bass.

Willer, P. (1992). Student affairs professionals as international educators. In D. McIntire & P. Willer (Eds.), *Working with international students and scholars on American campuses* (pp. 161–167). Washington: National Association of Student Personnel Administrators.

Wilson, E. K. (1966). The entering student: Attributes and agents of change. In T. M. Newcomb & E. K. Wilson (Eds.), *College peer groups* (pp. 71–106). Chicago: Aldine.

Winston, R. B., & Saunders, S. A. (1987). The Greek experience: Friend or foe of student development? In R. B. Winston, W. R. Nettles, & J. H. Opper, (Eds.), *Fraternities and sororities on the contemporary college campus* (pp. 5–20). San Francisco: Jossey-Bass.

Chapter 12

STUDENT FINANCIAL AID

Michael D. Coomes

From the rather meager beginnings of a single £100 scholarship, student aid in the United States has grown to incorporate dozens of federally funded programs, hundreds of state programs, and countless institutional and private programs with resources in excess of $89 billion in 2001–2002 (College Entrance Examination Board, 2002b). In 2001, more than 8.1 million students received over $61 billion in federal assistance in helping them meet their college costs (U.S. Department of Education, 2001). The early years of the twenty-first century mark an important turning point for the student aid profession. Changing goals, new delivery systems, expanded access, and new professional and institutional roles have changed the scope of aid programs that were created, for the most part, in the decades of the 1960s and 1970s. These changes are leading to creation of a new student aid industry and will have a significant impact on student access and success and institutional enrollment for years to come.

A HISTORY OF STUDENT FINANCIAL AID

As is the case with many aspects of higher education, student aid in the United States starts with Harvard College. In 1643, Lady Ann Radcliff Mowlson bequeathed to Harvard College £100 for the "yea(rly) maintenance of some poor scholler" (sic) ("Scholarship & beneficiary aid," in Godzicki, 1975, p. 15). The scholarship, funded through the gifts of alumni and other generous benefactors, employment opportunities for needy students, and tuition remission constituted student aid programs prior to the Civil War (Fenske, 1983). These programs of funded grants, tuition remission, and student employment established a number of trends (e.g., providing aid to the needy, multiple sources and types of aid, and institutional commitments of student assistance) that would influence the development of student aid programs sponsored by the states and the federal government.

Comprehensive, far-reaching, federal involvement in higher education is primarily a modern phenomenon (Coomes, 1994). The National Youth

Administration (NYA) was created in the 1930s to facilitate employment and is considered by some to be the first major program of direct federal aid to students (Brubacher & Rudy, 1976). The NYA was followed in 1944 by the Serviceman's Readjustment Act, more commonly known as the GI Bill. Like other programs that preceded it (NYA) and were to follow, the GI Bill was enacted for noneducational reasons: to reward the veterans of World War II for their service and to ease the burden on a fragile economy that a substantial increase in the number of employable men would represent (Rivlin, 1961).

In 1958, prompted by the 1957 launching of the *Sputnik* satellite and by a number of national reports outlining the nation's need for improved scientific and technical education, Congress passed the National Defense Education Act (NDEA). The NDEA authorized funds for colleges to improve the teaching of modern foreign languages, created a graduate fellowship program, and authorized funds for the dissemination of scientific information. The cornerstone of the act was a student loan program (the National Defense Student Loan—NDSL) for students planning teaching careers or pursuing programs in science, mathematics, or modern foreign languages (Conlan, 1981). In addition to creating the first program of generally available federal student aid, NDEA moved the federal government toward guaranteeing opportunity for education and established the precedent for making students, and not institutions, the primary beneficiaries of federal education funds (Conlan, 1981).

The next major piece of student aid legislation, the Higher Education Act (HEA) of 1965, was an outgrowth of an increasing national concern for the welfare of the underprivileged. The HEA created the Supplemental Educational Opportunity Grant (SEOG) and Guaranteed Student Loan (GSL) programs and transferred the College Work Study (CWS) program to the Office of Education (Moore, 1983). Enacted in a watershed year for federal domestic legislation, HEA "embodied for the first time an explicit commitment to equalizing college opportunities for needy students through grants and through such programs as Talent Search designed to facilitate access for the college-able poor" (Gladieux, 1983, p. 410).

With the passage of the Education Amendments of 1972, two new programs were created: the Basic Educational Opportunity Grant (BEOG, since renamed the Federal Pell Grant Program) and the State Student Incentive Grant (SSIG, subsequently renamed the Leveraging Educational Assistantship Partnerships—LEAP) program. The BEOG program was intended to serve as the foundation for a student's financial aid package and, when combined with the previously authorized programs (NDSL, SEOG, CWS, and GSL), stands as the zenith of federal support for educational access. Perhaps at no time before or since has the goal of student aid been so clear: to assist students who, for financial reasons, could not afford to attend a postsecondary institution. However, this goal was to be short-lived as new goals, including institutional choice and financial convenience, were to be accommodated by policy makers (Coomes, 2000a)

The passage of the Middle Income Student Assistance Act in 1978 extended participation in the federal student aid programs to the children of middle-class families. Not only would the financially disadvantaged be able to attend the postsecondary institution of their choice, but also middle income students now would be able to (Finn, 1985). The Education Amendments of 1980 further expanded the federal student aid programs through the creation of a new loan program, the Parents Loan for Undergraduate Study (PLUS).

Student aid legislation during the 1980s focused on the rising costs of federal student aid and on program efficiency issues. During the administrations of Ronald Reagan and George H. W. Bush, efforts were focused on reducing federal involvement in higher education and on limiting funding, not on creating new programs. While only one student aid program (i.e., Social Security Educational Benefits) was eliminated during the tenure of those presidents, constant efforts to reduce funding for the federal student aid programs resulted in very modest program growth (Coomes, 1994; Eaton, 1991).

The 1990s were marked by the creation of new programs, the development of new funding mechanisms, and the further extension of program eligibility to students from a wide range of income levels. In 1992, the Guaranteed Student Loan program was renamed the Federal Family Education Loan program, and in the following year, the Student Loan Reform Act of 1993 created the Federal Direct Student Loan program. In 1997, Congress passed the Taxpayer Relief Act. Based on policies instigated by then President William Jefferson Clinton and intended to meet the goal of making education universal through the thirteenth and fourteenth years, the act utilized tuition tax credits to offset the cost of higher education for students at a wide range of income levels (DeBard, 2000; Kosters, 1999; Roth, 2001). However, since the programs created by the Taxpayers Relief Act consist of tax credits against taxes paid, they seldom benefit low-income students who may come from families with modest or nonexistent tax liabilities (Kosters, 1999). As was the case with the Middle Income Student Assistance Act in 1978, the Tax Payers Relief Act of 1997 represents additional aid to middle-income families and further drift from the original goals of much of the federal government's student aid policies (Wolanin, 2001).

As the previous century drew to a close and a new one began, much of the public policy discourse on student aid was focused on the increasing cost of college attendance and on using aid to strategically impact institutional enrollments (Advisory Committee on Student Financial Assistance, 2001; Clotfelter, 1996; College Entrance Examination Board, 2002a; Cunningham, Wellman, Clinedinst, Merisotis, & Carroll, 2001a, 2001b; Russo & Coomes, 2000). Both of these issues are addressed in subsequent sections of this chapter.

In addition to federal involvement, the states have been involved in the creation and implementation of student aid programs. Many of the early state aid programs were created to assist students of high ability. The creation of state aid programs based on financial need with the intention of equalizing opportunity occurred concurrently with the development of the federal role in student aid (Marmaduke, 1983). Nineteen state aid programs existed prior to the 1969–1970 academic year, and by 1979 the remaining states and territories had instituted programs (Marmaduke, 1983). A major impetus for the development of state grant programs was the creation of the SSIG program in 1972 (the current LEAP program), which provided federal matching funds, intended to encourage states to create their own grant programs. In addition to state scholarship programs, state governments also funded loans and student employment programs. The most significant additions to state aid programs in the past 10 years have been the development of state supported merit scholarship programs, state tax breaks for college attendance, and college savings plans (Heller, 2002; Roth, 2001).

PHILOSOPHY AND PURPOSE

Historically, student aid has lacked a consistent philosophy. This is particularly the case at the federal level, where student aid has been used to realize goals only tangentially related to higher education (Coomes, 1994; Hansen, 1991). Student assistance programs have been used to reward members of the military for their service; as a means to encourage students to register for the draft, conduct community service, and avoid drug use; and as a means to force institutions to comply with a wide range of consumer information requirements (e.g., placement and graduation rates, campus safety statistics). This lack of a clearly and intentionally developed philosophy has resulted in a system that is at times overly confusing, cumbersome, and replete with duplicative programs (Coomes, 1994). In 1996, Coomes suggested that, while no intentional philosophy for student aid is present, it is possible to discern a set of goals that have emerged over time as policy makers have attempted to develop programs to meet the financing needs of postsecondary students. Some of these goals, as identified by Finn (1985). are to increase the supply of well-educated and highly skilled manpower in society;

> to nurture extraordinary individual talent . . .; to encourage the study of particular subjects or disciplines . . .; to increase social mobility, foster equality of opportunity, and diminish the importance of private wealth; [and] to advance interests of members of designated groups judged to be deprived in part by lack of access to or participation in higher education (pp. 2–3).

From 1965 through the mid-1970s, these last two goals were the primary purposes of federal student assistance and are frequently interpreted as improved equity and increased access to postsecondary education opportunities. However, since the mid-1970s, the contract between students and colleges has been breached, and the breaching of that contact has resulted in the two frequently conflicting purposes of maximizing resources for students and families and maximizing enrollments for institutions (Longanecker, 2002; McPherson & Shapiro, 1998, 2002). Many students (regardless of income level) now see student aid as both a necessity and an entitlement. This sense of entitlement has led to a consumer approach to the student aid system where students and their families bargain with institutions to secure the most favorable financial aid package (Monks, 2000, Russo & Coomes, 2000; White & Frishberg, 1997). Conversely, many institutions use student aid, through a process called preferential packaging, to attract students to meet a wide range of enrollment goals (e.g., increasing the number of high-achieving students, or students from specific racial or ethnic groups) (McPherson & Shapiro, 1998; Redd, 2001; White & Frishberg, 1997).

NEEDS ANALYSIS, BUDGET CONSTRUCTION, AND PACKAGING

Realizing the goals of equity and access for needy students requires a delivery system that equitably establishes the student's, and where appropriate the family's, ability to pay; determines the student's cost of education; and provides a package of resources to meet their calculated financial need. According to Case (1993), needs analysis is predicated on a number of important principles. First and foremost among those is that the student and, if the student is a dependent student, the student's parent(s) have the primary responsibility for paying for the student's education. Independent students are also required to use their income and assets to meet necessary educational and living expenses. The determination of a student's family financial situation should be "an objective assessment of their present [financial] circumstance" (Case, 1993, p. 2). Financial contributions should be built on progressive assessment rates; those with greater financial resources are required to make greater contributions toward their educational costs than those with more meager resources. Finally, "needs analysis procedures recognize that part of family resources must be devoted to taxes, basic living costs, and other unavoidable expenses; other expenditures that are a matter of family choice are usually not included as allowance against available income or discretionary net worth" (Case, 1993, p. 2). Each of these principles can be, and frequently are, challenged by applicants for financial aid, and while arguments can be proffered, one central concept is unassailable: Need-based financial aid should be awarded to those who cannot afford to attend college without that support. "Need" should not be confused with "want." Some families will be unwilling to tap their discretionary income and use those resources for educational costs; this does not make them financially needy. Discretionary income is just that—discretionary, and student aid policy makers believe the first use for discretionary income should be meeting educational costs.

Operationally, financial need is the difference between the student's cost of attendance (COA) and the student and/or family's expected family contribution (EFC). Since 1992, the EFC that must be used in establishing eligibility for the federal student aid programs has been calculated using the Federal Methodology (FM) established through data collected from the Free Application for Federal Student Aid (FAFSA). Data used in the FM to calculate the EFC include, but are not limited to:

- Student information (e.g., dependency status, student's year in college, student's marital status)
- Parent's information for dependent students (e.g., family size, number of tax exemptions)
- Family income, including both the parent's and the student's income
- Taxes paid; allowances for employment of both spouses in a two-parent family;
- An income protection allowance;
- Medical and dental expenses; and
- Family assets (e.g., savings; investments; but, as of the 1993–1994 award year, not home equity).

While determination of EFC for the federal student aid programs is determined by the FAFSA, the National Association of Student Aid Administrators has advanced the idea of "resource analysis," which "represents a reasonable measure of the family's ability to contribute toward postsecondary education costs and may be used by institutions, agencies, and donor organizations" (Case, 1993, p. 1). Resource analysis is most frequently accomplished through the application of the Institutional Methodology (IM) developed by the College Entrance Examination Board, and many student aid administrators consider it a more realistic assessment of the families ability to pay for a postsecondary education (Bandre, 2001a; College Board, 2002).

Needs analysis raises a number of interesting and important philosophical questions: Should a needs analysis system "objectively" determine the family's ability to pay or should it be used as a means to ration limited student aid resources? What family resources should be included in determining the EFC? How should a student's dependency status be determined? Which data elements should aid officers be allowed to change "for cause," and how should aid officers employ their professional judgment in making changes to needs analysis calculations? Should individual institutions be required to use FM for determining student eligibility for need-based institutional funds? Readers wishing to explore the answers to these questions as well as philosophical reasons for, and policy implications of, needs analysis are directed to Bandre (2001a, 2001b); Case (1993); Fitzgerald (1991); Guthrie (2001); and Heffron (1990).

The second element of need determination is the establishment of the student's cost of attendance. For federal student financial aid programs, cost includes tuition and fees, an allowance for room and board, allowances for books and supplies, transportation, and miscellaneous personal expenses (Research Publications Group, 2001). While costs are rather rigidly controlled by statutory guidelines, student aid officers do have the authority to utilize their professional judgment to adjust the cost of attendance on a case-by-case basis if they think that such an adjustment is warranted (Research Publications Group, 2001). Additional information on the process of constructing student budgets can be found in *Constructing Student Expenses Budgets* (National Association of Student Financial Aid Administrators, 1993a) and the *Student Financial Aid Handbook* (Research Publications Group, 2001).

Few students receive only one type of aid; rather, most students receive a combination of grants, loans, and student employment funds, referred to as a financial aid package. Like the determination of the family's and/or student's ability to pay and the establishment of realistic expense budgets, financial aid packaging is a complex process. Federal Pell Grants usually form the foundation of a student's financial aid package, and Federal Supplement Education Opportunity Grants (FSEOG) and Federal Perkins Loans (FPLs) must be awarded to exceptionally needy students (Research Publications Group, 2001). Once Pell Grants, FSEOG, and Perkins Loans have been awarded, remaining need can be met with a combination of Federal Work Study, institutional aid, loans from either the Federal Family Education Loan Program or the William D. Ford Federal Direct Loan Program, state assistance, and/or institutional aid. Students who receive funding from private sources (e.g., private scholarships) must have that aid included in their financial aid package. It must be remembered that if a student is receiving need-based financial aid, the sum total of a student's financial aid cannot exceed the student's demonstrated financial need.

STUDENT AID PROGRAMS

Traditionally, student aid has come in three types: grants, loans, and employment (Coomes, 1988). As noted earlier, these traditional types of aid have been supplemented in recent years by tuition tax credits and incentives as alternative means of financing higher education (DeBard, 2000). This section examines the three general aid types, discusses the typical funding sources for student aid programs, and describes the generally available federal student aid programs.

Grants are nonrepayable student aid resources or gift aid. Dannells (1977) identified five different types of gift aid: (1) grants, which are non-repayable awards based on financial need (e.g., Pell Grant, Ohio Instructional Grants); (2) merit/honors scholarships, which are based on the student's past performance, future promise, exceptional intellectual potential, or outstanding leadership abilities (Finn, 1985); (3) graduate fellowships for graduate study (Dannells, 1977); (4) tuition remission and subsidized tuition, which is frequently awarded to the spouses or children of university employees (Finn, 1985); and (5) service awards given to students for services rendered or in anticipation of future services (e.g., athletic scholarships and performing arts scholarships) (Finn, 1985).

Of special note are grants awarded at the institutional level, especially grants intended to assist in attracting students to college. Colleges that utilize institutional funds engage in the process of tuition discounting (Allan 2001; Redd, 2000). According to Allan, tuition discounts are financial aid (they must be considered as part of the student's aid package); can be awarded for need-based or merit purposes; are not an institutional expense, but a reduction in revenue; and are not part of an institution's general subsidy. Furthermore, tuition discounts are viewed differently by different constituent groups. Administrators (e.g., admissions officers) frequently see these programs as ways of generating revenue by increasing enrollments, whereas institutional finance officers see tuition discounts as a potential drain on the overall health of the institution. The value of tuition discounting has been called into question. Redd (2000) noted that between 1991 and 1999 institutions with the greatest tuition discount rates showed a net loss on average of over $306 per full-time student in net tuition revenue. In the same study, Redd noted that tuition discounting "was most successful at helping institutions achieve their goals of providing greater access to higher education for low-income students than attracting more academically talented freshmen" (p. 3).

Loan funds require repayment and can be made to either the student or, where appropriate, the student's parent(s). The repayment of many loans is deferred until the student leaves school, but some programs require repayment while the student is enrolled. Many student loans carry interest rates lower than the rates for other types of loans because the interest rate is subsidized by a lender or by state or federal governments. Most loans are made to pay general educational expenses and are awarded as part of the student aid package. However, many institutions maintain short-term loan programs that are intended to aid students in meeting emergency expenses. As federal, state, and institutional aid has failed to keep pace with rising postsecondary costs and student financial need, many private lenders have developed educational loan programs, frequently referred to as alternative loans. These private loan programs generally carry higher interest rates than the governmental loan programs. Estimates of the percentage of undergraduates receiving alternative loans in the 1999–2000 academic year vary from 7 percent to 11 percent (Redd & Miller 2002). For the 2001–2002 academic year, an estimated $5.6 billion was lent to students in the form of nongovernmental loans, an increase of $4.1 billion or 265 percent since 1996 (College Entrance Examination Board, 2002b).

Student employment funds may be either need-based or non–need-based. Although many students work while attending a postsecondary institution, only those jobs provided or arranged by the institution are rightfully considered student aid (Dannells, 1977). Student employment positions can exist in both on- and off-campus settings, and financial aid officers frequently attempt to place students in jobs that complement their academic interests.

FUNDING SOURCES

Funding for the various student aid programs comes from a variety of sources. In 1975, the National Task Force on Student Aid Problems identified the following sources of student aid: the federal government; state governments; postsecondary institutions; and private sources, including corporations, service clubs, and philanthropic organizations (Binder, 1983).

The federal government is the largest source of aid for students. For the 2002 academic year, federal funding for student aid totaled an estimated $62 billion, or 69 percent of all aid awarded (College Entrance Examination Board, 2002b). Funding for the generally available student aid programs for the same year totaled an estimated $543 billion (College Entrance Examination Board, 2002b). From the 1992 academic year to the 2002 academic year, funding for generally available federal student assistance increased (in inflation-adjusted dollars) by $26 billion, or 92 percent (College Entrance Examination Board, 2001b). Since the early 1980s, the largest federal programs have been the federal student loan programs (most specifically the William D. Direct and Federal Family Education Loan Programs). In 2002, federal student loan funds accounted for 78 percent of all federally supported generally available aid and 47 percent of funds from all federal, state, and institutional sources (College Entrance Examination Board, 2002b). From the 1992 academic year to the 2002 academic year, funding for the federal loan programs grew (in inflation-adjusted dollars) by $23 billion or 121 percent (College Entrance Examination Board, 2002b). During that time period, federal grant assistance increased (in inflation-adjusted dollars) by $2.5 billion, or 31 percent (College Entrance Examination Board, 2002b). It is abundantly clear from these data that students and families are taking on a significantly larger share of their college expenses by borrowing against the future through the student loan programs (Fossey & Bateman, 1998).

All 50 states as well as the District of Columbia and Puerto Rico support some type of student aid programs (DeSalvatore & Hughes, 2002). State aid programs vary widely in terms of type (e.g., need-based and merit grants, loans, and student employment) and in terms of the amount allocated to those programs by state legislatures. Nationally, state-supported aid totaled $5.9 billion in academic year 2001 (DeSalvatore & Hughes, 2002). The vast majority of those funds ($4.7 billion) came in the form of need-based and non–need-based grants to students (DeSalvatore & Hughes, 2002). From the 1995 academic year to the 2000 academic year, state grant aid increased (in current dollars) by $1.75 billion (60%). Funding for student aid programs with a merit component totaled $1.6 billion in 2001 (DeSalvatore & Hughes, 2002). According to the College Board (College Entrance Examination Board, 2001a),

> Since the early 1990s, the states have taken a sharp turn in the direction of non-need merit scholarships. Non-need state aid has grown 336% while need-based aid has grown by 88%. (p. 5)

Funding from individual states varies widely and is generally a function of the number of students enrolled in the state's postsecondary institutions. New York has the oldest and largest state-supported grant program. In academic year 2001, New York awarded $664 million in state aid (DeSalvatore & Hughes, 2002)

Like the other sources, institutions support the full range of grant, loan, and student employment programs. In 2002, institutional awards totaled $17 billion (College Entrance Examination Board, 2002b). From 1992 to 2002, institutional aid increased (in inflation-adjusted dollars) by $8.7 billion, or 105%. Much of that increase can be attributed to the need to offset rapidly increasing costs of attendance and to an increase in merit-based institutional aid. According to the College Board (College Entrance Examination Board, 2001), "the largest increases in average institutional grants at private institutions in the 1980s and 1990s were for middle-income and upper-income students" (p. 5).

THE FEDERAL STUDENT AID PROGRAMS

This section provides a broad overview of generally available federal student aid programs[1] as well as information on institutional and student eligibility. For more detailed program descriptions and detailed information on

---

1. The federal government offers a wide range of programs to assist students with meeting their educational costs (e.g., Paul Douglas Teacher Scholarships, Reserve Officers Training Corp Scholarships, veterans benefits). However, for purposes of this chapter, discussion will be limited to generally available student financial aid programs authorized under Title IV of Higher Education Act of 1965 and its amendments.

administering the federal student aid programs, student affairs practitioners are directed to the current editions of *The Student Financial Aid Handbook* (Research Publications Group, 2001, updated annually and available at www.ifap.ed.gov/IFAPWebApp/currentSFAHandbooksPag.jsp) and *The NASFAA Encyclopedia of Student Financial Aid* (Burns, 1984, updated annually).

Institutional Eligibility

For students to receive federal student financial aid, they must attend an eligible postsecondary institution. Institutions of higher education (e.g., colleges and universities), proprietary institutions (e.g., private, for-profit educational institutions), and postsecondary vocational institutions are all eligible to participate in the federal student financial aid programs (Research Publications Group, 2001). Eligible participating institutions must comply with a wide range of administrative standards (e.g., establish an institutional drug abuse prevention policy) if they wish to continue to participate in federal financial assistance programs. Institutions must provide applicants with information on the types and amounts of student aid available at the institution: how eligibility is determined and aid is awarded; institutional degree programs; satisfactory academic progress standards; and instructional personnel and physical facilities (Research Publications Group, 2001). In addition, schools participating in the student assistance programs must comply with the requirements of the following protective policy laws: the Family Educational Rights and Privacy Act, the Student Consumer Information Act and its amendments, the Equity in Athletic Disclosure Act, the Student-Right-to-Know and Campus Security Act (including the Sexual Assault Victim's Bill of Rights), and the Drug Free Workplace Act of 1988 (Research Publications Group, 2001). Participating institutions must also ensure that the aid program is effectively managed, that counseling is offered to students, that adequate staff is available to meet student needs, that they avoid excess loan default rates, and that they participate in all electronic processes required by the Department of Education (Research Publications Group, 2001).

Student Eligibility

In addition to institutional compliance, students must meet certain criteria if they wish to receive assistance from the federal government. Students must be U.S. citizens or nationals, permanent residents of the United States, or citizens of the Freely Associate States (i.e., the Marshall Islands, the Federated States of Micronesia and Palua). Certain students who are noncitizens—refugees and individuals granted permanent asylum in the United States—are also eligible to participate in the programs (Research Publications Group, 2001). To receive federal assistance, students must be enrolled in an eligible program of study; possess a high school diploma or its equivalent, or demonstrate the ability to benefit from a postsecondary education; maintain satisfactory academic progress; generally not be in default on a federal loan or owe a repayment of a federal grant; posses a valid social security number; and if required, be registered with the Selective Service System (Research Publications Group, 2001).

Federal Pell Grants

First authorized by the Education Amendments of 1972 and originally titled the Basic Educational Opportunity Grant (BEOG) program, Federal Pell Grants were intended to serve as the foundation of a student's financial aid award (Coomes, 1994). This need-based grant program was envisioned by its creators as a quasi-entitlement program, that is, "grants were to be made to every student who was determined eligible under a formula that assessed the family's ability to contribute toward a student's cost of education" (Moore, 1983, p. 37). However, appropriations for Federal Pell Grants have seldom been adequate to fully fund the grant program. A second major difference between the Federal Pell Grant and other federal grants is its portability. Awards are made directly to students, who can use the award at any eligible institution they choose to attend. The maximum amount of individual grants is determined each year based on yearly appropriations from Congress. As the foundation of the students financial aid package, Federal Pell Grants are intended to be awarded to low-income recipients. In 1999–2000, 84 percent of recipients came from families with incomes of less than $30,000, and the median income for all recipients was $15,118 (National Association of Student Financial Aid Administrators, 2001a).

William D. Ford Direct and Federal Family Education Loan Programs

In 1965, Congress created the Guaranteed Student Loan (GSL) program, a program of subsidized low-interest loans (Coomes, 1994). The program was renamed the Federal Family Education Loan Program (FFEL) in 1992 (Research Publications Group, 2001). In 1993, the Student Loan Reform Act created the William D. Ford Direct Loan Program (Research Publications Group, 2001). The Direct Loan program was created to simplify the existing loan program and to reduce interest subsidies and default payments to lenders and guarantee agencies and thus the cost to the federal government.

Both the Direct Loan program and the FFEL program provide low-interest loans to undergraduate and graduate students (Research Publications Group, 2001). The major difference between the William D. Ford Direct Loan Program and Federal Family Education Loan Program (FFEL) program is who makes the loans to students. Under the Direct Loan program, students and/or parents apply directly to their institution for a loan and the institution determines eligibility for and the amount of the loan. Once approved, payments are made to the student and/or the parent through the institution. Eligibility for the FFEL program is determined by the student's institution, but funds are lent by private lenders such as banks or credit unions, and repayment is made to those lending agencies. Students, and the parents' of students, who attend institutions that do not participate in the Direct Loan program participate in the FFEL program. Loan limits vary, depending on dependency level and year in school, and interest rates vary across programs and are adjusted each year.

Campus-Based Programs

The campus-based programs are the Federal Supplemental Educational Opportunity Grant (FSEOG), Federal Work Study (FWS), and the Federal Perkins Loan programs. All three programs are managed at the campus level. Funds for the three programs are allocated by the federal government directly to the institution, and eligibility for awards and award amounts are determined by the campus aid officer using the FAFSA. The federal government has established statutory limits on the amount of aid a student may receive from each of the campus-based programs as well as general administrative responsibilities that apply to all three programs (Research Publications Group, 2001).

The FSEOG is intended for low-income undergraduate students and first priority for awarding FSEOG funds must be given to students who have received Pell Grants. In academic year 2000, 86 percent of recipients came from families with annual incomes of less than $30,000 (National Association of Student Financial Aid Administrators, 2001a).

Federal Work Study is self-help program; students must work for an eligible employer to earn FWS funds. In 2002, 48 percent of the 1 million students receiving FWS awards came from families with incomes less than $30,000 (National Association of Student Financial Aid Administrators, 2002). As of 1992, certain colleges that have earned the designation "work colleges" have been allowed to utilize a percentage of their FWS and Federal Perkins Loan funding to facilitate comprehensive work programs and service learning programs on their campuses (Research Publications Group, 2001).

The oldest of the Title IV federal student aid programs is the Federal Perkins Loan program. Created in 1958 as the National Defense Student Loan, the program provides fixed-rate, low-interest loans to financially needy graduate and undergraduate students. Funds come from federal appropriations, institutional matching funds, and repayments from borrowers. In 1999–2000, approximately 700,000 graduate and undergraduate students received FPLs. Of those students, 52 percent came from families with incomes less than $30,000.

ADMINISTERING STUDENT AID

SOUND FINANCIAL AID PRACTICE

The student aid profession has been directed by various statements of professional practice since the early 1950s (Hart, 1991). The most recent of such statements was adopted by the members of the National Association of Student Financial Aid Officers (NASFAA) in April 1999. That statement reads:

> The primary goal of the financial aid professional is to help students achieve their educational potential by providing appropriate financial resources. To this end, this Statement provides the Financial Aid Professional with a set of principles that serves as a common foundation for accepted standards of conduct. The Financial Aid Professional shall:
>
> 1. Be committed to removing financial barriers for those who wish to pursue postsecondary learning.
> 2. Make every effort to assist students with financial need.
> 3. Be aware of the issues affecting students and advocate their interests at the institutional, state, and federal levels.
> 4. Support efforts to encourage students, as early as the elementary grades, to aspire to and plan for education beyond high school.
> 5. Educate students and families through quality consumer information.
> 6. Respect the dignity and protect the privacy of students, and ensure the confidentiality of student records and personal circumstances.
> 7. Ensure equity by applying all need analysis formulas consistently across the institution's full population of student financial aid applicants.
> 8. Provide services that do not discriminate on the basis of race, gender, ethnicity, sexual orientation, religion, disability, age, or economic status.
> 9. Recognize the need for professional development and continuing education opportunities.
> 10. Promote the free expression of ideas and opinions, and foster respect for diverse viewpoints within the profession.
> 11. Commit to the highest level of ethical behavior and refrain from conflict of interest or the perception thereof.
> 12. Maintain the highest level of professionalism, reflecting a commitment to the goals of the National Association of Student Financial Aid Administrators (National Association of Student Financial Aid Administrators, 1999).

RESPONSIBILITIES AND ROLES

Johnstone and Huff (1983) suggested that the financial aid administrator must fulfill the following responsibilities: serving students, informing the institutional community, promoting the programs efficiently, ensuring program integrity, and educating students and others. A similar list was developed by the College Scholarship service in 1973 and included the additional responsibility of research and professional development (College Scholarship Service, 1989).

The traditional roles for the student aid officer have been counseling and administrative management (Lange, 1983). Since much of financial aid administration involves the interpretation and communication of regulations, application processes, and award details to students and the management of personnel and programs, these two roles have maintained their centrality. However, the roles of student aid administrators have become more complex as the number and types of students and programs have grown in the past 30 years (Gordon, 1994; Hart, 1991). "Today . . . the financial aid world is full of individuals who emphasize computer savvy, legislation literacy, and numerical knowledge" (Gordon, 1994, p. 16). The most important trend that has shaped student aid administrators' current role is the advent of technology. Other factors that have necessitated a changing role for student aid administrators include increasing campus diversity necessitating "specialized counseling techniques and financial assistance programs" (Gordon, 1994, p. 16); increasingly complex and diverse student aid programs; and customer needs and the need to integrate with other campus offices in a total enrollment management plan (Hossler, 2000; Russo & Coomes, 2000).

STRUCTURE AND STAFFING

A 1999 (Williams) report of student aid officers indicated that student financial aid offices reported to one to the following administrative units: student affairs (38%), enrollment management (19%), campus executive or general administration (18%), business and finance (11%), and academic affairs (7%). Differences do exist when examining reporting lines by institutional sector and type. Financial aid offices are most frequently part of the student services division at four-year public institutions (45%) and two-year public colleges (77%). At four-year private colleges, the student aid function is most likely part of an enrollment services division (38%) indicating the important role student aid plays in ensuring adequate enrollments at private colleges. Finally, at proprietary institutions, the student aid office most frequently (83%) reports directly to the institution's chief executive officer.

Valid reasons exist for placing the aid office in any of the aforementioned divisions. Johnstone and Huff (1983) provided an eloquent rationale for housing student aid in the student affairs division: "The office of financial aid reports to the dean of students or vice president for student affairs not merely because it is manifestly a 'helping' service but because it must have extensive communication with all the offices that deal closely with the out-of-class-room problems of students; also, it must share the basic 'helping' orientation traditionally associated with student affairs" (p. 249). The value of linking student aid to the enrollment management function of the university is examined in the section on practice paradigms. As is the case with many organizational decisions, the final disposition of the student aid office within the organization will be a result of institutional mission (DeJarnett, 1975), the personal preference and expertise of the aid administrator (Adams, 1975), historical accident, or institutional politics.

A 2001 examination of student aid staffing patterns (Redd & Miller, 2002) disclosed that the average student aid office consisted of 6 full-time staff members; four-year public institutions had the largest staffs (11 full-time staff members), while two-year private colleges had the smallest staffs (1 full-time staff members). The majority (54%) of chief financial aid administrators responding to the survey indicated that their highest level of educational attainment was the master's degree, 34 percent held the bachelor's degree, and only 0.4 percent held a doctoral degree (Redd & Miller, 2002).

PRACTICE MODELS

Unlike many other student affairs areas, student aid clearly sees itself as a student service. Rather than dealing with the central issues of many student affairs programs, such as student learning, growth, and development, financial aid offices play an important maintenance role on college campuses. Limited applications of student development and learning theory to student aid practice have been developed (e.g., Coomes, 1992). Most of the student aid literature has focused on improving student aid services (Russo & Coomes, 2000), counseling skills, and the integration of student aid into enrollment management models (Coomes, 2000b). This latter paradigm, while relatively recent, has become much more prevalent on college campuses and warrants further discussion.

Enrollment management as an organizational philosophy and structural model has existed since the late 1970s (Hossler, 1996). The definition of enrollment management, the reasons for its development, and suggestions for implementing enrollment management within an institutional setting are offered in this volume by Hossler (Chapter 3). This section explores the role of student aid in that process. The efficient delivery of student aid resources has important implications for student matriculation and persistence (Graff, 1986). The financial aid office must work with the offices of admissions to ensure that students receive all the aid for which they are eligible and that students "receive their awards in a timely fashion" (Hossler & Bean, 1990, p. 8). By improving services to students and ensuring effective cooperation and communication between other service areas (e.g., bursar and registrar), the financial aid office can assist in the removal of structural barriers that may influence student persistence. Finally, the financial aid office has an important responsibility within the enrollment management paradigm to participate in the development of research on the relationship of student aid to student recruitment and persistence and the accomplishment of institutional objectives (Huff, 1989, Nelson & Fenske, 1983; Wilcox, 1991).

Enrollment management models similar to those described by Hossler (1984, 1986a) appear to provide student aid offices with the most useful practice paradigm. Such an approach not only ensures that student aid is playing a critical role in the recruitment and retention of students but also ensures that it is supporting the overall mission of the institution. When coupled with concepts that focus on customer service (Lackey & Pugh, 1994) and the development of new student aid products, the student financial services model may be reaching a new level of maturity (Russo & Coomes, 2000).

TECHNOLOGY

This section explores three different aspects of the application of technology to the student aid arena. The first aspect focuses on how technology is being utilized to deliver student aid to students. The second aspect explores how students and families are utilizing readily available web-based resources to make the application process more open and accessible and presents some caveats on web-based resources. That discussion is followed by a listing of web-based resources that may be of use to practitioners, researchers, and applicants for student aid.

The highly quantitative, formalized, and routinized (Hage & Aiken, 1970) nature of much of student aid work makes it an area that is particularly appropriate for the application of technology. Because of the complexities of the student aid programs and the numbers of students applying for and receiving assistance, it is nearly impossible, even at small institutions, to administer the student aid programs without the use of a wide range of technological resources. In addition, all institutions are required to employ some level of technological sophistication to participate in the federal (and some state) student aid programs. Currently, the federal student aid system utilizes computerized systems to conduct needs analysis (the FAFSA on the web), transmit student eligibility data through the Institutional Student Information Report (ISIR), and report Pell Grant expenditures through the Recipient and Financial Management System (RFMS), to name just a few activities. Redd and Miller (2002) reported that access to "the World Wide Web, electronic mail (e-mail), and the National Student Loan Data System (NSLDS) has become nearly universal in the financial aid office" (p. 30). Other types of technology (e.g., instant messaging) were utilized less widely across different types of institutions.

Kennedy, Cornell, Fox, Osswald, Williams, Wilson, Zuzack, and Gelinas (2000) present a very detailed examination of the ways in which student aid offices can use technology in a fully automated and integrated enrollment management system. According to Kennedy et al., student aid administrators must carefully evaluate their technological needs before implementing new systems or modifying existing ones. They suggest that such an evaluation consider the system's ability to enhance student services, its flexibility and adaptability, and its openness to accommodating and incorporating newer technologies. They further go on to delineate an extensive list of activities that an integrated system should accomplish, including fund management and auditing; establishment of cost of attendance, needs analysis, student aid packaging, award notification, disbursement and student correspondence; loan processing; maintenance of award histories; data importing and exporting (with the federal government, state agencies, lenders, and guarantee agencies); professional judgment; report development; and satisfactory academic progress monitoring, to name just a few. The complexities of the student aid system make it necessary for student aid administrators to continually modify their existing technology applications and add new services. As Kennedy et al. (2000) noted,

> System acquisition, maintenance, and enhancement are components of a *continual process* [emphasis in original]; understanding this allows a school to meet the demands of all its constituents, and to remain competitive in the changing environment. (p. 19)

Meeting constituent demands and attaining a competitive edge are important outcomes, but the implementation of technology in student aid services has not come without attendant costs. As early as 1994, Sears contended that student aid administrators have become technocrats who are more interested in "information than ideas" (p. 18). Many aid administrators have become more "process-oriented," attending to the demands of programs rather than "client-services oriented," attending to the needs of students (Gordon, 1994). An unfortunate side effect of this process and program orientation is the perception that student aid officers are bureaucratic information managers who are interested more in regulatory compliance and legislative interpretation, than educators interested in meeting the needs of students. Technological applications in student financial aid have traditionally been targeted at information management systems designed to increase efficiency and effectiveness (Gordon, 1992). This use of technology to handle complex but relatively routinized tasks should ensure that student aid officers have more time to spend counseling students with more complex needs. As Gibbons (2002) noted,

> The single most important service we can provide is direct human contact to address student inquiries. Voice messaging and online information can be effective in handling certain routine questions, but at some point, students want and expect to speak directly with a financial aid counselor. . . . We should remember the fundamental, human aspects of providing access to higher education and financial aid services to students. Critical thinking, empathic

counseling , and professional judgment may be enhanced by technology, but they cannot be replaced by it (p. 8).

One final note on the application of technology to the operation of student aid offices is necessary. As Kennedy et al. (2000) noted, technology is not evenly distributed across socioeconomic groups. Many poor students may not have ready access to the Internet, thus limiting their ability to avail themselves of computer-mediated student aid resources. For that reason, the federal government, the state, and institutions must continue to make alternative resources available.

Student aid offices are not the only ones to become more dependent on technology. Students and families have become quite adept at utilizing various online resources to calculate financial need, shop for the best student loan interest rates, search and apply for scholarships, and track their institutional student aid awards. The FAFSA on the Web has already been discussed as the primary means for applying for student aid. This free and universally available service has been supplemented by a wide range of free and for-profit web-based student aid search engines.

Students and families need to be very careful in employing online (or face-to-face) scholarship search services because a fair degree of fraud exists. A search of the World Wide Web in 2003 using the descriptor "scholarship data bases" yielded more than 48,400 hits. Certainly, many of these resources are legitimate, but many would fall under the heading of scholarship scams. The issue of scholarship scams became such a concern to Congress that it passed the Scholarship Fraud Prevention Act in 2000. This legislation resulted in increased penalties for individuals and organizations that engage in fraudulent activities, eliminated certain bankruptcy protections for scam artists, and required that the Departments of Education and Justice and the Federal Trade Commission (FTC) report annually to Congress on scholarship fraud. The first such report was issued in May 2002 (U.S. Department of Justice, Department of Education, & Federal Trade Commission). That report noted that the incidence of scholarship fraud had declined since the passage of the act in 2000 and that the types of fraud had changed from those perpetrated by telemarketers to fraudulent activities perpetrated through direct mailings and by financial aid consulting firms. Finally, the report presented information on 11 companies and 30 individuals who were the "subject of federal court orders prohibiting future misrepresentations" (U.S. Department of Justice, Department of Education, & Federal Trade Commission, 2002, p. iii). Future editions of the report will allow policy makers and consumers to track the level of fraud associated with scholarship programs. Students and families wishing to utilize scholarship search firms or web-based search engines should be encouraged to do so with caution and only after carefully researching the appropriate firms and sites. Consumers should avail themselves of resources such as those provided by the U.S. Department of Education (http://www.ed.gov/

prog_info/SFA/LSA) with its link to the FTC's Project Scholarscam web page and resources available on the FinAid: The SmartStudent Guide to Financial Aid webpage (http://www.finaid.com). Available information on scholarship databases, financial aid consultants, and search services is available for student aid professionals at http://www.finaid.org./educators and through the NASFFA web page at http://www.nasfaa.org/publications/2000/consultantsservices.asp.

Numerous student aid web sites exist that may be of interest to policy makers, student aid scholars, and the general public. The following is a short listing of sites, including sites sponsored by governmental agencies, nongovernmental organizations, and professional associations, and general information sites.

Governmental Web Sites

Department of Education (http://www.ed.gov/index.jsp). This entry portal for the Department of Education contains information and links to all of the department's agencies and initiatives. Of particular interest are the student aid–related sites, which include information on finding and applying for student aid (FAFSA On the Web) and loan repayment and consolidation. Resources for financial aid professionals, including the FSA (Federal Student Aid) Library, the FSA News, and FSA Training, are available at http://www.ifap.ed.gov/IFAPWebApp/index.jsp).

National Center for Education Statistics (http://nces.ed.gov/). A wealth of information and data on education from preschool through graduate school. Of particular use to scholars and administrators is the information generated through the Integrated Postsecondary Education Data System (IPEDS), which includes the annual *Digest of Education Statistics* and the National Postsecondary Student Aid Study (NPSAS) available at http://nces.ed.gov/surveys/npsas/index.asp.

Advisory Committee on Student Financial Assistance (http://www.ed.gov/offices/AC/ACSFA/index.html). This independent committee was created by Congress in 1986 and began operation in 1988. The site contains valuable information on student aid simplification, distance learning, early awareness programs, and other important issues related to the operation of the federal student aid programs.

Nongovernmental Organizations and Professional Associations

National Association of Student Financial Aid Administrators—NASFAA (http://www.nasfaa.org). The home site for NASFAA provides a wealth of information for students, families, and practicing professionals. The last group is particularly well supported through resources that include a daily newsletter, management and training materials, bibliographies, federal regulations, a job classified data bank, and position papers developed by the association. This site should be the first one visited by any professional wishing to gain information about student aid.

National Association of State Student Grant and Aid Programs—NASSGAP (http://www.nassgap.org). This association's site contains the Annual NASSGAP Survey report, which contains data on state-sponsored grant programs as well as other state-supported student aid programs. It also contains links to a range of student aid–related sites, position papers authored by the association, and information for members.

National Council of Higher Education Loan Programs—NCHELP (http://www.nchelp.org). NCHELP represents a nationwide network of guaranty agencies, secondary markets, lenders, loan servicers, collection agencies, schools, and other organizations involved in the administration of the Federal Family Education Loan Program (FFELP). The site contains links to a variety of reports and policy briefings on the FFELP program.

The College Board (http://www.collegeboard.com). The College Board is a nonprofit membership association that has focused its work on admissions and financial aid since 1900. Their web site provides information on college admissions, admissions testing, needs analysis (including a fee-based needs analysis application), and resources on student aid for educational professionals. Of particular importance are two annual reports published by the College Board, *Trends in College Pricing* and *Trends in Student Aid*.

General Information Sites

FinAid (http://www.finaid.org). One of the oldest web sites focusing on student aid issues, FinAid was founded in 1994. This comprehensive site offers information and links for student, parents, financial aid administrators, and educators. Of particular note is the important and reliable information it provides on scholarships and on how to avoid scholarship scams.

FastWeb (http://www.fastweb.com). FastWeb is the largest of a number of independent and free scholarship databases on the web. It contains information on more than $1 billion in financial assistance as well as advice on selecting a college.

PROFESSIONAL DEVELOPMENT

PROFESSIONAL ASSOCIATIONS

The National Association of Student Financial Aid Administrators (NASFAA) was founded as the National Student Aid Council in October 1966 (Brooks, 1986). NASFAA had its roots in a number of organizations, including the College Scholarship Service and its parent organization, the College Board; Commission V of the American College Personnel Association; and a number of regional student aid officer associations (e.g., Midwest Association of Student Financial Aid Administrators). The development of NASFAA was a result of the increasingly complex nature of student aid brought about by the creation of such programs as the National Direct Student Loan and the Supplemental Educational Opportunity Grant and by the emergence of campus administrative units focusing specifically on the administration of student aid resources.

According to their mission statement, the NASFFA represents

> . . . the student financial aid interests of institutions of postsecondary education in the United States. The primary goal of the Association is to promote maximum funding and effective delivery of financial assistance to students who are in need of additional funds to pursue their education beyond high school. (National Association of Student Financial Aid Administrators, 1993b, paragraph 1).

To realize this goal, the association serves as a forum for the discussion of student aid–related issues, sponsors research on student aid and its impact on students and institutions, offers a wide range of training opportunities and materials for new and experienced aid officers, advocates on behalf of students and institutions with student aid policy makers, and facilitates the development of professional identity through publications and national conferences.

NASFAA is governed by an Executive Board and an Executive Administration that consists of four divisions, (1) Finance and Membership Services, (2) Governmental Affairs, (3) Program Planning and Development, and (4) Training and Technical Assistance. The Executive Board is responsible for setting organizational policy. while the Executive Administration sees to the

> . . . day-to-day administrative tasks of the Association, . . . develops materials and coordinates arrangements for . . . leadership and national conferences, . . . coordinates the development of the five-year strategic plan, [the] activities of the Board of Directors, the Standards of Excellence Review Program" and oversees the organizations elections. (National Association of Student Financial Aid Administrators, 2002)

The Finance and Membership division is responsible for basic administrative functions, including membership services. The Governmental Affairs and Training and Technical Assistance divisions are primarily responsible for fulfilling one to the Association's most important functions—governmental advocacy. Because of the highly complex and technical nature of many of the student aid programs, NASFAA has carefully built and nurtured a reputation as the voice of expertise with many student aid policy makers. Few other student affairs associations can point to as successful a record in shaping and influencing federal education policy as can NASFAA.

In addition to their advocacy responsibilities, the Training and Technical Assistance division in conjunction with the Program Planning and

Development division, advance the association's other major role, that of providing professional development and training to its members. To realize this goal, the Association holds an annual national conference, conducts a wide range of technical training programs, and produces a number of print and electronic publications. The *NASFAA Encyclopedia* (available in print and online versions) is one of the most comprehensive sources of information on the federal student aid programs available, while the *Journal of Student Financial Aid* presents research on student aid related issues. Opinion and practice-oriented articles see print in the Association's magazine the *Student Aid Transcript.*

The work of NASFAA is complemented by six regional student aid associations (e.g., the Midwest Association of Student Financial Aid Administrators, the Western Association of Student Financial Aid Administrators). In addition, each of the 50 states, Puerto Rico, and the District of Columbia have their own associations of student aid administrators. Regional and state associations focus on issues of importance to their specific areas and ensure that student aid resources such as newsletters, training meetings, and conferences are available to administrators who may not be able to take advantage of or participate in activities sponsored by the national association.

ISSUES AND TRENDS

The issues and trends facing student aid policy makers and administrators are the same issues and trends facing higher education in general. These include demands from the public and their elected representatives for increased accountability; rising costs; limited resources; a rapidly changing student clientele that is becoming increasingly diverse on a number of dimensions (e.g., race and ethnicity, socioeconomic status, academic perpetration and ability); the technological revolution; and declining public confidence in the value of a postsecondary education.

In 1988, Coomes identified the following issues as having particular salience for the student aid field: overregulation; changing student populations; student debt levels; limits on access to postsecondary education brought about reductions in aid for the neediest students; a growing financial need gap; and deficit reduction (an issue thought dead in the 1990s, but certain to reemerge in the 2000s). In 1996, Coomes added the following issues: the creation of alternative financing plans for postsecondary education (e.g., increased support for merit scholarships or college savings and prepayment plans); program complexity; the credentialing and professional preparation of student aid administrators; student loan default issues; increasing technological demands, and fiscal accountability. As many of those issues are still salient, readers are encouraged to read the discussions of each in earlier versions of this chapter. To these lists could be added rising educational costs, the impact of the terrorist attacks of September 11, 2001, and the abrogation of the original mission of the student aid programs.

ESCALATING COSTS

The 1990s and early 2000s were periods when the cost of attending college rapidly outpaced the rate of inflation, and those rising costs become a source of considerable concern for parents, students, and public policy makers (Clotfelter, 1996; National Commission on the Cost of Higher Education, 1998; Vogelstein, 1998). According to the College Entrance Examination Board (2002a),

> Over the 10-year period ending in 2002–2003, after adjusting for inflation, average tuition at both public and private four year colleges and universities rose 38%, much more slowly than the preceding decade. Still charges in both sectors have grown over the last two years at relatively high rates by historical standards (p. 4).

Exploring rising costs is a complex process and requires savvy practitioners and consumers to be able to differentiate between cost, price, and general subsidy (National Commission on the Cost of Higher Education, 1998). Simply put, cost is what institutions spend to provide an education to students and cost per student is the total educational cost divided by the number of full-time equivalent students enrolled at a postsecondary institution. Price is a more complex concept. According to the National Commission on the Cost of Higher Education (1998), price can be considered three different ways: (1) sticker price, or the amount an institution charges a student for attendance and the amount they list in their publication; (2) total price of attendance, which is analogous to COA used for calculating a students need and which incorporates tuition fees, room and board, books, and other expenses; and (3) net price, which is the amount "students pay after financial aid has been subtracted from the total price of attendance" (p. 4).

For those wishing to understand the impact of student aid on college attendance and persistence, it is useful to understand the nuances of net price by exploring the concepts of affordability and access. Affordability is total price less the grants a student receives. This calculation yields an amount the student (and for a dependent student, the student's family) pays to attend college. Access is the total price of attendance less all student aid—grants, loans, and student employment, or the out-of-pocket cost of attendance. "This concept provides a measure of access, because, even though loans must be repaid, they allow a student to attend college" (National Commission on the Cost of Higher Education, 1998, p. 4). Finally, general subsidy is the difference between what it costs an institution to provide an education to students ("cost per student") and the tuition charged those same students ("sticker price"). All of these ways of looking at cost must be understood.

Families frequently make enrollment decisions based on sticker price, eliminating some colleges as too expensive before even applying for student aid. For some students and families, what is important is whether a college is affordable (once grants are subtracted, the family can afford to meet the expenses of attendance), whereas for others, accessibility is the key (see, Hosler, Schmit, & Vesper, 1999; King, 2002). From the institution's standpoint, general subsidy is the best indicator of institutional fiscal health. The distinction between concepts of cost to institutions and price to students has been blurred and has caused considerable confusion. The work of the National Commission on the Cost of Higher Education has helped greatly in clarifying that confusion. Readers seeking additional insights into the nature of college costs and student price are directed to the College Entrance Examination Board's annual report *Trends in College Pricing* and Cunningham, Wellman, Clinedinst, Merisotis, and Carroll (2001a, 2001b). The latter document is particularly helpful because it contains seven commissioned papers addressing a wide range of college cost issues by a number of important higher education policy scholars.

STUDENT AID POST–SEPTEMBER 11, 2001

The tragic events of September 11, 2001, have had, and will continue to have, an impact on all aspects of American society, including higher education. Short-term effects of September 11 include the creation of new scholarship programs to aid the victims and the families of the victims of the terrorist attacks and the implementation of regulations impacting existing federal and state programs. Long-term effects, while difficult to predict, could include the creation of new veteran's benefit programs or the expansion of existing programs to cover the increased number of military personnel involved in the war on terrorism and subsequent related conflicts and the impact of protracted hostilities on the federal budget and the nation's economy.

According the U.S. General Accounting Office (2002), more than $24 billion was raised by 34 large charities for victims' relief by October 2002. A significant portion of those resources was raised in the form of postsecondary scholarships. As of January 2003, NASFAA reported that more than 25 organizations (including philanthropic organizations, corporations, and unions) and more than 40 colleges had created September 11 scholarships (National Association of Student Financial Aid Administrators, 2001d). One of the largest of these programs is the Families of Freedom Scholarship Fund, which was created by Citizen's Scholarship Foundation of America on September 17, 2001. Within a year of its creation, more than $100 million was raised for scholarships. It is anticipated that these scholarships would be distributed to the victims' family members for the next 25 to 30 years (Citizen's Scholarship Foundation of America, 2002). To coordinate many of these programs, the September 11 Scholarship Alliance was created to manage

> . . . scholarship funds created to assist families of people killed or permanently disabled in the terrorist attacks on America on September 11, 2001, including airplane crews and passengers, World Trade Center and Pentagon workers and visitors, and relief workers. . . . [By serving] as an information clearing-house to help ensure that financial assistance for post-high school education, such as college, university, and vocational-technical schools, gets into the hands of those who need it most with minimal paperwork and frustration. (*September 11*, Overview, 1; About the Alliance 1)

The events of September 11 have also had an impact at the federal level. For example, certain categories of borrowers (reservists called to active duty and/or those who worked or resided in the designated disaster area in New York City) under the FFEL programs may be eligible for deferments or discharge of payments (NASFAA, 2001b; 2001c). In addition, the passage on October 26, 2001, of the USA Patriot Act made significant changes in the conditions of the Family Educational Right to Privacy Act (FERPA), making it possible, under certain conditions, for colleges to not note the disclosure of student information to the Attorney General of the United State in a student's file.

The long-term effects of the events of September 11 are less clear. Certainly, a protracted war against terrorism and the states that support terrorism will be a drain on the nation's economy and the federal budget. One could anticipate a negative economic impact of such a war on the student aid programs. These programs are large-ticket items, generally supported by policy makers and the public. And yet, if the federal deficit were to grow substantially or if federal funds needed to be reallocated to the war effort, student aid funding would certainly come under increased scrutiny.

ABROGATION OF MISSION

The student aid system was created in the 1950s and 1960s, largely as an outgrowth of the Great Society initiatives of the Lyndon Johnson administration. While it is true that student aid has been used to accomplish a number of educational and noneducation policy goals, it did for many years have a clear central purpose. That purpose, especially with the federal student aid programs, was to assist students who do not have adequate personal resources in meeting the cost of postsecondary education attendance. Since the mid-1970s, the goals of educational equity and access have shifted to accommodate affordability and choice. The expansion of many student aid programs to meet the needs of middle-class and upper-middle-class students, the shift in funding from grants to loans, and the use of preferential packaging techniques by colleges have all led to a movement away from the original purpose of student aid.

This shift in purpose and its impact on the ability of low-income students to attend college has emerged as a major issue for educational policy makers. Reports such as *Access Denied: Restoring the Nation's Commitment to Equal Educational Opportunity* (Advisory Committee on Student Financial Assistance, 2001), *Losing Ground: A National Status Report on the Affordability of Higher Education* (National Center for Public Policy and Higher Education, 2002), *Empty Promises: The Myth of College Access in America* (Advisory Committee on Student Financial Assistance, 2002), and *Unequal Opportunity: Disparities in College Access Among the 50 States* (Kipp, Price, & Wohlford, 2002) have all decried the loss of opportunities for the truly needy to attend college. As the Advisory Committee on Student Financial Assistance noted in 2002,

> This year alone due to record-high financial barriers, nearly one-half of all college-qualified, low- and moderate-income high school graduates—over 400,000 students fully prepared to attend a four year college—will be unable to do so, and 170,000 of those students will attend no college at all. Over this decade, 4.4 million of these high school graduates will not attend four-year college and 2 million will attend no college at all. (p. v)

The fact that, more than 35 years after the passage of the Higher Education Act, millions of students will be denied a postsecondary education for financial reasons is a policy and moral failure of the first magnitude. In times of limited economic growth and budget deficits, policy choices must be considered carefully. However, the nation cannot afford to waste the human capital represented by the 2 million low-income students who will be inadequately prepared to contribute to the nation's rapidly changing information-based economy. Policy makers at the federal, state, and institutional levels need to recommit themselves to achieving President Lyndon Johnson's goal of ensuring that

> . . . a high school senior in this great land of ours can apply to any college or any university in any of the 50 states and not be turned away because his [sic] family is poor. . . . Tell them [the nations young people] that the leaders of your country believed it is the obligation of your Nation to provide and permit and assist every child born in these borders to receive all the education that he [sic] can take. (Johnson, 1965, p. 467)

REFERENCES

Adams, F. C. (1975). Administering the office of student work and financial assistance. In R. Keene, F. C., Adams, & J. E. King, *Money, marbles, or chalk: Student financial support in higher education* (pp. 214–228). Carbondale, IL: Southern Illinois University Press.

Advisory Committee on Student Financial Assistance. (2001). *Access denied: Restoring the nation's commitment to equal educational opportunity.* Washington, DC: Author.

Advisory Committee on Student Financial Assistance. (2002). *Empty promises: The myth of college access in America.* Washington, DC: Author.

Allan, R. G. (2001, Fall). A background briefing on tuition discounting. *Student Aid Transcript, 13(1)*, 58–61.

Bandre. M. A. (2001a, Winter). Who needs analysis? *Student aid transcript, 12(2)*, 6–8.

Bandre. M. A. (2001b, Winter). Understanding income. *Student aid transcript, 12(2)*, 9.

Berkes, J. (1989, Spring). A guide to packaging principles. *Student aid transcript, 2(1)*, 10–12.

Binder, S. F. (1983). Meeting student needs with different types of financial aid awards. In R. H. Fenske, R. P. Huff, & Associates, *Handbook of student financial aid: Programs, procedures and policies* (pp. 149–168). San Francisco: Jossey-Bass.

Brooks, S. (1986). *NASFAA—The first twenty years: An organizational history of the National Association of Student Financial Aid Administrators, 1966–1986.* Washington, DC: National Association of Student Financial Aid Administrators.

Brubacher, J. S., & Rudy, W. (1976). *Higher education in transition: A history of American colleges and universities, 1963–1976.* New York: Harper & Row.

Burns, R. K. (1984). *The NASFAA encyclopedia of student financial aid.* Washington, DC: National Association of Student Financial Aid Administrators.

Case, J. P. (1983). Determining financial need. In R. H. Fenske, R. P. Huff, & Associates, *Handbook of student financial aid: Programs, procedures and policies* (pp. 124–148). San Francisco: Jossey-Bass.

Case, J. P. (1993). *Professional judgment in eligibility determination and resource analysis* (NASFAA Monograph No. 9, Rev. ed.). Washington, DC: National Association of Student Financial Aid Administrators.

Citizen's Scholarship Foundation of America. (2002). *2002 Annual Report. Education: Building America's future.* St. Peter, MN: Author.

Clotfelter, C. (1996). *Buying the best: Cost escalation in elite higher education.* Princeton, NJ: Princeton University Press.

College Board. (2002). *Your EFC: FAQs.* Retrieved January 9, 2003 from www.collegeboard.com/article/0,1120,6-30-57-40,900.html.

College Entrance Examination Board. (2001). *Trends in student aid: 2002.* New York: Author.

College Entrance Examination Board. (2002a). *Trends in college pricing: 2002.* New York: Author.

College Entrance Examination Board. (2002b). *Trends in student aid: 2002.* New York: Author.

College Scholarship Service. (1989). *Manual for student aid administrators: 1990–1991 policies and procedures.* New York: College Entrance Examination Board.

Conlan, T. J. (1981). *The federal role in the federal system: The dynamics of growth. The evolution of a problematic partnership: The feds and higher ed.* Washington, DC: Advisory Commission on Intergovernmental Relations.

Coomes, M. D. (1988). Student financial aid. In A. Rentz & G. L. Saddlemire (Eds.), *Student affairs functions in higher education* (pp. 155–184). Springfield, IL: Charles C Thomas.

Coomes, M. D. (1992). Understanding students: A developmental approach to financial aid services. *Journal of Student Financial Aid, 22(2)*, 23–31.

Coomes, M. D. (1994). A history of federal involvement in the lives of students. In M. D. Coomes & D. D. Gehring, (Eds.), *Student services in a changing federal climate* (New Directions for Student Services, No. 68, pp. 5–27). San Francisco: Jossey-Bass.

Coomes, M. D. (1996). Student financial aid. In A. L. Rentz & Associates, *Student affairs practice in higher education.* (pp. 334–364). Springfield, IL: Charles C Thomas.

Coomes, M. D. (2000a). The historical roots of enrollment management. In M. D. Coomes, (Ed.), *The role student aid plays in enrollment management* (New Directions for Student Services, No. 89, pp. 5–18). San Francisco: Jossey-Bass.

Coomes, M. D. (Ed.). (2000b). *The role student aid plays in enrollment management* (New Directions for Student Services, No. 89, pp. 5–18). San Francisco: Jossey-Bass.

Cunningham, A. F., Wellman, J. V., Clinedinst, M. E., Merisotis, J. P., & Carroll, C. D. (2001a). *Study of college costs and prices, 1988–89 to 1997–98, Volume 1* (National Center for Education Statistics Rep. No. NCES 2002-157). Washington, DC: U.S. Department of Education.

Cunningham, A. F., Wellman, J. V., Clinedinst, M. E., Merisotis, J. P., & Carroll, C. D. (2001b). *Study of college costs and prices, 1988–89 to 1997–98, Volume 2: Commissioned papers* (National Center for Education Statistics Rep. No. NCES 2002-158). Washington, DC: U.S. Department of Education.

Dannells, M. (1977). Financial aid. In W. T. Packwood (Ed.), *College student personnel services* (pp. 51–91). Springfield, IL: Charles C Thomas.

DeBard, R. (2000). Alternative financing methods for college. In M. D. Coomes, (Ed.), *The role student aid plays in enrollment management* (New Directions for Student Services, No. 89, pp. 47–59). San Francisco: Jossey-Bass.

DeJarnett, R. P. (1975). The organization of student support programs in institutions of higher learning. In R. Keene, F.C., Adams, & J. E. King, *Money, marbles, or chalk: Student financial support in higher education* (pp. 206–213). Carbondale, IL: Southern Illinois University Press.

DeSalvatore, K., & Hughes, L. (2002). *NASSGAP 32nd annual survey report: 2000–2001 academic year.* Albany, NY: New York Higher Education Services Corporation.

Eaton, J. S. (1991). *The unfinished agenda: Higher education in the 1980s.* New York: Macmillan.

Fenske, R. H. (1983). Student aid past and present. In R. H. Fenske, R. P. Huff, & Associates, *Handbook of student financial aid: Programs, procedures and policies* (pp. 5–26). San Francisco: Jossey-Bass.

Finn, C. E., Jr. (1985). Why do we need financial aid? or, Desanctifying student assistance. In College Entrance Examination Board, *An agenda for the year 2000: Thirtieth anniversary colloquia proceeding* (pp. 1–23). New York: College Entrance Examination Board.

Fitzgerald, B. K. (1991). Simplification of need analysis and aid delivery: Imperatives and opportunities. In J. P. Merisotis, (Ed.), *The changing dimensions of student aid* (New Directions for Higher Education, No 74, pp. 43–63), San Francisco: Jossey-Bass.

Fossey, R., & Bateman, M. (Eds.). (1998), *Condemning students to debt: College loans and public policy.* New York: Teachers College Press.

Gibbons, K. (2002). *Balancing technology and the human touch in financial aid.* Retrieved June 5, 2002 from http://www.finaid.org/educators/techsoc.phtml).

Gladieux, L. E. (1983). Future directions of student aid. In R. H. Fenske, R. P. Huff, & Associates, *Handbook of student financial aid: Programs, procedures and policies* (pp. 399–433). San Francisco: Jossey-Bass.

Godzicki, R. J. (1975). A history of financial aids in the United States. In R. Keene, F. C. Adams, & J. E. King, *Money, marbles, or chalk: Student financial support in higher education* (pp. 14–21). Carbondale, IL: Southern Illinois University Press.

Gordon, L. E. (1992, Summer). The computing generation gap. *Student Aid Transcript, 5 (1)*, 7–9.

Gordon, L. E. (1994, Spring). Sounding board: From counselor to technician. *Student Aid Transcript, 6(2).* 16–17.

Graff, A. S. (1986). Organizing the resources that can be effective. In D. Hossler, (Ed.). *Managing college enrollments* (New Directions for Higher Education, No. 53, pp. 89–101). San Francisco: Jossey-Bass.

Guthrie, M. (2001, Winter). A brief federal needs analysis timeline. *Student Aid Transcript, 12(2)*, 8.

Hage, J., & Aiken, M. (1970). *Social change in complex organizations.* New York: Random House.

Hansen, J. (1991). The roots of federal student aid policy. In J. P. Merisotis, (Ed.), *The changing dimensions of student aid* (New Directions for Higher Education, No 74, pp. 3–19), San Francisco: Jossey-Bass.

Hart, N. K. (1991). Constant response to change: The role of the financial aid office. In J. P. Merisotis, (Ed.), *The changing dimensions of student aid* (New Directions for Higher Education, No 74, pp. 65–73), San Francisco: Jossey-Bass.

Heffron, M. (1990, Spring). Philosophy behind needs analysis methods. *Journal of Student Financial Aid, 20 (2)*, 37–39.

Heller, D. E. (2002). State merit scholarship programs: An introduction. In D. E. Heller & P. Marin, (Eds.), *Who should we help? The negative social consequences of merit scholarships.* Cambridge, MA: The Civil Rights Project of Harvard University.

Hossler, D. (1984). *Enrollment management: An integrated approach.* New York: College Entrance Examination Board.

Hossler, D. (1986). *Creating effective enrollment management systems.* New York: College Entrance Examination Board.

Hossler, D. (1996). From admission to enrollment management. In A. L. Rentz, (Ed.), *Student affairs practice in higher education.* Springfield, IL: Charles C Thomas.

Hossler, D. (2000). The role of financial aid in enrollment management. In M. D. Coomes, (Ed.), *The role student aid plays in enrollment management* (New Directions for Student Services, No. 89, pp. 77–90). San Francisco: Jossey-Bass.

Hossler, D, & Bean, J. P. (1990). Principles and objectives. In D. Hossler & J. P. Bean, (Eds.), *The strategic management of college enrollments* (pp. 3–20). San Francisco: Jossey-Bass.

Hossler, D., Schmit, J., & Vesper, N. (1999). *Going to college: How social, economic, and educational factors influence the decisions students make.* Baltimore, MD: Johns Hopkins University Press.

Huff, R. P. (1989). Facilitating and applying research in student financial aid to institutional objectives. In R. H. Fenske, (Ed.), *Studying the impact of student aid on institutions* (New Directions for Institutional Research, No. 62, pp. 5–16). San Francisco: Jossey-Bass.

Johnson, L. B. (1965). The Higher Education Act of 1965: The President's remarks upon signing the bill at Southwest Texas State College. In Weekly Compilation of Presidential Documents, Monday, November 15, 1965 (pp. 467–496). Washington, DC: Office of the Federal Register.

Johnstone, D. B., & Huff, R. P. (1983). Relationship of student aid to other college programs and services. In R. H. Fenske, R. P. Huff, & Associates, *Handbook of student financial aid: Programs, procedures and policies* (pp. 237–257). San Francisco: Jossey-Bass.

Kennedy, P., Cornell, C., Fox, S. L., Osswald, A., Williams, M., Wilson, M., Zuzack, C., & Gelinas, D. (2000). *E-Aid office 2000: Financial aid software selection, implementation, and operation* (NASFAA Monograph #12). Washington, DC: NASFAA.

King, J. E. (2002). *Crucial choices: How student's financial decisions affect their academic success.* Washington, DC: American Council on Education.

Kipp, S. M., III, Price, D. V., & Wohlford, J. K. (2002). *Unequal opportunity Disparities in college access among the 50 states* (New Agenda Series, Vol. 4, No. 3). Indianapolis, IN: Lumina Foundation for Education.

Kosters, M. H. (1999). *Financing college tuition: Government policies & educational priorities.* Washington, DC: AIE Press.

Lackey, C. W., & Pugh, S. L. (1994). With TQM less is more for students. *Student Aid Transcript, 6(2)*, 7–11.

Lange, M. L. (1983). Factors in organizing and effective student aid office. In R. H. Fenske, R. P. Huff, & Associates, *Handbook of student financial aid: Programs, procedures and policies* (pp. 221–236). San Francisco: Jossey-Bass.

Longanecker, D. (2002, March/April). Is merit-based aid really trumping need-based aid. *Change, 34(2)*, 30–37.

Marmaduke, A. S. (1983). State student aid programs. In R. H. Fenske, R. P. Huff, & Associates, *Handbook of student financial aid: Programs, procedures and policies* (pp. 55–76). San Francisco: Jossey-Bass.

McPherson, M. S., & Shapiro, M. O. (1998). *The student aid game: Meeting need and rewarding talent in American higher education.* Princeton, NJ: Princeton University Press.

McPherson, M. S., & Shapiro, M. O. (2002, March/April). The blurring line between merit and need in financial aid. *Change, 34(2)*, 39–46.

Monks, J. (2000, August). Is this the beginning of the end of need-based financial aid? The *College Board Review, 191*, 12–15.

Moore, J. W. (1983). Purposes and provisions of federal programs. In R. H. Fenske, R. P. Huff, & Associates, *Handbook of student financial aid: Programs, procedures and policies* (pp. 27–54). San Francisco: Jossey-Bass.

National Association of Student Financial Aid Administrators. (1993b, July). *NASFAA mission statement.* Retrieved January 16, 2003 from http://www.nasfaa.org/publications/1998/nasfaa%20mission%20statement.htm

National Association of Student Financial Aid Administrators. (1999). *NASFAA statement of ethical principles.* Washington, DC: Author. Retrieved January 20, 2003 from http://www.nasfaa.org/publications/1999/NEthical599.html).

National Association of Student Financial Aid Administrators. (2001a). *Federal student financial aid: A national profile of programs in Title IV of the Higher Education Act.* Washington, DC: Author. Retrieved January 20, 2003 from http://www.nasfaa.org/AnnualPubs/TRNationalProfile101601.html.

National Association of Student Financial Aid Administrators. (2001b). News from NASFAA: GEN-01-11: Recent terrorist attacks—Relief for borrowers in the Title IV loan programs . Retrieved January 14, 2003, from http://www.nasfaa.org/publications/2001/gen0111.html

National Association of Student Financial Aid Administrators. (2001c). News from NASFAA: Persons affected by military mobilization. Retrieved January 14, 2003, from http://www.nasfaa.org/publication/publications/2001/GEN0113.html

National Association of Student Financial Aid Administrators. (2001d). News from NASFAA: List of scholarship funds created for families of victims of terrorist attack. Retrieved January 14, 2003, from http://www.nasfaa.org/publication/publications/2001/ARScholarshipFundsDetailed11070.html

National Center for Public Policy and Higher Education. (2002). *Losing ground: A national status report on the affordability of higher education.* Washington, DC: Author.

National Commission on the Cost of Higher Education. (1998). *Straight talk about college costs.* Phoenix, AZ: Oryx Press.

Nelson, J. E., & Fenske, R. H. (1983). Strategies for improving research, projections, and policy development. In R. H. Fenske, R. P. Huff, & Associates, *Handbook of student financial aid: Programs, procedures and policies* (pp. 285–306). San Francisco: Jossey-Bass.

Redd, K. E. (2000). *Discounting toward disaster: Tuition discounting, college finances, and enrollments of low-income undergraduates* (New Agenda Series, Vol. 3, No. 2). Indianapolis, IN: USA Group Foundation.

Redd, K. E., & Miller, C. (2002). *Financial aid professionals at work in 1999–2000: Results from the 2001 Survey of undergraduate financial aid policies, practices, and procedures.* Washington, DC: College Entrance Examination Board and National Association of Student Financial Aid Officers.

Research Publications Group. (2001). *Student financial aid handbook; 2001–2002.* Washington DC: U.S. Department of Education. (Also available online at: www.ifap.ed.gov)

Rivlin, A. (1961). *The role of the federal government in financing higher education.* Washington, DC: Brookings Institute.

Roth, A. P. (2001). *Saving for college & the tax code: A new spin on the "Who benefits for higher education?" debate.* New York: Garland Publishing.

Russo, J. A., & Coomes, M. D. (2000). Enrollment management, institutional resources, and the private college. In M. D. Coomes, (Ed.), *The role student aid plays in enrollment management* (New Directions for Student Services, No. 89, pp. 33–46). San Francisco: Jossey-Bass.

Sears, K. R. (1994, Spring). Sounding board: How we evolved. *Financial Aid Transcript, 6(2),* 18–19.

September 11 Scholarship Alliance. (n.d.). *September 11 scholarship alliance.* Retrieved January 14, 2003, from http://www.scholarships911.org

U.S. Department of Education. (2001). *Counselor's handbook for postsecondary schools.* Washington, DC: United States Government Printing Office (Available at: www.ifap.ed.gov.

U.S. Department of Justice, Department of Education, & Federal Trade Commission. (2002, May). *College Scholarship Fraud Prevention Act of 2000: First annual report to congress.* Washington, DC: Author.

U.S. General Accounting Office. *September 11: Interim report on the response of charities.* (GAO Report No. 02-1037). Washington, DC: Author.

Vogelstein, F. (1998). Paying for college: How high can tuition go? *U.S. News and World Report, 125(9),* 68–70.

White, P., & Frishberg, E. (1997). Why money drives the private college admissions process. *Student Aid Transcript, 8(3),* 32–34.

Wilcox, L. (1991). Evaluating the impact of financial aid on student recruitment. In D. Hossler, (Ed.), *Evaluating student recruitment and retention programs* (New Directions for Institutional Research, No. 70, pp. 47–60). San Francisco: Jossey-Bass.

Williams, M. S. (1999). *Staffing issues in student financial aid: A report on the NASFAA 1998 staff and salary survey.* Washington, DC: National Association of Student Financial Aid Administrators.

Wolanin, T. R. (2001). *Rhetoric and reality: Effects and consequences of the HOPE scholarship.* Washington, DC: Institute for Higher Education Policy.

Chapter 13

STUDENT HEALTH

Josh Kaplan, Edward G. Whipple, Jeanne M. Wright, and Rena K. Murphy

HISTORY

Student health care has been a part of American higher education since the beginning days at Harvard. However, from the 1660s to the mid-1850s, the health of students was viewed as the responsibility of the student, with the institutions assuming no responsibility. Depending on students' socioeconomic class, students were expected to seek aid from medical personnel in surrounding communities or were left to turn to the charitable nature of a local citizen who might offer financial assistance (Farnsworth, 1965, as cited in Saddlemire, 1988).

The gymnastic period of higher education, starting about 1825, was an opportunity to introduce German and Scandinavian methods to promote physical exercise to American college and university campuses (Packwood, 1977). At Amherst College in 1859, Dr. Edward Hitchcock, labeled the father of college health by Boynton (1962), was the first professor of hygiene to provide student health services. The philosophy that guided his practice and treatment of students was that the "body and mind should work together harmoniously" (Saddlemire, 1988, p. 185). Later in 1861, Amherst created the first comprehensive department of hygiene and physical education. The college provided for annual examinations, instruction on hygiene, regular physical exercise, and statistics on student illness and treatment (Boynton, 1971).

Concerns among the faculty for campus living conditions, the potential threats from contagious diseases, and an interest in promoting mental health led to the creation of faculty committees that began inspecting student living quarters. As athletic programs grew in size and stature, teams were provided with what today is known as a "team doctor" who began to treat nonathletes as well. Student infirmaries were soon created to care for students who were unable to remain in their rooms. Princeton University claims the first higher education infirmary in 1893, followed by the first student health service in 1901 at the University of California (Boynton, 1962).

The American College Health Association (ACHA), founded in 1920 as the American Student Health Association, has been instrumental in promoting health education, providing medical services, and addressing current health-related issues. The ACHA's most recent *Guidelines for a College Health Program* (1999) listed the following as general characteristics of a college health program: community responsibility—health service roles; ethical principles; mission and values; student and staff—shared responsibilities; and student participation and relations.

Student health services grew slowly until the 1960s. During this period, there was a focus on public health care and prevention. Students frequently turned to health sources other than their campus service for information and help with venereal diseases, drug use, mental health issues, and contraception. Consequently, college health centers became more comprehensive, as reflected in the following areas of recommended programs suggested by the ACHA in 1977; "(1) outpatient and inpatient services, (2) mental health, (3) athletic medicine, (4) dental services, (5) rehabilitation/physical medicine, (6) preventive medicine, (7) health education and promotion, (8) environmental health and safety, and (9) occupational health" (Saddlemire, 1988, p. 187). The need for colleges and universities to establish and provide health care for their students was evident:

> The mission for health centers remained relatively unchanged until the late 1960s and early 1970s, when the social and cultural revolution sweeping our nation altered forever the way colleges and universities dealt with students. The sexual liberation movement, the popularization of drug and alcohol use on campuses, and an aggressive new student activism brought change to the student health agenda. These new issues demanded new approaches: drug and alcohol treatment and education programs; specialized services, such as women's clinics offering gynecologic and contraceptive services; and many others. And during this period, students became much more vocal in expressing their discontent with campus agencies or services that were not meeting their needs. All of these forces served as catalysts leading to the health centers that we see on today's campuses (Bridwell & Kinder, 1993, pp. 481–482).

During the 1990s, college and university student health services were affected by many of the issues facing health care in the United States. Citing the increasing complexity of higher education campuses, the American College Health Association wrote in *College Health 2000: Strategies of the Future* (1991),

> Higher education, and more specifically college health, can be effective only to the degree that those in the field are responsive to the needs of the larger community in which they operate. College and university campuses, reflecting changes occurring throughout the nation, are becoming increasingly rich in their diversity. Campuses are becoming more heterogeneous environments with respect to ethnicity, age, and religious preference, and more open with respect to sexual orientation. Health services must increase their sensitivity

and assume leadership in understanding the issues and special needs of the many different populations comprising the campus community (p. 1).

College health during the first decade of the twenty-first century encompasses an even broader array of services to students including

- health promotion and prevention;
- mental health, counseling, and psychotherapy;
- consumer services (students' rights and responsibilities and insurance);
- immediate/urgent care;
- pharmaceutical;
- laboratory;
- diagnostic and therapeutic imaging;
- emergency;
- surgical and anesthesia services;
- inpatient/infirmary;
- athletic, sports, and recreational medicine;
- dental health;
- environment health and safety; and
- occupational health services (American College Health Association, 1999).

A majority of these services are addressed in this chapter.

MISSION

The *Guidelines for a College Health Program* (1999) issued by the American College Health Association (ACHA) identified the mission of college health programs simply as "to advance the health of students" (p. 3). This mission guides the college health practitioner in providing health services for students and health and safety services for institutions. Carrying out this mission is based on three important assumptions: (1) that physical and mental health have an important impact on social issues; (2) that college health services can play a major role in encouraging students to attend to these issues; and (3) that college students are particularly receptive to education and self-exploration. It is essential that the scope of health services extend beyond treatment of illness, to encompass disease prevention and health promotion. Furthermore, health services must meet the special needs of diverse student populations, including international students; single parents; returning students; gay, lesbian and bisexual students; the physically and mentally challenged; and students with special health needs.

Disease prevention and health promotion require a broad range of activities. Health services must contribute to the development of policies for immunization requirements, policies on alcohol and other drug abuse, policies on suicide and homicide threats, and policies on sexual harassment and assault. Health services should participate in planning emergency response protocols and in programs to deal with potential hazards, such as food services, sanitation, and chemical and biological hazards. Health services must support intercollegiate athletics, intramurals, recreational athletics, and physical education by developing programs for prevention, conditioning, early recognition of injury, treatment, and rehabilitation. Health education programs should address alcohol and other drug abuse, nutrition, sexuality issues, prevention of sexually transmitted disease (STD), and stress management. Clinical counseling and/or psychotherapy services must be used for prevention, in addition to early intervention and treatment, through outreach and educational programs.

The illnesses that may be presented to a college health service encompass all aspects of medicine. Many problems are minor, but severe problems occur as well. For example, in a single year, a typical college health service might see students with cancer, inflammatory bowel disease, endocrine disorders, and neurological or psychiatric disease, all potentially severe. Fingar (1989) reported that in one year, a single college health physician saw 5,748 patients with 505 different diagnoses. However, 50 percent of the visits were accounted for by just 23 diagnoses. When specific diagnoses were grouped, 70 percent of visits were accounted for by the following 13 groups:

1. respiratory infection,
2. routine gynecological exams,
3. gynecological disorders,
4. viral infection,
5. urinary disorders,
6. dermatitis,
7. joint pain,
8. conjunctivitis,
9. sprains,
10. psychological disorders,
11. abdominal pain,
12. ulcer/gastritis, and
13. superficial injury.

ADMINISTRATIVE STRUCTURE AND STAFFING

A college health service may provide care only to students, or it may serve an entire university community, including faculty, staff, and dependents. The range of health care services may vary widely as well. Smaller health services may provide only first aid and referral. At the other end of the spectrum are comprehensive clinics that may provide a pharmacy, radiological imaging, laboratory, physical therapy, dentistry, psychiatric services, and care by medical and surgical specialists. Factors that predispose toward more comprehensive services include a larger student body, a residential campus, and a lower availability of services in the immediate surrounding community.

The extreme variation in size and services is reflected in diverse administrative structures and staffing. Health services usually are located within the student affairs division. Larger health services most commonly are directed by a health care administrator, a physician, or a psychologist; many smaller health services are directed by a nurse. The director should have authority to administer effectively the college health program and to participate actively in the development of institutional policies affecting health and safety (American College Health Association, 1999). Regardless of staff size, two critical activities must be in place to minimize staff conflict and enhance teamwork: (1) hiring the right people; and (2) helping the entire staff work in a manner that is consistent with the department's mission and goals (Meilman, 2001).

Staffing needs can be estimated from a study of the 10 largest public American universities and the 10 largest private American universities (Patrick, 1988.) For each 10,000 students, public institutions averaged 3.2 physicians and 23.2 total health service staff, and private institutions averaged 4.1 physicians and 31.5 total staff. These staffs provided an average of 2.0 visits per student per year at public institutions and 2.5 visits per year at private institutions.

College health services usually are financed primarily by prepaid fees. This approach serves to maximize preventive care and ensures access to treatment without financial barriers (Kraft, 1993.) A 1991 Blue Cross/Blue Shield survey of 400 college health services revealed that 85 percent of their funding was prepaid (46% from general fees and 39% from student health fees). Another 5 percent of the funding was derived from fee-for-service income; the remainder would be primarily from insurance, with very small amounts from other miscellaneous sources. The average annual budget was $102 per full-time student ($81 at commuter schools and $128 at residential campuses).

EMERGING ISSUES

Few endeavors are more precarious than attempting to predict the future. Previous editions of this chapter (Saddlemire, 1988; Kaplan, Whipple, & Wright, 1996) postulated several general trends in college health: an increasing role for preventive services; an increasing role for psychological support services; increasing development of antibiotic-resistant disease, with particular concern for the possibility of a worldwide epidemic of multiple drug–resistant tuberculosis; a revolutionary impact from genetic research, with therapy for many diseases including, diabetes and cancer, being provided through insertion of custom-modified genes (*Lancet*, 1995); expanded use of electronic communication, including the use of the Internet for health education; and providing specialist consultation to remote sites by "telemedicine."

In the area of preventive services, optimism was expressed for multiple new vaccines and better contraceptives. So far, for the most part, these predictions have not been fulfilled. Contraception remains essentially unchanged. Women can now take injectable contraceptives; these are perhaps more convenient, but risks, efficacy, and side effects remain unchanged. The new vaccines for hepatitis A and chicken pox will not revolutionize health care; vaccines for AIDS and tuberculosis, which would do so, do not appear imminent. However, with regard to vaccines, one significant series of events should be noted. In the 1990s, there was an increase in the number of cases of bacterial meningitis in young adults, particularly college freshmen living in residence halls. In response to this, the American College Health Association (1997) drafted a recommendation that the vaccine for this disease be made available to college students, that college students be informed about bacterial meningitis and the vaccine, and that they be advised to consider receiving the vaccine. Because of the relative infrequency of the disease and the relatively high cost of the vaccine, even this relatively mild recommendation was highly controversial when it was first released. However, nearly three years later, an almost identical recommendation was released by the U.S. Centers for Disease Control and Prevention (2000).

Antibiotic-resistant bacteria continue to be a concern, but so far new antibiotics have kept pace, and the feared epidemics have not yet come to pass. Similarly, genetic research has so far failed to achieve its promise and has not yet had a significant impact on the practice of clinical medicine.

With regard to an increasing role for psychological support services, the anticipated improvements in risk factor identification, motivational tools, and neuropharmacology have not yet come to pass. In fact, health insurers are demanding proof of efficacy and are subjecting traditional therapies to increasing scrutiny.

The Internet has had a major impact on student health. Students derive much of their information about diseases and health from the Internet, from sources of widely varying quality. Some of these sources are produced by student health services, including a far-reaching and frank site produced by the University of Columbia called "Go Ask Alice." Providers are increasingly able to obtain up-to-date information from a variety of excellent Internet databases. Providers are also able to communicate with patients by e-mail, and institutions have been forced to develop new policies to address such communication. A major challenge for student health services is complying with federally mandated requirements for protecting patient privacy in electronic communications, as delineated in recent regulations under the Health Insurance Portability and Accountability Act (1996).

With the understanding that *conjecture* may be a better term than *prediction*, there are some current trends in medicine that seem worth noting.

An area of major concern to almost all college campuses is alcohol use, particularly a pattern of extremely heavy use referred to as high-risk drinking. Alcohol abuse interferes with the academic mission of the college or university. It is also responsible for a significant number of physical assaults, sexual assaults, unplanned sex, unwanted pregnancy, and sexually transmitted disease. Current theories for intervention are focusing on the concept of peer misperceptions (Robinson, 2001). This theory suggests that students' behaviors are greatly influenced by what they believe other students do, but that their perceptions of what other students do are often greatly exaggerated. Thus, education about what is, in fact, normative behavior can be highly effective in curbing abuse. The next few years should provide evidence as to whether this theory has value.

Men's health clinics are a relatively recent phenomenon. These clinics serve men's needs for sexual health care, strength and conditioning, nutrition, and stress management, and they address men's traditional resistance to utilizing health facilities (Sabo, 2000). They can also serve as one way to address issues of peer pressure that encourage aggressive and violent behavior. In addition, a number of campuses are sponsoring Men's Health Fairs or Days to educate men about the student health center and encourage them to utilize the services offered.

Another relatively recent phenomenon is the emergence of travel medicine clinics. These clinics serve the needs of students, and often faculty, who travel outside North America and northern Europe. Travelers to developing countries, especially to the Tropics, are confronted by a number of major health risks. Travel medicine clinics provide advice for avoiding disease, education about food and water consumption, preventive medicines, and vaccines. At a few institutions, such clinics are also open to the general public, providing both a source of external revenue and enhanced college and community relations.

HEALTH CARE REFORM

One area where change is having a great current effect on college health services is not in technology but rather in the business of health insurance and health care delivery. Skyrocketing health care costs have become a major national issue. In the early 1990s, it seemed likely that there would be significant changes in health care delivery based on federal health care reform. It now appears that legislative reform will occur primarily at the state level, if at all. But regardless of what happens in the state and national legislatures, market forces almost certainly will continue to produce sweeping changes in American health care delivery. Student health services, which have been somewhat sheltered so far, can expect to be dramatically affected and have already started to prepare.

The driving force behind marketplace reform is the desire of employers to reduce, or at least limit, the cost of providing employee health care. Early approaches included fee schedules, mandatory second opinions, close scrutiny of catastrophic cases (case management), and increasing demands for documentation of the need for tests and treatment. More recently, a growing number of employee insurance plans are embracing managed care approaches that limit the choice of provider. The basic concept is simple: insurers, representing large numbers of patients, are able to negotiate with health care providers. In return for directing patients to specific providers, insurers can negotiate discounted rates and may in some cases even impose standards of care. One structure is a preferred provider organization (PPO) of independent providers who may be associated with several plans. Another is a health maintenance organization (HMO) whose staff serves only HMO clients.

How does this affect student health services? Traditional indemnity insurance plans coordinate well with student health services. Such plans usually pay for tests and hospital care and typically have deductibles that apply to office visits, so that students do not object to the prepaid health fee that covers office visits. Now, however, students are often covered by insurance with managed care components that restrict their choice of provider. Tests done at the student health service may not be reimbursed. And the plan may cover office visits, but only when provided by designated providers or clinics. These plans pose problems for both the student and the student health service. From the student's perspective, there may not be adequate access to care. The student is required to obtain primary care not from the student health service, but instead from providers who are off campus and quite possibly out of town. Moreover, these providers may not provide the appropriate focus on prevention and education issues, such as alcohol and drug abuse, sexually transmitted disease, and eating disorders. From the health service's perspective, there is decreased utilization and decreased opportunity to pursue its mission. Furthermore, students who can not be reimbursed for tests or treatment provided at their student health service and who can not be referred to specialists by their student health service are going to resist paying student health fees. This is, in effect, a threat to the health service's continued existence.

Many of the concerns of both payers and consumers are addressed by the traditional student health model. Student health services are nonprofit, usually provide service on a prepaid basis, and use salaried providers. These features allow universal access without financial barriers, remove financial incentives to provide unnecessary care, and remove profit incentives to inappropriately limit care. However, this model health care delivery system is far from comprehensive. Many student health services do charge for laboratory and radiology services, as well as for pharmaceuticals. Others simply do not provide these services. And with few exceptions, student health services do not provide specialty care or hospital care. What is needed is a system that incorporates this model into a comprehensive health care program under the new rules of managed care.

It is perhaps easier to say what *should* happen than what *will* happen. Insurers should make provisions for students to have access to health care while they are in school. And students should have access to plans that meet their unique needs for education and preventive services. Whether this will happen will depend on how well student health services adapt to the new marketplace. One way for student health services to survive is to form alliances with groups of specialists and with hospitals in order to be able to offer students comprehensive care plans. It is extremely encouraging that in recent years student health insurance plans have been able to buy into provider group arrangements, obtaining for students the same kind of provider discounts that were previously available only to members of large employee groups. Another approach is to subcontract with an HMO to provide primary care services to those HMO members who are students. Student health services are already taking steps to prepare for these inevitable changes.

ACCREDITATION

Health services are seeking formal accreditation in unprecedented numbers. There are two major accrediting bodies for outpatient health care facilities: the Joint Commission on Accreditation of Healthcare Organizations (JCAHO) and the Accreditation Association for Ambulatory Health Care (AAAHC). Accreditation, while not required by law, may be valuable in negotiation with insurers or HMOs; accreditation also provides demonstrable evidence of quality when a school considers outsourcing student health care. The accreditation standard that requires a formal quality assurance program usually is the one that requires the most change.

CAMPUS HEALTH PROMOTION: INTEGRATING WELLNESS CONCEPTS INTO STUDENT HEALTH SERVICES

Wellness is a critical element of student health services and encompasses aspects of physical, emotional, intellectual, occupational, spiritual, and social health. From the beginning, a primary goal of wellness programming has been to foster positive student attitudes toward health and the adoption of healthful lifestyle behaviors. Student affairs administrators have the unique opportunity to impact college health behaviors by spearheading university initiatives to increase students' accessibility to vital health and wellness services. College health delivery and wellness services vary greatly, as do student and parental expectations concerning appropriate interventions for treating and preventing illnesses (Haltiwanger, Hayden, Weber, Evans, & Possner, 2001). Traditionally, college health promotion programming has contributed to students' increased awareness of health hazards associated with eating disorders, obesity, inadequate nutrition, insufficient exercise, violence, substance abuse, and stress. The addition of university wellness centers has augmented existing preventive services related to chronic disease management, substance abuse issues, dietary concerns, sexual health, and infectious diseases.

A national effort to guide prevention practices, Healthy People 2010 (United States Department of Health and Human Services [USDHHS, 2000] identified age-related goals and objectives to decrease preventable illnesses, injuries, and disabilities. Developed by the U.S. Department of Health and Human Services (USDHHS, 2000), Healthy People 2010 outlines health objectives for the nation for a 10-year period that began in the year 2000. For the first decade of this new millennium, its framework clearly delineates the challenges facing the higher education community in areas of college health promotion. The two major overlapping health goals of Healthy People 2010 are to (1) increase the quality and years of healthy life, and (2) eliminate health disparities. The 10 leading health indicators which will be used to mark the progress of the Nation's health include:

1. physical activity,
2. overweight and obesity,
3. tobacco use,
4. substance abuse,
5. responsible sexual behavior,
6. mental health,
7. injury and violence,
8. environmental quality,
9. immunization, and
10. access to care.

College student affairs administrators can play an important role in addressing these numerous health indicators by fostering a variety of educational and environmental program strategies as well as institutional policies to support a healthier college campus (USDHHS, 2000).

To enhance the quality and years of life among student populations, Healthy People 2010 (USDHHS, 2000) Objective 7-3 recommended that specific health information be integrated into a college or university setting.

Universities and colleges are requested to provide health information on these six priority health risk behavior areas:

1. injuries (unintentional and intentional);
2. tobacco use;
3. alcohol and illicit drug use;
4. sexual behaviors that cause unintended pregnancies;
5. sexually transmitted diseases; and
6. dietary patterns that cause disease and inadequate physical activity.

Along with these priority areas, postsecondary institutions have also been requested to implement health promotion activities that would increase health literacy levels among students. Taking into consideration student diversity factors, (disability status, sexual orientation, gender appropriateness, and racial and/or cultural factors), college and university administrators have also been asked to target broader student issues related to environmental health, mental health, emotional health, personal health, and consumer health (USDHHS, 2000).

Health practitioners continue to debate whether campus health promotion programs and services have effectively considered gender differences and cultural perspectives. Rogers, Harb, Lappin, and Colbert (2000) suggested that gender-appropriate marketing strategies be aimed at males who do not routinely access existing campus health services. A comprehensive health promotion plan to attract male students should include a thorough needs assessment of health services desired by males, a supportive interdisciplinary health care setting, and implementation of gender-specific health risk screenings for differing age groups (Rogers, Harb, Lappin, & Colbert, 2000). Student health and wellness professionals are also encouraged to integrate a variety of multicultural interventions that adequately reflect the needs of diverse student populations. Recruiting peer educators with multicultural backgrounds, selecting representation from various racial groups, and incorporating existing cultural practices into health programming are essential. Moreover, the health needs of international college students should be carefully evaluated. Among international students in higher education, Bradley (2000) emphasized that cultural adaptations are not uniform and individual differences should be considered. Diverse college populations also encompass students with special health needs who may have physical and mental impairments. Comprehensive policies regarding disabilities are recommended to break down barriers for college students attempting to access student services (Patterson & Lanier, 1999). Student affairs practitioners have the responsibility to merge social, cultural, and political systems that can empower college students to fully attain their life goals (Rhoades & Black, 1995).

The impact of adolescent years should be considered for incoming freshmen who will be entering college immediately after completing high school. As early as the adolescent years, health risk behaviors related to unintentional injuries, homicides, and suicides have been cited as the major causes of death (Resnick et al., 1997). High-risk behaviors, including unsafe sexual practices and substance abuse, continue into the college years. However, raising students' awareness of the health hazards associated with cigarette smoking and excessive alcohol intake often do not deter students from initiating smoking and binge drinking behaviors (Simantov, Schoen, & Klein, 2000). To counter risky behaviors, Turrisi, Padilla, and Wiersma (2000) proposed that health interventions be tailored to address differing beliefs and motivations that can affect college students' lifestyle choices. To effectively reduce the transmission of HIV-STD infections, prevention programs and reinforcement strategies should be aimed at specific health risk activities (no existing risk behaviors, low-risk behaviors, and high-risk behaviors) (Holtgrave et al., 1995). Furthermore, Bennett and Bauman (2000) encouraged student health practitioners to carefully assess potential psychosocial factors that may contribute to high-risk behaviors. Prior to entering college, many students have relied on parental advice for health-seeking behaviors (Haltiwanger, Hayden, Weber, Evans, & Possner, 2001). Therefore, many college students have not had the opportunity to independently engage in health prevention practices or to take an active part in health care decision-making. Even though these college students might be conversant with disease terminology, Oprendek and Malcarne (1997) found that college students participating in their study did not uniformly comprehend the full significance of their illnesses or their role in disease prevention. In order to assist students in developing a more thorough understanding of lifestyle choices and disease relationships, these researchers suggested incorporating role-playing techniques into disease education and prevention (Oprendek & Malcarne). Role-playing exercises frequently are integrated into wellness programming and trained peer educators have the ability to integrate effective problem-solving techniques and patient-provider negotiation strategies into their outreach presentations.

Previous health promotion efforts had been aimed primarily at changing the individual student's health behaviors while largely ignoring the social and environmental influences. In recent years, the influence of social norms on alcohol consumption and drug misuse among college students has been investigated. Within specific peer groups, including athletes, fraternities, and sororities, students often perceive that the amount of alcohol consumed is higher than the actual amount ingested (Thombs, 2000). As a result of these misconceptions, Thombs (2000) reported that students may intentionally increase their consumption of alcohol, attempting to meet perceived expectations of these peer groups. Moreover, media's portrayal of binge drinking among college social groups continues to impact perceived norms. Inadvertently, news stories reporting greater alcohol consumption among college athletes, may actually bolster drinking behaviors among incoming student athletes seeking to follow reported norms. Higher education institutional environments, in collaboration with the surrounding community, can strongly influence students' perceptions of healthy, normative behaviors.

The misuse of alcohol and other drugs also increases the risks of violence, high-risk sexual behaviors, and sexual assaults (USDHHS, 2000). In the event of a sexual assault, university student health and counseling centers frequently provide numerous student support and health intervention services. Campus wellness centers are often perceived as nonthreatening environments from which student referrals can be made to health care professionals for specific health issues. According to Dunn, Vail-Smith, and Knight (1999), some survivors of acquaintance rape may not divulge any information about the rape incident until another related event occurs, and the majority will turn to a friend for this initial disclosure. Trained peer educators are in a unique position to increase the number of student referrals to health professionals. Frequently, peer educators have more access to a greater number of college students because of their peer identity and role in campus outreach programming. During campus outreach presentations, peer educators not only provide education on health and wellness issues, but also are able to promote essential campus health services. Santelli, Kouzis, and Newcomber (1996) found that peers who were familiar with school health services significantly affected other students' attitudes about school-based health centers. In the future, peer education programs will continue to be an integral part of wellness programming. Therefore, continual recruitment, selection, and training of peer educators will be required. Moreover, potential peer educators will need to be carefully assessed to determine if their existing traits, experiences, and academic preparation are appropriate to the specific health promotion activity and/or program (Keeley & Engstrom, 1993).

Addressing the growing number of emergent infections continues to present unique challenges to student affairs practitioners. Guidelines and recommendations concerning the planning and response to infectious disease agents continue to evolve. Along with the threats of HIV infection, college students are at a greater risk for contracting other sexually transmitted diseases, including hepatitis B infection (USDHHS, 2000). Prevalence rates of hepatitis B remain higher among adolescents and young adults, as compared with the general population, even though a hepatitis B vaccine is available (Ganguly, Marty, Herold, & Maria, 1998).

To reduce the incidence of infectious disease on college campuses, health and wellness centers can offer assessments of students' vaccination status, provide easy access to needed vaccines, and disseminate information regarding current recommendations. Promoting the benefits of vaccinations and providing immunizations have the potential to decrease premature morbidity and mortality. Whether meningococcal vaccines should be routinely offered through college health centers remains controversial. Analyzing retrospective data from a Maryland cohort, Jeansonne (2000) noted that college students who lived on campus were at a higher risk for meningococcal infections. Recent reports of fatal meningococcal infections among college students have fueled debates as to whether to aggressively promote meningococcal vaccines for those residing in on-campus housing units.

When developing a healthful school environment and school health curricula, Rudd and Walsh (1993) endorsed the public health ecological model and recommended that normative, environmental, and policy influences be carefully considered. For example, university environments can significantly impact student eating behaviors and overall nutritional status. Horacek and Betts (1998) surveyed 400 college students to determine what factors influenced their dietary behaviors. Primary determinants of food choices included taste, convenience, availability, and cost factors. Therefore, actively engaging university students in the food selection decision process is essential. College students should be encouraged to participate in taste-testing campus recipes, provide suggestions for new menu items, and recommend ways to increase healthful, inexpensive food selections. University settings can offer convenient access to a variety of healthful and tasty food choices in dining units and vending machines for reasonable costs.

Student affairs professionals can effectively collaborate with university and community members to generate health-promoting environmental and social policies. For example, food vending machine merchants, resident advisors, dining unit managers, nutritionists, and student peer educators can collectively plan strategies for disseminating nutritional information and providing heart-healthy food items in residence halls. To eliminate campus safety hazards associated with poor visibility at night, facility management personnel, university students, campus safety staff, exterior lighting merchants, parking personnel, and student affairs professionals can collectively design improved lighting strategies. Additionally, university coalitions comprised of faculty, staff, students, and community members can address campus safety and health issues related to acquaintance rape and formulate university policies to decrease incidences of sexual assault. Similarly, city officials, university judicial affairs personnel, campus police, municipal court staff, and resident advisors can effectively develop alcohol sanctions that encompass constructive educational programming and community service options.

As health priorities continue to change throughout the decades, student health and wellness centers reprioritize existing services to meet these demands (Auer, 1999). Evolving holistic therapies have also impacted college health prevention practices. Analogously, technological advances have greatly influenced college health interventions, including comprehensive health management databases, computerized wellness assessments, and Internet connections for global access to college health information.

Because of variations in college health and wellness services, Stephenson (1999) stressed the importance of developing a thorough marketing plan to adequately promote the variety of services offered to students. Patrick (1997) acknowledged that college health professionals have the capacity to confront these challenges and need to effectively communicate the value of college health and wellness services to the larger community.

Whereas the number of health and wellness issues affecting students in higher education continues to escalate, it is highly unlikely that revenues will increase to support expanded programming. Cost-effective measures that can yield effective health outcomes among diverse college populations will continue to challenge wellness program planners. In addition, the rapid expansion of college health and wellness services will grow in complexity. For these reasons, student affairs administrators and health practitioners will continue to deliberate over ethical issues surrounding health care standards, confidentiality, and legal responsibilities (Stiles, 1998). In order to maintain or adopt a high level of well-being, a variety of individual wellness strategies must continually be available to assist students in coping with ever-changing life stressors. The future of college and university wellness programming depends on a greater integration of resources; stronger community collaborations; holistic approaches targeting diverse needs; attention to expanding informational systems; and dynamic interactions with social, cultural, and political systems, which impact overall health.

ADDITIONAL SERVICES AND CONCERNS

This chapter has provided only an overview of college health. The 1999 edition of *Guidelines for a College Health Program* provided information about additional services. These recommendations addressed care for international students, athletes, and physically challenged students. They also addressed additional services including dental, pharmacy, laboratory, diagnostic imaging (X-ray), emergency, surgery, occupational health, and inpatient infirmaries.

TECHNOLOGY RESOURCES

The American College Health Association not only identifies additional areas of concern for college health, but also serves as an authoritative source of information and advice. The ACHA web site http://www.ACHA.org lists a number of special publications:

- College Health: A Model for Our Nation's Health;
- General Statement of Ethical Principles and Guidelines;
- General Statements on Institutional Response to AIDS;

- Statements on AIDS and International Education Issues;
- Responding to HIV Infection and AIDS: Campus Assessment Inventory;
- Suggestions for Implementing the Drug-Free Schools and Campuses Regulations;
- Position Statement on Tobacco Use on College and University Campuses—Updated 2000;
- Recommendations for Institutional Prematriculation Immunizations—Updated 2000;
- Recommended Standards: Alcohol and Other Drug Use, Misuse, and Dependency;
- Standards for Student Health Insurance/Benefits Programs—Updated 2000;
- Health Insurance for International Students and Scholars and Their Dependents;
- Drug Education/Testing of Student Athletes;
- Cultural Competency Statement—New 2000; and
- Tuberculosis Screening on Campus—Updated 2000.

Additional resources for learning about the breadth of concerns of college health personnel are the *Journal of American College Health* (Heldref Publications), the annual meetings of the American College Health Association, and an Internet user group, SHS, which is open to all. To join, send e-mail to the address <listserv@listserv.utk.edu>, under the SUBJECT type Subscription, and in the MESSAGE type SUB SHS (Your Name).

REFERENCES

American College Health Association, (1997). Available at http://www.acha.org.

American College Health Association, Standards Revision Work Group (1999). *Guidelines for a college health program.* Baltimore, MD: Author.

Auer, J. (1999). School health: Yesterday, today and tomorrow. *The Nurse Practitioner, 24(4),* 20–23.

Bennett, D. L., & Bauman, A. (2000). Adolescent mental health and risky sexual behavior: Young people need health care that covers psychological, sexual, and social areas. *British Medical Journal, 321,* 251–252.

Boynton, R. E. (1962). Historical development of college health services. *Student Medicine, 10,* 354–359.

Boynton, R. E. (1971). The first fifty years: A history of the American College Health Association. *Journal of the American College Health Association, 19,* 269–285.

Bradley, G. (2000). Responding effectively to the mental health needs of international students. *Higher Education, 39,* 417–433.

Bridwell, M. W., & Kinder, S. P. (1993). Confronting health issues. In M. J. Barr and Associates (Eds.), *The handbook of student affairs administration* (pp. 481–492). San Francisco: Jossey-Bass.

Dunn, P. C., Vail-Smith, K., & Knight, S. M. (1999) What date/acquaintance rape victims tell others: A study of college student recipients of disclosure. *Journal of American College Health, 47(5)*, 213–220.

Fingar, A. R., (1989). Patient problems encountered at a student health service. *Journal of American College Health, 38(3)*, 142–144.

Ganguly, R., Marty, P. J., Herold, A. H., & Maria, A. (1998). Hepatitis B immunizations in a university student population. *Journal of American College Health, 46(4)*, 181–184.

Haltiwanger, K. A., Hayden, G. F., Weber, T., Evans, B. A., & Possner, A. B. (2001). Antibiotic-seeking behavior in college students: What do they really expect? *Journal of American College Health, 50(1)*, 9–14.

Health Insurance Portability and Accountability Act (1996). 45 C.F.R. § 160–164.

Holtgrave, D. R. et al. (1995). An overview of effectiveness and efficiency of HIV prevention programs. *Public Health Reports, 110 (2)*, 134–146.

Horacek, T. M., & Betts, N. M. (1998). Students cluster into 4 groups according to the factors influencing their dietary intake. *Journal of the American Dietetic Association, 98 (12)*, 1464–1467.

Jeansonne, S. W. (2000). Risk of meningococcal infection in college students. *Clinical Pediatrics, 39*, 125–132.

Kaplan, J., Whipple, E. G., & Wright, J. (1996). Health services. In A. L. Rentz, (Ed.), *Student affairs practice in higher education* (2nd ed.). Springfield, IL: Charles C Thomas.

Keeley, R., & Engstrom, E. (1993). Refining your peer education group. *Journal of American College Health, 41*, 255–257.

Kraft, D. P. (1993). College health: A model for our nation's health. *Journal of American College Health, 42(2)*, 77–78.

Lancet, (March 25, 1995). Editorial. 345(8952), pp. 739–740.

Meilman, P. W. (2001). Human resources issues in university health services. *Journal of American College Health, 501*, 43–47.

National Center for Health Statistics (2001). *Healthy people 2000 final review*. Hyattsville, MD: Public Health Service.

Oprendek, S. T., & Malcarne, V. L., (1997). College student reasoning about illness and psychological concepts. *Journal of American College Health, 46*, 1–20.

Packwood, W. T. (1977). Health. In W. T. Packwood (Ed.), *College student personnel services* (pp. 298–339). Springfield, IL: Charles C Thomas.

Patrick, K. (1997). Assuring college student health. *Journal of American College Health, 45(6)*, 235–237.

Patrick, K. (1988). Student health, medical care within institutions of higher education. *Journal of the American Medical Association, 260(22)*, 3301–3305.

Patterson, D. L., & Lanier, C. (1999). Adolescent health transitions: Focus group study of teens and young adults with special health care needs. *Family and Community Health, 22(2)*, 43–58.

Rentz, A. L., & Associates (Eds.) (1996). *Student affairs practice in higher education* (2nd ed.). Springfield, IL: Charles C Thomas.

Rhoads, R., & Black, M. A. (1995) Student affairs practitioners as transformative educators: Advancing a critical cultural perspective. *Journal of College Student Development, 36(5)*, 413–421.

Robinson, F. (2001). Campaigns for conformity. *Journal of American College Health, 49(6)*, 316–317.

Rogers, W. M., Harb, K., Lappin, M., & Colbert, J. (2000). College men's health in practice: A multidisciplinary approach. *Journal of American College Health, 48(6),* 283–289.

Rudd, R. E., & Walsh, D. C. (1993). Schools as healthful environments: Prerequisite to comprehensive school health. *Preventive Medicine, 22,* 499–506.

Sabo, D. (2000). Men's health studies: Origins and trends. *Journal of American College Health, 493,* 133–142.

Saddlemire, G. (1988). Health services. In A. L. Rentz, & G. Saddlemire (Eds.), *Student affairs practice in higher education* (pp. 185–202). Springfield, IL: Charles C Thomas.

Santelli, J., Kouzis, A., & Newcomer, S. (1996). Student attitudes toward school-based health centers. *Journal of Adolescent Health, 18,* 349–356.

Simantov, E., Schoen, C., & Klein, J. D. (2000). Health-compromising behaviors: Why do adolescents smoke or drink? *Archives of Pediatrics & Adolescent Medicine, 154(10),* 1025–1033.

Stephenson, M. T. (1999). Using formative research to conceptualize and develop a marketing plan for student health services. *Journal of American College Health, 47(5),* 237–240.

Stiles, C. A. (1998). Ethical decision making: A challenge to college health practitioners. *Journal of American College Health, 47(1),* 47–49.

Thombs, D. L. (2000). A test of perceived norms model to explain drinking patterns among university student athletes. *Journal of American College Health, 49,* 75–84.

Turrisi, R., Padilla, K. K., & Wiersma, K. A. (2000). College student drinking: An examination of theoretical models of drinking tendencies in freshmen and upperclassmen. *Journal of Studies on Alcohol, 61(4),* 598–602.

United States Centers for Disease Control and Prevention (2000). Advisory Committee for Immunization Practices Recommendations. Available at http://www.cdc.gov.

United States Department of Health and Human Services (2000). *Healthy People 2010: Understanding and improving health and objectives for improving health* (DHHS Publication No. 017-001-00547-9). Washington, DC: U. S. Government Printing Office.

Chapter 14

ISSUES IN STUDENT AFFAIRS

Fiona J. D. MacKinnon, Ellen M. Broido, and Maureen E. Wilson

Issues in student affairs mirror the concerns of students and professionals, as well as matters of importance to the larger society. Although seemingly inconsequential, they may float somewhere in the background of the campus and then unexpectedly ascend into prominence. However, provocative issues provide student affairs professionals with unique teachable moments that can change the lives of students. For example, concerns such as free speech, removal of tuition caps, underpreparation of students, underage drinking, or affirmative action resurface in different forms year after year and provide professionals with persuasive teachable moments.

Cues in both the internal and the external environment require vigilant attention with a mindful eye. Unfortunately, automatic responses frequently become the quick reaction or convenient answer to difficult situations (Seymour, 1992). The best and considered approach to solution of campus issues comes from listening with careful mindfulness (Langer, 1997). What is the mindful response? According to Langer, "the mindful approach to any activity has three characteristics: (1) the continuous creation of new categories, (2) openness to new information, and (3) an implicit awareness of more than one perspective" (p. 4). The mindful response allows professionals to observe with deliberate tentativeness using multiple filters for making informed judgments.

Both formal and informal occasions provide promising opportunities for listening to the up-to-the-minute concern or current trend and for hearing students' points of view. The latest rumor, conversations over coffee, and casual exchanges provide just as many clues to issues as do the board of trustees' meeting, the president's convocation, or the faculty senate meeting. Issues cross all boundaries of student and academic affairs.

Student affairs professionals are never at a loss for challenging issues on which to focus. For this chapter, three continuing concerns that affect the student affairs profession, higher education generally, and society's expectations for a value added experience for students in higher education have been selected. The first issue, the role of social justice in higher education, has been a continuous part of the nation's agenda. Access to higher education and a quality education for all students has been crucial to the undergirding structure of the democratic way of life. In the global economy and the technologically sophisticated information society, access to higher education becomes central to the well-being of individuals, society, and the social contract. The section on social justice raises compelling questions about the legacy of social justice within student affairs.

The second issue, the educator role and student learning, challenges student affairs practitioners as equal partners in the teaching and learning agenda of higher education. The student affairs role of educator has always been a fundamental competency of student affairs work. Broadening the scope of the learning agenda to include content (course content and student affairs content areas) as well as process (learning how to learn) is key to the value-added aspects of student affairs and the lasting impact of the higher education experience on students.

The third issue, professionalism, resonates with student affairs practitioners at every level of career development. It also addresses issues that stakeholders of higher education view as central to guiding the pathways and decision points for students within the system. New professionals as they enter the field must be particularly cognizant of their professionalism—as individuals, as role models, as employees of a college or university system, and as representatives of the profession. As college costs rise, as state legislators question the value and public cost of a college education, and as students demand quality educational experiences, professionalism provides the support for understanding multiple perspectives and for striving for excellence.

WORKING TOWARD SOCIAL JUSTICE IN STUDENT AFFAIRS

"We must always take sides. Neutrality helps the oppressor, never the victim. Silence encourages the tormentor, never the tormented" (Wiesel, cited in Shor, 2000, p. 1). Words such as "oppressor," "tormentor" and "victim" might seem a long way from the day-to-day work of student affairs. Few of us became student affairs professionals with the goal of addressing social injustices. Yet, because of our daily interactions with students in all the roles they take on campus—as members of student organizations, residents in residence halls, seekers of career and academic advice—we constantly shape the experiences, ideas, and values of the students we serve. Whether we intend to or not, the ways we conduct our work influence social justice.

Social justice is the condition in which there is the full and equal participation of all groups in a society that is mutually shaped to meet their needs . . . the distribution of resources is equitable and all members are physically and psychologically safe and secure . . . individuals are both self-determining (able to develop their full capacities), and interdependent (capable of interacting democratically with others) . . . [people] have a sense of their own agency as well as a sense of social responsibility toward and with others and the society as a whole. (Bell, 1997, p. 1)

If we are to work toward social justice in the context of our efforts as student affairs professionals, this means that through our interactions with students, colleagues, and policies, we aim to create settings in which all students (and members of the larger campus community) are physically and psychologically safe and secure, where students have a voice in decisions affecting them, where they learn to interact effectively and respectfully with people both similar to and different from themselves, and where they learn to understand the consequences of their actions on the world as a whole. This is no small task, but as the quote from Wiesel indicates, failure to work toward these ends means supporting a status quo in which power and privileges are unequally distributed.

As student affairs professionals, we are in a position to work for social justice on at least three fronts. The first is providing support for underrepresented and historically disenfranchised students, which includes racial and ethnic minority students; women; students with disabilities; lesbian, gay, bisexual, and transgender students; and students coming from working class or economically poor backgrounds, among others. The second is educating all students, those who are members of groups with more social power (e.g., White students, male students, etc.) and those with less power about the existence of oppression, working with them to create a campus climate that affirms intergroup relations and values difference, and teaching them to be effective advocates for their own and for others' liberation. The third is working to change institutional structures and policies that perpetuate oppression, be it classism, heterosexism, racism, sexism, or other form of oppression.

CALLS FOR A SOCIAL JUSTICE ORIENTATION WITHIN THE STUDENT AFFAIRS PROFESSION

Student affairs work has long been concerned with issues of social justice, although it was rarely stated as such. The 1949 version of the Student Personnel Point of View (SPPV) (American Council on Education, 1994b/1947) identified as among the "new goals" of higher education "Education for a fuller realization of democracy in every phase of living; . . . [and] education for the application of creative imagination and trained intelligence to the solution of social problems" (p. 25). Later in the same document, "Through his [sic] college experiences he [sic] should acquire an appreciation of cultural values, the ability to adapt to changing social conditions, motivation to seek and to created desirable social changes" (p. 26).

Although the call to address social justice issues goes back more than 75 years, this issue has moved to the forefront in the past 15 years. In 1987, the National Association of Student Personnel Administrators published *A Perspective on Student Affairs*, in which they reaffirmed the values stated in the SPPV and stated a core set of beliefs and values that shape contemporary student affairs work. Among these beliefs and values are: "Each person has worth and dignity," "bigotry cannot be tolerated," and "a supportive and friendly community helps students learn" (pp. 10–12). The report *Campus Life: In Search of Community* (Carnegie Foundation, 1990) proposed six principles to guide colleges and universities in the development of campus climates supportive of their missions. One of those six principles was the development of "a just community," which it defined as "a place where the sacredness of each person is honored and where diversity is aggressively pursued" (p. 25). As the report made clear, "the issue is more than access; it has to do with the lack of support minority students feel once they have enrolled" (p. 26).

Chickering and Reisser (1997) highlighted the development of cross-cultural competence in their redefinition of aspects of students' psychosocial development. Their description of the fourth vector, developing mature interpersonal relationships, has "toleration and appreciation of differences" as one of its two components. Chickering and Reisser noted,

> Development involves reassessing assumptions about people we do not know. It means moving beyond initial disapproval or impetuous labeling to try to understand the basis for the difference, and even to appreciate how it is a contributing part of a larger whole. Now that multicultural communities are growing, academic institutions have a responsibility to equip their graduates with tolerance and empathy as essential survival skills (p. 150).

More recently, ACPA and NASPA, in their jointly published *Principles of Good Practice for Students Affairs* (1997), stated, "Good practice in student affairs builds supportive and inclusive communities. Student learning occurs best in communities that value diversity, promote social responsibility, encourage discussion and debate, recognize accomplishments, and foster a sense of belonging among their members" (p. 6). The authors noted that among the core values evident in student affairs work over its history is a commitment to developing "citizens capable of contributing to the betterment of society . . . an acceptance and appreciation of individual differences . . . ; [and] pluralism and multiculturalism" (p. 2).

APPROACHES TO SOCIAL JUSTICE IN STUDENT AFFAIRS WORK

When first thinking about diversity and social justice issues it is easy to identify explicitly, overtly discriminatory behaviors and assume that our only role, if any, is to rid our institutions of those obvious barriers and educate those particular individuals whose behavior clearly has no relation to our own. But in identifying the problem as that of particular individuals and their specific behaviors, we miss the fact that everyday, "normal" ways of behaving reinforce a status quo that privileges some social groups at the expense of others. What is easy to miss is that oppression not only is the work of mean-spirited individuals, but also is built into the institutions and structures of our society. It also is easy to presume that the way to achieve social justice is just to learn about "others" who are different from ourselves. While this is an important first step, we must not forget that not all forms of difference are equally valued, and we must understand how various forms of difference have very different amounts of power.

One obvious area in which to work for change is that of structural diversity. Structural diversity has been defined as the "numerical representation of various racial/ethnic groups" (Hurtado, Milem, Clayton-Pederson, & Allen, 1999, p. 5), although the concept is easily extended to all forms of social group membership. Do all levels of your institution (students, staff, faculty, and administration) represent the range of identities present in your community? In the country? Are particular groups of people concentrated in various places? How do institutional policies and practices create and maintain these groupings?

These questions are one way to begin working for social justice on our campuses. Ask them of yourself, of your colleagues, of your students, of your supervisors, of your faculty, and of your senior administrators. Think about the answers you receive: Do they meet your standards for a socially just campus? Do all members of the community give the same answer? What additional questions need to be asked? Next find a preliminary, incomplete list of other questions you might consider.

- Who is considered a "normal" student? What assumptions do we make about that student's gender, race, sexual orientation, socioeconomic status, religion, physical, learning, and psychiatric abilities and disabilities? Who is missing for our conception of the "usual" student? Are all members of the campus community treated equitably? How are their unique needs and interests accommodated and respected?
- How do we recognize and support students' development of their racial and ethnic identities? Do our organizations, forms, and practices recognize the growing numbers of bi- and multiracial students on our campuses? Is our programming reflective of the range of cultures on our campus? In what ways do we acknowledge the range of ethnicities within pan-ethnic identity labels such as Asian American, Hispanic, Black, or Native American?
- What are our institutional policies regarding affirmative action? Do we fully understand how it is and is not utilized? Understanding the historical and legal basis and extent of affirmative action, what are our own views on its use?

- How do we foster the development of students as allies for social justice? Do we support men who speak out against sexism? In what ways are we teaching White students to fight against racism? Do we support the heterosexual students challenging heterosexism and homophobia or do we quietly question their sexual orientation?

- Are our campuses fully accessible to students, staff, and faculty who have disabilities, be they physical, learning, or psychological, remembering that accessibility is more than curb cuts, ramps, and interpreters, although that would be a start in many cases. Do we actively recruit people with disabilities into our student bodies, administrative positions, and the profession? Do we include disability issues when we consider diversity? Are people with disabilities considered "victims" or "heroic" rather than just people? Are necessary accommodations made without fanfare or special request?

- Are there patterns to positions held by women and men on campus? To their advancement? Are women and men presumed to be equally talented and interested in all roles, majors, or administrative positions? Do policies allow both women and men the flexibility needed to raise children? How are issues of sexual and domestic violence addressed on campus?

- How are the concerns of transgender students, staff, and faculty addressed? How are single-sex settings (bathrooms, locker rooms, residence hall floors, student organizations) negotiated by those whose gender identity may differ from their biological sex? Are there stated or unstated rules or norms about gender expression (e.g., would a male administrator be able to wear a skirt to work without negative repercussions? Are women expected to wear pantyhose, makeup, and so forth?)

- Is the winter holiday party the Christmas party, just retitled, with a Hanukkah song thrown in? Are important campus events scheduled on the holy days of non-Christian religions? Do dining halls open early and late to accommodate those students observing Ramadan? Are paper plates and plastic utensils available for those who keep kosher or halal?

- Are all students presumed to be heterosexual? Do lesbian, gay, and bisexual students feel safe? Can they show affection in the same ways that heterosexual couples may without being harassed or attacked? Are campus health care providers aware of the specific health care needs of those whose sexual partners are the same sex? Are the career counselors aware of the career issues facing gay, lesbian, and bisexual students? How are university benefits provided? Are all forms of relationships given the same status and benefits? Do same-sex partners have access to family housing?

- What assumptions do we make about the economic resources available to our students? What costs are incurred by students that are not included in published statements about tuition and fees? Do our housing, meal plan, course load, and financial aid policies allow for students who must contribute to the income of their families? What restrictions are placed on part-time students?

As students affairs educators, we have many ways to help our students understand issues of diversity and social justice and to help make our campuses inclusive, supportive, and effective educational environments for all students. Such efforts are consistent with the historical and contemporary mandates of our profession. We are fortunate to have work that provides us with daily opportunities to work toward the social good. The educator role of student affairs is key to the success of a responsive social justice agenda.

THE EDUCATOR ROLE IN STUDENT AFFAIRS

Students learn best (about social justice and other student affairs agendas) when they find their classwork or out-of-class involvement relevant to their own life experiences. When they join with mentors and peers who share their excitement about ideas and help construct meanings that set off sparks of recognition, students enjoy learning (Light, 2001). Learning in student affairs is generally an energizing, collaborative experience—an involving process that includes interested mentors and co-learners. through which students actively and carefully examine their prior knowledge in light of current life experiences.

The student affairs learning agenda has two essential goals: (1) to ensure excitement about the world of ideas, and (2) to assist learners in developing competence and performance goals related to their academic work, as well as their personal agenda, as they engage actively with complex ideas and the broader world (Association of American Colleges and Universities, 2003; Chickering & Reisser, 1993; Kegan, 1994). When academic challenges are overwhelming, the possibilities for engagement with ideas and opportunities for student development are stifled. The exciting reality of learning in student affairs is that competence in learning skills (e.g., teaching study or time management skills) can go hand in hand with the learning agenda in any functional area. The cocurriculum is intentionally designed for this dual purpose (Baxter Magolda, 2003; MacKinnon-Slaney, 1994).

The marvel of the student affairs learning agenda is that it has the potential to go beyond false distinctions of cognitive, affective, social, physical, and spiritual domains to develop holistic conceptual connections in both the academic and out-of-class curricula (Love & Love, 1995). The sad thing is that student affairs professionals have relegated the academic agenda to the faculty and have consequently tended to renounce responsibility for the learning agenda in out-of-class experiences. Student affairs practitioners have bought into the mythology of the faculty monopoly of the learning agenda. In other words, student affairs professionals have frequently removed the intellectual domain from their holistic thinking about students.

The educator role in student affairs provides support for learners to become self-authoring (Kegan, 1994). Student affairs professionals, in non-threatening ways, nudge students beyond the simple "what are you thinking about" of reflective consciousness, to "why are you thinking this, what is your rationale, and what are the implications" of critical consciousness (Kegan, 1994). Through the student affairs agenda, learners are encouraged to grapple with meaningful connections between their own experiences and ideas learned in class as well as cocurricular activities. In the cocurriculum, students learn that ideas and personal values are the basis for action in all student activities. Learning in student affairs,

> Speaks not of what ought to be, but of what is real for us, of what is true. It says things like 'This is what fits you and this is what doesn't.' 'This is who you are and this is who you are not.' 'This is what gives you life and this is what kills your spirit' (Palmer, 1997, p. 20).

The broad-based learning agenda is vital not only to the welfare of students, but also to the efficacy and viability of the student affairs profession (Kuh, 1996; Light, 2001; Love & Love, 1995; Terenzini, Pascarella, & Blimling, 1996).

TEACHING AND LEARNING DOMAINS IN STUDENT AFFAIRS

The teaching and learning domains of student affairs focus on knowledge, skills, and attitudes that evolve from the classic student affairs literature: cognitive competence, intrapersonal competence, interpersonal competence, practical competence, content knowledge competence, and citizenship competence (Baxter Magolda, 1999; Light, 2001; MacKinnon-Slaney, 1994). The six domains require teaching and content expertise on the part of practitioners. "Fostering student learning in all its complexity requires integration of all domains of learning and involvement of all educators, regardless of their campus role" (Baxter Magolda, 1999, p. 39).

The first domain is cognitive competence, or meta-learning, sometimes known as relearning how to learn (Baxter Magolda, 1999; MacKinnon-Slaney, 1994). To help students achieve content and process mastery in this domain, student affairs educators assist students in becoming self-conscious learners. This domain requires professionals to be experts in learning theory, learning styles, motivation theory, beginner and expert learning models, dialectical thinking, andragogy, critical thinking, study skills, the politics of the classroom, and so forth. For example, students need to realize that contextual relativism, or the fourth order of consciousness, plays a critical role in their success in the classroom, in student activities, in the residence halls, and in all adult experiences (Chickering & Reisser, 1993; Kegan, 1994; MacKinnon-Slaney, 1994).

To reinforce this learning domain, professionals in any functional area may ask students to write a brief, quick, free-writing paper on "my most difficult learning challenge this week" and "my learning success this week" to be shared and discussed at the beginning of the cocurricular experience (MacKinnon-Slaney, 1991). Asking students to generate "time logs" to record activities on a half-hour basis over a two-week period sheds light on the time delegated to tasks, values, and goals. It encourages meta-learning (Light, 2001).

The second domain for teaching and learning in student affairs is intrapersonal competence (Baxter Magolda, 1999). Within this domain student affairs professionals focus on helping students reflect on personal areas of life, such as a sense of identity, clarification of values and ethical systems, definition and awareness of personal boundaries, stresses, and the total sense of self (MacKinnon-Slaney, 1994). An understanding of academic self-efficacy, for instance, helps students become attuned to their own potential for success in the classroom or student affairs activity.

To create an environment conducive to concentrating on the intrapersonal domain, students may be asked at the beginning of cocurricular activities, "On a scale of one to ten this week, how competent do you feel as a learner? Why?" followed by discussion. Intrapersonal competence can be stimulated by taking a group of students to see a hit movie, a theater production, or an art show. The ensuing discussion should center on personal reactions and interpretations. At the end of any student leadership meeting students may be asked such questions as, "What did you agree with or disagree with in today's discussion? Why?" Intrapersonal awareness (of values, attitudes, conflicts, challenges, and celebrations) is an important part of all cocurricular activities.

The third domain, interpersonal competence, concentrates on awareness of the self "in relationship to others" as well as "the capacity for interdependence and collaboration, appreciation of diversity, communication, problem-solving and conflict management skills" (Baxter Magolda, 1999, p. 39). Knowledge of interpersonal competence, group dynamics, group process, process consultation, and social learning are central to success in the classroom, student activities, residence life, and relationships with family members (MacKinnon-Slaney, 1994). Students should be taught the theory and research that support this domain.

The fourth domain emphasizes practical competence, which is defined as "managing one's daily life and tasks, career and personal decision making" (Baxter Magolda, 1999, p. 39). Practical competence is also a component of intelligence, indeed wisdom, that develops with experience and maturity (Merriam & Caffarella, 1998). Discussions about practical concerns, such as renting an apartment, obtaining a loan, hiring a speaker, planning a dual career, searching for a summer job, and so forth, fall within this domain. Practical competence is readily incorporated into a gestalt "here and now" exercise at the beginning of a student affairs meeting. The Internet is a great tool for exploring individually relevant topics that can be shared to benefit the group as a whole.

The fifth domain, content knowledge competence, is related to comprehensive understanding and appreciation of academic subject areas as well as relevant student affairs content. Most student affairs professionals have undergraduate and graduate degrees, and consequently academic backgrounds in liberal education, particular expertise in an undergraduate major, and in expert knowledge within a graduate degree. Professionals can intentionally encourage students to acknowledge the content and process of the academic curriculum in order to construct complex and mature meanings and to expand their understanding of past experiences with present knowledge in the cocurriculum.

At the beginning of an activity, student affairs educators can make use of an adaptation of the "one minute paper" (Angelo & Cross, 1994) elaborating on "one idea you encountered in your classes this week that really had meaning for you" or "one idea that has relevance for our group" and "one idea that seemed confusing." Professionals in all functional areas can help students make connections between life events and academic concerns. Common experiences (common reading, attendance at special campus speakers, sports events, and informal discussions) can strategically evolve into conversations about history, political theory, and sociology—and provide stimulus for reflection on self and the world. Involvement in this domain is rooted in an appreciation for the world of ideas.

The sixth domain, citizenship competence, involves awareness of the role of citizens in this democracy, as well as the responsibilities and rights that accompany the role. As delineated in the Student Personnel Point of View (1949), citizenship education prepares students for continuous concern and action within the political arena for the greater good.

The social contract, a key student development concept, is central to the well-being of individuals and groups within every residence hall, commuter lounge, university or college, and the nation. Each student organization meeting can be framed with a discussion of pertinent current events, especially given the availability of newspaper reading programs in residence halls. Informal discussions of current events at lunch or an analysis of issues such as safety on campus and civility in the classroom encourage awareness, responsibility, and competence in this domain.

The six domains provide the foundation of teaching and learning in student affairs. Every interaction with students is predicated on intentional learning goals that are based on one of the six domains. Student contact in all functional areas is potentially an opportunity to encourage an integration of the academic and student affairs learning agenda to benefit students (Love & Love, 1995).

Students spend more time out of class than in class; consequently, student affairs educators have many opportunities to support the learning agenda of students as well as the mission of the institution. Student affairs professionals have the flexibility and resourcefulness to create lively and attractive intellectual pursuits for students as part of the cocurriculum. The student affairs intentional learning agenda is an important part of the professionalism of the field and has the potential to be transformative for students and the learning environment.

PROFESSIONALISM IN STUDENT AFFAIRS

Preceding chapters have addressed the philosophy and history of student affairs, along with a number of functional areas that fall under its umbrella. While each area serves specific needs and purposes, they are linked together by a common mission of supporting and promoting student learning, growth, and development. Having well-trained staffs who engage in professional and ethical practice to meet that mission is another bond that joins those departments on campuses. After examining characteristics of effective professional practice in student affairs, suggestions for professional practice and development, particularly for new professionals, are offered.

Creamer, Winston, and Miller (2001) argued that professional student affairs administrators must integrate their roles as educators, leaders, and managers to meet the needs of their students and institutions. They identified five important characteristics of student affairs professionals. First, they engage in theory-based practice. Those theories—including theories of student and organizational development and the influences of gender, sexual orientation, ethnicity, and culture on them—explain why professionals do what they do. Strange (1994) contended, "What distinguishes professionals at work is their ability to bring reasoned explanations, grounded in evidence, to the phenomena about which they claim expertise" (p. 584). In other words, knowledge and application of theory is a hallmark of professional practice.

Second, student affairs professionals adhere to ethical standards and principles. Professionals will face difficult, complex, and important choices that can have a powerful impact on those affected by administrative decisions. Consulting with professional codes, those published by ACPA or NASPA, for example, and with respected colleagues can help professionals make decisions that are professionally and ethically sound.

Third, professional involvement is an important characteristic of professional practice. Promoting the student affairs profession and extending its knowledge base can be accomplished via contributions to professional organizations (e.g., committee service and conference presentations) and literature (e. g., journals and monographs). Additionally, reading professional literature and using it as a foundation for practice is advisable.

Fourth, being an advocate for students is critical. This means that student affairs professionals work to protect the best interests of students and intervene when students' welfare is jeopardized through institutional policies, practices, or decisions.

Fifth, student affairs professionals contribute to the educational mission of their institutions. Professional practice makes direct or indirect contributions to student learning, a position supported by the *Student Learning Imperative* (ACPA, 1994). Collaborating with faculty to enhance student learning and development increases the likelihood of successful implementation of those goals.

Komives (1992) identified six desirable professional behaviors and attitudes. A professional *knows* (e.g., understands and uses diverse theory bases), *learns* (e.g., attends and participates in professional associations), *leads* (e.g., has vision and enhances motivation), *cares* (e.g., has genuine concern for students and colleagues), *communicates* (e.g., writes and speaks effectively), and *matures* (e.g., acts on personal and professional values). All of these require active and intentional engagement on the part of student affairs professionals.

Understanding characteristics of effective student affairs professionals is helpful, yet the processing of becoming a full-time professional is challenging. Transitions are difficult (Wilson, 2000). Graduation and the move to a new job mark the beginning of an important life transition. While transitions can be exciting, invigorating, and rewarding, they involve letting go of familiar people and surroundings, comfortable routines, and knowing how to get things done in a particular environment. In addition to the suggestions for good professional practice stated and implied previously, the following recommendations may be helpful to student affairs professionals.

- Find a mentor. Mentors generally are at least 10 years older than the mentee, experienced in the same profession or setting, and generally are not one's supervisor. Mentoring relationships are sustained, complex, and mutually chosen (Komives, 1992). Mentors can help professionals grow and advance their careers.
- Develop support networks internal and external to your campus. Internal supports can help you understand your current circumstances. External support can provide different perspectives from those not affected directly by campus events.
- Get to know colleagues within the department and across campus. Doing so increases your ability to understand the institution and helps to forge the relationships necessary to accomplish professional and programmatic goals.

- Work to develop a good relationship with your supervisor and be an effective supervisor. The ability to supervise a diverse range of employees is critically important in many student affairs positions. A strong supervisory relationship can be a powerful source of professional development and support.
- Learn about the institution's students, structure, norms, culture, quirks, and political realities prior to attempting to implement change. Before new colleagues are likely to be open to your suggestions for change, they need to know that you understand your current institution, and it takes considerable time to do that. What worked on one campus may not work on another and may indeed be inappropriate for a different setting. New professionals are advised to be good anthropologists. That is, they should spend time observing and talking with others to understand the new environment. Doing so increases the likelihood of promoting positive changes.
- Commit yourself to a professional development plan. Schedule time to read journals and other professional publications; join and contribute to state, regional, and/or national professional organizations; and participate in workshops and institutes. You may have to bear some or all of the cost for your professional development, but your career success may be enhanced by these efforts.
- Be confident and humble. You were hired because you demonstrated strengths and potential to contribute to the maintenance and growth of a program. At the same time, a level of humility is appropriate as you still have much to learn—and that will be the case at every stage of your career.
- Live a balanced life. Create a life beyond work, get involved in the community, and take time for yourself. A healthy lifestyle can help avoid on-the-job burnout and provide good role modeling for students and colleagues.

CONCLUSIONS

The student affairs profession is a demanding one; it is a profession for the thoughtful. It is not a profession for those who seek shortcuts and quick fixes. It is not a profession where boilerplate solutions can simply be transferred from one student problem to the next or from one campus to another (Seymour, 1992). Student affairs is a profession for those who like challenges, love learning, and thrive in the face of ambiguity.

Student affairs is a profession for those who take the time to develop a philosophy of life and work. It is the right profession for those who are willing to examine their own assumptions about learning and learning organizations and help others to do the same. It is a profession for those who view the college campus as a special place where people come to experience the life of the mind and to appreciate the power of knowledge.

Student affairs professionals are not people who tolerate mediocrity. They are not people who suffer an "If it ain't broke, then don't fix it" mentality. They are people who acknowledge that students' search for the value-added quality of higher education is motivated by today's realities.

> So a critical role for campus leaders is to 'get in the way' of each student, to help that young adult [and adult learner] evaluate and reevaluate his or her choices, always in the spirit of trying to do just a bit better the next time (Light, 2001, p. 210).

The value-added culture of excellence is important if students are to gain all that they can from their educational experience. From first-year student orientation and registration until graduation day, students must join in the quest for success, accomplishments, excellence, and quality in all experiences. The goal of student affairs professionals is to provide constant and consistent leadership in the campus community to create optimal learning experiences for all. This creative tension is not an accidental, hit-or-miss approach—it is carefully and strategically designed, planned, and implemented by members of an informed profession.

TECHNOLOGY RESOURCES

The following web sites provide helpful tools for further information about the issues discussed in the chapter:

1. Association of American Colleges and Universities— http://www.aacu.org—provides links to the "greater expectations" project that focuses on student engagement, inclusion, and achievement. AACU Diversity Web is also helpful—http://www. diversityweb.org/diversity_innovations/institutional_leadership/ institutional_statements_plans/index.cfm
2. American Association of Higher Education—http://www.aahe.org/— offers opportunities to engage with other professionals who are concerned with pertinent campus issues.
3. Information on intergroup relations may be found at http://www.intergrouprelations.uiuc.edu/DiversityResources.htm
4. The Understanding Prejudice web site at http://www.understanding-prejudice.org/ provides literature, exercises, demonstrations and useful links related to prejudice.
5. Diversity dialogues offer a effective intervention for raising campus issues—http://www.dialogues.umich.edu/

REFERENCES

American College Personnel Association. (1994). *The student learning imperative.* Washington DC: Author.

American College Personnel Association and National Association of Student Personnel Administrators. (1997). *Principles of good practice for student affairs: Statement and inventories.* Washington DC: Author.

American Council on Education, (1994a). The Student Personnel Point of View (1937). In A. L. Rentz (Ed.), *Student affairs: A profession's heritage* (pp. 66–78). Lanham, MD: University of America Press.

American Council on Education. (1994b). The Student Personnel Point of View (1949). In A. L. Rentz (Ed.), *Student affairs: A profession's heritage* (pp. 108–123). Lanham, MD: University of America Press.

Angclo, T. A., & Cross, K. P. (1994). *Classroom assessment techniques: A handbook for college teachers* (2nd ed.). San Francisco: Jossey-Bass.

Baxter Magolda, M. (1999). Defining and redefining student learning. In E. Whitt (Ed.), *Student learning as student affairs work: Responding to our imperative* (pp. 35–49). Washington, DC: NASPA.

Baxter Magolda, M. (2003). Identity and learning: Student affairs' role in transforming higher education. *Journal of College Student Development, 44(1),* 231–247.

Bell, L. A. (1997). Theoretical foundations for social justice education (pp. 1–15). In M. Adams, L. A. Bell, & P. Griffin (Eds.), *Teaching for diversity and social justice: A sourcebook.* New York: Routledge.

Carnegie Foundation for the Advancement of Teaching (1990). *Campus life: In search of community.* Lawrenceville, NJ: Princeton University Press.

Chickering, A. W., & Reisser, L. (1997). *Education and identity* (2nd ed). San Francisco: Jossey-Bass.

Creamer, D. G., Winston, R. B., Jr., & Miller, T. K. (2001). The professional student affairs administrator: Roles and functions. In R. B Winston, Jr., D. G. Creamer, T. K. Miller, & Associates. *The professional student affairs administrator: Educator, leader, and manager.* New York: Taylor & Francis.

Hurtado, S., Milem, J., Clayton-Pederson, A. & Allen, W. (1999). *Enacting diverse learning environments: Improving the climate for racial/ethnic diversity in higher education.* ASHE-ERIC Higher Education Report 26(8). Washington, DC: The George Washington University.

Kegan, R. (1994). *In over our heads: The mental demands of modern life.* Cambridge, MA: Harvard University Press.

Komives, S. R. (1992). The middles: Observations on professional competence and autonomy. *NASPA Journal, 29,* 83–90.

Kuh, G. D. (1996). Guiding principles for creating seamless learning environments for undergraduates. *Journal of College Student Development, 37,* 135–148.

Langer, E. J. (1997). *The power of mindful learning.* Reading, MA: Perseus.

Light, R. J. (2001). *Making the most of college: Students speak their minds.* Cambridge, MA: Harvard University Press.

Love, P. G., & Love, A. G. (1995). *Enhancing student learning: Intellectual, social, and emotional integration.* ASHE-ERIC Higher Education Report No. 4. Washington, DC: The George Washington University.

MacKinnon-Slaney, F. (1994) The Adult Persistence in Learning Model: A road map to counseling services for adult learners. *Journal of Counseling and Development 72,* 268–275.

MacKinnon-Slaney, F. (1991). Discovery writing in introductory college student personnel graduate courses. *Journal of College Student Development, 32,* 92–94.

Merriam, S. B., & Caffarella, R. S. (1998). *Learning in adulthood: A comprehensive guide* (2nd ed.). San Francisco: Jossey-Bass.

National Association of Student Personnel Administrators. (1987). *A perspective on student affairs: A statement issues on the 50th anniversary of The Student Personnel Point of View.* Washington, DC: Author.

Palmer, P. J. (1997, November/December). The heart of a teacher: Identity and integrity in teaching. *Change, 29(6),* 15–21.

Seymour, D. T. (1992). *On Q: Causing quality in higher education.* New York: American Council on Education/Macmillan.

Shor, I. (2000). Introduction: (Why) education is politics. In I. Shor & C. Pari (Eds.), *Education is politics: Critical teaching across differences, postsecondary* (pp. 1–14). Portsmouth, NH: Boynton/Cook.

Strange, C. (1994). The evolution and status of an essential idea. *Journal of College Student Development, 35,* 399–412.

Terenzini, P. T., Pascarella, E. T., & Blimling, G. S. (1996). Students' out-of-class experiences and their influence on learning and cognitive development: A literature review. *Journal of College Student Development, 37,* 149–162.

Wilson, M. E. (2000). Connection and transition: Influences of career mobility on the close friendships of women student affairs professionals. *Journal of College Student Development, 41,* 529–543.

AUTHOR INDEX

Marmaduke, A.S., 339, 366
Martinson, G., 59, 87
Marty, P.J., 381, 385
Masiel, J.M., 313, 334
Mason, T.W., 177
Math, M.G., 184, 186, 215
Matkin, J., 22, 26
Matusak, L.R., 320, 334
Maul, S.Y., 304, 334
Maurer, C., 124, 141
May, D.L., 199, 213
McBee, M.L., 195, 213
McCabe, D.L., 199, 214
McCalla-Riggins, B., 103, 106
McCann, J.C., 246, 252, 265
McCaulley, M.E., 92, 100, 105-106
McClellan, G.S., 278, 295
McDermott, D., 166, 176
McDonough, P.M., 64, 87
McEwen, M.K., 219-220, 222, 236
McFadden, M., 281, 294
McGillin, V.A., 98, 106
McIntire, D., 229, 236
McIntosh, J.G., 310, 334
McIntosh, S., 173
McKaig, R.N., 305, 334
McKeachie, W.J., 90, 106
McKinley, D., 146-147, 165, 175
McMahon, T.R., 320, 333
McMichael, J., 154, 165, 176
McPherson, M.S., 340, 366
McRee, T.K., 228, 236
Mead, T.M., 149-150, 173
Meilman, P.W., 373, 385
Mendenhall, W.R., 49, 56
Merisotis, J.P., 338, 360, 364
Merriam, S.B., 108, 141, 395, 401
Merseal, J., 243, 264
Metzinger, T., 166, 176
Meyer, L.D., 281, 295
Michel, J., 175
Milem, J., 391, 401
Miller, C., 344, 351-352, 367
Miller, D., 324, 334
Miller, G.A., 158, 175
Miller, M.T., 259, 264
Miller, S.J., 130, 141
Miller, T., 20, 25
Miller, T.E., 287, 295
Miller, T.K., 18, 26, 49-50, 56, 91-93, 95, 104, 107, 191, 214, 227, 237, 302-303, 310, 319, 333-334, 397, 401

Mills, D.B., 276, 295, 334
Miser, K.M., 206, 210
Mitchell, M.H., 174
Moberg, T.F., 172
Monks, J., 340, 366
Moore, J.W., 337, 347, 366
Moore, K.M., 90, 106, 270, 295
Moore, L.V., 324, 334
Moore, M., 103, 105, 279, 295
Morales, R.H., 91, 94, 105
Morison, S.E., 38, 56, 239, 265
Morrill, W.H., 146-147, 149, 175, 279, 295
Mosier, R., 279-280, 295, 297
Moyer, R.A., 230, 237
Mueller, K., 302, 334
Mueller, K.H., 28-29, 32-34, 38, 45, 56, 93, 106, 182, 214, 239, 241-242, 249, 265, 274, 295
Mullane, S.P., 206, 214
Mullen, R., 259, 263
Mullendore, R.H., 197, 209, 246, 256, 258, 265
Munger, S.C., 59, 87
Murdock, S.H., 239, 265
Murphy, R.K., vii, 298, 369
Murray, J.L., 252, 265
Murry, J.W. Jr., 192, 206, 211
Murty, K.S., 32, 34-35, 56

N

Nagle, R., 115-117, 119-121, 126-128, 130-132, 134, 141
Neal, G.W., 145-147, 158, 174
Nelson, J.E., 352, 367
Ness, M.E., 148, 150, 154-156, 158, 169-170, 174
Nestor, D., 22, 26
Newcomb, T.A., 91, 104
Newcomb, T.M., 243, 250, 263, 307, 332
Newcomer, S., 381, 386
Newell, W.H., 307, 334
Newton, 310, 332
Niles, S., 142
Niles, S.G., 120-121, 124-125, 131-132, 138, 142
Noel, L., 64, 87, 243, 246, 250, 262, 265
Nolfi, T., 320, 334
Noll, V.H., 140
Nora, A., 220, 238, 258, 262
Nord, D., 116, 140
Nuss, E., 182, 214
Nuss, E.M., 288, 295

SUBJECT INDEX